AFTER THE WILD GEESE

THE IRISH BRIGADES AND THE PURSUIT OF INDEPENDENCE

A British Perspective

JOHN YARNALL

Copyright © 2022 John Yarnall

The moral right of the author has been asserted.

Apart from any fair dealing for the purposes of research or private study, or criticism or review, as permitted under the Copyright, Designs and Patents Act 1988, this publication may only be reproduced, stored or transmitted, in any form or by any means, with the prior permission in writing of the publishers, or in the case of reprographic reproduction in accordance with the terms of licences issued by the Copyright Licensing Agency. Enquiries concerning reproduction outside those terms should be sent to the publishers.

Matador
Unit E2 Airfield Business Park,
Harrison Road, Market Harborough,
Leicestershire. LE16 7UL
Tel: 0116 2792299
Email: books@troubador.co.uk
Web: www.troubador.co.uk/matador
Twitter: @matadorbooks

ISBN 978 1803133 010

British Library Cataloguing in Publication Data.
A catalogue record for this book is available from the British Library.

Printed and bound by CPI Group (UK) Ltd, Croydon, CR0 4YY
Typeset in 11pt Adobe Caslon Pro by Troubador Publishing Ltd, Leicester, UK

Matador is an imprint of Troubador Publishing Ltd

AFTER THE WILD GEESE

CONTENTS

PART ONE

Introduction ix

One	Meagher and the American Civil War	1
Two	John MacBride and the Irish Transvaal Brigade	38
Three	Arthur Lynch and the Second Irish Brigade	62

PART TWO

Four	Roger Casement – British Consul	95
Five	Casement the Nationalist	140
Six	The German Irish Brigade	156
Seven	Return to Ireland	196
Eight	Trial, Retribution and Legacy	221

PART THREE

Nine	Dowling and the German Plot – The Final Act	289
Ten	Aftermath	334
Eleven	Epilogue	343

Endnotes	*351*
Bibliography	*373*
Acknowledgements	*387*
Index	*389*

PART ONE

INTRODUCTION

In 1691, the Catholic armies in Ireland, under their commander Patrick Sarsfield, 1st Earl of Lucan, surrendered at Limerick, ceding victory to William of Orange in the Jacobite war. The ensuing Treaty of Limerick, signed on 3 October and drawn up by the English Commander-in-Chief, Lieutenant General Baron Godert de Ginkel (later to become the 1st Earl of Athlone), provided for Sarsfield, and any of his forces who wished to go with him, to go into exile in France.[1] Some 12,000 troops (together with 4,000 women) were transported to France as a result. The event became famously known as the "Flight of the Wild Geese"[2]. At first, the "Wild Geese" continued to serve in James II's army in exile, until this was disbanded in 1697. They then merged with the remnants of five Jacobite regiments which had been sent from Ireland to France in 1690 in exchange for a larger French Infantry contingent, and which had been formed into an "Irish Brigade", serving with the French army. The resulting force became known as the "Irish Brigade of the Wild Geese". An Irish Brigade lived on in the French army for the next hundred years, until it was disbanded following the French Revolution. Replenishment of the brigade after Limerick was mainly accomplished by French ships smuggling brandy and wine into the west coast of Ireland and returning with recruits listed as "Wild Geese" in the ships' paperwork. The brigade played a conspicuous part in the French victory over the British at the Battle of Fontenoy in 1745, where around 4,000 Irish troops were deployed. According to one estimate, as many as half a million or more Irishmen died fighting for France in the century after Limerick. "Wild Geese" also served in other armies, in particular those of Austria and Spain.[3] While many joined foreign armies simply to earn a living, many joined with the specific purpose of fighting against England. For his part in the Limerick campaigns, Sarsfield came to be regarded as a hero, representing a new, emerging, Irish nation[4].

The "Wild Geese" and the Irish Brigade – with its alleged battle cry, "*Cuimnidh ar Luimneach agus ar Feall na Sasanach!*", "Remember Limerick and the Saxon Faith" (i.e., English betrayal) – were to live on in the minds of nationalists who were increasingly looking for alternative ways to assert, if not actually secure, Irish independence. New Irish Brigades were established on four separate occasions between the French Revolution and the period of the First World War. The first fought on the Union side in the American Civil War. It was set up by Thomas Francis Meagher, an erstwhile "Young Irelander" who had been a leading fomenter of the "cabbage patch rebellion" at Ballingarry in 1848. For his part in the rebellion, Meagher had been sentenced in a British court to transportation for life to Van Diemen's Land from where he had escaped to the United States in 1852. A hero of Irish nationalists among the large Irish-American immigrant community in New York, Meagher established and led an Irish Brigade which fought

INTRODUCTION

with distinction. While deeming it right to fight for the country which had given him a new home, Meagher's more personal objective was to cultivate the United States Government as an "ally" in any future war for Irish independence and to secure military training for Irish Americans which would be put to use in any such fight. Meagher looked back to Sarsfield, the Wild Geese and Fontenoy as his inspiration. Such inspiration also motivated John MacBride, the son of an Irish Fenian born in Westport, Co Mayo, who emigrated to South Africa in 1896, and at the start of the South African War formed an Irish Brigade to fight with the Boers against the British. Like its predecessor in the American Civil War, the Irish (Transvaal) Brigade, as it was called, also fought with distinction. MacBride received the personal thanks of President Kruger and inspired nationalists in Ireland. He was to re-emerge later – reputedly by accident – as a participant in the 1916 Easter Rising, for which he was executed. In MacBride's shadow, a Second Irish Brigade fought for the Boers under the leadership of Alfred Arthur Lynch, a polymath and adventurer born in Australia to an Irish Catholic father and a Scottish mother. On his return to Ireland after the war, Lynch secured election as an MP, deliberately provoking the authorities to put him on trial for high treason where he was found guilty and sentenced to death. His sentence was immediately commuted to penal servitude for life and he was eventually granted a free pardon. The last of the four new brigades was the "German Irish Brigade", recruited by Sir Roger Casement, a former British Consul, from among Irish prisoners of war in Germany during the First World War. Casement's efforts proved to be a failure, with fewer than sixty prisoners being recruited and the Brigade never fighting as a unit. He was, nevertheless, tried for high treason and executed for seducing British soldiers away for their allegiance to the Crown in order to fight against the British Government. This and his consequent association with the Easter Rising caused him to be regarded by many in nationalist circles as a martyr. A member of Casement's Brigade, Joseph Patrick Dowling, became the last member of any Irish brigade to be actively involved in the fight for independence, having landed in Ireland from a German submarine in 1918 and been sentenced to penal servitude for life amid accusations that he had been involved in the famous "German Plot" of that year.

The contribution of these latter-day "Irish Brigades" to the cause of independence was in many respects incidental, and their individual stories have been told before. Taken together, however, the history of the brigades – and their leaders – provides an interesting insight into one aspect of the pursuit of independence. This study explores their contribution to "the cause", and in particular the reactions they provoked from the British authorities, itself an important part of the whole story.

ONE

MEAGHER AND THE AMERICAN CIVIL WAR

... I look upon the sword as a sacred weapon.
Meagher, "Sword Speech", 28 July 1846

...if only one in ten of us come back when this war is over, the military experience gained by that one will be of more service in the fight for Ireland's freedom than would that of the entire ten as they are now!
Meagher on his Irish Brigade in the American Civil War

Thomas Francis Meagher is mainly remembered for his participation in the Young Irelander Rebellion of 1848 and for his part in creating the first Irish national flag. He is less well remembered for his subsequent and continuing fight for Irish freedom in the unlikely role of Irish brigadier in the American Civil War.

Meagher was born in Waterford in 1823. His father, also Thomas Francis but known as Thomas, was a wealthy merchant who was twice elected mayor of the city (in 1843 and 1844), the first Catholic to occupy the post following emancipation under the Roman Catholic Relief Act of 1829. From July 1847 to March 1857, Meagher senior also served as one of the two MPs which the constituency of Waterford City was entitled to return to Westminster. As an MP, he appears to have played little part in the politics of Westminster and to have had little impact there, intervening on only twelve occasions in the business of the House during the ten years he served as an MP – once with a question about the navigation of the Danube with his remaining contributions relating solely to technical aspects of Irish domestic affairs. Thomas Meagher's personal objective was to ensure that his son had a top-class Catholic education, which he secured by sending him first to Clongowes Wood College in County Kildare (later famously attended by James Joyce) and then to Stonyhurst College in Lancashire, both leading Jesuit institutions. Thomas Francis completed his education in 1843, having gained a reputation at both institutions as a skilled orator.

On returning to Ireland, Thomas Francis went to Dublin intending to study law, but quickly became involved with Daniel O'Connell's Repeal Association (O'Connell was a family friend of the Meaghers[1]) and in particular with a group of young writers for the *Nation* newspaper, which included John Dillon and Gavan Duffy, known collectively as the "Young Irelanders". The Young Irelanders represented a militant wing of the Association, whose views were becoming increasingly at odds with O'Connell's objective of securing the repeal of the Act of Union and its replacement by Irish Home Rule through peaceful means. The Young Irelanders wanted full independence, not independence limited to Home Rule, and appeared to be far from peaceful in intent. Furthermore, by 1846, the Young Irelanders' suspicions were growing that even the Association's own objective was becoming diluted; it appeared to be moving towards an agreement with the Whig Government in London to put right the civic and social wrongs that had been inflicted on Ireland in the past, with the consequence that progress towards repeal and Home Rule would be stalled. As the tensions between the two wings mounted, the Association's leadership decided to organise a Conference to consolidate their position and to flush out the incipient militancy represented by the Young Irelanders. In this they were successful, but with consequences that they had almost certainly not intended.

The conference was held at O'Connell's Conciliation Hall in Dublin on 27 and 28 July 1846. Before its start, O'Connell had circulated draft resolutions specifically denouncing the use of force as a means to gain independence. Meagher's rejection of these "peace resolutions" established him, at the age of twenty-three, as a significant force in nationalist politics. In a forceful yet remarkably eloquent speech, Meagher met all the contentious points between the two sides head-on, starting with an attack on the notion that Ireland's salvation could be secured simply by the Whig Government improving conditions –

> *My Lord Mayor… A Whig Minister, I admit, may improve the province – he will not restore the nation. Franchises, "equal laws", tenant compensation bills, "liberal appointments", in a word, "full justice" (as they say) may ameliorate. They will not exalt. They may meet the necessities – they will not call forth the abilities of the country. The errors of the past may be repaired – the hopes of the future will not be fulfilled. With a vote in one pocket, a lease in the other, and "full justice" before him at the Petty Sessions, in the shape of a "restored magistrate", the humblest person may be told that he is free; but… he will not have the character of a freeman – his spirit to dare, his energy to act.*

And –

> *A good government may, indeed, redress the grievances of an injured people; but a strong people alone can build up a great nation. To be strong a people must be self-reliant, self-ruled, self-sustained. The dependency of one people on another, even for the benefits of legislation, is the deepest source of national weakness.*

Meagher was careful to acknowledge the debt of gratitude owed to O'Connell ("the great man") while disagreeing with him about the way forward. He accepted that in present circumstances any attempt to repeal the Act of Union by force of arms would be bound to fail. But he could not accept that this would be the position forever, and he did not oppose the use of arms in the vindication of national rights. He then went on to laud nations, in particular Belgium and America, that had secured their independence through force of arms –

> *Be it for the defence, or be it for the assertion of a nation's liberty, I look upon the sword as a sacred weapon. And if, my lord [Mayor], it has sometimes reddened the shroud of the oppressor – like the anointed rod of the high priest – it has, as often, blossomed into flowers to deck the freeman's brow. Abhor the sword? Stigmatise the sword? No, my lord, for in the passes of the Tyrol it cut to pieces the banner of the Bavarian, and through those cragged passes cut a path to fame for the peasant insurrectionist of Innsbruck. Abhor the sword? Stigmatise the sword? No, my lord, for at its blow, and in the quivering of its crimson light a giant nation sprang up from the waters of the Atlantic, and by its redeeming magic the fettered colony became a daring, free Republic. Abhor the sword? Stigmatise the sword? No, my lord, for it swept the Dutch marauders out of the fine old towns of Belgium – swept them back to their phlegmatic swamps, and knocked their flag and sceptre, their laws and bayonets, into the sluggish waters of the Scheldt.*

> *My lord, I learned that it was the right of a nation to govern itself – not in this Hall, but upon the ramparts of Antwerp.*
>
> *This, the first article of a nation's creed, I learned upon those ramparts, where freedom was justly estimated, and where the possession of the precious gift was purchased by the effusion of generous blood. My lord, I honour the Belgians, I admire the Belgians, I love the Belgians for their enthusiasm, their courage, their success, and I, for one, will not stigmatise, for I do not abhor, the means by which they obtained a Citizen King, a Chamber of Deputies.*[2]

Meagher's words were met with enthusiasm and applause by some sections of the audience, but at this point he was silenced by John O'Connell (son of David O'Connell), who rose to say that he could not listen to the expression of such sentiments. Either Meagher or he should leave the Association.[3] Meagher's comments had gone right to the heart of the difference between the mainstream "moral force" Repealers and the "physical force" Young Irelanders. He had effectively repudiated the Association's leadership. Following some kerfuffle, Meagher and his colleagues left both the hall and the Association, never to return. In a contribution to *Punch* magazine, the novelist Thackery attempted to ridicule Meagher by dubbing him "Meagher of the Sword", and the term "of the sword" continued to be used as a term of sarcasm when referring to Meagher in the English press. But among Irish nationalists and Meagher's supporters everywhere, the sobriquet became a term of admiration.[4]

In January 1847, the Young Irelanders, together with other defectors from the Repeal Association, formed the "Irish Confederation" to pursue their objective of securing independence by whatever means. Meagher was elected to the governing council and set about touring the country, making speeches to wide acclaim and advancing the Confederation's cause. The Confederation unsuccessfully contested the 1847 parliamentary by-election at Galway, losing by four votes to the government candidate, while

Meagher similarly failed to secure a vacant seat at Waterford in early 1848.[5] The Young Irelanders became increasingly vocal on the effects of the Irish famine, unsuccessfully demanding the closure of the ports to the export of corn while the famine continued.[6] Their growing militancy was given further impetus by the emerging unrest across Europe and the revolutions of 1848. When the French ousted Louis Philippe at the start of the year, the leaders of the Confederation seized on the opportunity to support the new republic with a view to securing some help for their own cause in return. At a Confederation meeting at Dublin's Music Hall on 15 March, it was agreed to send a delegation to France with a congratulatory message to the new government there. The delegation would include Meagher, William Smith O'Brien and Edward Hollywood (Richard O'Gorman Jnr and John Dillon were added later).[7] In a speech made during the meeting, Meagher again demonstrated his power as an orator, with his comments this time directed towards the British Government. In supporting a proposition that elected delegates from the chief towns and cities of Ireland should go to London and "demand an interview with the Queen", he commented –

> *If this demand be refused, then, I say, let the Irish deputies pick up their court dresses, as Benjamin Franklin did when repulsed from the Court of George III; and then and there let them take solemn oath, that next time they demand admission to the court of St James's, it shall be through the credited ambassador of an Irish Republic.*

He went on that if the demand were conceded, the Queen should be asked to convene an Irish Parliament in Dublin. But –

> *…should the throne stand as a barrier between the Irish people and the supreme right – then loyalty will be a crime, and obedience to the Executive will be treason to the country. I say it seriously*

– *I say it deliberately – it will then be our duty to fight, and desperately. I have only a word to say, if gentlemen, you will listen to me. If nothing comes of this – if the constitution open to us no path to freedom – if the Union will be maintained despite the will of the Irish people – if the Government of Ireland insist in being a Government of dragoons, of bombardiers, of detectives, of light infantry – then I say, up with the barricades, and invoke the God of Battles. Should we succeed, think of the joy, the ecstasy, the glory of this old Irish nation, which in that hour will at last grow young and strong again. Should we fail, the country will not be worse than it is now.*[8]

This was too much for the authorities to let go unchallenged, and six days later, on 21 March, Meagher was arrested and charged with seditious libel. Also arrested and charged in respect of speeches made at the same meeting were O'Brien and John Mitchel, the proprietor of *The United Irishman*, a newspaper with an established record of militancy whose title echoed the name given to the rebels of 1798.

Pending the ensuing trials, the delegation went to Paris as planned. One of their aims is said to have been to secure agreement to raise a new "Irish Brigade" on French soil. It is not clear whether this idea was seriously discussed with the new French Government, but if it was and was turned down, this would not be surprising. However sympathetic the French might have been towards the Irish cause, they would have had no desire to upset the British Government through such a provocative act.[9] According to Arthur Griffith, "Lamartine [the French Minister of Foreign Affairs] received them [the delegation] courteously but coldly. He had been threatened by the British Government with the possible breaking-off of diplomatic relations if he offered encouragement to Ireland".[10] But the delegation did not return entirely empty-handed. At meetings in Ireland to celebrate the French Revolution,

Irish tricolours had begun to appear alongside the iconic tricolour of France. In March, Meagher had flown an Irish tricolour from the Wolfe Tone Confederate Club in Waterford for a week before it was removed by the authorities. On his return from Paris, he brought with him an Irish tricolour said to have been woven in the finest French silk by women sympathetic to the Irish cause. In presenting this to a meeting in Dublin, Meagher outlined its significance – "The white in the centre signifies a lasting truce between Orange and Green and I trust that beneath its folds the hands of Irish Protestants and Irish Catholics may be clasped in generous and heroic brotherhood." The tricolour came to be accepted as the national flag in 1916 after being raised above the General Post Office during the Easter Rising. It was adopted as the flag of the Irish Free State in 1922 and subsequently confirmed in the 1937 constitution.[11]

The trials of O'Brien and Meagher took place in Dublin between 15 and 17 May 1848 before a packed court, with crowds of up to 2,000 supporters accompanying them to and from the proceedings. The Irish Attorney General led for the prosecution. The case against O'Brien was that his speech on 15 March had been delivered, "for the purpose of exciting hatred and contempt against the Queen in Ireland, and inducing the people to rise in rebellion". Specific passages in the speech could only be construed as inviting acts of treason, particularly as they had been made in the context of the overthrow of the French monarchy and the establishment of a republic less than a fortnight before. The Attorney General noted remarks by O'Brien that if England were threatened by invasion, the Irish people would not, "lift a hand to assist them", and that in the absence of an Irish Parliament, "the French army would not be considered by the people of Ireland invaders of their soil". He also noted that O'Brien had advocated establishing an Irish Brigade in America, whose purpose he surmised would be to assist in the establishment of an Irish Republic. The case presented in

O'Brien's defence was essentially that he had done no more than argue legitimately for repeal.[12] Following an overnight retirement, the jury returned the following morning to say that they were unable to reach a verdict. O'Brien was set free.[13]

Meagher's trial immediately followed, the charge in this case being that Meagher's speech on 15 March had been delivered with one or more specific intents – "to disturb the peace, to incite the subjects of the Queen to entertain hatred and dislike of her person and Government – to excite her subjects to endeavour to obtain changes in the Government and Constitution by force and violence – and to incite the people to insurrection and rebellion". Again, the Attorney General drew attention to the fact that Meagher's remarks had been made specifically in the context of the French Revolution. The jury deliberated overnight and again failed to reach a verdict. One of the jurors told the Chief Justice, 'We are all agreed, my lord, but one, and he is a Roman Catholic.' The juror was not only a Catholic but also a Repealer. Meagher was set free and left the court to cheers, accompanied by O'Brien and others in a procession to the office of the Irish Confederation, where Meagher told the crowd that the results of the trials were a "triumph of liberty and the people".[14] Needless to say, this was not a view universally shared. In the opinion of *The Times*, "Trial by jury has received a blow from which it cannot soon recover. It is proved that a fair trial in Ireland is impossible".[15] It noted that the failure applied in relation to "two out of three of perhaps the most popular mob leaders that ever outraged the peace of this or any other country", with the result that "the hero of the sword breathed the air of liberty".[16]

The trial of John Mitchel, the third of the "popular mob leaders", had meanwhile been delayed as a result of motions submitted by his defence lawyer. Unfortunately for Mitchel, this enabled the authorities to re-arrest him and charge him with treason felony, a new offence created by the Treason Felony

Act, passed on 22 April. The new offence was more serious than seditious libel – a common law misdemeanour – and had been constructed specifically to deal with the situation in Ireland. The new charge related to material published in *The United Irishman* since the passing of the Act. The earlier charges lay on the file and Mitchel was found guilty of treason felony at his trial on 27 May. He was sentenced to deportation for a period of fourteen years. There were widespread protests against Mitchel's trial and sentence in Ireland, which also spread to England. Chartist meetings held on 25, 26 and 29 May and on 4 June drew crowds of "thousands" at Clerkenwell Green and elsewhere, resulting in six of the Chartist leaders being charged with "wickedly, maliciously, and seditiously uttering and pronouncing certain scandalous and seditious words of and concerning our lady the Queen and Government". At a hearing at Bow Street, the court was told of seditious speeches made by both Chartists and Irish Confederation members. At the trial itself, the Chartist John Fussell was said to have told a crowd on 29 May that, 'If the Queen forgets to recognise the people, the people must forget to recognise the Queen. If John Mitchel is sent out of the country, every Irishman must rise and reverse the insult, or they will be no longer worthy of the name of men.' All six of the Chartists were found guilty and each was sentenced to two years in prison, plus various fines. On receiving his sentence on 10 July, another leader, Ernest Jones, told the judge, 'I wish your Lordship good night, and may you sleep with the motto of the Charter round your neck, and no surrender.'[17]

The progress of events had begun seriously to unnerve the British Government. On 22 July, the Prime Minister, Lord John Russell, announced the Government's intention to suspend *habeas corpus* in Ireland until March the following year. He told the House of Commons that suspension was absolutely necessary in order to prevent bloodshed and to stop an incipient insurrection, on grounds that, "the present state of things in Ireland is fraught with evil – that it threatens danger – and that we are on the eve of an outbreak if it is not timely prevented". He said that the decision was not based on any secret reports or intelligence, but on the basis of activities in Ireland which were plain for all to see. The Irish Confederation's objective of securing "a total separation of Ireland from the Dominions of the Crown" by means of "physical force" meant no less than "rebellion against the Crown of this kingdom". He went on to accuse the Confederation of taking advantage of the potato famine – "the misfortune which fell on Ireland of the blight of the potato crop" – as a means to inflame the passions of the people and to provide the basis for seditious harangues. The Confederation had been encouraged in its aims by the revolution in France and had sent a deputation there to seek assistance against the authority of the British Government. This had been refused – "The Government of that country, although sprung out of a revolution, felt that its duties towards neighbouring countries were paramount, and refused to lend its aid to their designs". He then noted the sympathy that had been shown to Mitchel by his supporters in Ireland which indicated that they identified themselves with the views set out in the *United Irishman*. Reports were being received from the Irish Constabulary that meetings of Confederation clubs were now being held in secret, with the police being excluded without a warrant, and at Bree on 2 July, a certain Mr Devlin, "produced a pattern of a cheap pike for poor persons, urged the people to arm and drill, and suggested methods of attack". He referred to Meagher, who had been arrested again on 11 July –

> *A Mr Meagher, who is one well known for having used language frequently exciting the people to rebellion and insurrection, was arrested at Waterford, on a charge of sedition. Several thousand persons collected together wished to rescue Mr Meagher, but he declared that it would be wasting the blood of the Irish people to*

attempt such a thing. The Roman Catholic clergy, I am bound to say, used all their efforts to keep the peace, and Mr Meagher was conveyed without resistance out of the town of Waterford. There was soon afterwards a meeting, which assembled on a mountain well known in the political history of Ireland, called Slievenamon, which was attended, some say, by 10,000, and others by 15,000 persons, to hear Mr Meagher, Mr Doheny, and others. When Mr Meagher returned to Waterford from that meeting, he was waited for by several thousand persons, who wished to give him a welcome...

Russell went on to say that the general view of those who had witnessed the events at Waterford was that while people of property, and the clergy (both Protestant and Catholic) were against any outbreak, they could exert no effective influence in deterring "many thousand persons of the younger men of every class, but more especially of the farmer and peasant class, who are determined to rise in insurrection". Suspension of *habeas corpus* was needed because any attempt merely to ban the clubs would simply be evaded. During debate, one MP argued that the Government had, "as usual", opted for coercion first and conciliation afterwards, while another, supporting suspension, claimed that the situation in Ireland was most alarming, with houses in Tipperary and Clonmel being stripped of their lead to make bullets. The Government secured the support of the House by 271 votes to 8.[18]

While it was true that the Confederation leaders had been organising themselves for a rising, spurred on by the reception given to Meagher at Slievenamon, they were completely wrong-footed by the decision to suspend *habeas corpus*. They had been working on the assumption that they had until August or September to complete preparations for a rebellion, but they were now put in the position of having to act immediately – before they were ready – or, because of the implications of suspension, not at all.[19] Within the Confederation clubs, suspension was met with bitterness and anger and expectations of some form of retaliation[20], but when the Confederation's leaders went out to canvass their views on a possible rising, they found little support. In Carrick-on-Suir, believed to be a suitable well-armed stronghold from which to launch a rising, the local leadership were found to be against any action. In Waterford, Meagher found the local clergy also to be against a rising.[21] The British authorities, meanwhile, pressed home their advantage by posting Proclamations on 28 July offering a five hundred pound reward for the detention of Smith O'Brien, and three hundred pounds each for the detention of Meagher, John Dillon and Michael Doheny.[22] The following day, the Irish Constabulary came across O'Brien, at the head of a band of 300 supporters – mainly farmers and miners – at Ballingarry, South Tipperary.[23] Though armed only with pikes, mining and farming tools, plus a few guns with sparse ammunition, the supporters seriously outnumbered the police contingent of an Inspector and forty-six men, who immediately retreated to a nearby cottage owned by "the widow McCormack".[24] The widow was out at the time, though her five children were at home. O'Brien and his supporters, plus a large crowd of onlookers, laid siege to the cottage for several hours until police reinforcements arrived and O'Brien and his supporters fled. Shots had been exchanged during the encounter, resulting in the deaths of two of the besiegers and the wounding of several others.[25]

The "Battle of Ballingarry" (or "the battle of Widow MacCormack's cabbage garden"[26]) constituted the sum total of the "Young Irelander Rebellion" of 1848. O'Brien and other Confederation leaders, including Meagher, were caught and arrested. Meagher blamed the failure of the rebellion squarely on the fact that they had been forced into action precipitately by the British Government. Their failure to anticipate the suspension of *habeas corpus* had been a grievous mistake. Meagher's own father, he noted, had argued that to stage a rising when the clergy were against it and the clubs not organised, "would be to rush, with naked hands, upon the bayonets of the police and soldiery". Nevertheless, "I saw we were driven, by a master-stroke, to the last point upon the board; and that, either we must surrender without a parley, or fight without arms and arrangement. We are driven to it – I said to Smyth [a friend] – there is nothing for us now but to go out; and we have not gone far enough to succeed, and yet, too far to retreat". But Meagher had no regrets –

> *There again, had we not gone out upon the Suspension Act, and written our protest on the standard of Rebellion, the English officials would have been led to believe that the privileges of Irish citizens might be abused, not only with perfect impunity, but without one manly symptom of resentment. We preferred risking our lives, rather than suffer this contemptuous impression to go abroad.*[27]

The "State Trials" of O'Brien and other Confederation leaders – for "levying war against the Queen" – took place at Clonmel over a five-week period starting on 28 September. O'Brien was tried first and found guilty on 9 October, with a plea by the jury for the exercise of "the mercy of the Crown". In response to the usual invitation to speak before sentence was passed, O'Brien eschewed the opportunity to vindicate his actions, other than to say that he had only done what it was the duty of any Irishman to have done and that he was, "now prepared to abide by the consequences of my having performed my duty to my native land". After noting that the jury's plea for clemency was a matter for the Lord Lieutenant, to whom the matter would be referred, the Lord Chief Justice then passed on O'Brien the traditional sentence for high treason of death by hanging, drawing and quartering.[28] The trials of McManus and O'Donoghue then followed immediately, and they too were found guilty with recommendations for mercy.

Meagher was the last of the leaders to be brought before the court on 16 October, for a lengthy trial lasting five days.[29] The charge against him was that he had conspired with others to bring about the Ballingarry rising and knew of O'Brien's intentions. The Irish Attorney General told the court that in law the fact that Meagher had not been present at Ballingarry was irrelevant, as – "A man who incited, advised, encouraged, or sent out others for the purpose of levying war was himself guilty of the offence", and, "…a man might be guilty of levying war, though he himself had not left his own dwelling". The case was that sometime in the early part of 1848, the Confederation leaders – "none more conspicuous than Mr Meagher" – had "formed the design of effecting a revolution by force of arms". The evidence against Meagher started with his support for the French Revolution and his "God of Battles" speech of 15 March; he had then gone on to make other speeches around the country inciting rebellion. In July, discussions within the Confederation focused on whether the time had now arrived to attempt a revolution, resulting in a decision to form an executive council – a council of war – to oversee operations. The prosecution brought before the court a witness – a Mr Dobbin, a member of the "Red Hand Club" – who claimed to have been present at a meeting on 21 July, when the five, including Meagher, had been elected, the other four being John Dillon, Richard O'Gorman Jnr, Thomas Darcy McGhee and Thomas Devin Reilly. According to Dobbin, immediately after the election, a resolution was proposed that the revolution should not be delayed beyond 8 August. Meagher had refused to give a positive pledge to that effect but had committed to do all in his power to expedite a rising before that day. The prosecution brought before the court police witnesses testifying to Meagher's movements in the week before Ballingarry, including Police Constable Hamilton, who reported a speech given by Meagher at Carrick-on-Suir on 24 July, in which he had asked the crowd –

Were they ready to stand before the military? The English Government had trampled on all laws; it had refused to grant the people law; with packed juries and bloody judges they had persecuted the bravest of Ireland's young citizens… and

They were about to renew the bloody scenes of '98. Then they had men of talent to stand by them. Then too, those talented men were persecuted. Then, too, they had packed juries and bloody judges. Then, too, they had a suspension of the Habeas Corpus Act. Then, too, the judges with folded arms, presided over those scenes red with the blood of their victims, and returned to their festivities satisfied with having done their duty to their Government.

Counsel for Meagher conducted a lengthy defence, challenging the lawfulness of the charge, the reasonableness of using his old speeches against him, the reliability of Dobbin's uncorroborated evidence (and his questionable character) and the accuracy of the reports of the various police witnesses. The jury proceeded nevertheless to find Meagher guilty, with a unanimous recommendation of mercy due to "the prisoner's youth and for other reasons".

Meagher, McManus and O'Donoghue were sentenced together on 23 October and given the same punishment as O'Brien. Their responses in advance of sentence have entered folklore as examples of defiant bravery in the face of death. McManus spoke first, noting that at no time in the course of his activities had he been actuated by animosity towards Englishmen, among whom he had spent the happiest days of his life – "Therefore I have only to say, it is not for having loved England less, but for having loved Ireland more that I now stand before you". O'Donoghue followed with, "I beg to say that the Attorney-General and the Solicitor-General have conducted the case against me fairly but strictly, and that I find no fault with either, nor with the evidence given against me, as far as it was stated to the jury"; and while complaining that the jury had been stacked against him and that he could be found guilty of treason by assisting O'Brien even if he had not known of O'Brien's intent, he concluded that, "It is not fit at this solemn moment to defend my opinions and conduct. I will, therefore, only say that these opinions have always been tolerant, sincere and consistent".

Meagher's "Speech from the Dock" has gone down alongside his "Sword Speech" as one of the finest examples of his rhetoric, as demonstrated by the following extracts –

My Lords, it is my intention to say only a few words. I desire that the last act of a proceeding which has occupied so much of the public time, shall be of short duration. Nor have I the indelicate wish to close the dreary ceremony of a State prosecution with a vain display of words. Did I fear that hereafter when I shall be no more, the country which I have tried to serve, would think ill of me, I might indeed avail myself of this solemn moment to vindicate my sentiments and my conduct. But I have no such fear. The country will judge of those sentiments and that conduct in a light far different from that in which the jury by which I have been convicted have viewed them; and, by the country, the sentence which you, my Lords, are about to pronounce, will be remembered only as the severe and solemn attestation of my rectitude and truth...

My Lords, you may deem this language unbecoming in me, and perhaps it might seal my fate. But I am here to speak the truth, whatever it may cost. I am here to regret nothing I have done, – to retract nothing I have ever said. I am here to crave with no lying lip, the life I consecrate to the liberty of my country... To lift this island up, – to make her a benefactor to humanity, instead of being the meanest beggar in the world, – to restore her to her native power and her ancient constitution – this has been my ambition, and my ambition has been my crime. Judged by the law of England, I know this crime entails the penalty of death; but the history of Ireland explains this crime, and justifies it. ... And in conclusion –

> *Pronounce then, my Lords, the sentence which the law directs – I am prepared to hear it. I trust that I shall be prepared to meet its execution. I hope to be able, with a pure heart, and perfect composure, to appear before a higher tribunal – a tribunal where a Judge of infinite goodness, as well as of justice, will preside, and where, my Lords, many many of the judgments of this world will be reversed.*[30]

Some sources claim that Meagher also said, with the words in square brackets being included in some versions –

> *My Lord, this is our first offence, but not our last. If you will be easy with us this once, we promise on our word as Gentlemen to try to do better next time. [And next time – sure we won't be fools enough to get caught.]*

The provenance of this particular claim is unclear, as these words are not included in any of the authoritative records of Meagher's speech. The only other recorded occasion when Meagher was invited to speak during the trial was when the Lord Chief Justice asked him if he wished to address the jury following the final summary by his defence counsel. Meagher simply replied, 'My Lords, I don't wish to address anything to the jury. I have committed my case to the counsel and I am perfectly satisfied with the way in which they have conducted it.' It seems unlikely therefore that the words are genuine, but for many they have come to form part of the Meagher legend.

The prisoners' words were indeed defiant, as they could afford them to be. By the end of the trials, few thought that the death sentences would actually be carried out. *The Times* noted, "The prospect of a mitigated and very mild punishment had grown into such a certainty in the course of the trials, as to import a mock heroic air to the speeches before sentence". Alluding to the expected alternative of transportation, it commented that "everybody feels that wholesome discipline at Bermuda, or some other safe retirement, would suit Mr Meagher's complaint much better than the gallows". Even in the case of O'Brien, *The Times* noted, "For one reason or another no one was prepared to see Smith O'Brien dying the death of a malefactor. The scaffold was either too ignominious, too dignified, or too grave for so silly and contemptible an offender".[31] That leniency would be granted had already been indicated when in response to a "memorial" from a deputation headed by the Lord Mayor of Dublin on 17 October, praying for a commutation of the sentence passed on O'Brien, the Lord Lieutenant had given an assurance that "full weight" would be given to the recommendation of the "highly respectable" jury who had presided at O'Brien's trial[32]. But first it was necessary to await the result of appeals against conviction lodged by O'Brien and the others on technical legal grounds, under a process known as "writ of error". The prisoners' arguments were rejected by the Court of the Queen's Bench in January, following which Meagher dropped out of the process, according to *The Times* due to lack of money, "declining all offers of pecuniary assistance, although urgently pressed on him by family and friends". O'Donoghue seems also to have decided not to take things further. An appeal to the House of Lords by O'Brien and McManus was then finally rejected in May, leaving the way open for the exercise of the Royal Prerogative.[33] Without delay, on 5 June 1849, a letter was sent to the Governor of Richmond Prison in Dublin, where the prisoners were being held, notifying the decision that their death sentences were to be commuted to transportation for life.

The substitution of transportation for the death sentence was common practice at the time. O'Brien had clearly prepared for this eventuality and immediately protested that in the specific case of treason, the law in Ireland did not permit transportation to be substituted for the death sentence. He demanded that the matter be brought before the courts. The other prisoners then also refused to accept the commutation.[34] Public support for the prisoners was extensive, with some 150,000 people signing memorials petitioning for mercy. Many believed that even transportation was excessive and that the right course was a free pardon. But this would have been a step too far for the Government, which decided instead to put the matter to rest by introducing a bill (the "Transportation for Treason (Ireland) Bill") to enshrine the right of the Crown or the Lord Lieutenant to commute capital sentences to transportation without any right of objection on the part of those convicted. Despite a petition by the four against the Bill (strongly supported in the Commons by John O'Connell), it was quickly passed by both Houses.[35] Some accounts have suggested that the prisoners rejected transportation because they favoured martyrdom through death, though there was never any real danger of this. The key driving force was that transportation would have separated them from their families forever; life imprisonment would in this respect have been a better alternative.

While waiting in prison, Meagher wrote that he and the others had been led into captivity without glory – "We suffer not for a rebellion but for a blunder".[36] But his spirits had improved by 9 July 1849, when, under heavy escort, the prisoners were transferred from Richmond Prison to the ship that would transport them to exile in Van Diemen's Land. According to *The Times*, a number of relatives and friends had assembled in the prison yard from an early hour, "to take the last sad farewell before the "law" had done its work". Meagher told them, 'My last words on leaving the country shall be, don't give up on the good old cause'; and in taking his place in the prison van, 'I feel a prouder man leaving the country even thus, than many who remain in it.' O'Donoghue is then reported to have said, 'And so do I,' while the others remained silent.[37]

On reaching Van Diemen's Land, Meagher took advantage of the offer of a "Ticket of Leave" – a form of parole enabling him to live outside prison in return for an undertaking not to attempt to escape. But by the beginning of 1852, life in exile had become too much, causing him to write to the local magistrate on 3 January that he intended to resign his Ticket of Leave at noon the following day. He then made his escape, travelling via South America to New York, arriving there on 26 May 1852.[38] Whether Meagher might have achieved a long-term result more satisfying to him by staying in exile a little longer is perhaps a moot point. On 26 April, *The Times* reproduced a petition to the Lord Lieutenant from a number of influential Conservatives in Ireland, requesting him to ask the Queen to grant clemency to "William Smith O'Brien and his companions in penal exile". Immediately following this, it noted, "Somewhat *mal apropos* for the chances of an extension of the Royal Clemency towards these misguided men, the *Nation* of this day contains the somewhat startling announcement that Mr Thomas Francis Meagher has taken French leave of Sir William Denison [Lieutenant Governor of Van Diemen's Land] and that in all human probability by this time the champion of "the sword" has joined his more fortunate brother patriots who had for special reasons chosen the free soil of America as their country of adoption".[39] The petition was turned down with reference to the fact that the convicts had "never expressed contrition for their crime".[40] On this basis, it seems almost certain that the petition would not have succeeded even if Meagher had not made his escape.

Meagher was welcomed in New York as a brave freedom fighter against British oppression. Over 7,000 people (including the 69th New York State Militia (Second Irish Regiment)) gathered outside the home of Richard O'Gorman, who had escaped to America following the suspension of *habeas corpus,* to celebrate Meagher's arrival. Pro-Meagher demonstrations were held in a number of cities, and resolutions in his honour were passed by various state legislatures. "Meagher Clubs" were established in New York and Boston and in July he was invited to review the New York State Militia and local Irish military organisations.[41] As things settled down, Meagher began to carve out a new life, earning a living by extensive lecture tours and as a lawyer after qualifying for the New York Bar in 1855. In 1856, he returned to journalism by establishing a weekly periodical, *The Irish News*. In 1857, he became a US citizen. From then until the outbreak of the Civil War in April 1861, he went on to divide his time between journalism, the Bar and latterly undertaking trips to Central America – Costa Rica in particular – developing a detailed knowledge of the region which he put to good use in lectures, journalistic articles and as a commercial adviser and facilitator.

At the start of the Civil War, the Union state governors were asked to provide volunteers from their militias – to serve initially for three months.[42] The 69th New York Militia, under the command of Colonel Michael Corcoran, a leading Fenian, set off for Washington within two weeks, on 23 April 1861. Despite having no military experience, Meagher decided to join the fight and to form his own company of Irish volunteers. He agreed with Corcoran that his company could fight as a company of the 69th (for which there was a vacancy) and that it would be designated the "Irish Zouaves". (The naming of volunteer units as "Zouaves", after French light infantry regiments in North Africa, and dressing them accordingly, became common in both the North and the South.[43]) Recruitment was sufficiently rapid to enable Meagher's company to join the 69th in Washington before the end of May.[44] The 69th was quick to see action at the First Battle of Bull Run in July, where, in the face of the surprise Confederate victory, Meagher acquitted himself well. His fellow officers reported afterwards that acting as Major of the regiment, and special aid to Colonel Corcoran, Meagher's exertions were "incessant". He rode "coolly and deliberately" along the line and in front of the enemy's batteries; when his horse was "torn to pieces by a cannon shot", he took his place with his company of Zouaves (conspicuous targets in their bright red uniforms) on foot; and "in the face of the deadliest of fire, with his head uncovered, he stood his ground, waved his sword, and rallied the Sixty-ninth "in the name of Ireland"".[45] When the 69th returned to New York, Meagher was welcomed as a hero. On 3 August, the 69th was "mustered out", having served the stipulated three months, and discharged from the service of the United States. Meagher was offered a captaincy in the regular army and then a post as aide-de-camp to Major-General Fremont with the rank of colonel. He declined both, preferring instead to remain with his old comrades in the 69th who were contemplating the establishment of a distinctive Irish Brigade. On their behalf, Meagher obtained the agreement of the War Department to the offer of the "69th Infantry Regiment", plus four other regiments, to form a Brigade in the US army for a period of three years. In the event, the Brigade, some 3,000 strong, was to comprise only three regiments – the 69th, 63rd and 88th New York Volunteers, plus two Batteries of Artillery – the governors of Massachusetts and Pennsylvania having refused to allow the Irish commands recruited in those states to join it.[46] The intention had been for the Irish veteran General Shields to command the Brigade, but when communication problems put this in doubt, the officers of the Brigade nominated Meagher to take his place. Meagher was confirmed as Brigadier-General, with Shields' warm support, on 3 February 1862.[47]

The Irish Brigade's first experience in the field was on 1 June 1862 at the Battle of Fair Oaks, whose result was inconclusive. The Brigade's losses were light – seven killed, thirty-one wounded and one missing – but it achieved all the objectives it had been set.[48] This was followed by further encounters, concluding at Malvern Hill on 1 July, where the Brigade engaged in some of its fiercest fighting, ironically much of it against fellow Irishmen. Called up to reinforce a line under severe pressure, the 69th regiment and the 88th ("Mrs Meagher's Own") came under fire from "fearful volleys" in response to which they stood "like a stonewall… returning a fire more destructive than it received".[49] There then followed a charge on the Brigade by the Confederate 10th Louisiana regiment ("The Lousiana Tigers"), made up largely of Irish Americans, recruited from around New Orleans. This started with heavy rifle and artillery fire from both sides and concluded with ruthless hand-to-hand fighting. Meagher's brigade held the line, with the North emerging as victors.[50]

The fighting up to and including Malvern Hill had cost the Irish Brigade dearly. The 69th, 88th and 63rd had lost about twenty per cent of their numbers.[51] In order to bring the Brigade back up to strength, Meagher returned to New York during a lull in the fighting to undertake a recruiting drive. Here he found that outside the Brigade, enthusiasm for joining the fight had started to pall. Generous offers from private and commercial interests failed to provide enough new recruits to fill the ranks. Among these was a scheme put forward by the New York Corn Exchange, whose members had raised sufficient funds by private subscription to offer ten dollars each to the first 300 men to volunteer; an offer by Austin Kelly & Co to give ten dollars to each of the first fifty recruits, plus "constant employment during the war" for their wives and daughters; and an offer of ten dollars a head for up to sixteen new recruits by Isaac Selligman of the firm Selligman and Stettheimer.[52] In all, the recruitment drive produced less than 200 new recruits, woefully short of the 800 or so needed.[53] It was thus with still depleted ranks that the Brigade joined the Battle of Antietam (also known as Sharpsburg), the bloodiest battle of the Civil War, in September 1862. Antietam was described by one officer as the Brigade's "crowning glory". As before, Meagher joined in the fighting and once again had his horse shot from under him. His men engaged the enemy with heavy musketry fire, holding the notorious "sunken road" to the end of the fight, "losing not a prisoner, having not one straggler, but at a loss of life which was appalling".[54] Accurate statistics are elusive but Meagher stated afterwards that fewer than 500 men of the Brigade left the field.[55] Some figures show that sixty-one per cent of the 69th and fifty-nine per cent of the 63rd were killed or wounded. This was not the heaviest casualty rate of the battle (on the Confederate side, eighty per cent of the 1st Texas were killed or wounded[56]), but Antietam sustained the Brigade's reputation for hard fighting and bravery.

By the time of its next main encounter at Fredericksburg in December 1862, the Brigade had been reconfigured to include the 116th Pennsylvania Volunteers and the 28th Massachusetts Volunteers. The 28th had been recruited mainly from Irishmen around Boston and had adopted as its regimental motto "*Faugh-a-Ballagh* ("Clear the Way"), a battle cry first coined in the Peninsular War which was later to become directly associated with the Brigade itself. The cry evoked the days of the Young Irelanders, "*Faugh-a-Ballagh*" being the title of a poem attributed to Gavan Duffy which had appeared in the first edition of *The Nation* in 1844.[57] Before the battle, Meagher continued to secure his place in Irish nationalist history by ordering his officers and men into battle each wearing a sprig of evergreen (boxwood) in their caps – "the colors of their Fatherland" – in place of the usual regimental colours which were currently being refurbished. The scene and its aftermath were vividly recounted in a letter written by a captain of the 88th the day after the battle, reproduced in *The Times*. The officer had reportedly given up a job in "the Custom-house" paying 1,300 dollars a year to raise a company –

... The destruction of life has been fearful, and nothing gained. The battle opened about 10 o'clock yesterday morning with a terrible fire of artillery. As we were drawn up in the line of battle on the front of the city General Meagher addressed us in words of inspiration and eloquence I never heard equalled, after which he ordered every one of the brigade to place a bunch of green boxwood at the side of his cap, showing the example himself. Every man appeared fired with determined zeal and a firm resolution, which the result proves to have been carried out in a manner scarcely paralleled in the annals of war. The 88th Regiment this morning numbers 10 officers and 41 men; the 69th, 7 officers and 59 men; the 63rd, 6 officers and 64 men; the 116th, 13 officers and 57 men. The 28th Massachusetts also suffered heavily, but I have not the returns. Irish blood and Irish bones cover that terrible field today, for Irish regiments were placed foremost, as the reports and returns will prove...[58]

Meagher had addressed each of the regiments in turn. His inspirational and eloquent words to the 88th were –

Officers and soldiers of the Eighty-eighth Regiment – In a few moments you will engage the enemy in a most terrible battle, which will probably decide the fate of this glorious, great and good country – the home of your adoption. Soldiers – This is my wife's own regiment, "her own Eighty-eighth" she calls it, and I know, and have confidence, that with clear woman's smile upon you, and for woman's sake, this day you will strike a deadly blow to those wicked traitors who are now but a few hundred yards from you, and bring back to this distracted country its former prestige and glory. This may be my last speech to you, but I will be with you when the battle is fiercest; and, if I fall, I can say I did my duty, and fell fighting in the most glorious of causes.[59]

In the event, Meagher failed to play the fully active part in the battle that he envisaged due to a burst abscess on his knee. Divisional commander General Hancock noted in his Official Report of the Battle that Meagher had "led his brigade to the field under fire; but, owing to a serious lameness making it difficult for him to either ride or walk, he was unable to bear that prominently active part which is usual with him". Hancock went on to note that the Brigade had gone into action with ninety-two officers and 1,323 men and had lost fifty-three officers and 488 men.[60] At the close of the war, in an interview with a former chaplain of an Ohio regiment, General Robert E Lee, Commanding-General of the Confederate army, spoke highly of the fighting quality of Irish Americans on both sides, including a comparison between Meagher and the highly regarded Confederate General Patrick Cleburne, born in County Cork and formerly of the British Army –

> *Meagher on your side, though not Cleburne's equal in military genius, rivalled him in bravery and the affection of his soldiers. The gallant stand which his bold brigade made on the heights of Fredericksburg is well known.* **Never were men so brave**. *They ennobled their race by their splendid gallantry on that desperate occasion. Though totally routed, they reaped harvests of glory. Their brilliant, though hopeless, assaults on our lines, excited the hearty applause of our officers and soldiers.*[61]

Following Fredericksburg, Meagher sought agreement to remove the 69th, 88th and 63rd New York Volunteers temporarily from the field to enable their numbers to be brought back to strength. Other commands had already been allowed to return home during the four months that the army was lying inactive in winter quarters. In a detailed memorandum to the Secretary of War on 19 February 1863, Meagher drew attention to the fact that the three New York regiments had been active since November 1861, and that no Brigade had "more assiduously, unremittingly, bravely, nobly done its duty". The strength of the three New York regiments had, however, been reduced to only ninety-one officers and 531 men. Meagher received no reply. The Brigade accordingly went on to fight at Chancellorsville in early May, but immediately following the battle, Meagher resigned his command. In his resignation letter of 8 May 1863, he noted that what was once known as the Irish Brigade "no longer existed" and observed bitterly that his earlier memorandum to the Secretary of War had not even been acknowledged. He stated nevertheless that his services, "in any capacity that can prove useful, are freely at the summons and disposition of the Government of the United States".[62]

This offer was soon taken up in an unexpected way. In October, Meagher's help was enlisted in dissuading Irish voters in Ohio from voting for the "Copperhead" leader and lawyer Clement Vallandigham in the election for State Governor. The Copperheads (named after a particularly venomous variety of snake) comprised a small minority of Northern Democrats opposed to the Civil War who wanted a negotiated peace, allowing the South to secede.[63] Vallandigham had at first been imprisoned and then banished behind Confederate lines for taking this "treasonous" position, and conducted his election campaign from Canada. In the event, his controversial views and the Union victories at Gettysburg and Vicksburg in the summer of 1863 went against him, and he lost the election by around 100,000 votes.[64] (Following his defeat, Vallandigham continued in active Democratic Party politics, returning to the US in 1864 untroubled by the authorities. His notoriety was finally secured by his untimely death in 1871, while he was preparing the defence of an accused murderer. Acting out his view of what had occurred at the crime scene, Vallandigham took a pistol he was using as a prop and, thinking it was unloaded, pointed it at himself and pulled the trigger, leaving him mortally wounded.) For his part, Meagher's role in securing

Vallandigham's defeat in the 1863 Ohio election was likely to have been an aggravating factor rather than anything more decisive, but he clearly did make an impact, as acknowledged by *The Times*. Quoting from a long letter by Meagher to the Union Committee of Ohio in denunciation of the Southern "rebels" and of Mr Vallandigham, *The Times* noted that Meagher had indulged in "a vast amount of Hibernian eloquence" and had demonstrated that his long stay in America had not "deprived his phraseology of its native characteristics". Though the sentiments in the article were generally contemptuous of Meagher, *The Times* nevertheless concluded that he had "been rather shabbily used by the Federal Government" in not being allowed to replenish the ranks of the Irish Brigade, and that, "if, after his letter to the people of Ohio, he be not again appointed to a command, Mr Lincoln will be as ungrateful as all Princes are supposed to be…"[65]

But Lincoln and the army had been ungrateful and continued to be so. The precise reason why Meagher so obviously fell out of favour with the authorities after Fredericksburg has been the subject of much debate. The response to his letter of resignation of 8 May 1863 could not have been more perfunctory. On 14 May, the Assistant Adjutant-General wrote simply, "Sir, Your resignation has been accepted by the President of the United States, to take effect this day".[66] That he was held in low regard by some of his fellow officers is not in doubt. As a newcomer with no previous military experience, he was viewed with suspicion, not helped by his flamboyant style of command and rhetoric which contrasted starkly with the natural reserve of many of his fellow (professional) generals. Such suspicion was compounded by resentment at the praise heaped upon him for what many considered to be the unnecessary exposure of his men to danger in the pursuit of personal glory,[67] a trait exacerbated by his heavy drinking.[68] An officer of the 5th New Hampshire Regiment – Colonel Cross – wrote after Fredericksburg, "After more than one year's observation in the field, there is not in the United States, certainly not in the Army of the Potomac, another such a consummate humbug, charlatan, impostor, pretending to be a soldier as Thos Francis Meagher! Nor do I believe him to be a *brave* man since in every battlefield he has been *drunk* and not with his brigade…"[69] Another source records that at Antietam, Meagher had left the field on a stretcher, being so drunk that he had fallen from his horse, and at Fredericksburg, he had engaged in "skulking", the abscess on his knee being simply a pretext for not joining.[70] At the same time as making enemies within the military, Meagher seems also to have been reckless in making enemies of Republican politicians by, for example, publicly criticising the White House over its sacking of General McClellan as commander of the Army of the Potomac after Antietam.[71] All in all, the indications are that after Fredericksburg, both the army and the political administration had simply lost confidence in Meagher's competence and his value as a general.

Following his resignation, the Irish Brigade fought on without him in various forms, and at varying strengths. Its reputation for hard fighting and gallantry was sustained particularly at the Battle of Gettysburg in July 1863, where about 320 of the Brigade's remaining 500 soldiers were killed. (There are monuments in honour of the Brigade at Antietam and Gettysburg.) Meanwhile, Meagher himself secured Lincoln's agreement in June 1863 to raise an Irish regiment of 3,000 men, but nothing came of this.[72] And in the summer of 1864, he eroded any low standing he had still further during a visit to General Hancock. Provost Marshal General Marsena Patrick records in his diary entry for 18 August 1864, "General Meagher is lying in the tent of the Chaplain of the 20th as drunk as a beast, and has been sending out his servant for liquor and keeping his bed wet and filthy. I have directed Col Gates to ship him tomorrow if he does not clear out".[73] It should be noted here, however, that Patrick was a Presbyterian teetotaller with a reputation for taking a stern approach to any amusement, especially if it involved alcohol. He had previously stated in relation to a St Patrick's Day celebration that, "In accordance with a Special request from [Gen. Joseph] Hooker, I agreed to go over & witness some of the festivities at the Head Quarters of Meagher's Irish Brigade. We brought up in the midst of a grand steeple chase, from which the crowd soon adjourned to drink punch at Meagher's Head Quarters – Everybody got tight & I found it was no place for me – so I came home".[74]

After repeated requests and much lobbying, Meagher was finally called back into service on 13 September 1864, when as Acting Major-General he was given the backwater command of the Military District of Etowah, Tennessee, whose HQ was based in Chattanooga. From there, in January 1865, Meagher was ordered to move his troops to North Carolina, *en route* to join the army of General Sherman at Savannah on its famous "March to the Sea". *The Times* reported that upon leaving, "He was the recipient of high compliments from General Steadman [Steedman], commanding, on his administration of affairs in the district of Etowa [*sic*], and his success in protecting steamboats and railroad transportation".[75] But during the journey, a Major Robert Scott, the officer responsible for coordinating ship transport from Annapolis to North Carolina, reported that on the evening of 5 February, when he had attempted to give Meagher certain orders, he found him too drunk to understand what was being said. Following his arrival at New Bern, North Carolina, Meagher was relieved of his command by the Secretary of State of War on 24 February and told to return home, thereby bringing to an end his military career.[76] For his part, Meagher subsequently claimed that he had actually resigned his commission out of disapproval of Sherman's "excessive" form of warfare which showed no respect for crops, cattle, houses or other property[77] – a policy which would subsequently make him the "most hated Northerner in the Confederacy".[78]

*

Many of the criticisms levelled at Meagher undoubtedly contain some truth. His reputation for heavy drinking is irrefutable, though the extent to which this was excessive to the point of unnecessarily endangering his men is less clear. Also, as a completely inexperienced general, it is not surprising that his competence might be called into question by his more professional peers, though criticisms of military competence were by no means confined to Meagher. Captain D P Conyngham, Meagher's aide-de-camp at Chancellorsville, records, for example, that "jealousies and private piques" among some of his generals marred the well-laid plans of General Joseph Hooker, the commander of the Army of the Potomac, and "converted what promised to be a glorious victory into a shameful defeat", before going on to note that, "Sedgwick, who commanded the left wing at Fredericksburg, by unaccountable delay, lost an opportunity of occupying the heights, and his retreat across the river does not appear to be in accordance with his instructions".[79] Accusations of "skulking" and avoiding personal danger in battle do, on the other hand, seem far wide of the mark and unsustainable in the face of the many reports of Meagher's bravery. Conyngham's report on Chancellorsville adds to those already recorded –

> *As we marched through the columns that lined the way, we were loudly and repeatedly cheered. With our general at its head, the Brigade marched as steadily and coolly as if on parade. As we marched through the woods, shot and shell were poured like hail upon us. When the general reached the end of the road, he turned the head of the column and deployed into the woods. His escapes here were almost miraculous; for, though men were falling on every side, he boldly rode on, all the time cheering the men by word and example. Here a shell burst behind him, where he had just left, killing four of our men.*[80]

Conyngham's words do nothing if not demonstrate the high regard in which Meagher was held by his men. Regardless of his skills as a military tactician and his brash temperament, he displayed the same mixture of vision and oratorical skills in leading the Irish Brigade as he had as a Young Irelander at the start of his career. His success in this regard is amply demonstrated by his parting from the Brigade following his resignation in May 1863. Addressing the remnants of the Brigade from inside a hollow square formed for the occasion, Meagher's words included –

> *Sharing with the humblest soldier freely and heavily all the dangers of the battle-field – never having ordered an advance that I did take the lead myself – I thank God I have been spared to do justice to those whose heroism deserves from me a great commemoration; and that I have been preserved to bring comfort to those who have lost fathers, husbands, and brothers in the soldiers who have fallen for a noble government under the green flag. (Meagher then shook hands with each soldier individually.)*[81]

A written farewell address to Meagher from the officers of the 69th, 63rd and 88th a few days later included –

> *[We desire]… to express to you the sorrow we personally feel at your departure, and the sincere and heartfelt affection we entertain, and shall ever entertain for you under all circumstances, and changes of time and place.*
>
> *We regard you, General, as the originator of the Irish Brigade in the service of the United States; we know that to your influence and energy the success which it earned during its organization is mainly due; we have seen you since it first took the field – some eighteen months since – sharing its perils and hardships in the battle-field and in the bivouac; always at your post, always inspiring your command with that courage and*

devotedness which has made the Brigade historical, and by word and example cheering us on when fatigue and dangers beset our path…

… rest assured, General, that you take with you the confidence and affection of every man in our regiments, as well as the esteem and love of the officers of your late command.[82]

There then followed another farewell address from the non-commissioned officers of the 88th, which included –

Seldom, if ever, has a more mournful duty devolved on a soldier than now devolves on a few of that devoted band of Irishmen that rallied at your call around the green flag of our native land, and who are here now to evince their sincere and heartfelt sorrow at the loss of an indomitable leader, a brave companion, and a stern patriot, as well as to extend their congratulations at your returning in all your manly pride and spotless integrity to the domestic scenes of your own fireside.

And –

The first to lead us to victory, we fondly hoped it would be your proudest honor, as it was your highest ambition, to lead us back again to our homes; but, through the inscrutable wisdom of an all-wise War Department, it will be reserved for you instead to welcome back what has been, or will be, left of what was once known, and proudly so, as Meagher's Irish Brigade…[83]

A third farewell came from the officers of the 116th Pennsylvania Volunteers, whose resolution included –

…we have been deprived of a leader whom we would have followed to the death…

And –

> ... in the discharge of his official duties he [Meagher] exhibited alike those qualities which only a true soldier can possess – when on duty a strict disciplinarian, and when off-duty an affable, agreeable, and kind companion.[84]

At a subsequent banquet in New York in January 1864, given by the officers of the Brigade to the enlisted men and honourably discharged veterans, Meagher again praised the bravery of his men in a characteristically eloquent address and thanked them for their loyalty. When they thanked him in response, he returned to what was clearly a sensitive subject for him, asking all those present in relation to a charge that "had been privately circulating" whether he had recklessly exposed the lives of his officers and men – to which the cry was "no"; whether he had ever brought them into danger, except when he had been ordered there – to which the cry was also "no"; and whether, when he had brought them into danger, was he not first in himself at the head of the column? – to which the cry was "yes". Meagher thanked them for their contradiction of the "malicious falsehoods that had been asserted against him".[85] At a Grand Review of the Union army in Washington on 22 May 1865, the men of the Irish Brigade units wore green sprigs of boxwood in their caps in commemoration of Meagher's famous order at Fredericksburg.[86] Whatever the external criticisms, there appears to be no doubt that the members of the Brigade remained truly loyal to him.

Meagher's decision to fight on the Union side had been something of an about turn. Before the war, his sympathies had been with the South, a stance compatible with his position as a Catholic and Democrat and lifelong supporter of self-determination. As *The Times* was later to observe, "Had he not been a rebel he would have been nothing",[87] though Meagher himself eschewed the term "rebel" in the Southern cause commenting that, "You cannot call eight millions of white freemen *"rebels"*... you may call them *revolutionists* if you will".[88] But when the war came, he took a pragmatic line, arguing that support for the Union was a good investment for the best long-term interests of Ireland – "We could not hope to succeed in our effort to make Ireland a Republic without the moral and material aid of the liberty-loving citizens of the United States" – which he argued would be forthcoming after the present struggle was over. Meanwhile, in the shorter term, Irishmen fighting in the war would provide invaluable experience for the time when the battle could be taken to Ireland itself –

> *It is a moral certainty that many of our countrymen who enlist in the struggle for the maintenance of the Union will fall in the contest. But, even so; I hold that if only one in ten of us come back when this war is over, the military experience gained by that one will be of more service in the fight for Ireland's freedom than would that of the entire ten as they are now!*[89]

The Brigade's fighting strength represented a tiny proportion of the total number of Irish Americans who fought in the war. In all, some 150,000 Irish Americans enlisted in the Union armies, while some 30,000 fought for the Confederacy. The reasons for their participation were complex. Irish Americans generally did not appear to support the North out of any sense of commitment to its cause but rather, perhaps, because this represented an opportunity to express patriotism for their new homeland. In many cases, enlistment was no doubt also seized on as an opportunity to escape poverty. Emancipation was certainly not a driving force, as many Irish immigrants already regarded black Americans as their competitors for jobs, a situation which could only be made worse by the freeing of the slaves. Matters were brought to a head by Lincoln's Emancipation Proclamation in January 1863, which created great unrest among Irish Americans. When this was closely followed by the introduction of conscription, a largely Irish mob rioted in New York for three days in July 1863; black Americans were lynched, property destroyed, and a Negro orphan asylum was burnt down.[90] After 1863, many Irish Americans turned against the war, leading to difficulties in voluntary recruitment, as has already been noted even in relation to the Irish Brigade itself. Despite the military success of the Brigade and the accolades awarded to it in the United States, its objectives and aspirations failed to resonate widely in Ireland itself. Opinion there was also against the war, with many viewing the prospect of Irishmen fighting Irishmen on foreign soil with abhorrence. Within nationalist circles, however, the legacy of Meagher and the Irish Brigade was the reinforcement of the Irish reputation for hard fighting, and the perpetuation of the holy legends of the Wild Geese and Fontenoy.

In the summer of 1865, Meagher was appointed by President Andrew Johnson as Secretary to the territory of Montana, where he later became Acting Governor. On 1 July 1867, in the absence of any witnesses, he fell off a ship in the Missouri River and drowned. His body was never recovered. Even if he had lived, he would have been too old to fight with the next re-formation of an "Irish Brigade".

TWO
JOHN MACBRIDE AND THE IRISH TRANSVAAL BRIGADE

To fight for the liberty of any land could only be a happiness and an honour for an Irishman, but to fight for the liberty of a land whose enemy is also our own is the birthright of an Irish Brigade.
John MacBride to President Kruger, November 1900

Suddenly they heard McManus shout, 'Hands up or I'll run you through.'
He thought it was a Yorkshire "Tyke" – 'twas Corporal Donoghue!
McGarry took O'Leary, O'Brien got McNamee,
That's how the "English fought the Dutch" at the Battle of Dundee.
Extract from an anonymous Boer verse following the battle of Dundee

While the American Civil War may have failed to capture the imagination of the Irish public, this was not so in the case of the Boer War (or "South African War"). Here, Irish nationalists immediately saw the close parallel between their fight for independence and that of the small Boer Republics, especially with England as the common enemy. Just as Meagher had done in the US, another charismatic figure – John MacBride – came forward to provide the focus for nationalist attention. Though also charismatic, MacBride was a quite different character to Meagher, possessing neither his eloquence nor his higher political ambitions. By contrast, MacBride, known as "Foxy Jack" because of his wiry features, red hair and long nose, was a rough adventurer with his feet firmly grounded in the practicalities of Irish nationalism.

John MacBride was born into a Fenian family in Westport, County Mayo, in 1865, the youngest of five brothers.[1] His father, Patrick, was a shopkeeper and trader, his mother, Honoria, a grocer and publican who (according to early police reports) also dealt in dynamite detonators held in a magazine at Westport Quay. John MacBride's brother, Dr Anthony MacBride, moved to London in 1893, where he managed a GP surgery for Dr Mark Ryan, an organiser for the Irish Republican Brotherhood (IRB) and later a member of its Supreme Council. Ryan became leader of the Irish Nationalist Alliance (INA) on its foundation in 1895. According to police reports, Anthony MacBride "took a prominent part in every Irish movement" following his arrival in London, among other things, serving as Treasurer of the Amnesty Association and of the INA. Another brother, Joseph MacBride, became Secretary to the Harbour Commissioners at Westport after failed careers in the Ulster Bank and as a coal and grain dealer (resulting in a spell in Australia allegedly to escape his creditors). The police noted that though not previously engaged in "Secret Society Work", Joseph MacBride became actively involved in the formation of local INA branches. John MacBride himself was educated at Christian Brothers' School, Westport and at St Malachy's College, Belfast. Having given up medical studies, he worked as a clerk for a wholesale chemist firm in Dublin. He was sworn into the IRB by Ryan and attended the Chicago Convention in 1895 at which the INA was inaugurated.[2]

In 1896, John MacBride left Ireland for the gold mines of South Africa, where he secured a job as an assayer. He persuaded his friend Arthur Griffith (later to be a founder of Sinn Féin and briefly Irish President) to join him there for a short period in 1897 and 1898.[3] Together they formed an Irish Society in Johannesburg and collected money for the Amnesty Association in London from the large number of young Irishmen in Pretoria and Johannesburg. In the light of the Jameson Raid, MacBride had decided to join the Boer cause, telling meetings of Irish residents that it was the duty of Irishmen not only to fight for their own freedom but also to help safeguard the liberties of others. He became a Boer citizen and when war appeared inevitable, drafted a manifesto for an Irish Brigade to fight alongside the Boers.[4] Like Meagher in the American Civil War, MacBride made clear that his objective in establishing the brigade stretched beyond the immediate conflict towards the longer-term fight for Irish independence. He wanted to ensure that in the future there would be Irishmen ready to fight "the hereditary enemy, the oppressor of our race" at a time when "they could not unfortunately do so at home".[5] The brigade's manifesto, issued by MacBride shortly before the war began, made clear that the fight would be just as much for Ireland as for the Boers –

> *The Government of the Transvaal being now threatened with extinction by our ancient foe, England, it is the duty of Irishmen to throw in their lot with the former, and be prepared by force of arms to maintain the independence of the country that has given them a home, at the same time seizing the opportunity to strike a good and effective blow at the merciless tyrannic power that has so long held our people in bondage.*

And later on, after references to Drogheda and Cromwell –

England has been a vampire, and has drained Ireland's life-blood for centuries, and now her difficulty is Ireland's opportunity. The time is at hand to avenge your Irish dead. England's hands are red with blood, and her coffers filled with the spoil of Irish people, and we call upon you to rise as one man and seize upon the present glorious opportunity of retaliating upon your ancient foe...[6]

As the instigator and chairman of the organising committee, MacBride was offered command of the brigade by his supporters, a position which he declined because of his lack of military training and experience. Instead, he proposed the appointment of John Blake, a former US Cavalry Officer, born in Missouri in 1856.[7] Blake had attended West Point and had served in the Apache wars. He is said to have escorted the Apache War Chief Geronimo as a prisoner from Fort Bowie in Arizona to Fort Pickens in Pensacola, Florida, and during the journey to have been converted to the cause of freedom and liberty for all nations. He had also learned from the Apache the skills and effectiveness of guerrilla warfare.[8] After leaving the army as a 1st Lieutenant in 1889, Blake unsuccessfully attempted a business career before moving to South Africa as a gold prospector, arriving there in January 1895.[9] Blake was strongly pro-Irish, pro-Boer and anti-British. MacBride's proposal that he should take command of the brigade was accepted and he was elected Colonel to what became formally the Irish Transvaal Brigade in September 1899. The embryonic brigade, comprising at the time a hundred men, was able to take part in a military parade to celebrate President Kruger's birthday on 10 October 1899.[10] MacBride was elected to the rank of Major and received his commission from Kruger the same month.[11]

Like its predecessor in the American Civil War, the Irish Transvaal Brigade was to fight with distinction, though the term brigade was something of a misnomer because it probably never comprised more than 500 men – mostly Irish or Irish Americans. Because of the mining background of many of its members, the brigade was able to specialise in the demolition of bridges and railway culverts and other acts of sabotage on the battlefield, for which it also became known as the "Wreckers Corps",[12] though this in turn seems to have been based on a mistranslation of the name given to it by the Boers – "Het Wrekers Korps", strictly meaning "The Avengers Corps".[13] Although it was formally under Blake's command, in practice the brigade became generally known as "MacBride's Irish Brigade". The brigade's first serious encounter was at the Battle of Dundee (or Talana Hill) in October 1899. In November, it achieved its first distinguished success at Modderspruit (the Modder River), where Blake had been wounded. Here, the Boer guns had been carried up by the brigade under heavy fire, earning special thanks from General Joubert. The brigade had a permanent camp outside Ladysmith and had taken part in numerous attacks there; two companies had also taken part in the Battle of Colenso.[14] The contemporary periodical *With the Flag to Pretoria*, an illustrated history of the war, reported that the brigade was present in Johannesburg at the time of the town's surrender and suggested that it had been a major source of disturbance in the town, leading to a Boer request for a twenty-four hour delay before its occupation by British forces[15] (the formal ground for the request being to allow the Boer forces sufficient time to leave in order to avoid unnecessary hand-to-hand fighting[16]).

Whatever sensitivities may have existed about Irishmen fighting Irishmen in the American Civil War, these do not seem to have had much influence in the Boer War, where England's involvement made the dividing lines between loyalists and separatists clear. This is exemplified in a popular anonymous Boer verse written after the battle at Dundee, where MacBride's Brigade had faced the 1st Royal Irish Fusiliers and the 2nd Royal Dublin Fusiliers –

> *"On the mountain side the battle raged, there was no stop or stay;*
> *Mackin captured Private Burke and Ensign Michael Shea,*

Fitzgerald got Fitzpatrick, Brannigan found O'Rourke;
Finnigan took a man named Fay – and a couple of lads from Cork.
Suddenly they heard McManus shout, 'Hands up or I'll run you through.'
He thought it was a Yorkshire "Tyke" – 'twas Corporal Donoghue!
McGarry took O'Leary, O'Brien got McNamee,
That's how the "English fought the Dutch" at the Battle of Dundee.

Then someone brought in Casey, O'Connor took O'Neil;
Riley captured Cavanagh, while trying to make a steal.
Hagan caught McFadden, Carrigan caught McBride
And Brennan made a handsome touch when Kelly tried to slide.
Dicey took a lad named Welsh; Dooley got McGurk;
Gilligan turned in Fahey's boy – for his father he used to work.
They had marched to fight the English – but Irish were all they could see –
That's how the "English fought the Dutch" at the Battle of Dundee.

The sun was sinking slowly, the battle rolling along;
The man that Murphy "handed in" was a cousin of Maud Gonne,
Then Flanagan dropped his rifle, shook hands with Bill Maguire,
For both had carried a piece of turf to light the schoolroom fire.
Then Rafferty took in Flaherty; O'Connell got Major McGue;
O'Keefe got hold of Sergeant Joyce and a Belfast lad or two.
Some swore that "Old Man Kruger" had come down to see the fun;
But the man they thought was "Uncle Paul" was a Galway man named Dunn.
Though war may have worse horrors, 'twas a frightful sight to see
The way the "English fought the Dutch" at the Battle of Dundee."[17]

Following the annexation of the Transvaal in September 1900, the Irish Brigade was disbanded. MacBride went to Paris, where his attendance at a reception given by Kruger for delegates of the Irish

Transvaal Committee was reported in *The Times*.[18] Kruger was effusive in his praise of MacBride –

> *To you I owe a personal and special thanks, for you and the brave men of your brigade have personally aided us in our struggle for the cause of justice. I shall never forget, and my countrymen will never forget, how the Irish Brigade stood by the men of the Transvaal in their hour of need. Again, I thank you, Major MacBride.*

To which MacBride replied –

> *To fight for the liberty of any land could only be a happiness and an honour for an Irishman, but to fight for the liberty of a land whose enemy is also our own is the birthright of an Irish Brigade.*

In answer to a question about his impending trip to New York and his future movements, he responded –

> *I am not much of a speechmaker. I believe more in the efficacy of one well-directed bullet than in that of a hundred appeals to the foreign Parliament that has its seat in Westminster, but I may give some lectures in America.*

MacBride's exploits had a great impact on nationalist opinion in Ireland. "MacBride Clubs" were formed, ballads were written about him, and a movement was established in Dublin to present him with an address and a sword of honour.[19] In nationalist circles, he became a hero, as indicated by the following report in the *Western People* on 3 November 1900 –

> *Major John McBride* [sic], *the gallant leader of the Irish Brigade in the Transvaal, arrived in Paris on Wednesday by the Marseilles express, and was met at the station by his mother,*

his brother, Dr McBride [sic], *London; Dr Mark Ryan, Dr Barry, Mr J W O'Beirne, of Dublin and several French deputies, journalists, and other leading and representative men. The gallant major was accorded a most enthusiastic welcome. He looked wonderfully well, notwithstanding all that he had gone through during the past 12 months. Thousands of his friends in Mayo and throughout the country and the still vaster numbers of our exiled race everywhere will rejoice to know that this brave soldier of liberty, whose name will live in their hearts with a love born of admiration for heroic deeds given in the most holy of causes, has come back scathless from the war in which his brigade has borne such a glorious part in all the chief battles that will make it memorable.*[20]

During the same year, despite his disparaging comments about the Westminster Parliament, MacBride's reputation was so high that he allowed his name to be put forward (and stood unsuccessfully) against the Home Rule candidate in the South Mayo by-election caused by the resignation of Michael Davitt in protest against the Boer War.[21]

MacBride's charisma was given a further boost when he married Maude Gonne, the wealthy Irish nationalist actress and close friend of the poet W B Yeats, in Paris on 21 February 1903. Gonne had met MacBride through Arthur Griffith in 1900. She had been introduced to Fenianism by John O'Leary, an erstwhile associate of Thomas Francis Meagher, who had tried to rescue the leaders of the failed Ballingarry rising from Clonmel Gaol in 1848. It was also O'Leary who in 1889 had introduced Gonne to Yeats and who is remembered in Yeats' poem *September 1913* – "Romantic Ireland's dead and gone; it's with O'Leary in his grave". Gonne, who was born in England of Anglo-Irish descent, had first risen to prominence in Ireland as an organiser of protests against slum landlords and harsh eviction laws and then against the celebrations for Queen Victoria's Diamond Jubilee in 1897. In October 1899, she co-founded the Irish Transvaal Committee with Arthur Griffith. The committee's objects were to send an ambulance to the Transvaal, to collect money and to draw up a list of names of people willing to fight for the Boers. At Gonne's suggestion, the committee also started a campaign against Irishmen enlisting in the British Army.[22] In 1900, she co-founded the "Daughters of Erin" (*Inghinidhe na hÉireann),* a nationalist revolutionary organisation for women, and in April 1902 starred in the nationalist play *Cathleen ní Houlihan,* specially written for her by Yeats. By the time that she married MacBride, she had already turned down at least two proposals of marriage from Yeats, who was, and was to remain, infatuated with her. It is often stated that she turned down Yeats because she regarded herself as his muse and believed that this would irrevocably change if they were married, arguing that they should be friends – "the world would thank her for not marrying him".[23] In truth, she seems simply not to have been in love with him, writing in February 1903, "…I fear that you are sad and yet our friendship need not suffer by my marriage". How much she actually loved MacBride is also questionable. Writing in the same letter, she said about her decision to marry, "I did not quite understand things but I *know* that I am fulfilling a destiny".[24] She believed that by marrying MacBride, a national hero, "she was marrying Ireland".[25]

In reality, marrying Ireland and marrying MacBride turned out to be two quite different things. Right from the start, things went badly. According to Gonne, their honeymoon in Spain was a cover for a plot to assassinate King Edward VII during a visit to Gibraltar. While Gonne was to act as a decoy for the police shadowing them, the plan was for MacBride to join others to carry out the assassination. She records that having set out for this purpose, MacBride returned to their hotel the same night, drunk and refusing to say what had happened. (He subsequently confirmed to his brother Anthony that "he had not set foot in Gibraltar".) Gonne promptly ended their honeymoon the following day and they both returned to Paris.[26] MacBride's heavy drinking continued to be a problem. Gonne was subsequently to state that she had two phobias: madness, which she had struggled to conquer; and drunkenness, which she considered, "a danger to the national movement", a horror of which therefore seemed "quite normal and right".[27] But MacBride's heavy drinking was not all. Gonne was subsequently to write to Yeats that from the start of their marriage she had suffered from MacBride's insane jealousy – "…he has accused, at some time or other, every man who he has ever heard of being my friend or whose photo he has ever seen at my house of having been my lover. On one occasion he told me he had intended to kill you…"[28]

Matters were to come to a head less than two years into their marriage. On returning to their home in Paris in October 1904, Gonne was met with complaints of drunken and indecent behaviour by MacBride towards various members of their domestic staff. In addition, it was suggested that he had also frightened Gonne's ten-year-old daughter by a previous relationship (Iseult) in a similar fashion. Gonne moved for a separation, which was not disputed by MacBride *per se*, but which faltered over custody and visiting rights in relation to their son Seán, who had been born the previous January. Lengthy and acrimonious court proceedings then followed in Paris during which MacBride refuted the allegations of sexual impropriety – "If I wanted a woman I had plenty of money in my pocket and would have no difficulty in making a suitable choice in Paris, without trying to rape a hideously ugly old cook in my wife's house", and in the case of another accusation that he, "would not be seen dead with her in a five-acre field".[29] He also brought forward witnesses who testified against accusations of drunkenness. The matter dragged on until a final court judgement in August 1906, which found that a charge of drunkenness against MacBride had been proved but the charges of immorality had not. As MacBride had proved to the court his Irish nationality and domicile, the court was unable to grant a divorce because this was not permitted in Ireland. The court agreed a judicial separation under which Gonne was given the right of guardianship of Seán, with weekly visiting rights given to MacBride[30]. The affair tainted the reputation and standing of both, though MacBride's was to suffer the most through an enduring reputation for heavy drinking.

*

MacBride's activities with the Irish Brigade were understandably viewed differently by the British Government and others outside nationalist circles. On 21 March 1900, *The Times* carried the following report from Cape Colony –

> *From reports which have reached here it is evident that St Patrick's Day was celebrated with unusual enthusiasm all over South Africa as well as in Cape Town. At meetings and dinners everywhere sentiments of loyalty and a keen desire to preserve the supremacy of the Empire in South Africa were displayed, while disapproval of the attitude of the Nationalist members of Parliament and detestation of the Transvaal Irish Brigade* [sic], *so called, were expressed…*[31]

On 2 January 1901, a report from *The Times*' Dublin correspondent included –

> *Nationalism was, indeed, generous of "resolutions" in favour of the Boers but it spent its money on pipes and socks for the Connaught Rangers, and had neither subscriptions nor recruits for that melancholy imposture, the "Irish Transvaal Brigade.*[32]

MacBride's activities and public utterances could hardly be construed by the general public as anything but treasonous. But public opinion in the Boer War was so closely focused on the bigger picture of England and the Empire that the activities of foreigners and a few traitors warranted little more than passing note. Thus, when an Englishman was found among some captured Boer prisoners, *With the Flag to Pretoria* wrote –

> *Among the few Boer prisoners taken in this engagement was a double-dyed traitor and thief named Greener. This man, a Sergeant-Major of the Royal Engineers, had been detected in wholesale theft at Aldershot. Deserting the colours and betraying the country which had given him birth, he fled to South Africa and took service with the Boers. So far as we can discover, the extraordinary leniency of the British suffered this rogue to retain his life. By any other nation he would have been summarily executed under the orders of a drum-head court martial.*

And when a British chaplain was allowed after an action to move among the Boers to bury the British dead, he told a reporter –

> *...that there were Englishmen, Irishmen and Scotchmen among them, as well as the mercenary German and Scandinavians, serving for a gold krüger a day – which is to say, a pound sterling Dutch. ... Everybody was courteous.*[33]

Another reason why MacBride's escapades were of little general concern was that, despite the Irish Transvaal Committee's best efforts, far more Irishmen fought with the British Army than against it. A "real" Irish Brigade within the British Army (the 5th), comprising the 1st Connaught Rangers, the 1st and 2nd Royal Dublin Fusiliers, the 1st Royal Inniskilling Fusiliers and the 1st Border Regiment gained its own reputation for bravery and hard fighting. They fought under the command of Major-General Arthur Fitzroy Hart, "a cool-eyed veteran with a moustache extending in waxed points across the breadth of either cheek"[34], and, "a fiery Irishman, beautifully dressed, a master of field tactics, who believed in the traditional virtues of close order and dash".[35] Hart's tactics epitomised the "Boys' Own" style of leadership which came to characterise the British in the Boer War. He acquired the nickname "General No-Bobs" (as opposed to the Commander-in-Chief, Lord Roberts ("Bobs")) because of his refusal to duck his head when shells came over and his practice of exposing himself to rifle fire as he rode along on his charger. No one could criticise Hart on the grounds of his own personal courage, but his failure to adapt his tactics to the nature of the war needlessly exposed his men to danger. His requirement that they should march in columns of four and follow parade ground formation, for example, fully exposed them to the hidden enemy, resulting in high and pointless casualties. At the Battle of Colenso on 15 December 1899, through such tactics compounded by a series of errors, Hart led his men to disaster.[36] Then at Hart's Hill on 23 February 1900, during the Battle of the Tugela Heights, the Irish Brigade suffered 500 casualties, with the colonels of both the Dublins and the Inniskillings being killed. The Inniskillings had lost in total seventy-two per cent of their officers and twenty-seven per cent of their men, the highest proportion of any regiment so far in the war.[37] Queen Victoria was directly moved by the losses sustained by the brigade and the gallantry displayed by its men in the many battles which it had fought. Following the relief of Ladysmith, *With the Flag to Pretoria* noted –

> *From the Queen came thanks to the general and his troops, and especial recognition of the valour of the Irishmen, whose deeds were henceforward to be commemorated by the "wearing of the green" on St Patrick's Day and by the creation of a regiment of Irish*

> Guards. It was noted that, for probably the first time in history, the green flag made its appearance everywhere in England side by side with the Union Jack.[38]

This gratitude for the contribution of Irish soldiers in the war also directly inspired the Queen to visit Ireland in April 1900, for the first time in thirty-nine years, where the formalities of her decisions could be concluded.[39] These events eclipsed the activities of MacBride and his men in the general public mind.

MacBride's own position was nevertheless a matter of concern to the authorities. He was clearly safe from arrest for treason while he kept away from Ireland, though his movements were monitored as far as it was practicable to do so. Rumours circulated that he had successfully evaded the police in November 1900 and had spent ten days in Ireland talking to a number of prominent Irishmen, though the police had doubts whether this was actually true. A copy of an address given by MacBride to *Clan na Gael* (the US wing of the IRB) in New York in December 1900, in the presence of its leader, John Devoy, was placed on file. There was also a suggestion that "a considerable sum of money" had been given by Kruger to Michael Davitt in France and that some of this money was being utilised by the IRB in Ireland. There was even a report that MacBride and others were involved in a plot to kill Lord Kitchener in South Africa. The Royal Irish Constabulary (RIC) said of MacBride in February 1901 that, "If he should visit Ireland he would be a most dangerous conspirator".[40] But things then remained quiet until 1903, when the Metropolitan Police in Dublin asked their counterparts in London whether a warrant had been issued for MacBride's arrest in connection with his activities in South Africa. The police in London said that they were not aware that this had been considered and that they had no evidence bearing on the subject. They continued that, "McBride [sic] went to the Transvaal about May 1896 and it is reasonable to suppose he took the precaution of being naturalized before the outbreak of hostilities to save himself from the consequences attaching to a rebel, if taken prisoner and as a bar to prosecution for treason".[41] Whether Boer citizenship had in fact given him or others immunity from prosecution was later to become a matter for debate, and as we have seen, MacBride himself subsequently went on to establish before a court that he was an Irish citizen for the purpose of his divorce and separation proceedings.

Eventually, MacBride returned to Ireland, arriving at Westport Quay on 25 November 1904. The event was recorded by Sergeant Sheridan of the RIC, who reported that MacBride had arrived at 4 pm and was staying at his mother's house, where he intended to remain for a few weeks. Sir Neville Chamberlain, the Inspector General of the RIC, noted that if MacBride had been a British subject at the time, his activities in South Africa would represent a very clear case of high treason. In recording that MacBride had returned to Ireland for the first time since the Boer War, however, a subsequent note to the Under Secretary, Dublin Castle, commented that, "Even if there should be evidence that he fought against the British, it is doubtful whether he is worth notice now…"[42] And a month later, on 29 December 1904, an informant reported that MacBride's return to Ireland had no particular significance and that he would be giving no further trouble either at home or abroad. The informer went on to say that MacBride was looking for a position with the Dublin Corporation and that when this had been secured, very little would be heard of him again. A covering note to the Under Secretary commented that the contents of the report showed "the wisdom of the decision taken in this case".[43] The file does not indicate what that decision was, though it seems reasonable to assume that it was a decision to take no action against MacBride. That no action was to be taken was confirmed in June 1906, when John Lonsdale, the Irish Unionist MP for Armagh, put down a question in the Commons asking the

Chief Secretary to the Lord Lieutenant of Ireland, "whether it was with the cognisance and permission of the police authorities that Major McBride [*sic*] was present in Dublin on June 1st." In reply, James Bryce said that he was not aware of any reason why the permission of the police should be necessary. When Lonsdale then asked whether the right honourable gentleman, "was aware that Major MacBride fought on the side of our enemies in the Boer War and was therefore guilty of high treason", Bryce responded by saying that he had no information on that point.[44] This was an incredible response, perhaps designed to shut down the debate and signalling that the Government did not want to pursue the matter. Whatever the Government might or might not have been prepared to say in public, the briefing given to Bryce should certainly have told him the full background to the allegations against MacBride and his activities in the Transvaal, even assuming that he had not already read these in the newspapers. The exchange brought the following response from none other than MacBride himself in a letter to the editor of the *Freeman's Journal*, sent from Gardiner's Place, Dublin –

> *Sir*
>
> *I am at a loss to understand why Mr Lonsdale – who I am informed is one of the Orange deadheads – wants to know if I was in Dublin on 1st June. Why the 1st June, any more than the 1st January, or the 12th July?*
>
> *I returned to my country on November 25th, 1904, and have been in permanent residence here since. I am on no "visit". I may inform Mr Lonsdale, and all others concerned, that I did fight with the Boers against the forces of the so-called "mighty" British Empire, and am proud of the fact.*
>
> *Yours truly,*
> *John MacBride*

Whether it had in the event been wise not to pursue the question of MacBride's arrest further is a matter for debate. Certainly, the course of history would have been changed, even if only slightly perhaps, had he been put on trial. As it was, MacBride continued with his nationalist activities despite securing a job with Dublin Corporation (as a water bailiff) and the informant's claim that "very little would be heard from him again". In May 1910, MacBride gave a major speech at the City Hall in Cork. A police plant in the audience produced a report of the speech running to about ten pages which carefully noted that MacBride had said nothing "political" about the present sovereign. The speech covered the escapades of the Irish Transvaal Brigade in detail while belittling the role of the British forces. MacBride told his audience that before the Brigade finished, it blew up the "Long Toms" it was responsible for safeguarding and took pains to surrender to the Portuguese rather than "the English". He concluded with, "Ireland is today fighting the possessors of as villainous an Empire as ever encountered on God's earth".[45] He was received by the audience with loud cheers.[46] In 1911, he led the way in preventing a loyal address by the Dublin Corporation during a royal visit, and in the same year was elected for a short time onto the Supreme Council of the IRB. MacBride's activities attracted the criticism of British politicians who repeatedly queried why no action had been taken against him. During debate on the Parliament Bill in the House of Lords in 1911, Lord Farnham stated –

> *Loyalty to the Throne, fair-play to minorities, and the strengthening of the Empire is what we are told Home Rule means. Yet we find a Major McBride* [sic] *of South African fame, but who, mark you, at the present moment is a favourite protégé of the RedmoniteCorporation of Dublin – we find him being received with loud applause by a large Nationalist gathering in*

Dublin when he declared – 'They should strike how they might and when they might against the Throne and the cursed British Empire, and for the freedom of Ireland.'[47]

In another debate on the Government of Ireland Bill in the House of Commons on 31 December 1912, after a dispute with John Redmond who (rightly) denied that MacBride had ever been a member of the Nationalist party or a supporter of Home Rule, Captain Craig said the following –

The strongest Nationalist body in Ireland is the Dublin Corporation, and they gave him [MacBride] a place because, I presume, they had not got a place in Parliament for him. At any rate, what I say is this, that this class of man has a large following in Ireland, and it is not fair for hon Members to get up and say, 'Oh, So-and-so is outside our pale.' These men in the public life of Ireland represent a large section, and in their speeches and sentiments they voice the opinion of a large section of Ireland, and here is what this gentleman said:– England was not his country; the English King; was not his King. He owed no allegiance to England, and he indignantly repudiated the idea of an Englishman posing as censor of his words and acts in Ireland. The English King would undoubtedly receive a reception from his garrison and from the men who believed they had a country to sell, but the manhood of Ireland would take no part in that reception…[48]

MacBride continued to attract attention at the start of the First World War, now as an anti-enlistment campaigner and supporter of the Irish Volunteers. A speech given by him in Cork on 30 November 1914 was described by Viscount Midleton (leader of the Irish Unionist Alliance) in the House of Lords as "the worst speech that has been made". He reported that MacBride had said –

Irishmen would sing throughout the land "Live Ireland. To hell with the Empire". To his mind the Irishman who fought for England would be a meaner wretch than a Belgian who fought for Germany. The war on the continent had nothing to do with Irishmen; they should stay at home and mind their own business. Let Englishmen do their own fighting and get killed and be damned to them.

And –

I would again ask, why are Colonel Warburton and Major MacBride still at large? Why have steps not been taken to make them amenable to the law? I cannot help saying that the conduct of the Government has been both tardy and timorous in this respect.[49]

Viscount Midleton returned to the same theme in a debate on the Easter Rising in May 1916, when he commented –

In the November following – November, 1914 – the so-called Major MacBride delivered a seditious and treasonous speech in the South of Ireland. It was the subject of great public comment, but no action of any sort was taken against him by the Government.[50]

By then, action had, in fact, been taken against MacBride. During the Easter Rising, on Easter Monday 1916, MacBride had joined a group of Irish Volunteers and marched with them to the Jacobs Biscuit Factory. There he had been appointed second-in-command, eventually of some one hundred men. The rebels surrendered the factory six days later, at 5 pm on Sunday, 30 April, following which MacBride had been court-martialled.[51] He had been found guilty and executed on 5 May.

It seems generally accepted that MacBride took no part in planning the Rising, nor, perhaps, that he was even aware of it.[52] According to his statement presented to the court martial, MacBride had left his home on Easter Monday to meet his brother, who was coming to Dublin to get married. On his way, he had met by chance a band of Irish Volunteers – some of whom he knew personally – who told him that "an Irish Republic was virtually proclaimed". His statement went on to say that, "although I had no previous connection with the Irish Volunteers I considered it my duty to join them".[53] He marched with them to the Jacobs Factory where during the course of the week he gradually assumed the practical leadership of his party, exhibiting the skills for which he had been praised as commander of the Irish Transvaal Brigade – the Volunteers referred to him as "the Major" out of respect and admiration.[54] MacBride's statement to the court martial concluded, "I could have escaped from Jacobs Factory before the surrender had I so desired but I considered it a dishonourable thing to do. I do not say this with the idea of mitigating any penalty they may impose but in order [to] make clear my position in the matter".

Most of the death sentences imposed on the rebels were eventually commuted. As MacBride had not in any way been a leader or plotter of the Rising, it might well have been expected that his sentence too would have been reduced. But his activities in the Transvaal appear finally to have caught up with him – a point of no surprise to MacBride himself, who is reported to have said to fellow rebel Sean O'Kelly after his court martial, 'Nothing will save me, Sean. This is the end. Remember this is the second time I have sinned against them.'[55] Following the court martial, his sentence was quickly confirmed by Major-General Sir John Maxwell, GOC, Ireland. That MacBride's time in South Africa tilted the balance against him is evidenced by a subsequent report from Maxwell to Asquith on those who had been executed following the Rising. This began with the following –

> *This man* [MacBride] *fought on the side of the Boers in the South African war of 1899 and held the rank of Major in that Army, being in command of a body known as the Irish Brigade. He was always one of the most active advocates of the anti-enlistment propaganda and the Irish Volunteer movement…*

MacBride's final exchanges with those involved in his execution have become part of the folklore surrounding the Rising. There are varying accounts of what actually happened, but the most authentic version seems to be that of Father Augustine, a Capuchin friar who relates that he was awoken at 2 am on 5 May 1916, by a soldier who told him that a prisoner at Kilmainham Gaol who was about to be executed had asked to see him. After taking MacBride's confession, Father Augustine waited with him until the time of execution. When this came, MacBride –

> *… asked quietly not to have his hands bound and promised to remain perfectly still. 'Sorry Sir,' the soldier said, 'but these are my orders.' Then he requested not to be blindfolded and a similar answer was given.*
>
> *Turning slightly aside he said to me, quite naturally in a soft voice: 'You know, Father Augustine, I've often looked down their guns before.'*[56]

MacBride's aside echoed a similar comment he had allegedly already made at the end of his court martial –

> *I thank the officers of the court for the fair trial I have had, and the Crown counsel for the way he met every application I made. I have looked down the muzzles of too many guns in the South African War to fear death, and now please carry out your sentence.*[57]

Although over the years MacBride had continued to have a reputation for heavy drinking, which in turn had brought into question his reliability and discretion,[58] his final contribution to the nationalist cause in Easter Week redeemed his tarnished reputation. But not everyone was impressed. Tom Kettle, a committed nationalist and former IPP Westminster MP, who had distributed pro-Boer leaflets in Dublin at the start of the South African War,[59] had time neither for MacBride nor the Easter Rising. His version of events was that MacBride had told the firing squad, 'Fire away. I've been looking down the barrels of rifles all my life,' on which Kettle commented, 'That was a lie, a magnificent lie,' adding, 'He had been looking down the necks of porter bottles all his life.'[60] A different version again is attributed to W B Yeats, who on hearing of MacBride's last words (in this case, 'I've been staring down rifle *butts* all my life') is alleged to have remarked that, 'he might better have said that he had been staring down pintpots all his life.'[61] Yeats' sister Lily was even more acerbic, writing to John Butler Yeats on 7 May 1916, "Maud Gonne is at last a widow, made so by an English bullet. It must have been some humourist who got him the job of water bailiff to the corporation".

Gonne herself was gracious, writing to W B Yeats on 9 May that she had read in the newspapers the announcement of MacBride's execution, commenting that he "had died for Ireland". In a further letter on 11 May she wrote that, "Major MacBride by his Death [sic] has left a name for Seagan [Seàn] to be proud of. Those who die for Ireland are sacred". And in response to what she described as a vile and inaccurate attack on MacBride's role in the South African War in the Paris edition of the *Daily Mail* on 8 May, which had included the comment that the Boers were finally glad to get rid of him because he had stolen some horses, Gonne wrote to the French press to set the record straight, referring to the unanimous praise given to MacBride by President Kruger and other Boer leaders publicly in Paris, commenting that, "I separated from my husband for personal reasons, but I don't want the memory of him to be dishonoured".[62] Her defence of MacBride's memory continued later in the year in response to Yeats' poem *Easter 1916*, in which he referred to MacBride as, "A drunken vainglorious lout". She wrote, "No, I don't like your poem, it isn't worthy of you & above all it isn't worthy of the subject ... sacrifice has never yet turned a heart to stone though it has immortalised many & through it alone mankind can rise to God... As for my husband he has entered Eternity by the great door of sacrifice which Christ opened & has therefore atoned for all..."[63]

The attitude of the British Government towards John MacBride's activities in South Africa and then on his return to Ireland is interesting, and on the face of things surprising. It was criticised by many. His action in taking arms against the British must in any practical sense be regarded as treasonous. Had he been brought to trial – as many thought he should – his status as a Boer citizen might have provided a legal argument in his defence, though it seems barely credible that he would have wanted to defend his activities as an Irish nationalist on the basis that he was not an Irish citizen. In any event, there seems no surviving evidence that this question was seriously examined by the law officers. The reality seems to be that there was simply no appetite for action along these lines. Unlike 1848, when the Government thought (albeit wrongly) that it was facing mass protest and rebellion in Ireland which needed to be quelled, the prospect of Home Rule was now on the agenda. To have entered into a contentious court case with the danger of creating a martyr was something which the Government was no doubt keen to avoid. There was, however, another more pragmatic reason for not wanting to proceed. By the time MacBride returned to Ireland in 1904, a similar case had already been brought before the courts – as set out in the next chapter – resulting in little advantage to anyone.

As a postscript, MacBride and Gonne's son Seán was to have his own notable nationalist career, among other things as Acting

JOHN MACBRIDE

Chief of Staff to the IRA, founder of the republican party *Clann na Poblachta*, TD, and Minister for External Affairs in the Irish Government. His most distinguished work was to be carried out in the field of international justice, most notably as a founding member of Amnesty International. In 1974, he was awarded the Nobel Peace Prize.

THREE
ARTHUR LYNCH AND THE SECOND IRISH BRIGADE

Never since Fontenoy have Irishmen been so blessed by fortune. Remember how that name has resounded in Irish history. Remember that Irishmen who fall in this war will be joined in Irish memories for ever with Sarsfield, with Wolfe Tone, and with Robert Emmet.
    Recruiting advertisement by Arthur Lynch, 21 March 1900

Do not strike me, but hear me
    Arthur Lynch to a hostile House of Commons (1902)

References to the "Irish Brigade" in the Boer War, or the "Irish Transvaal Brigade", invariably relate to the unit commanded by Blake and MacBride. There was, however, a lesser-known "Second Irish Brigade" established during the war under the command of "Colonel" Arthur Alfred Lynch.

Lynch was a near contemporary of MacBride, having been born in Australia in 1861 to an Irish Catholic father and a Scottish mother. His father (John Lynch) had been prominent in the "diggers'" (miners') insurrection at the Eureka stockade in 1854, for which he had been temporarily imprisoned before going on to become a magistrate and chairman of his local council. Arthur Lynch attended the universities of Melbourne and Berlin and then moved to Paris to study medicine. In 1888, while in Berlin, he met an Irish student, Annie Powell, whom he went on to marry in 1895.[1] During the period of his courtship, perhaps stimulated by trips to Ireland to meet his future wife, Lynch became an active Irish nationalist. In 1892, he unsuccessfully contested Galway City as a Parnellite in the general election of that year. He gathered a reputation sufficient to feature on the "Register of Suspects" held by the Irish Special Branch at Dublin Castle. This noted that he had been an IRB delegate to *Clan na Gael*, and had visited all their camps in America where, in November 1893, he had been observed in the company of prominent IRB suspects. It went on to record that following this, he had attended a meeting of the IRB in Toome, Co Antrim, before moving on to Dublin, Galway and London. In London, he had associated with Dr Mark Ryan of the IRB, whose GP surgery was managed by John MacBride's brother Anthony, as set out in the previous chapter. The entry in the suspects' register went on to say that in January 1894 he had visited Limerick and Ennis for the reorganisation of the party of Irish National Independence, "and to stir up the leading spirits in those centres to renewed exertions in that direction", noting that he had met with very little success. In April 1894, Lynch resigned the presidency of the Amnesty Association on being elected President of the Irish National League of Great Britain. Major Gosselin, head of the Home Office Special Irish Branch, noted in December 1893 that, "no man of such importance in a revolutionary sense had visited Ireland for the past 8 or 9 years".[2]

For a while, Lynch earned a living as a journalist and freelance writer in London, before being appointed Paris correspondent of the *Daily Mail* in August 1896. In Paris, he became active in the "Paris Young Ireland Society", formed by Maud Gonne and W B Yeats from among the Irish living there.[3] In November 1899, Gonne and others went on to set up a "Boer Franco-Irish Committee", and Lynch decided to visit the Transvaal himself. He wrote the same month to Dr Leyds, the Boer emissary in Europe, to say that he had completed arrangements to enable him to travel to the Transvaal, being "extremely anxious to do good work" there. On 29 November, J Pierson, the Boer Consul General in Paris, sent Lynch 500 *francs* to cover his expenses.[4] The exact nature of the "good work" he intended to carry out in the Transvaal was to be the subject of debate in the future, with some speculating that the Boers had paid him to secure the services of a trained engineer.[5] Lynch always insisted, however, that his sole intention in going to the Transvaal had been to act as a war correspondent.[6] He left for South Africa at the beginning of 1900, travelling on the German passenger ship *Hertzog*. In his subsequent memoirs, he claimed that the journey to South Africa had been something of an adventure itself when some Germans travelling to South Africa to fight for the Boers had plotted to throw him overboard as a British spy, though he had taken no action to report this.[7]

On his arrival in Pretoria, Lynch quickly contacted Count Villebois-Mareuil, a former colonel in the French army. Villebois-Mareuil had a particular antagonism towards the British following France's humiliation at Fashoda in 1898. He had arrived in South Africa from France in November 1899 and had already fought for the Boers at the Battle of Colenso. In March 1900, he was to be given the rank of Brigadier-General and put in command of all foreign forces in the Boer army. Meanwhile, in addition to his other activities, Villebois-Mareuil acted as correspondent for the *Revue des Deux Mondes*, the *Correspondant* and *La Liberté*. Lynch introduced himself to Villebois-Mareuil in a letter sent from the Transvaal Hotel, Pretoria, on 15 January 1900. In that letter (written in French), Lynch said that, "Colonel Monteil, one of my friends in Paris, has honoured me with a letter of introduction to you, but I had to destroy it when the *Hertzog* was captured, because I expected to be arrested in Durban, and the letter contained some compromising sentences about me". (This is a reference to the *Hertzog* having been stopped at sea by the Royal Navy in search of contraband – none was found.[8]) Lynch said that he had come with a mission from Dr Leyds to observe any facts, "such as the employment of natives by the English – which would be useful to make known in Europe with a view to influencing public opinion". He had accordingly arranged to act as a correspondent for *Le Journal* in Paris. Lynch described himself as an Irishman who had lived in Paris for three years and (curiously) that prior to his departure he had applied for naturalisation as a French subject, "which I expect has now been granted to me".[9] There appears to be no record elsewhere of this application or its fate, and it may be that Lynch made the claim simply to dissociate himself from any "Britishness" and to ingratiate himself with Villebois-Mareuil. Lynch concluded by passing on Monteil's "enthusiastic congratulations for the part you have played in the war".

Within three days of writing to Villebois-Mareuil, Lynch had taken the Boer Oath of Allegiance and had become a fully enfranchised Burgher of the South African Republic. According to Lynch's account given in 1902, this was simply to enable him to carry out his work as a reporter and to accompany Villebois-Mareuil in the latter's capacity as correspondent for *La Liberté* –

> *I agreed to accompany him and I became naturalised as a Burgher and took the oaths of allegiance that were necessary for this purpose in order that I might have unrestricted liberty to go practically everywhere I wished among the Boer forces and their positions,*

even though it would necessarily involve my becoming acquainted with military secrets. I had no intention of fighting and no idea of being asked to command a troop when I was naturalised. I was naturalised solely for the advantages it would secure me as a journalist.

But Lynch then describes how he was drawn into the conflict itself –

Colonel Villebois-Mareuil left for Colesberg where I intended to rejoin him, but a delay occurred owing to my horse getting fever, and while waiting I was informed that a new troop, composed principally of Afrikanders of Irish origin, was in the process of formation at Johannesburg. I went thither to observe in a general way the state of affairs in that city, and while there I met Louis Botha who had just come up from the Front. It was after a conversation with him that I decided to assist in the organization of the troop mentioned which became known as the Second Irish Brigade.

Subsequently they came to me and asked me to command the troop, with the title conferred by the Executive and approved by Commandant-General Joubert, of Colonel of the Second Irish Brigade. When I arrived on the scene the troop numbered about fifty horsemen and it was decided to make a beginning with that. Soon after taking the field the numbers had doubled, and subsequently the roll shewed considerably more than two hundred. It was impossible, however, owing to the exigencies of the campaign to get all the men together at any one time. I was a member of the Krijgs-Raad (or War Council) and I always acted in concert with the Boer Generals.[10]

In his memoirs twenty-two years later, Lynch was to give a slightly different version of events, claiming that on their meeting he immediately struck up a friendship with Botha, who intimated that it would not be possible for Lynch to act as a war correspondent because this would be the equivalent of him communicating directly with the British Government from behind the Boer lines. At this, Lynch says that he proposed to Botha that he should be given a command on his staff and that Botha had said that Lynch could best serve the cause of the republic by helping the "organisation" of a troop which was being put together in Johannesburg.[11] With absolutely no military experience, Lynch expressed himself confident that he could lead such a troop. (Commenting on all this separately, Kruger was to remark caustically, 'All these men are mad after military titles, and we have a topsy-turvy condition. There are some men who have seen some real fighting and they have kept with their former titles of Lieutenant or what not, although they are commanding troops, and here is a man [Lynch] who has never commanded at all and wants to be a Colonel.'[12]) Lynch was granted his request and on 10 February was appointed Special Justice of the Peace to enable him to administer the Oath to new recruits.

On taking over the new brigade, Lynch quickly embarked on a recruiting drive, invoking the legends of Sarsfield and the Wild Geese and Fontenoy as Meagher had done before him, by means of an advertisement in the *Standard and Diggers' News* –

From Arthur Lynch, Colonel: Irish Brigade II, by Krugersdorp Laager, Near Glencoe, 21 March 1900 –

TO IRISHMEN

The events of the war are daily becoming more critical and important. We Irish burghers of the two republics are fighting not only for the country but for liberty, honour, and all that men hold dear. The time has come for all to be up and doing. Irishmen and men of Irish descent have never been backward when battle has sounded its clarion call, and never has the need been greater or the opportunity more glorious for the display of Irish chivalry.

> Irishmen, rally to the Green Flag! Make your strength greater in unity, and the part of Ireland in this war more disastrous to your enemies and more inspiring to your friends. Never since Fontenoy have Irishmen been so blessed by fortune. Remember how that name has resounded in Irish history. Remember that Irishmen who fall in this war will be joined in Irish memories for ever with Sarsfield, with Wolfe Tone, and with Robert Emmet. Remember that all Ireland and all Irish America are looking at your actions, and that your valour has already sent the electric thrill of enthusiasm throughout the ranks "of the Sea-divided Gael" and raised the prestige of the Irish name.
>
> Communicate with M F Hogan care of H S Lombaard Field Cornet of Johannesburg, or direct to me.[13]

There appears to be no authoritative record of how successful Lynch's recruiting efforts were, but despite his own claim that the brigade's roll eventually totalled over 200 men, estimates from various other sources put its strength during its three months in the field at between 50 and 150.[14] There were also differing views about the quality of the recruits and the character of the brigade. A news article in *The Times* over a year later referred to it as "a cosmopolitan body, whose constitution was far more Teutonic than Celtic",[15] while a contemporary source (one of MacBride's men) described it as, "fifty or sixty soreheads, greasers, half breeds and dagos" and, "the laughing stock and contempt of every commando in the neighbourhood". There was even a claim that Lynch recruited men from the cells of Johannesburg Gaol.[16] Ex-MP Michael Davitt, on the other hand, visited the Transvaal following his resignation from Westminster and put a much more positive slant on things –

> He [Lynch] was elected to the post of colonel, and being an able linguist, speaking French and German with fluency, he succeeded in enlisting about 150 "Irishmen" from several European

> nationalities, not hitherto reckoned as subordinate members of the Celtic racial family. Colonel Lynch soon earned such a reputation for capacity and for looking carefully after the comforts of his men that numbers of volunteers from other commandos were induced to join the second "Irish" Brigade, which in this way became at one time as strong numerically as that organised by Major MacBride.

And –

> ...this unique brigade had representations from every European country, with one or two Americans, completing the most thoroughly cosmopolitan body which was ever commanded by an Irish or any other officer. There was Ireland, America, Australia, the Transvaal, Free State, Cape Colony, France, Germany, Holland, Italy, Austria, Russia, Greece, and Bulgaria represented in this second "Irish" corps, which, to complete its unprecedented representativeness, embraced a solitary Englishman, who fought for right and justice against his own country's forces. I visited Colonel Lynch's laager while in Natal early in May, 1900, and can bear personal testimony to the true soldierly manner in which his well-equipped camp was organised, and to his popularity as an officer among his Continental and universal "Irishmen".[17]

The brigade does not seem to have seen much action during its existence, though it did attract some praise for an action at Biggarsberg in May 1900, when it fought well and delayed General Buller's advance out of Ladysmith. (Lynch was subsequently concussed by a British shell at Laing's Nek before moving on to Johannesburg.) *The Times* noted that, "Mr Lynch's military qualities are said to have earned the admiration of General Botha, and it is stated that he was instrumental in saving several Boer guns in the retreat after the relief of Ladysmith.[18] But there were also allegations that Lynch had to beat his men into obedience and that he rarely or never joined them in the front line.[19] The brigade was also mired in controversy over allegations that Lynch had been involved in a racket selling horses back to the Boer suppliers and personally pocketing the proceeds. (The allegation of horse stealing levied against MacBride in the *Daily Mail* and objected to by Maude Gonne, *see previous chapter*, was probably based on this episode and wrongly attributed.) Lynch's final movements in the war are unclear, though his exploits with the brigade seem likely to have finished by the end of May 1900.[20]

On leaving South Africa, Lynch returned to Paris via the United States. From there, he decided to renew his attempt to enter national politics and won the support of William Redmond (son of John Redmond, the leader of the Irish Parliamentary Party) to his nomination as IPP candidate for the parliamentary by-election at Galway in November 1901. This time, he was successful, but to have fought against Britain and then secure election to its parliament was inevitably contentious; any suggestion that he had capitalised on the former to ensure the latter could only make matters worse. Lynch himself tried to separate the two issues by playing down his role in the Boer War, arguing that his candidature was a straightforward attempt to enter the House of Commons, "on the basis of National principles and a programme of National betterment". His election address issued from Paris on 5 November 1901 concentrated solely on the state of Ireland, making no reference to South Africa.[21] He insisted that it was his opponents who had "first agitated the Boer question", in response to which he had not denied his activities in South Africa.[22] According to *The Times*, at the meeting where Lynch had been selected as the IPP candidate, William Redmond dealt with this question directly, seeing no problem at all –

> "…*he* [Redmond] *ridiculed the rumour that Mr Lynch might not be eligible as a candidate, even if the convention selected him, that he would be unable to land on the shores of Ireland, and*

that there was something mysterious about him. To hear this, Mr Redmond is reported to have said, one would think he was guilty of some dark and mysterious crime. What was the fact? It was said that he went to South Africa and raised an army and did his best on the side of struggling liberty in Africa in defence of the cause of the Boer Republic. Was that a crime in the minds of the Nationalists in Galway? (Cries of 'No.') Was that a reason why he should not receive their support? No; quite the contrary, and he misjudged their feelings if they were not the same as those of every true Nationalist throughout the country, the feelings of honour and of pride at having an opportunity of showing how they could respect Irishmen who risked their liberty, and perhaps their lives, in protecting the causes of liberty when attacked by Britain. (Cheers.)[23]

Understandably, not everyone shared these views. Many considered that Lynch should not be allowed to escape the consequences of what they saw as his obvious treason. In January 1902, the Conservative MP Earl Percy (supported by Winston Churchill) argued in the House of Commons that in publicly claiming to have "assisted the King's enemies" in the war, and this fact having become the crux of his election, Lynch had deliberately insulted the House. This in turn represented a breach of privilege and a Special Committee should be formed to consider what action should be taken against him. This move was rejected by the Speaker, leading another Conservative MP, Francis Horner, to give notice that he would move that the oath should not be administered to Lynch if he presented himself in the House for that purpose. On the following day, in response to further questions, A J Balfour, then Leader of the House, announced that "Mr Lynch will be arrested as soon as he lands".[24]

Nothing then happened until *The Times* reported on 6 June that it had received in an envelope from Paris – without any covering letter – what purported to be a copy of a letter dated 4 June from Lynch to the Speaker. In that letter (which proved genuine), Lynch notified the Speaker that now the war was over, he intended to attend the House of Commons to take up his duties as MP –

> *I have waited for the conclusion of the South African war, as I thought it meet to refrain from any attempt to enter the House while a matter which had excited such deep feelings was still undecided. The proclamation of peace marks an epoch in the history of the British Empire, and, no doubt, in the history of the world. The Boers, arms in hand, have signed the instrument that makes them British subjects, and which vastly increases the domain subject to British law. That event must have a profound influence on all the diverse parts of the Empire; the adamantine gates have closed on the past, and a new phase of national life begun. Ireland alone remains unsatisfied, but I hope that it will be found possible to devise a measure of autonomy for that country that will bring about a spirit of peace there also.*

Lynch went on to say that he was aware that his activities in South Africa had been "brought under the notice of the law" and that, "how far he had overstepped the bounds of legality must be left to the proper tribunal". In a rambling attempt to justify his actions, he said that he had been driven by "no base feelings" but merely out of sympathy with the Boers and their struggle for independence. His actions had been mainly influenced by his hopes that attention might be called to the state of Ireland, "so that remedial measures might be passed to remove the grounds of discontent". In his intentions, he "had been guilty of no treason". He did not believe that he was opposing the true interests of the English people (without commenting on how this could be compatible with killing them in battle). He had hoped that the amnesty afforded under the Boer Treaty would be general. As to the future, he "would not insist upon the causes of sympathy with the Boers and of resistance to the policy of the Government". He wished to place himself at the Speaker's service. Concluding, Lynch offered a paraphrase of the Themistocles quote "Strike, if you will, but hear", to those members of the House who were hostile to him – "Do not strike me, but hear me". The following day, *The Times* remarked that while nationalist members of Parliament had no doubt about the genuineness of the letter, it must be borne in mind that "owing to the precautionary measures which have been taken by the Scotland-yard authorities, Mr Lynch may be frustrated in his endeavour to reach Westminster".[25] And so it was. On 11 June, Lynch was arrested on his arrival at Dover and charged with high treason. He was brought before a hearing at Bow Street police court on Saturday, 14 June, and was then remanded in custody until being brought to trial at the High Court of Justice on 21 January 1903.

The trial was held before the Lord Chief Justice (Lord Alverstone), sitting with Mr Justice Wills and Mr Justice Channell. The prosecution was led by Sir R B Finlay, KC, the Attorney General, and Sir E Carson, KC, the Solicitor General. The defence was led by Mr Shee, KC and Mr Avory, KC.[26] According to *The Times*, the Court was fully occupied well before the start of proceedings and remained crowded throughout its duration.[27] The trial was to last three days, with most of the argument surrounding points of law, starting with an unsuccessful attempt by the defence to have the indictment quashed on the grounds that no offence had actually been committed. The Edward III statute under which the indictment had been drawn stated that the crime of treason was committed, "If a man do levy war against our Lord the King in his realm, or be adherent to the King's enemies in his realm, giving to them aid and comfort, in the realm or elsewhere". As Lynch's actions had all taken place outside the realm, the defence argued that there was no case to answer. The Lord Chief Justice declined to accept the defence motion and the trial proceeded with Lynch entering a plea of "Not guilty". The Attorney General outlined the case for the prosecution, starting with the fact that within three days of writing to Villebois-Mareuil from Pretoria, Lynch had taken the following oaths of allegiance to and support for the South African Government –

I, the undersigned Arthur Alfred Lynch, up to the present an Irishman (British Subject) born at Australia in-habitant of the South African Republic since 5 days, hereby declare my willingness to take up arms for this Republic in order to maintain and defend its independence, which now is, or in the future may be threatened, and therefore desire to take an OATH of allegiance as a FULL BURGHER of the South African Republic. Signed at Pretoria on the 18th of January 1900.

AND –

I ARTHUR ALFRED LYNCH up to the present an Irishman (British Subject) born in Australia desiring to become a fully enfranchised burgher of the South African Republic in terms of Hon. First Volksraad's Resolution, Art 1442, dated 29 Sept 1899, swear (or solemnly declare that the taking of an oath is not allowed by my creed and solemnly promise) in all sincerity, that I shall be faithful to this State, shall respect and support its independence, shall submit to the "Grond Wet" and other laws and lawful authorities of the country, and shall in every way conduct myself as becomes a faithful burgher of the State. SO TRULY HELP ME GOD. (or (THAT I PROMISE SOLEMNLY) (sgd) Arthur Lynch, Sworn 18 January 1900.

The Attorney General noted that, "There could be no greater instances of the crime of high treason than these acts". He continued that on 10 February, Lynch took charge of the Second

Irish Brigade and in consequence took two further oaths, one to be faithful to the South African Republic as a commander and the other to be faithful as a Special Justice of the Peace (to enable him to administer the oath to recruits). Lynch then left Pretoria with his Brigade, "for the seat of war in Natal", setting up camp near Glencoe on 3 March where he stayed until 12 May – "The mere fact of the prisoner's presence there during the war was, of course, an act of adherence to the enemies of the Queen, and was so charged in the indictment". The prosecution outlined further incidents of what it regarded as high treason, as set out in the indictment. The first was the advertisement Lynch had placed in the *Standard and Diggers' News* inciting Irishmen to join the war – "a direct act of inciting Irishmen to take part against this country" – "It mattered not whether it was addressed to Irish burghers of the Transvaal or to Irishmen who were British subjects. Such an appeal, to subjects or to foreigners, constituted the crime of high treason". He then outlined other alleged acts set out in the indictment – on 10 April, Lynch commanded the brigade at an engagement at Sunday Rivers Bridge, where he both directed fire and himself fired against British troops; on 20 May, he took part in a Boer inquiry into the conduct of alleged British spies at Vereeniging; and on 24 May, he was engaged in the Boer recruiting office and in commandeering Boer supplies. The Attorney General concluded – "This was the narrative which spoke for itself and needed no commentary".

The prosecution brought forward witnesses who had served with the brigade to testify to these events, one stating specifically that he had been present when Lynch had fired a Mauser pistol towards the British forces at Sunday Rivers Bridge. Another, an American citizen, described how he and two friends (one American, the other a burgher) had been arrested by the Boer forces at Vereeniging. *The Times* reported the witness's testimony as follows –

> *They [the three] were searched, and all papers and money taken from them. They were told they were supposed to be spies. They were examined in the presence of Commandant Schoeman, his secretary, the prisoner [Lynch], and several Boers. Lynch asked them the questions like an attorney conducting a case. He asked them whether any of the three of them had seen him before. They said no. He said to Holder [the burgher], 'Weren't you a member of the Johannesburg Town Council?' Holder said he was. Lynch said, 'Don't you remember my being introduced to you?' Holder said, 'O, you are Captain Lynch.' The prisoner said, 'Colonel Lynch, if you please,' and said to the secretary, 'Put that answer down.' Lynch then examined him, and said to the commandant, 'I will prove to you that these are British spies, and should be shot.' The other two were examined, and they were all told that they had been accused, and would have to be taken to Johannesburg to be released by Dr Krause, the Public Prosecutor. They were taken to Johannesburg and released the next morning.*[28]

The defence objected to the admission of this evidence on the grounds that the witness had previously stated that Lynch had used the word "spies" and not "British spies". The Solicitor General said that he would not press the matter. A deposition by an American citizen who was too ill to attend the Court was then read out. In this, the American described how he first saw the Second Irish Brigade on 3 March 1900 when they retreated from Ladysmith to Glencoe. The witness said that the brigade had destroyed a lot of property and he remonstrated with Lynch, pointing out that the property belonged to his employer, a storekeeper. Lynch had replied that the property did not belong to the employer but to the Boers, commenting that he was a British subject as well as the witness, and knew the law as well as he did. The witness then said, 'If you are a British subject, why are you fighting for the Boers?', to which Lynch replied, 'For fun.'

The defence case consisted mainly of legal argument. The generality of the acts alleged to have been committed by Lynch was not disputed. The defence argued instead that those acts did not constitute high treason under the law. In addition to their earlier contention that the statute of Edward III did not cover acts committed outside the realm, they argued that Lynch was not guilty of treason because when he carried them out he was a citizen of the South African Republic by naturalisation. They argued that central to this were Lynch's intentions when he first set out for South Africa; when he had set out, he had no intention of joining the Boer forces but had gone there solely to carry out his work as a journalist. Going to South Africa for this purpose was not a treasonable act. When he got there, however, he had become carried away by the prevailing atmosphere of excitement. His Counsel drew a parallel with the atmosphere of excitement in London at the time, and argued that though Lynch's attitude towards naturalisation may seem odd to many, he had a cosmopolitan background which gave him a different outlook –

> *None of the jury was probably a naturalized Englishman; doubtless they were all born Englishmen, with exclusively English associations. None of them probably ever thought of changing their nationality. Mr Lynch's history was widely different; he was the son of an emigrant born in America. He had studied at the University of Berlin, then the University of Paris, where he had long been resident. In effect he was a cosmopolitan journalist, and in that capacity he went to South Africa, where he wanted to make a name for himself in his profession. He had already contemplated becoming a Frenchman and had applied in Paris for letters of naturalization.*

Lynch wanted to be naturalised so that he could be in the Boer army, which did not have –

> ...*correspondents among it who were sending dispatches to Paris, [in order] to see clearly the inner life of the Boer forces – to see the work of the Boer generals – to identify himself with the Boers for descriptive purposes – those were the objectives which he had in view.*

His Counsel continued that in his own statements, Lynch had acknowledged that when he took over the Second Irish Brigade, "he had gone further perhaps than he ought to have gone". But having taken the oath of allegiance on 18 January, he "honestly believed that he was a Boer and had the fullest right to fight for the Boer armies".

In his statements, Lynch had also insisted that when they first met in Pretoria, Villebois-Mareuil had been simply a correspondent for *La Liberté* and had no position in the Boer army. And referring to his comment in the letter to Villebois-Mareuil that he had had to destroy an introductory letter from Monteil, Lynch asserted that nothing written by Monteil would have compromised him or justified him being arrested; he had used the French word "*arrêter*" in the letter to mean "stop" rather than "arrest". Lynch also stated that he had no mission from Dr Leyds personally when he had gone to the Transvaal.[29] The defence called witnesses to attest to Lynch's intentions. Mr H Letelier, part owner of *Le Journal*, testified that Lynch had been sent out as a correspondent for them. The paper had paid for his passage out and had received articles from Lynch for which they had paid him 3,600F in total. Mr Valerian Gribayedoff said that he lived in Paris and had suggested to Lynch that he write articles and provide pictures for the American papers. He subsequently arranged that Lynch should send copies to *Collier's Weekly*, an American paper, and *Black and White* in London. He said that Lynch bought a camera with a view to learning how to take photographs. Lynch's sister-in-law, Mrs Frances Powell, testified that he had gone to the Ashanti War to act as a correspondent in 1896.

In his summing up for the jury, the Lord Chief Justice stated that the case constructed by the defence was largely invalid in terms of the law. As far as Lynch's original intentions were concerned, the letter to Villebois-Mareuil was of little importance in itself, though his comments that he had destroyed documents "because he might be stopped", and that he had come to South Africa on a mission from Dr Leyds, a man known to be hostile to British rule, might help point to the real intention behind his original mission. Whatever that intention might have been, however, if a man joined the King's enemies in time of war, whether for his own purposes or not, he was guilty of an unlawful offence. The taking of the oath of allegiance on 18 January was itself a treasonable act. Whether Lynch believed he was naturalised on 18 January or not, this made no difference to his subsequent culpability. The Lord Chief Justice concluded –

> *I remind you again that the charge is that of aiding the King's enemies and I have already told you that if that which has been proved before you amounts to the aiding of the King's enemies wherever it was done, whether in Africa or elsewhere, it is an offence in respect of which if proved the Defendant is by you to be found guilty under this Indictment.*

The jury retired at 2.40 pm on 23 January 1903 and returned at 3.06 pm, with a verdict of guilty on each count. When asked if he had anything to say, Lynch replied simply, 'No, thank you. I will say nothing.' Lynch was sentenced to death by hanging.[30] The following day, the sentence was commuted to Penal Servitude for Life.[31]

The general public viewed the verdict as inevitable at the same time as considering that it ought to be tempered by a degree of clemency. Before it became known that the sentence had been commuted, the nationalist *Daily Irish Independent* accepted the legitimacy of the punishment, while adding a plea for mercy on grounds of political expediency. *The Times* noted that this was an important admission – "It says that the law of high treason is practically the same in all civilized countries, and that Mr Lynch has only experienced the same treatment which would be meted out to any Frenchman, German, Italian, Russian, or Pole, who bore arms against the established Government of their countries".[32] Not everyone was so happy, however. The Strokestown District Council in Roscommon declared that, "Nothing but extreme measures seem able to satiate England's greed for revenge whenever Irishmen are so unfortunate as to be the victims".[33] The Galway District Council resolved, "that we, the Galway District Council, condemn the action of the Government in the treatment meted out to Colonel Lynch in only commuting his sentence from capital punishment to penal servitude for life, as such treatment unfavourably compares with the treatment Dr Jameson met at the hands of Dr Kruger".[34]

Some wanted even more punishment to be meted out. Having been found guilty of high treason, Lynch was automatically disqualified from his seat in the House under the Forfeiture Act 1870.[35] But when in March 1903 the Attorney General moved the issue of a writ for an election to fill the consequent vacancy, this was opposed by a number of MPs led by Sir George Christopher Trout Bartley, a Conservative MP (for Islington North) who had been in South Africa at the beginning of the war.[36] Bartley argued that the Galway electorate knew that Lynch was a traitor and had deliberately and provocatively elected him for this reason. As punishment, the constituency should be disenfranchised for the remainder of the present session of Parliament. In support of his argument, Bartley cited a number of press reports and articles that had appeared during the course of the election campaign. These included a quote from a telegram sent by John Redmond MP to John Dillon MP, reported in *The Freeman's Journal* on 18 November 1901 – "We call upon the people of Galway to strike a blow for Irish freedom by electing triumphantly the Nationalist candidate, the soldier of freedom, Colonel Arthur Lynch". *The Freeman's Journal* also reported that at a meeting in Galway the previous day ex-MP Michael Davitt had said, 'What was the case of Colonel Lynch? They knew that he fought as gallantly and loyally for the Boers as MacBride.' And even more provocatively, William Redmond MP also at a meeting on 18 November had noted, 'Colonel Lynch could not have come to Galway because there was a price on his head, but if he was made MP for Galway, the British Government would not be able to touch him.' After the election, the Latterfrack Branch of the United Irish League resolved – "That we, members of the Latterfrack Branch of the United Irish League, hail with delight the result of the Galway election, and the return of Colonel Arthur Lynch, who fought against British tyranny and for the freedom of the South African Republics". Bartley concluded, "…surely it stands to reason that we should disenfranchise a constituency when we know they are steeped in treason, and when we know perfectly well that at the present moment they do not regret or repent what they did". Lord Hugh Cecil considered that – "This constituency committed a wrong which nearly resulted in a great insult to Parliament… and I say we ought to punish the constituency in order to prevent the danger of a recurrence of such an outrage".

In the event, Bartley and his supporters failed. A J Balfour (then Prime Minister) said that while he personally believed that Lynch's activities in South Africa *had* helped him get elected, he would not himself want to be judged by the leading articles written about him. Remarking on the reports and articles read to the House by Bartley, Balfour commented – "…the experience of my hon. friend [Bartley] and other hon. Members must be happier than mine if they wish to be judged by the speeches made on their own platform in their favour. I think it is dangerous ground…" For his part, the Attorney General said that while he was sympathetic and understood the strong feeling and resentment at what had occurred, he also considered that it would be a very dangerous precedent to disenfranchise a constituency because it returned to the House of Commons a person whose conduct or whose views were obnoxious to the views of the majority of the House. Past instances of disenfranchisement had mainly centred around cases where there had been very general bribery and corruption in the constituency concerned. In other cases he had examined, however, "the chain of precedents is unbroken in showing that in such circumstances as the present the issue of the writ ought not to be suspended by way of a punishment to the constituency". He cited five such cases since 1849, which included those of O'Donovan Rossa and Michael Davitt. In 1865, O'Donovan Rossa had been found guilty of high treason for plotting a Fenian rising and had been sentenced to penal servitude for life. In an 1869 by-election, he had been returned as MP for Tipperary. The election was declared invalid. Similarly, in 1882, Michael Davitt had been returned as MP for County Meath but was disqualified because he had been sentenced to fifteen years penal servitude in 1870 for treason felony, having been arrested at Paddington Station while awaiting a delivery of arms. Neither in these nor in the other three cases cited had the writ been delayed as now proposed. The Government won the vote by 248 to 45. Charles Ramsay Devlin (IPP and secretary general of the United Irish League) took Lynch's place.

As soon as Lynch had begun to serve out his sentence, lobbying took place for his release. In November 1903, J G Swift MacNeill MP (IPP) – later to become Professor of the Law of Public Wrongs at the National University of Ireland – wrote to the Home Secretary asking for Lynch's release, pointing out that there was a wide expectation that this would take place as part of the general amnesty granted to political prisoners following the King's recent visit to Ireland.[37] Then, on 23 January 1904, exactly one year after he had been sentenced, Lynch was released from Lewis Gaol on licence by order of the Home Secretary. *The Times* took a conciliatory line, pointing out that similar offenders in Cape Colony had been amnestied on average after eighteen months, while Lynch had spent eight months in prison while awaiting trial in addition to the twelve months he had served since being sentenced. It also noted that while he was on licence, Lynch remained disqualified from Parliament and, if necessary, could be called back at any time to complete his sentence.[38] On his release, Lynch moved to Paris. Then, on receiving a free pardon on 6 July 1907,[39] he returned to London where he completed his earlier medical studies and took up practice as a GP on Haverstock Hill in 1908. The receipt of the free pardon removed the disqualification from him serving as an MP and, despite discouragement from John Redmond, he finally secured a seat in Parliament in 1909, standing as an Irish Nationalist candidate in an uncontested by-election at West Clare. Lynch's parliamentary career lasted from 3 September 1909 to 14 December 1918, during which time he actively participated in the business of the House, making some 1,924 contributions in total on a variety of issues.[40]

*

Though he was active in Parliament, Lynch had little impact there on the nationalist cause. He was distrusted by his party and fellow nationalist MPs and was not called upon to lead or speak in nationalist debates. At the onset of the First World War, he supported the position of Redmond and the IPP that Ireland should support the fight against Germany. But in maintaining this position as events in Ireland moved on during the war, he became further alienated from the hardliners. It cut little ice that he described those involved in the Easter Rising as "heroes and martyrs"[41] and it is in any event questionable how seriously he meant this. He clearly showed little sensitivity on the matter when he visited Maud Gonne in Paris in June 1916, shortly after the execution of MacBride. Gonne wrote to W B Yeats, "Arthur Lynch is here but has no news, can you believe he wanted to discuss Greek literature today!"[42] The hardliners were right not to trust him. At the height of the conscription crisis in 1918, Lloyd George reported to the War Cabinet on a meeting that he had had with Lynch about the likely activities of Sinn Féin.[43] He noted that Lynch "was passionately pro-French, and consequently passionately pro-Ally", and that he had lately seen a good deal of the Sinn Féiners in Ireland. Lynch regarded them as "rather *tête monté*" – they really thought that they could beat the British Army by guerrilla methods – "Side by side with a certain childishness they had a lot of natural cunning, and Mr Lynch had thought that this might be easily underestimated. They did not intend to fight in the towns, but to withdraw at once to the country where they had lots of clever guerrilla leaders. They had a large number of rifles, having received small consignments steadily during the last year or two. … Mr Lynch thought that the insurrection might be delayed for two months, although it might come off within a fortnight".

Astonishingly, Lynch persuaded Lloyd George to allow him to form and lead a new "Irish Brigade" in the British Army, an idea that was accepted because of its propaganda value rather than any military contribution it might make. On 27 June 1918, Lynch was given a temporary commission as Colonel to help with recruiting, while remaining an MP. The instruction to grant the commission had come by word of mouth from 10 Downing Street with no associated papers and had been implemented by the Military Secretary. All this caused consternation within the War Office, which had not been consulted. In briefing the Secretary of State for War on 14 August, the Adjutant General said that the War Office knew little of what Colonel Lynch was supposed to be doing, as any arrangements had been made between the Prime Minister and the Secretary for Ireland. He noted that current policy was against raising new battalions; these could not be accommodated and experience indicated that as soon as any were raised, they quickly became depleted and had to be topped up from elsewhere, taking away their original character. He went on to comment that Lynch appeared from the files to be "a thorn in the side of the Irish Recruiting Committee", but the only plan to avoid friction would be for Colonel Lynch to place his services at the disposal of that committee. This attempt to sideline Lynch failed. The Secretary of State met Lynch the following day and agreed that it should be made clear that Lynch had been authorised to raise a new battalion by the Army Council, and that the battalion HQ should be located as near as possible to his constituency in County Clare.

On 29 August, the Commander-in-Chief, Forces in Ireland, notified the War Office that Lynch's battalion HQ would be at Ballyvonare. Lynch wanted it to be raised as a unit of the Royal Munster Fusiliers and its officers to be Irishmen who had served in the war. He had agreed that if insufficient men were raised to form a battalion, they should be made available to Irish Infantry Regiments. Lynch was also, "very anxious that a Colonial pattern hat be approved with a badge of a harp looping up at one side, and that green shoulder straps be worn. He would like a green plume or hackle to be worn with the hat. He also desires that pipers be authorised and that they should wear the Irish Kilt". To bring the wheel full circle, in a final characteristic display of vanity, Lynch wanted the unit to bear the name "Lynch's Brigade", as he attached "much sentimental importance to the word Brigade". The title settled on was the 10th (Service) Battalion, Royal Munster Fusiliers (Lynch's Brigade).

Not surprisingly, in the general climate of the time, Lynch met with little success in finding volunteers. In Dublin, a hostile crowd was quick to compare him unfavourably to MacBride, a martyr of the Rising, chanting, "What about MacBride? Why weren't you with him?" Lynch was forced to leave the recruiting meeting under police protection. A statement by him at another meeting that he had, "endured great trials and faced great dangers in the cause of home rule", generated the response, "Why not stop in Ireland and share our dangers?" The crowd, many now looking for something more than mere home rule, accused him of, "hiding his cowardice behind the high-sounding name of patriotism".[44] Lynch did have one final, fleeting, moment of glory. During the Armistice celebrations, he was cheered by the crowd and carried shoulder-high to Trinity College by British soldiers.[45] "Lynch's Brigade" was finally disbanded on 25 January 1919, never having seen active service.[46] Meanwhile, in the general election of 1918, Lynch left Irish politics for the Independent Labour Party, unsuccessfully contesting the seat of South Battersea. He returned to general practice and writing until his death in 1934.

Whether or not it was Lynch's intention to fight for the Boers from the beginning is unclear. Except for the purposes of providing a subterfuge for his journey to South Africa and later a defence at his trial, his insistence that his original intention had been solely to act as a war correspondent hardly mattered one way or the other. It certainly did not matter to the prosecution, as the Solicitor General made clear during the trial – "I am prepared… to admit that Mr Lynch went to the Transvaal in the capacity of a journalist, and in the capacity of a journalist alone. That is not one of the charges here", before adding, "But he says further that he was merely naturalized for 'Press purposes'. Naturalized for Press purposes!" Even on the basis of his own account, however, it is curious that the Boers should have paid Lynch's expenses to travel to South Africa for a purpose that was in the event, he claimed, vetoed by Botha. It is also odd that the Boers should have even been contemplating a second Irish brigade at the time of his arrival, given that MacBride's brigade was hardly overwhelmed with recruits. Blake and MacBride were unaware of any proposal for a second brigade until after Lynch's arrival in South Africa, and when they did hear about it they argued that it was unnecessary and foolish, given that in reality they did not have enough men for the existing brigade. Lynch ignored their invitation to discuss the matter, which may not have been surprising as he and MacBride had already met in London and had not got on. Lynch would almost certainly not have wished to serve as a subordinate to Blake and MacBride.[47] It is at least plausible that, having seen the success that MacBride had achieved in the Transvaal, Lynch intended from the outset to emulate or better this with a brigade of his own. Lynch's entire character, evident at the time and becoming more so later, was of a man convinced of his own superiority pursuing a path of self-aggrandisement. It was in keeping with this that he should have been deluded enough to think that he could subsequently take up his seat in the House of Commons with no repercussions. Such a provocative act was bound to produce a response from the authorities, however reluctant they almost certainly were to go down that road.

In the longer term, Lynch was able to salvage a political career, but his defence at his trial, where he did everything to exonerate himself from blame for his own actions, did nothing to sustain his credibility (already suspect in the eyes of many) among staunch Irish nationalists. In his 1901 election address, he had again invoked the memory of Meagher – 'I hope that one day I will be able to say without contradiction, in the words of Thomas Francis Meagher: "To lift this Island up – this has been my ambition".'[48] But his conduct during the trial showed none of the exalting defiance exhibited by Meagher in his "Speech from the Dock" and elsewhere, nor that displayed by John MacBride at his court martial and before the firing squad. Afterwards, his position shifted further and further away from that of the physical force nationalist so feared by the Special Branch in 1893. His continuing support for the war after the Easter Rising, and finally his decision to join the British Army to help counter the activities of Sinn Féin, who were campaigning against further Irish enlistment, completed the process. On his death in 1934, *The Times* described Lynch not as an Irish nationalist but as a "philosophical Republican" who always maintained that he had not been motivated by any hatred of England.[49] More recently, one author, writing about his role in the Boer War, described Lynch as an interloper. This is perhaps the most apt description of him both as an Irish nationalist and as an "Irish brigadier".[50]

Thomas Francis Meagher – Young Irelander

Thomas Francis Meagher – US Civil War

John MacBride – Irish Transvaal Brigade

Arthur Lynch and the Second Irish Brigade

PART TWO

FOUR
ROGER CASEMENT – BRITISH CONSUL

...only another proof of the methods of those in Pretoria, to leave no weapon untried to induce men loyal to their Queen to be false to their own allegiance, and to be false to themselves.

Casement on the recruitment of Irish prisoners to fight against the British in the Boer War

I find it difficult to choose the words, in which to make acknowledgment of the honour done to me by the King... convey to him my deep appreciation of the honour he has been so graciously pleased to confer on me.

Casement to Sir Edward Grey on receipt of his knighthood

Unlike Meagher, MacBride and Lynch before him, Casement came to the cause of Irish nationalism late, having previously achieved notable success as a member of the British consular service and international acclaim as a humanitarian. His transition from a loyal servant of the British Crown to a committed nationalist forms a key part of his story and sets the context for many of his subsequent activities and the official reaction to them. His practical contribution to the cause of independence was mixed, by any yardstick, but it was his decision to try to establish what became known as a "German Irish Brigade" from among Irish prisoners of war in Germany that finally brought about his execution for high treason. Ironically, it was not Fontenoy and the Wild Geese that inspired Casement to follow this road, but a meeting with John MacBride, whose tales of the Irish Transvaal Brigade inspired him and touched on his romantic notions of nationalism. The irony is magnified by the fact that as a Crown servant during the South African War, Casement had loftily criticised the Boers for inducing Irishmen to join MacBride and abandon their allegiance.

Casement was born in 1864 at Sandycove near Dublin into a well-known Protestant landowning family which had moved from the Isle of Man to County Antrim at the beginning of the eighteenth century. His father (also Roger) had been a captain with the 3rd Dragoon Guards and subsequently a member of the North Antrim Militia. Captain Casement had been something of an adventurer, having travelled to take part as a volunteer in the 1848 Hungarian rising against Austrian rule. By the time he arrived, the Hungarians had already surrendered at Világos in August 1849, and Kossuth, their "Regent-President", had crossed the Ottoman frontier as a fugitive, where he had been hospitably received. Captain Casement is reputed to have immediately ridden back to London, where he secured an interview with Lord Palmerston to press for British intervention to prevent Kossuth's extradition back to Austria. This was forthcoming and the Ottoman authorities, with British support, were able to resist Austrian pressures for Kossuth to be given up.[1] There are suggestions that Captain Casement later expressed sympathy with the Fenians' attempted uprising in

1867, though there appears no evidence that he took any active part in Irish nationalist affairs.[2] Roger Casement's mother, Anne Jephson, also from Dublin, came from a Roman Catholic branch of a Protestant family from Mallow, County Cork. She had four children – three sons and a daughter – of whom Roger was the youngest. Although the children were brought up as Protestants, she secretly had Roger baptised as a Roman Catholic in 1868.[3] The family moved to England before Casement reached the age of three, and lived in Worthing until his mother died when he was nine. The family then returned to Ireland to live in Antrim. Casement's father died when he was thirteen, following which he was looked after by relatives. He was educated at the Diocesan School, Ballymena, which he left aged sixteen to return to England.

In England, Casement went to live with his mother's sister Grace and her family. Grace had married Edward Bannister, the agent in West Africa for a Liverpool trading company. Through Edward, Casement secured a job as a shipping clerk with the Elder Dempster shipping line. After three years, he sailed as purser on one of the company's ships to Boma, in the Congo, where Bannister was stationed. He returned to the Congo the following year to work as a volunteer for Henry Morton Stanley and the International Association of the Congo, a Belgian organisation set up to explore the area and exploit its resources. When the Independent State of the Congo (the Congo Free State) was established under King Leopold II of Belgium at the Berlin Conference of 1885, and the Association made responsible for its government, Casement stayed on, carrying out surveying and other commercial activities until 1888, when he took a job for a few months as a lay employee at a Congo Mission Station under the English Baptist missionary William Holman Bentley. In 1890, he negotiated a year's contract as manager and labour recruiter for a company formed to construct the Matadi-Leopoldville (Kinshasa) railway, before returning to Ireland. In all these tasks, Casement acquitted himself well and gathered a sound reputation. He was widely regarded as the perfect gentleman: cultured and hardworking, ever-helpful and condemning cruelty and injustice of all kinds. The writer Joseph Conrad said of Casement, whom he met at Matardi, "Thinks, speaks well, most intelligent and sympathetic", describing him as a "limpid personality". Bentley, commenting on Casement's work at the Mission Station, noted that his treatment of the natives appeared to be all that could be desired, his only criticism being that Casement "lacked ruthlessness" in haggling a sufficiently low price when buying food from the natives. Bentley also noted, "…I managed also very delicately to get an assurance that there had been nothing in his [Casement's] manner of life out here which would cast reflection on us…"[4] Whether or not seeking such an assurance was standard practice in relation to all new recruits, or whether it reflected possible concerns about Casement specifically, it is impossible to say. It would be much later that Casement's own diaries would reveal his homosexuality and how he indulged this through paid encounters with young men.

In 1892, Casement was back in Africa, this time as an employee of the British Government in the survey department of the Niger Coast Protectorate, whose task was to survey previously unexplored areas. Casement was given the job of examining commercial possibilities in the region and making peaceful contact with local chiefs. He was to survey the territory around Old Calebar (the Protectorate's seat of government), preparatory to the opening up of overland routes between the coastal ports and interior markets. As before, his reports displayed an eye for detail and – untypical for someone in his position at the time – a sympathetic approach towards native Africans.[5] The success of his conciliatory approach found favour with the Protectorate's administrator and within Whitehall, leading to real recognition in June 1895 when he was appointed her Majesty's Consul in the Portuguese Province of Lourenço Marques.

Casement's posting to Lourenço Marques coincided with increasing tensions between the British Government and the Transvaal in advance of the Jameson Raid, which was to take place in December the same year. In addition to carrying out normal consular duties, Casement had been brought in to gather intelligence, involving him directly for the first time in international diplomacy, espionage and official intrigue. His remit related particularly to the recently completed railway line between the Transvaal and Lourenço Marques (situated on the Delagoa Bay), which opened the way for people and goods to be moved easily into the Transvaal without crossing British colonial territory. This could obviously include arms, a matter of immediate concern to the British Government. Suspicions were heightened by the visit to Lourenço Marques of Transvaal President Kruger's emissary, Dr Leyds, in November. The intelligence sent by Casement to London included a report in June 1896 that there had been substantial arms movements into the Transvaal during the previous three months.[6] By the end of 1896, Joseph Chamberlain, the Colonial Secretary, was able to tell the Cabinet that in total the Boers had in their possession some 45,000 rifles, thirty million rounds of ammunition and seventy-six guns.[7] When the Boer War finally broke out three years later, Casement, who had by then moved to Luanda, was immediately sent back to Lourenço Marques to pick up the threads. He quickly established that the movement of arms through Delagoa Bay had by now effectively ceased, but to avoid the possibility of the rail route being used again for this purpose, he proposed an expedition into the Transvaal to cut the track.[8] Casement's scheme (including his proposal that he should accompany the expedition) was approved, and in April 1900 a force set out by sea from Cape Town to the Zululand coast, which it was intended would then march to Komati Port on the border between Portuguese East Africa and the Transvaal, where the line would be sabotaged. In the event, the expedition had to be abandoned when it became known that the Boers had advance intelligence of the attack.[9]

There being no further reason for Casement to stay in South Africa, his involvement in the Boer War ended. Unlike many other Irishmen, Casement remained a supporter of the war. He strongly disliked the Boers for the way they treated African natives. But beyond that, he regarded loyalty as paramount. So far as MacBride's Irish Transvaal Brigade was concerned, he noted that the recruitment of Irish prisoners of war to fight against the British seemed "only another proof of the methods of those in power in Pretoria, to leave no weapon untried to induce men loyal to their Queen to be false to their own allegiance, and to be false to themselves".[10] Casement was awarded the Queen's South Africa medal.

His posting to Luanda, between his two spells in South Africa, had taken place in July 1898, when he had been appointed "her Majesty's Consul for the Portuguese possessions in West Africa, south of the Gulf of Guinea, to be resident at Loanda *[sic]*; to be her Majesty's Consul in the Gabon; and to be her Majesty's Consul to the Independent State of the Congo".[11] He had been posted there principally to gather intelligence on possible French use of the Congo to move supplies to the trading post at Fashoda in the Sudan, which they had just occupied (as it turned out temporarily) in the face of British protests.[12] But his posting also reflected concern about the increasing number of reports coming out of the Congo Free State of restrictions being imposed on trade and of atrocities being committed against the Congolese natives.

*

When the Congo Free State had been created by international treaty at the Berlin Conference in 1885, its governance had been put in the hands of the International Association of the Congo under Leopold II, acting in a personal capacity rather than as King of Belgium. It was Leopold who created the name "Congo

Free State". The General Act of the Berlin Conference provided that, "The trade of all nations shall enjoy complete freedom", and, "All the powers exercising sovereign rights or influence... bind themselves to watch over the preservation of the native tribes, and to care for the improvement of the conditions of their moral and material well-being, and to help in supressing slavery..."[13] There was evidence almost from the beginning that neither of these objectives was being fully met. As early as 1890, a black American journalist, George Washington Williams, wrote an "open letter" to King Leopold, widely published and distributed throughout Europe, charging him with overseeing atrocities against the natives.[14] Williams had started with the intention of arranging for black Americans to go to the Congo to work and secure a better life than they could in the US.[15] He had met Leopold and was impressed, but following a six-month tour of the Congo declared himself in his letter to be "disenchanted, disappointed and disheartened". Far from the natives receiving "fostering care", he found that they were everywhere being ill-treated and exploited. While Arab slave trading may have been brought to an end in the Congo, slavery still existed in the form of forced labour now being imposed by the Free State itself on the natives. In subsequent correspondence, Williams is said by some to have been the first to use the now established phrase, "crimes against humanity" in his charges against Leopold.[16] Reports of ill-treatment continued to flow out of the Congo, as did reports of the exclusion of non-Belgian nationals from trade. In 1895, a British trader, Charles Stokes, was arrested in the Congo by a Belgian, Captain Lothaire, charged with gun-running and executed without right of appeal following an illegal trial. An American missionary, John B Murphy, subsequently reported that the real reason for the action against Stokes had been that he was trading directly with natives, rather than through a recognised agent, which was now a requirement. He went on to describe how natives were being forced to collect quotas of rubber, with those refusing being shot and their bodies mutilated.[17] In September 1896, another American missionary, E V Sjöblom, wrote to the Stockholm press, criticising the Congo administration.[18]

In response to the adverse publicity, Leopold promptly set up a "Commission for the Protection of Natives". A decree dated 18 September 1896[19] prescribed that the Commission would comprise six members appointed for a two-year term – three Protestant and three Catholic – drawn "from among the representatives of philanthropic and religious Associations". In a subsequent "letter of instruction" to the Governor General at Boma, EDM van Eetvelde, Secretary of State, noted specifically, "It has seemed advisable that selected and impartial men, without official or administrative connection, should be placed in a position to form a perfectly independent opinion in regard to any acts of violence of which the natives may have to complain".[20] Two of the six appointed came from the Baptist Missionary Society Corporation – William Holman Bentley, at whose Congo Mission Station Casement had served in 1888–89, and George Grenfell, who was to act as Commission Secretary. The third Protestant was Dr A Sims, of the American Baptist Missionary Union. The three Catholics were Mgr van Ronslé, Bishop of Thymbrium, Vicar Apostolic of the Congo Independent State (President); Father van Hencxthoven, J., Superior of the Jesuit Mission at Leopoldville; and Father de Cleene, of the congregation of Scheut. The Commission's remit (individually as well as collectively) was to, "inform the judicial authorities of any acts of violence of which the natives may be the victims", with the right to communicate directly with the Governor General. Van Eetvelde further instructed that in order to strengthen the guarantee of protection given to the natives by the decree, "…all offences against the persons of natives, and all attempts against their liberties committed by Europeans, shall be remitted exclusively to the Court of First Instance at Boma, that is to say, before a Court sitting under the fullest conditions of publicity and control". In order to bring the new arrangements fully into line with the Berlin Act, Leopold's decree also dealt with abuses by the natives themselves as well as any by outsiders –

> *The Commission shall further indicate to the Government the measures to be taken to prevent slave-trading, to render more effective the prohibition or restriction of the trade in spirituous liquors, and gradually to bring about the barbarous customs, such as cannibalism, human sacrifices, ordeal by poison, &c.*[21]

With regard to the latter point, a subsequent circular to District Commissioners and others on 21 February 1897, noted that while a number of measures taken so far had resulted in cannibalism being less frequent, the time was now right to deal with the practice through greater "repression", and accordingly cannibalism and ordeal by poison had now been made specific offences. The aim would be to prosecute cases to check and extirpate this custom.[22]

The establishment of the Commission had an instant effect on public opinion; by the end of October 1896, press interest had completely ceased.[23] But major weaknesses in its structure and remit were clear from the outset. In reply to his letter of appointment, Grenfell noted that while he was honoured to accept the appointment, "…I regret to say that I do not see how the new Commission will be able to work, seeing that the members live far apart from one another and communication is very difficult. In Europe a distance of 700 kilom. [*sic*] would offer no impediment, but the postal service between Boma and Bolobo takes three weeks to a month. In these circumstances, we shall, I think, find it impossible to meet".[24] There was also the problem that most of the alleged atrocities against the natives had taken place in the interior, often at great distance from where the members of the Commission were based. Father van Hencxthoven alluded to this in his reply. While saying that the Government could count on his devotion, he added, "I feel bound, however, to say that, during the four years in which I have lived in the Pool District, I have never verified an act of violence which ought to have been brought to the notice of the higher authorities".[25] Holman Bentley, in his acceptance, struck a more positive note, commenting, "I need only express the hope that my modest efforts may promote a work of humanity and protection, and that the steady disappearance of the inhuman customs and barbarities of the natives, may be facilitated by the labours of the Commission".[26] Though positive, Bentley's comment indicates that his priority was the standard missionary objective of bringing Christianity and European values to the natives, rather than protecting the natives from the Europeans.

The Commission only met twice, with only three members attending on each occasion. At its first meeting on 17 May 1897, members reported that in their personal experience, since the Commission had been set up, the laws of the State had been administered well and in the interests of the well-being of the community; every case of injustice brought to the attention of the authorities had been immediately followed by measures "of the most energetic description". And, "The members of the Commission, recalling the days of "native rule", take this opportunity of recording their sincere appreciation of, and their gratitude for, the law and order introduced by the Independent State into the districts where they reside". Their report went on to record, "with the deepest satisfaction", that the laws forbidding the introduction of alcoholic liquor to the natives were being satisfactorily enforced; but at the same time it expressed regret that ordeal by poison, carried out in secret, continued. The report ended by calling attention to the fact that all of the Commission's members had been chosen from the Stanley Pool district and below and that no one had been chosen from the immense areas, "which are supposed to furnish the reason for the existence of the Commission". The Commissioners hoped for the early arrival of an inspector nominated by Leopold whose "powers of observation would be infinitely greater than their own".[27] At its second meeting on 23 November 1897,[28] the Commission focused on a commitment by Leopold in a decree dated 12 July 1890 to safeguard native women and children who had been freed from slavery or simply abandoned. The stipulation that the children should be, "collected together in agricultural and professional settlements, where provision would be made for their education and maintenance" was not happening. The Commission further noted that "great" native chiefs of the Lualaba-Kassai district had been recruiting by force of arms slaves of both sexes, not only with the knowledge but perhaps also at the instigation of government representatives in that region. Lastly, the Commission reported that some of its members had directly observed native porters being given loads which were too heavy for them because of their health, age or other weakness. The Commission's final recommendation was that its size should be increased to eight or ten, with the new members coming from the Upper Congo and Upper Kassai.

Apart from a circular issued by the Governor General on 7 February 1898, setting out detailed regulations on how abandoned or orphaned native children should be dealt with, no response to the Commission's recommendations is recorded and nothing then seems to have happened for two and a half years, until on 1 June 1900, Adolphe de Cuvelier, Leopold's Secretary General of Foreign Affairs for the Congo, wrote to the Congo Governor General in Boma about the lack of further Commission meetings, commenting –

> *I am inclined to believe that this inaction is really due to a conviction on the part of the members of the Commission that the Government have already taken all such measures as are practicable in the present social state of Africa to assure the material and moral progress of the natives.*

He went on to say that, "generally speaking", the Government considered that the Commission should be maintained, and asked for suggested names for new members, "animated by a spirit of justice and equity". Over six months later, on 8 February 1901, the Governor General replied that the choice of possible members was "somewhat limited", "since it is necessary, if the Commission is to be of any use as a deliberative body, and meet sufficiently often, that the residences of the members who may be appointed should not be too far from those of their colleagues". Bizarrely, in the light of what the members of the Commission had themselves said, he concluded that, "These conditions would be realized by the reappointment of the original members". On 23 March 1901, the original members were accordingly reappointed, with the exception of Father Cambier, who replaced Father de Cleene, both from the Congregation of Scheut.[29] There seems to be no record of the new Commission ever meeting.

Other than calming down press and public concern, the Commission achieved very little. It is, of course, possible that it was never intended that it should achieve anything beyond this. A more likely explanation, however, is that Brussels simply failed to grasp the nature of the problem, deliberately or otherwise. As de Cuvelier's note of 1 June 1900 indicates, it seems that Brussels was looking at any problem from the perspective of improving the lot of the natives in the round, by "westernising" them ("the white man's burden") rather than seeking to address detailed questions about their day-to-day treatment by Europeans. Much of the reason for the Commission's failure to explore the widely publicised atrocities allegedly committed against the natives was identified by its members themselves when they were appointed. But there was also a less obvious factor at play with regard to this apparent failure. The British missionary societies had generally held themselves aloof from the controversy surrounding the workings of the Free State. This was in recognition of the fact that they were dependent on Leopold's goodwill in order to carry out their work. Without this, they might not be there at all. Whatever reservations they had, therefore, they preferred to express privately, outside the public debate. Even at the time of the 1896 decree establishing the Commission, Sims, Bentley and Grenfell were cited in the press as defenders of the Free State. The dilemma facing the societies was to be neatly encapsulated in the words of the evangelical missionary Henry (Harry) Grattan Guinness, founder of the Congo Babolo Mission. The difficulty facing the missionary societies, he said, had been, "how to do good – without doing harm".[30]

*

If the missionary societies were ambivalent in their approach, so was the British Government. As early as 1890, at the time when George Washington Williams wrote his "open letter" to Leopold, the Foreign Office was receiving so many adverse reports about the Congo that it had established a dedicated file series – "Congo Free State: Administration: Atrocities, etc.".[31] But for reasons not dissimilar to those of the missionary societies, these were treated low-key. Belgium was an important European ally and the Government was loath to upset Leopold by appearing to interfere in the internal affairs of the Free State and to directly criticise his regime there. Disquiet was nevertheless mounting in the light of evidence being presented by campaigners, chief among them being E D Morel. Morel had joined the Elder Dempster Shipping line as a clerk in 1891, some ten years after Roger Casement before him. By the late 1890s, Elder Dempster had secured the contract with the Free State for movements between Antwerp and Boma. Morel, as a French speaker, had been appointed the company's representative in Belgium. In looking at the trade returns, he had noticed contradictions between the trade statistics published by the Free State and the company's own records. He found that the amount of rubber and ivory being brought out of the Free State on Elder Dempster's ships far exceeded the amounts in the Congo Government's returns, indicating that someone was skimming off an illegitimate profit. He also noted that most of the imports into the Congo (eighty per cent) could not realistically be construed as being for trading purposes, so "nothing was going in to pay for what was coming out".[32] Finally, he noted that apart from transport costs, almost the whole value of the rubber exported from the Congo was being shown as a credit. Labour costs were negligible, indicating that the labour force was not being paid.[33] Morel published these findings in a series of pamphlets in 1900, raising the profile of the Congo debate further. He also decided to become a full-time journalist and Congo reform campaigner. On resigning from Elder Dempster in 1902, he founded *The West African Mail* in order to provide a platform for his work.

During his brief stay in Luanda before returning to South Africa in 1899, Casement had also looked at the Congo trade returns, this time from the other end, i.e., in relation to goods moving through Matadi and Boma. He found that while massive amounts of rubber from the Upper Congo were being sent to Antwerp, effectively only guns and ammunition were being received in return. This indicated that the goods being imported were simply for the use of the security forces, and again that the natives were not being paid. Had they been, other goods would also have been imported for them to buy with their wages.[34] Before finally leaving South Africa, Casement had already developed strong views on the Congo regime, writing to the Foreign Office on 30 April 1900, that after the Boer War, "Britain might join Germany or any other interested power in putting an end to the veritable reign of terror in the Congo".[35] These views were developed in his next post as Consul in Boma. Although he was formally gazetted in August 1900, he did not actually arrive in Boma until December. In October, he was sent by the Foreign Office to Brussels to find out as much as possible about the Free State. While in Brussels, he was invited for lunch with King Leopold and to a follow-up meeting the next day. Leopold's objective was to preserve Anglo-Belgian relations, thus enabling Casement to ask questions about the reported atrocities. Leopold accepted that problems had occurred, but argued that the reports had been exaggerated. It was inevitable that things would sometimes go wrong given the number of people involved and the difficulty in ensuring that they were all suitable for the work. Nevertheless, Leopold emphasised that his objective was always to ensure the well-being of the natives, as he continually made clear to his officers. On the question of forced labour, Leopold argued that if the natives were to enjoy the benefits of civilisation, they had to make their own contribution through work – the labour was not forced but was imposed in lieu of a tax. He also denied that non-Belgian nationals were being shut out of the Congo and that free trade was being prevented.[36]

When Casement finally got to Boma, he quickly found that despite Leopold's denials, the critics had been correct. In despatches to London, he urged international action (at the same time as newspaper reports of atrocities were increasing), but the Foreign Office failed to respond. It was not until 1903 that matters finally came to a head. On 7 January, Casement wrote to Lord Lansdowne, the Foreign Secretary, about the Commission for the Protection of Natives and the real attitude of the Congo Government –

> *In a letter from Mr Grenfell, the senior Baptist Missionary member of the so-called Protection Commission, written from the Upper Congo some time ago, he spoke of the exactions of the Congo Government, and ended by lamenting that that Administration did not seem to realize that its true wealth lay in the welfare and happiness of its people.*
>
> *Certainly no one on the Congo, whatever European may be, treats the Commission for the Protection of natives seriously.*[37]

On 23 January, Lord Cromer, the widely respected British Consul General in Egypt, wrote similarly to Lansdowne following a journey he had himself made into the Free State –

> *I had heard so many and such contradictory accounts of the Belgian Administration that I was very desirous of ascertaining some concise and definite evidence on this subject. During a hurried visit, and with opportunities of observation confined to the banks of the river, I scarcely anticipated that I should be able to arrive at any independent opinion on the point at issue. I saw and heard, however, quite enough to give an insight into the spirit which pervades the administration.*

He recorded that on entering the Free State, in contrast to the other side of the border, he and his party had not met a single human being other than Belgian officers and men, and the wives and children of the latter. He had asked a Swedish officer at Kiro and an Italian officer at Lado whether they ever saw any natives and was told that the nearest native villages were a great distance away. Cromer continued –

> *The reason of all this is obvious enough. The Belgians are disliked. The people fly from them, and it is no wonder that they should do so, for I am informed that the soldiers are allowed full liberty to plunder, and that payments are rarely made for supplies. …I understand that no Belgian officer can move outside the settlements without a strong guard.*
>
> *It appears to me that the facts I have stated above afford ample evidence of the spirit which animates the Belgian Administration, if, indeed, Administration it can be called. The Government, so far as I could judge, is conducted almost exclusively on commercial principals, and, even judged by that standard, it would appear that those principles are somewhat short-sighted.*[38]

Within the UK, matters were to come to a head in a debate in the House of Commons on 20 May, instigated by the campaigning MPs Herbert Samuel and Sir Charles Dilke, on the following motion –

> *That the Government of the Congo Free State, having, at its inception, guaranteed the Powers that its native subjects should be governed with humanity, and that no trading monopoly or privilege should be permitted within its dominions, and both these guarantees having been constantly violated, this House requests His Majesty's Government to confer with the other Powers, signatories of the Berlin General Act by virtue of which the Free State exists, in order that measures may be adopted to abate the evils prevalent in that State.*

The Government's opening position in the debate was somewhat complacent, having no doubt been influenced by a last-minute briefing provided by Sir Constantine Phipps, the British Ambassador in Brussels. Phipps had been handed a package of material by de Cuvelier on the Commission for the Protection of Natives, from which Phipps had concluded (and was later to be criticised for) –

> [The correspondence] *undoubtedly leads to the conclusion that, if the operation of the Commission has not been so effective as might have been anticipated, the fault has rather been due to the great extent of territory which it had the duty to watch, and to the considerable distances by which its members were separated, and not to any deficiency of conception or absence of energy on the part of the Central Government.*[39]

But the Government was met with a more authoritative response than it had perhaps expected. Briefed by campaigners such as Morel, Henry Fox Bourne (Secretary of the Aborigines Protection Society) and the missionary societies who had now come on board, those speaking against the Free State gave specific and graphic examples of breaches of trading rules and atrocities against the natives. These painted a bleak picture which could hardly be ignored, leaving Lord Cranborne, Under Secretary of State for Foreign Affairs, having to concede that His Majesty's Government was, "disposed to think that the system which had been established, and which was prevalent in the Congo Free State, was not altogether in accordance with the obligation into which the Free State had entered", and that it "seemed reasonable" to sound out the views of the other signatories to the Berlin Act. So far as "the condition of the natives" was concerned, he noted that the laws of the Free State left little to be desired and were "full of provisions intended to protect the natives from ill-usage and to further their material advantage", but atrocities had clearly been committed. The Free State had set up a Commission to investigate the reports of ill-treatment, and Cranborne said he would recommend to the other signatories that they send any reports they had received about the ill-treatment of natives to the Free State for investigation by that Commission. Subject to the deletion of the words, "and both these guarantees have been constantly violated" (requested by the Prime Minister, A J Balfour, in order to "avoid direct criticism of a friendly government"), the motion was passed without dissent.[40]

On 8 August, Lansdowne followed up the debate with a note to the British representatives in Paris, Berlin, Rome, St Petersburg, Vienna, Madrid, Constantinople, Brussels, Lisbon, The Hague, Copenhagen and Stockholm. (It had clearly been delayed in drafting, as Casement noted in his diary as early as 15 June that he had been, "very busy correcting Lord L's proposed draft to Brussels".[41]) Lansdowne asked each representative to read the note to, and then leave a copy with, their respective Minister for Foreign Affairs. The note referred to allegations repeatedly drawn to the attention of HMG in recent years of ill-treatment and the existence of trade monopolies in the Congo, and enclosed a copy of the House of Commons Resolution. The note included –

It is reported that no efforts are made to fit the natives by training for industrial pursuits; that the method of obtaining men for labour or for military service is often but little different from that formerly employed to obtain slaves; and that force is now as much required to take the native to the place of service as it used to be to convey the captured slave. It is also reported that constant compulsion has to be exercised in order to exact the collection of the amount of forest produce allotted to each village as the equivalent of the number of days' labour due from the inhabitants, and that this compulsion is often exercised by irresponsible native soldiers uncontrolled by any European officer.

And –

[Information received indicates that] *no attempt at any administration of the natives is made, and that officers of the Government do not apparently concern themselves with such work, but devote all their energy to the collection of revenue. The natives are left entirely to themselves, so far as any assistance in their government or in their affairs is concerned. The Congo stations are shunned, the only natives seen being soldiers, prisoners, and men who are brought in to work. The neighbourhood of stations which are known to have been populous a few years ago is uninhabited, and emigration on a large scale takes place to the territory of neighbouring States, the natives usually averring that they are driven away from their homes by the tyranny and exaction of the soldiers.*

The note also stated that HMG did not consider that the present trading situation in the Congo was "in harmony" with the provisions of the Berlin Act, since nearly the whole territory was being claimed as the private property of the Free State or concession holders. The note concluded –

> *His Majesty's Government will be glad to receive any suggestions which the Governments of the Signatory Powers may be disposed to make in reference to this important question, which might, perhaps constitute, wholly or in part, the subject of a reference to the Tribunal at the Hague.*[42]

De Cuvelier responded to the note on 17 September, forcefully rebutting all criticisms of maladministration, arguing that the system in operation in the Congo was on a par with those operated by other colonial powers elsewhere.[43] He disagreed that the manner of administration in the Free State involved a systematic regime of "cruelty and repression" and also rejected any criticism that commerce in the Free State was being restricted contrary to the Berlin Act. It had only been when the State took off financially, he argued, that the anti-Congo movement had taken shape, relying on a few individual and isolated cases as a pretext in order to conceal the real object of covetousness. It had been necessary for the critics to bring forward a whole series of cases alleging violence against the natives, which had then been re-edited *ad infinitum*. The note went on to quote back at Lansdowne some words written by Casement to the Congo Governor General on 2 July 1901 –

> *I pray, believe me, when I express now, not only for myself, but for my many fellow-countrymen in this part of Africa, our very sincere appreciation of your efforts on behalf of the general community – efforts to promote goodwill among all and to bring together the various elements of our local life.*

With regard to the charge of forced labour, de Cuvelier argued that there was not a single country or colony in which the inhabitants did not contribute in one way or another towards public costs – "On what legitimate grounds could the exemption of natives from all taxes be based, seeing that they are the first to benefit by the material and moral advantages introduced into Africa? As they have no money, a contribution in the shape of labour is required from them. It has been said that, if Africa is ever to be redeemed from barbarism, it must be by getting the negro to understand the meaning of work by the obligation of paying taxes". Building on the words attributed to Casement, de Cuvelier quoted some further words allegedly spoken by Joseph Chamberlain, the Colonial Secretary[44] –

> *It* [native labour] *is a question which has engaged my most careful attention in connection with West Africa and the other Colonies. To listen to the right honourable gentleman, you would almost think that it would be a good thing for the native to be idle. I think it is a good thing for him to be industrious; and by every means in our power we must teach him to work. …No people have ever lived in the world's history who would not work. In the interest of the natives all over Africa, we have to teach them to work.*

And –

> *We are all taxed heavily. Is that a system of forced labour? It is perfectly fair to my mind that the native should contribute something to the cost of administering the country.*

De Cuvelier continued by saying that in every part of Africa, including British possessions, the native was taxed. The legality of a tax was not affected by its mode of payment, whether in money or in kind, so long as it was not excessive. It was certainly not excessive in the Congo, where the work done by the native did not exceed forty hours a month. So far as charges of ill-treatment were concerned, de Cuvelier accepted that crimes and offences had been committed, as in every other country or colony, but these cases had been brought before tribunals.

On a more general level, de Cuvelier considered the most unfair criticism of all to be that the State was simply not interested in the welfare or administration of the natives. He pointed out that Pickersgill, Casement's predecessor as British Consul, had observed as long ago as 1898 that the welfare of the African had improved through restricting the liquor trade, suppression of intertribal wars, diminution of cannibalism and of the traffic in human beings among the natives themselves. There were now railways, hospitals had been established and small pox had been diminished by means of vaccination. Cattle had been introduced into every district, sanitary commissions had been instituted and schools and hospitals had multiplied.

None of the other Powers replied to Lansdowne's note.

*

Casement's major contribution to the Congo affair, on which his subsequent reputation was to be based, was now about to be launched. Following the debate on 20 May, in addition to writing to the other Powers, Lansdowne had instructed Casement to go to the Upper Congo to find out the facts on the ground.[45] Casement accordingly embarked on an extensive two-and-a-half-month-long tour which he completed in September 1903. His resulting sixty-page report[46] provided the first official and comprehensive overview of actual conditions in the Congo. His tour involved in large part revisiting places he had last been to in 1887, so that he could see how things had changed since the days, "when the natives lived their own savage lives in anarchic and disorderly communities, uncontrolled by Europeans". He confirmed that there had indeed been many improvements: way stations had been built and were well maintained, a fleet of steamers had been introduced to navigate the main waterways, and a railway had been built to connect Stanley Pool with the ocean ports. Slavery had been abolished and, as an indication of just how primitive things had been in the past, so had cannibalism –

> *Cannibalism had gone hand in hand with slave raiding, and it was no uncommon spectacle to see gangs of human beings being conveyed for exposure and sale in the local markets. I had in the past, when travelling on the Lulongo River, more than once viewed such a scene. On one occasion a woman was killed in the village I was passing through, and her head and other portions of her were brought and offered for sale to some of the crew of the steamer I was on. Sights of this description are to-day impossible in any part of the country I traversed, and the full credit for their suppression must be given to the authorities of the Congo Government.*

But the improvements were overshadowed by all the other things that Casement found. Almost everywhere he went, he noted a "wholesale diminution of human life". Native communities which had previously been large and flourishing centres of population now no longer existed or were so reduced as to be unrecognisable. Much of the overall reduction in population, he noted, could be put down to the ravages of sleeping sickness, but the natives themselves attributed the principal cause to the treatment they had received at the hands of the colonialists. Typical of the many examples he cited was an area on the southern shores of Stanley Pool, whose previous population of 5,000 Bateke natives had reduced to about one hundred, with the majority fleeing overnight some twelve years previously to French territory on the north shores of Stanley Pool. Shops in Léopoldville stood empty because the natives had been paid in barter goods for which they had no use. The native hospital comprised dirty and dilapidated mud huts with most of their roofs missing. He found seventeen sleeping sickness patients there lying in "utmost dirt" and one patient lying dead in the open. Most of the villages in another settlement, which in

1887 had comprised up to 5,000 people but now no more than 500, were deserted and overgrown. Local villagers (some 240 men, women and children in total) were compelled to supply food for the local wood-cutting post for government steamers in the form of *"kwanga"* (boiled cassava puddings). They were required to supply 380 *kwanga*, each weighing 4.5lb to 6lb, every six days – an amount beyond their capacity – for a derisory sum. The requirement was also in excess of what the woodcutters needed, who then sold on the surplus to the crews of passing steamers. If any of the *kwanga* were not up to standard, or the villagers complained about the price received, they were subjected to beatings by the woodcutters and sometimes detention when they were required to chop firewood. In another settlement, forty adult males and families had to supply 400 *kwanga* each week – some 1,250lb weight of food – for 20 *francs* against a value of 40 *francs* for the raw materials alone. The requirement for natives to provide food formed an integral part of the system, as did punishment for failure to comply, which could often be extreme. In one instance cited by Casement, failure by villagers to supply livestock resulted in an expedition by government soldiers which resulted in sixteen villagers being murdered while another disappeared. A further ten villagers were taken away as prisoners and released (except for a child who died) on payment of sixteen goats. A further forty-eight goats and 225 fowl were also taken away, several houses burned and native property pillaged and destroyed. A derisory 950 *francs* was finally paid by the authorities (passed on as a "fine" to the officer in charge) for the total loss of property and life. One official admitted to Casement that he had been forced to flog men from the villages that failed in their weekly supplies, but that for some months he had stopped doing this. He now put defaulters in prison instead – "If a village which was held to supply, say, 200 rations of fish each week brought only 180 rations, he accepted no excuse, but put two men in "block". For each further ten rations short, another man would be incarcerated. The men stayed in custody until the full ration came in. In another locality, men who failed to meet the requirement of their "tax" were placed in a chain gang. As the number of natives in an area diminished, delivery of what was required inevitably became harder.

Forced labour had become the norm whenever manual work was required. In one settlement that ran close to a riverbank, those living there and up to 20 miles inland were required to keep a government telegraph line clear of undergrowth, for which they received no pay. Many had to work a long way from their homes, during which time they found it difficult to feed themselves. At Bolobo, Casement visited a new pier being constructed for government vessels. Some 1,500 to 2,000 trees and saplings had already been used in the construction, all cut down by men from the neighbouring towns. Most of the trees had had to be carried for some miles. The men had been required to do the work as a "public duty", for which they had received no remuneration. Labour was required for cutting wood, paddling canoes and generally supporting government activities. It was either poorly paid or not remunerated at all –

> *If the local official has to go on a sudden journey men are summoned on the instant to paddle his canoe, and a refusal entails imprisonment or beating. If the Government plantation or the kitchen garden require weeding, a soldier will be sent to call in the women from some of the neighbouring towns. To the official this is a necessary public duty which he cannot but impose, but to the women suddenly forced to leave their household tasks and to tramp off, hoe in hand, baby on back, with possibly an angry husband at home, the task is not a welcome one.*

The most brutal form of forced labour became the collection of rubber. Rubber collection was undertaken by private companies granted "concessions" by Leopold, usually in return for a fifty percent or more share of their takings. The system was enforced by Leopold's *Force Publique*, an 18,000-strong private army comprising African soldiers ostensibly commanded by European officers, and by "sentries" employed by the concessions. Technically, the use of armed men was regulated by the Government, which accorded the companies the "rights of police", though in practice the controls were widely ignored. The rule that black troops must not be deployed unaccompanied by a European officer, for example, was often breached. As in the case of food supply, natives were given often unrealistic quotas of rubber to collect. And as the supplies of rubber were exploited, the natives had to travel further and further from their homes. Among many examples cited by Casement was the case of three men who had to undertake a two-day journey to collect rubber, causing them to be away from their wives for six days at a time. The quantity of pure rubber collected by the three was not less than 7 kilogrammes, worth £2, for which they received goods, valued locally at 1s10d (about 9 pence). Prolonged absences from home left men with insufficient time to tend their own fields and the prospect of starvation. The goods in which they were paid, e.g., cotton reels or buttons, were often of no use. Failure to achieve quotas resulted in savage beatings, or floggings by means of a *chicotte*, a sharp whip made out of hippopotamus hide. Alternative punishments included putting men into penal servitude for a short period in factory prisons (known as "*maisons d'otages*"), holding their families hostage until the required amount of rubber was brought in, or allocating them to projects involving heavy labour. Casement described how he had come across eleven women, some pregnant and others with children being breastfed, who at nightfall were held tied together in a shed, either neck to neck or ankle to ankle, to secure them for the night. In another example, he related –

> *At Bondanga I saw thirty-three large tree trunks, each of which could not have weighed less than half a ton – some of them nearer one ton, which, I was told, had been felled and carried by the natives in building a new home* [for the use of the company's agent].

The agent confided that this work was a burden specifically imposed upon unwilling rubber workers, or "backward *récolteurs*".

Outright refusals to collect rubber resulted in those involved (including women and children) being shot down. Their right hands were then cut off by the soldiers or guards to provide proof to the authorities of the "legitimate" use of cartridges. Rumours of this were already widespread and Casement found evidence to substantiate these and the scale of the practice in a disused diary –

> *... MP [an officer in the Government service] said, 'Each time the corporal goes out to get rubber, cartridges are given to him. He must bring back all not used; and for every one used he must bring back a right hand.' MP told me that sometimes they shot a cartridge at an animal in hunting; they then cut off a hand from a living man. As to the extent to which this is carried on, he informed me that in six months they, the State, on the Momboyo River, had used 6,000 cartridges, which means that 6,000 people are killed or mutilated. It means more than 6,000, for the people have told me repeatedly that the soldiers kill children with the butt of their guns.*

Casement relayed even more gruesome tales, such as finding "a young man" both of whose hands had been beaten off with the butt ends of rifles against a tree, and of several men being put one behind the other and shot with a single cartridge.

Casement noted (in an echo of Leopold's justification that the natives were being put to work for their own good) that –

> *The summing up of the situation by the majority of those with whom I sought to discuss it was that, in fact, it was forced labour conceived in the true interest of the native, who, if not controlled in this way, would spend his days in idleness, unprofitable to himself and the general community.*

His own assessment was that, "all combined to convince me over and over again that during the last seven years, this *"domain privé"* of King Léopold has been a veritable hell on earth".

Even before his report was published, speculation began about Casement's findings. *The Times* reported on 7 December 1903 – under the heading, *The Treatment of Natives in the Congo Free State* – that his mission was originally to have lasted six months but had been aborted after only two because it was obvious by then that no further action was necessary. It noted that Casement was now in England writing his report, and secrecy about its contents was being maintained. Nevertheless –

> *It will be shown, on the undeniable authority of a British official, that the most horrible outrages are being perpetrated under the* **rubber régime** *[italics in original], and that slavery and barbarism in the most revolting forms exist today.*[47]

In contrast, *The Times* reported a few days later from Brussels that the leaked contents of Casement's report had aroused a good deal of feeling and that –

> *The Brussels Press argue that, whatever may be the conclusions arrived at by the British Consul, the public mind in England has been unfairly prejudiced before it has had a chance of hearing both sides of the case, which is necessary before passing judgment upon any question at issue.*[48]

There was some support for this view even in England, where the President of the Liverpool Chamber of Commerce, who had had an audience with Leopold for the purpose of gaining trade access to the Congo, noted that the King had expressed "great anxiety" to put down "any atrocities that might exist in the Congo".[49] Michael Holland, an experienced African pioneer and explorer writing to *The Times* from London EC, went into greater detail. (Holland had been the first European to find the exact location of the Katanga copper mines and had a close knowledge of that part of the Congo.[50]) His view echoed that of Brussels, i.e., that any atrocities were isolated and local rather than systemic –

> …*The local administration collects rubber and ivory from the natives and pays them for it. I have never heard of natives complain of ill-treatment from a white official on account of not bringing rubber or ivory in sufficient quantities, and I have always been on such friendly terms with the chiefs and people that cases of cruelty would have come to my ears.*
>
> *Isolated cases occurred, and also in both the Rhodesias and the British Central African Protectorate, where black soldiers, travelling through the country without a white official, beat and bullied the natives; but the local authorities in Katanga have issued orders that no armed party shall travel without a European in charge, and I think the same regulation holds good in British spheres…*

Holland went on to say that, "The science of ruling Central African natives can only be learned by a prolonged stay…"[51]

The controversy was nevertheless having an effect on the Belgian attitude. *The Times* reported on 19 December that the Congo Free State had decided that in future it would appoint inspectors drawn from foreign armies, either Scandinavian or Italian. Also, the army was to be reorganised so that soldiers would no longer be used for work other than military duties.[52] And when

Leopold visited Berlin in January, ostensibly in celebration of the Kaiser's birthday, *The Times* suggested that his real motive was to confer with the German Emperor "on the attitude of England in respect of the Congo State".[53]

Casement's report was finally published in mid-February 1904, and a copy sent to de Cuvelier. An accompanying FO memorandum set out HMG's view that the report supported the allegations that had been made about conditions in the Congo.[54] Far from moving the matter on, this became the start of a lengthy dispute between the two sides. In a twelve-page "rejoinder" dated 12 March,[55] the Free State complained that despite repeated requests, HMG had not supplied copies of any individual reports that it claimed provided evidence of systematic cruelty. It also criticised Casement for not producing any figures to back up his claims on population decline between 1887 and 1903. While the population had declined in certain areas, it argued that this was largely due to sleeping sickness, which was "decimating the population throughout equatorial Africa". Added to this, small-pox epidemics and the inability of tribes to top up their numbers by the purchase of slaves, and the ease with which natives could migrate, would explain how Casement and the missionaries could have been struck by the diminution of population. It quoted Mgr Van Ronslé, Vicar Apostolic of the Belgian Congo (and member of the Commission for the Protection of Natives) –

> *The people (slave) are for the most part originally prisoners of war. Since the Decree of emancipation they have simply returned to their own distant homes, knowing their owners have no power to recapture them. This is one reason why some people think the population is decreasing, and another reason is the vast exodus up and down river.*

And –

> *So long as the Slave Trade flourished the Bobangi flourished, but with its abolition they are tending to disappear, for their towns were replenished by slaves.*

The Free State went on to attack the basis of Casement's allegations of ill-treatment, arguing that along with the Protestant Missionaries, he had been seen by the natives as the righter of wrongs, and they had brought complaints to him, as he had inevitably been seen as "the antagonist of the established authorities". As an example of how he had been misled, it singled out the case of a boy named Epondo, whose hand had been cut off. The authorities had now staged a judicial inquiry into the allegation, and this revealed that Casement had been the object of a plot contrived by the natives, who, "in the hope of no longer being obliged to work, had agreed among themselves to represent Epondo as the victim of the inhuman conduct of one of the *"capitas"* of a commercial company". In reality, Epondo had been the victim of an accident while out hunting and had been bitten by a wild boar. His hand had been amputated because gangrene had set in. Casement had been wrong to extrapolate from this one case the conclusion that the system was at fault, and he had been wrong to accept at face value the narrative presented to him. Nevertheless, all the cases highlighted by Casement would be investigated.

In what was to become a running sore between HMG and the Free State and a long-term irritation to Casement himself, the rejoinder went on to "regret" that in his report as published, all names, places and dates had been omitted and substituted by a series of initials – "That Mr Casement should formulate so serious a charge without at the same time supporting it by absolute proof would seem to justify those who consider that his previous employment has not altogether been such as to qualify him for the duties of a Consul". The decision to anonymise the report had, in fact, been taken by the Foreign Office for the best of reasons, *viz.* to avoid coercion by those accused and victimisation of those natives who had put forward complaints. It had, nevertheless, been taken against Casement's own strong wishes. He too saw the damaging effect that this would have on the report's impact and credibility and that it would open him up to exactly the sort of criticism now being directed towards him by the Free State. The rejoinder concluded with the objection that Casement had exceeded his remit as a Consul in a foreign country – "It is obviously altogether outside the duties of a Consul to take upon himself, as Mr Casement has done, to institute inquiries, to summon natives, to submit them to interrogatories as if duly authorised thereto, and to deliver what may be styled judgments in regard to the guilt of the accused".

Public reaction in Belgium remained defiant. The newspaper *Indépendence Belge* accused the British Government of lending itself "to a campaign of calumny and defamation by the merchants of Liverpool". It had no confidence in the Casement report, considering such inquiries "devoid of weight unless emanating from an absolutely disinterested source…" While abuses had undeniably occurred in the Congo, it was "utterly false to allege that the Free State tolerates or connives at them".[56] On 15 March, the Free State published an interim response to the report in the form of a pamphlet, along the lines of the rejoinder, pending the outcome of an official inquiry. In the UK, *The Times* reported on 19 February that the Aborigines Protection Society had sent to Lord Lansdowne a first-hand report from a missionary, dated 7 November 1903, of atrocities witnessed in the Congo.[57] And in a letter published on 22 February, John Holt of John Holt & Company (Liverpool) Ltd, wrote that although he was a merchant operating in the Congo, his concerns were not related to the trading aspects of the arguments about the Free State –

> *I am not in any way interested as a trader in the Congo State. I am, however, strongly opposed to the doctrine propounded by King Leopold by which the native has been deprived of his natural right*

to the fruits of the soil, and has been robbed of those rights under the plea of obtaining taxes in the form of rubber. –

There is no more awful picture in our generation than that which has been painted so well and so terribly by Consul Casement.

And –

This unnecessary cruelty must be put an end to; it is too horrible to think it is possible that Europe can continue to remain indifferent to the woes of our helpless and voiceless fellow creatures in the Congo.[58]

Campaigners mobilised themselves behind Casement's report. Under the headline *Maladministration of the Congo*, *The Times* reported that on 19 April, 2,000 people had attended a public meeting at Exeter Hall in the Strand, chaired by T A Denny, a philanthropist and financial supporter of the Salvation Army, "to protest against the continuance of Congo State misrule".[59]

Despite his obvious success in producing a report that put the Congo affair at the centre of international attention and debate, Casement himself had become disillusioned by what he saw as a soft-pedalling approach by the Foreign Office, as exemplified by its refusal to allow names and other identifiers to be included in the published version of his report. He was also upset at having his competence and integrity traduced in the responses from Belgium and the Free State. The British Government had it in their hands to back up his findings by publishing the contents of the Foreign Office "atrocity" files, but Lansdowne refused to do this. As a civil servant, Casement was prevented from defending himself in public or actively campaigning in the cause, but having met Morel for the first time in December 1903, when the two men got on immediately, he pursued with him the idea of setting up "a single organisation, having a single purpose, systematically and continuously to strive to enlighten public opinion in Britain about the conditions in the Congo".⁶⁰ This gave rise to the birth of the Congo Reform Association (CRA), formally founded in March 1904, for which Morel then worked indefatigably. As well as Morel and Casement, the CRA's membership went on to include such international figures as Mark Twain, Booker T Washington, Sir Arthur Conan Doyle and Joseph Conrad. Morel himself was funded by the Quaker chocolate millionaire William Cadbury.⁶¹

On 8 June 1904, *The Times* reported that a conference of MPs and missionary and philanthropic societies had been held at Westminster Palace to consider Casement's report.⁶² On the following day, a further debate took place in the House of Commons.⁶³ In opening the debate, Sir Charles Dilke said that the conclusion to be drawn from Casement's findings was clear: the claim that had been made by Phipps that any problems in the Congo were, "not due to any deficiency of conception or absence of energy on the part of the central [Free State] Government", was false. HMG's note to the other Powers following that debate had made clear that the method of obtaining men for labour differed little from the previous method of obtaining slaves, and that compulsion in regard to bringing in produce was exercised by "irresponsible native soldiers uncontrolled by Europeans". It had been argued, he said, that things were getting better, but that was not the opinion of Casement, an "administrator of wide African experience", who "continually returned to the statement that things were getting far worse, and that large native trades which formerly existed had been destroyed, that the people were driven across borders, and that the country was becoming void of population". He noted that Casement's report had been foully attacked and ought to be defended, given that Casement had been selected by the Government as an official of great experience. He then went on to express regret at a suggestion which had been put to de Cuvalier by Lansdowne that an independent Special Commission should be set up to investigate Casement's findings, arguing that the facts were already known and this would simply put the clock back many years. Others contributors to the debate added their condemnation of the Congo system of government. Austin Taylor, Conservative MP for Liverpool East Toxteth, satirised the Belgian and French approach to colonial government –

> *An area of a couple of thousand square miles was marked off on a map of Africa and then the company obtaining the concession was told, 'Gentlemen, we, the Government of this African country, grant you and your associates everything of commercial value which grows within the area marked on the map of that country. You will, of course, make it convenient to pay the native some little trifle for his self-imposed labour in bringing you what you require. Gentlemen, good day; and never forget that we seek only one thing – the moral and material advancement of the dark races.'*

Taylor went on to compare this with the British system under which the native knew the fixed amount of his obligation, and, once discharged from it, was at liberty to seek where he would labour or leisure. In contrast, the Congo labourer might not even leave his village except as a fugitive, and was a "close bondsman to his endless tasks". Alfred Emmott, Liberal MP for Oldham, denied that what was going on in the Congo was actually "trade" at all –

> *The merchant, which is really the state, says, 'This land is mine, and the black native must gather the produce. I pay what I like for it, and this black man is to work as long as I wish for the collection of produce'... This was not trade at all, but slavery.*

Sir John Eldon Gorst, Conservative MP (and a former Solicitor General), compared the situation in the Congo to the old system of colonialism – such as the Spanish conquest of America – under which the riches and resources of a country belonged to the people who conquered and occupied it, with "the wretched people over whom they assumed the duties of the administration" being treated as slaves for the sole purpose of enriching the occupiers. By contrast, the basis of British principles was that –

> *...the resources and riches of the State belonged to the inhabitants of it, that the civilised power in its administration sought only to develop those resources for the development of the people, and that the welfare of the people was the sole object for which the administration was carried on. The gain this country derived from administration of that kind was restricted to the advantage of trade.*

In response, the Government was for the first time publicly unequivocal in its condemnation of the Free State. Earl Percy, Under Secretary of State for Foreign Affairs, noted that the tone of the debate had been favourable to HMG – "There has never been a policy of which it might be said as truly as of this one that it was the policy not so much of His Majesty's Government as the policy of the House of Commons". Some progress had been made. Orders had now been issued to the local administration in Boma to make an inquiry into forced labour contributions, including the conduct of *gardes forestières*; Italian officers had been appointed as State inspectors; the post of Royal High Commissioner had been created to ensure execution of orders given to protect the natives; and instructions had been given to the ABIR company forbidding restrictions on the freedom of commerce and to ensure the removal of any officials who ought to be removed. Regrettably, however, HMG had received no information about the nature of a promised inquiry into the cases raised in the Casement Report. Nor had any replies been received from the other Powers to the Foreign Office note issued following the debate on 20 May 1903. While it was believed that some were conducting inquiries of their own, most were not prepared to act. Italy, Turkey and the United States (who had been sent a copy of the Casement Report) were giving the UK's representations "their most earnest consideration", but most of the other governments, "took the view, which is to us quite incomprehensible, that their material interests are not sufficient in the Congo Basin to warrant any active participation in the matter". Percy concluded –

> *For good or evil the Congo State stand today in the eyes of millions of the heathen throughout the darkest regions of that unhappy continent as the mandatory of Europe, the sole exemplar and interpreter of Christian methods of government. What is at issue if that position is abused and that trust betrayed is not the question of the existence or the Sovereignty of a State – that is a matter on which the Congo Government may make its mind easy – but the fair fame of Western civilisation, and the reputation of the creed upon whose principles that civilisation is avowedly based.*

Sir Edward Grey closed for the Opposition, saying how rare it was for such unanimity in the House, "but it was a gruesome anonymity". The Congo Free State had done some good, but to say that the practices which had been described during the debate were not universal in the Congo State was neither here nor there. What was detestable was that they should exist at all –

> *It would be distressing to hear these things if they had existed a century ago; it was intolerable to hear about it in relation to contemporary history.*

On 13 June, *The Times* reported from Berlin that there had been little comment in Germany about the various British Ministerial statements. The *Cologne Gazette*, however, had expressed the view that the proposed "Special Commission" was an attempt by HMG to sustain Casement's report and possibly even to conceal the weakness of certain of his statements.[64]

Arguments over the Congo did not end with the debate. It would, in fact, take until 1908 for there to be a structural resolution of the problem, when irresistible international pressure finally resulted in the Congo being handed over by Leopold to the Belgian State and being renamed the Belgian Congo. During the twenty years or so of the Free State's existence, it is estimated that between three and ten million Congolese were killed.[65] Joseph Conrad, in his novel *Heart of Darkness*, which was based on his own experience in the Congo, wrote of one gang of adventurers, "To tear treasure out of the bowels of the land was their desire, with no more moral purpose at the back of it than there is in burglars breaking into a safe".[66]

*

Following the debate in June 1904, Casement continued to be involved in the Congo Reform Association, insofar as this was compatible with his role as a public servant, until the Association was finally wound up in 1913. He also continued his close relationship with Morel and other notable supporters of the Association and its aims, though there are signs that his friendship with Morel later began to pall.[67] Casement's official involvement in the Congo ended, however, shortly after the June debate, when he was appointed consul general in Lisbon. Though a prestigious posting, Casement was forced quickly to return on the grounds of ill health. On 1 January 1905, he successfully applied for leave without pay and was to be absent from duty for some eighteen months. (During his absence, he was awarded the CMG in Edward VII's 1905 Birthday Honours list.) On return to duty in August 1906, he was posted to Brazil as consul at Santos, transferring in December 1907 to Pará, and then in March 1909 to Rio de Janeiro as consul general. During these postings, he performed regular consular duties.

The closing chapter of Casement's consular career emerged in 1910, when he was asked by the Foreign Office to join a commission established to investigate reports of atrocities against native Indians in the rubber-collecting area of Putumayo, a region of the Amazon bounded by Peru, Colombia and Ecuador. The commission was being set up by the British directors of the Peruvian Amazon Company, registered in London but controlled by its Peruvian founder, Julio Cesar Arana. Reports had emerged that the native employees of that company were being subjected to treatment as inhumane as, or even more inhumane than, that which had applied to natives in the Congo. In addition to the fact that the company was registered in London, among its employees were a number of Barbadians – subjects of the Empire – providing the British Government with a further locus to intervene. Casement was the obvious candidate to represent the Government on the commission. He left England on 23 July 1910, arriving at La Chorrera, the principal station of the company, on 22 September. From there, he visited five of the company's outlying stations where he interviewed fourteen Barbadian employees, before returning home from Pará on 17 December and arriving back in Cherbourg on 31 December. In a preliminary report dated 7 January 1911, Casement noted that charges made against employees of the company by those he had interviewed were "of the most atrocious kind" and included murder, violation and constant flogging. These charges had been accepted without further investigation by Señor Juan Tizon, the company's representative in La Correra –

> *There was, moreover, the evidence of our own eyes and senses, for the Indians almost everywhere bore evidence of being flogged, in many cases of being brutally flogged, and the marks were not confined to men nor adults. Women, and even little children, were*

more than once found, their limbs scarred with weals left by the thong of twisted tapir-hide, which is the chief implement used for coercing and terrorising the native population of the region traversed.[68]

Two further reports followed. In a 16,000-word report dated 31 January 1911, Casement analysed the role played by Barbadians in rubber collection. Originally, in 1904, about 200 Barbadians had been recruited by the company as labourers; there were now substantially fewer. While their original contracts were for two years, the labourers worked effectively under a system of peonage, being encouraged to take on company debts at usurious interest rates, binding them to their employer until these were repaid. Though appointed as labourers, they were generally required to oversee the forced labour of native rubber collectors. While the Barbadians were themselves often subjected to ill-treatment, many in turn ill-treated the natives in the process of ensuring that they fulfilled their quotas for rubber collection. Casement's report contained detailed notes of interviews and case histories.[69] His full report to Sir Edward Grey, now Foreign Secretary, followed quickly on 17 March 1911.[70] This document, some 27,000 words long, plus transcripts of testimonies from thirty Barbadians, was – like his earlier report on the Congo – clear and comprehensive. Starting with background on the Putumayo, it noted that the Indian population there in 1906 had been estimated at 40,000 to 50,000. As early as 1903, a missionary had written to the Peruvian Minister of Justice that it had not been possible to establish a mission there owing to the abuses of the "*caucheros*" (rubber workers) against the Indians ("*los infiels*"), whom they maltreated and murdered for no reason, seizing their women and children. The Apostolic Prefect had also written to the Minister of Justice on 27 August 1907 – "…I wish to draw the attention of the Supreme Government to the infamous trade in buying and selling boys and girls which for years has been practised in these parts…"

Casement noted that no action had been taken on either of these reports and went on to describe the present situation with regard to rubber collection. He expanded on his preliminary comments about flogging – "…in the production of Putumayo rubber, the lash played an unceasing part". Less than six months before his visit, a native chief had been flogged to death and had died in actual confinement in the station "stocks" between his wife and one of his children. Indian women went around entirely naked, with the men wearing small loin cloths; of seven nude figures Casement had come across in La Chorrera, five were scarred across the buttocks and thighs with marks of the lash. Most of the people he saw subsequently – young, old, women, men and children – also bore marks of the lash. As a rule, the flogging of defaulting rubber collectors was performed by one or more of the salaried staff – "The general method of flogging as described to me by those who had administered the lash was to apply it to the bare buttocks, the back and thighs coming in for a share of the blows, while the victim, male or female, lay or was forcibly extended on the ground, sometimes pegged out", and – "In many cases the Indian rubber worker – who knew roughly what quantity of rubber was expected of him – when he brought his load to be weighed, seeing that the needle of the balance did not touch the required spot, would throw himself on the ground, and in that posture to await the blows". One man gave in evidence – "The Indian is so humble that as soon as he sees that the needle of the scale does not mark the 10 kilog., he himself stretches out his hands and throws himself on the ground to receive the punishment. Then the chief or a subordinate advances, bends down, takes the Indian by his hair, strikes him, raises his head, drops it face downwards on the ground, and after the face is beaten and kicked and covered with blood the Indian is scourged". And, "I was informed by a British subject who had himself often flogged the Indians that he had seen mothers flogged, on account of shortage of rubber by their little sons. These boys were held to be too small to chastise, and so, while the little boy stood terrified and crying, his mother would be beaten "just a few strokes" to make him a better worker". Seeing it as depressingly reminiscent of the situation in the Congo, Casement went on to describe further aspects of the regime of atrocities in the business of rubber collection. Attempted escape was a capital offence, as often resulting in torture and being put to death as being flogged. The fugitives were tracked down, however far they had got. Those hunting them down were paid by results – their crimes included pouring kerosene oil on men and women and setting them alight; burning men at the stake; dashing the brains out of children, and again and again cutting off the arms and legs of Indians and leaving them to die – "Men and women would be suspended by the arms, often twisted behind their backs and tied together at the wrists, and in this agonising posture, their feet hanging high above the ground, they were scourged on the nether limbs and lower back…" Other practices included drowning, pseudo-drowning and the stocks, with the legs distended in several holes apart.

Casement concluded by saying that he had reported the many allegations that had been made to him to the local prefect, some of which he had laid personally before him supported by the verbal testimony of eyewitnesses, one being a white Peruvian employee of the company. The prefect had given assurances that immediate action would be taken to protect the Indians in the future and that any of those found guilty of the crimes alleged would be adequately dealt with. And on returning to the Putumayo towards the end of 1911, Casement learned that following the despatch by the Peruvian Government of a Judicial Commission to the Putumayo, warrants had been issued against twenty-two individuals who had been charged with the crime of "flogging and flaying thirty Ocainas Indians and then burning them alive". But Casement was dubious about the slow rate of progress being made, concluding that the problem lay in the Putumayo simply having no background or tradition of systems of justice.[71] At the end of the year, he returned to Europe via Washington, where, with the help of the British Ambassador, he was able to meet US President Taft and present his evidence and his case against the Peruvian Amazon Company face to face. While this resulted in some pressure being placed by the US on the Peruvian Government, the bigger picture emerging very much echoed that which had applied in the Congo, i.e., however many assurances were given, little followed by way of practical action. The Peruvian Amazon Company denied that problems existed, while the Peruvian Government promised results that failed to materialise. While the United States indicated sympathy with the British concern, Grey was reluctant to press them too hard in the light of the Monroe Doctrine. Various attempts to break the impasse failed. Grey held back publication of the report for want of maintaining good relations with Peru. Through pressure from Grey, the Peruvian Amazon Company allowed Casement an ex officio place on their board, but he was unable to exert any practical influence. In August 1912, Casement returned to the Putumayo, where he learned that though 237 warrants had been issued only nine arrests had been made. A considerable number of the 237 continued to force Indians to bring rubber at stated intervals. The estimated Indian population of 50,000 in 1906 had, by 1911, fallen to 8,000 because of the ruthless system in place, but it appeared to be held that there were "still enough Indians to go round". In a letter to Sir Edward Grey on 5 February 1913, Casement noted –

> *The number of Indians killed by starvation – often purposely brought about by destruction of crops over whole districts or inflicted as a form of the death penalty on individuals who failed to bring in their quota of rubber – or by deliberate murder by bullet, fire, beheading, or flogging to death, and accompanied with a variety of atrocious tortures, during the course of these twelve years, in order to extort these 4,000 tons of rubber, cannot have been less than 30,000, and possibly came to many more.*[72]

The British Government had been unable to secure any tangible improvements despite growing pressure and despite the Peruvian Amazon Company being a British company. It finally published Casement's report as a Blue Book in July 1912,[73] which attracted much public attention and concern, including questions about whether action could be taken directly against the company's directors. This question was referred by Grey to a Parliamentary Select Committee which reported in February 1913, recommending that tighter controls should be considered for the activities and responsibilities of company directors. Casement had given evidence to the Committee as well as being involved in fundraising to set up a Catholic Mission in the Putumayo to protect the natives. The problem of ill-treatment of the native Indians was, however, never in terms resolved. The question died down partly through diminishing public interest but mainly through the world-wide switch from the collection of natural rubber to its managed cultivation and harvesting in plantations, notably in Malaysia. For Casement, the Putumayo effectively represented the final chapter of his diplomatic career, which had been capped in June 1911 by the award of a knighthood in the Birthday Honours list. His thank-you letter to Grey was fulsome and was to be oft-quoted against him in the future –

> *I find it very hard to choose the words, in which to make acknowledgment of the honour done to me by the King.*
>
> *I am much moved at the proof of confidence and appreciation of my services on the Putumayo, conveyed to me by your letter, wherein you tell me the King has been graciously pleased upon your recommendation to confer on me the honour of a knighthood.*
>
> *I am indeed grateful to you for this signal assurance of your personal esteem and support and very deeply sensible of the honour done me by His Majesty.*
>
> *I would beg that my humble duty might be presented to His*

Majesty, when you may do me the honour to convey to him my deep appreciation of the honour he has been so graciously pleased to confer on me.[74]

Casement's diplomatic career had by any measure been successful. His contribution had been above and beyond that of the average British consul. His reports on the Congo and the Putumayo were thorough, well written and dispassionate. The Congo report established him as a widely known and well-regarded diplomat and humanitarian. At the same time, during his career he had often displayed a difficult and recalcitrant personality, as well as having a tendency towards ill-health. Following his retirement from the diplomatic service, it was his personal weaknesses rather than his character strengths that came to the fore in his final role as an Irish nationalist.

FIVE
CASEMENT THE NATIONALIST

…henceforth and for aye I shall concentrate on Ireland alone
Casement on his retirement from the Foreign Office in July 1913

The true alliance to aim at for all who love peace is the friendly Union of Germany, America and Ireland. These are the true United States of the world.
                Casement, *The Elsewhere Empire*, article in *Irish Freedom*,
                                                            February 1914

The Germans <u>deserve</u> to win. They are making heroic sacrifices – without a word… The lies of the English press are colossal. The "atrocities" in Belgium are a horrid lie – I've been there and seen with my own eyes… Everyone is sorry for France and Belgium – it is only England, the originator and plotter of the war they loathe
    Casement in a letter to Gertrude Bannister, 2 December 1914

The timing of Casement's conversion to Irish nationalism and the reasons for it are unclear. His consular career had been successful and superficially there was no reason why it should not have continued. But he had always shown signs of being restive and became upset at the responses to his Congo report. He was angry with Leopold and the Congo administration for suggesting that his report was biased, and he was angry with Sir Constance Phipps for appearing to take the side of Leopold against him. Crucially, he also fell out with the Foreign Office for failing, as he saw it, to back him up over his report and the associated personal criticisms made against him. His absence from official duties from 1904 to 1906 is generally regarded as being in reaction to that. It was during his time away that he developed a growing interest in the "Gaelic Revival" and the cause of Irish Nationalism. (Some suggest that he may have drawn parallels between the colonialism that he had seen in action as a consul and the position of the people in Ireland.) He became involved in preparations for the first *Glens Feis*, at Glenariff (Waterfoot), County Antrim, in 1904, toured large parts of Ireland, especially in the Irish-speaking areas, and became heavily involved in the work of the Gaelic League to revive the Irish language. While he made financial contributions towards the work of the League, he failed to make much progress himself in learning the language. He also opened up what was to be an enduring association with the noted historian and Irish Nationalist, Alice Stopford Green. Their relationship began as the result of an approach from him in April 1904, soliciting her support for the Congo Reform Association. There then followed meetings at her home in London, where Casement was also to meet other leading figures of the day – such as Lord Haldane, Florence Nightingale and Winston Churchill – and to develop his thinking and contacts on the Irish cause.[1] His return to consular duties in South America in 1906 effectively put these activities on hold, though he did strike a minor blow for nationalism by changing the address on his private and official correspondence in Santos from "British Consulate" to "Consulate of Great Britain and Ireland".²

Following his return from the Putumayo, Casement showed no inclination to return to his consular duties and was put on half pay by the Foreign Office in July 1912.³ Then, following appearances before the Parliamentary Select Committee on the Putumayo on 13 November and 11 December, he applied for two months' sick leave. This was turned down by the Foreign Office, who told him to return to Rio,⁴ in response to which he sought an urgent consultation in London with Sir Lauder Brunton, a distinguished clinician married to Louisa Jane Stopford, a sister of Alice Stopford Green. The choice of Brunton seems to have been made for practical reasons, as there is no evidence that Brunton was a supporter of the nationalist cause. (In 1908, he had been co-signatory to a letter to *The Times* supporting the annexation of the Congo by Belgium,⁵ and in March 1914, he was reported in *The Times* to have signed the British Covenant against the Third Home Rule Bill.⁶) On 20 December, Brunton wrote –

> *I saw Sir Roger Casement on Dec 19th and examined him very carefully. I found him suffering from congestion of the liver, feeble circulation, gastro-intestinal catarrh and so much irritation and tenderness over the appendix as to render it questionable whether he ought to have his appendix removed.*
>
> *He was also suffering from much pain in the sciatic nerve and it is just possible there may be a calculus in his left kidney or ureter. He is in a condition requiring great care and I should certainly not advise him to go to any tropical climate at present, nor do I think he ought to be out of reach of surgical assistance in case an operation should become absolutely necessary.*

The following day, J W Thompson Walker – a noted urologist – having conducted a follow-up examination, wrote to Dr Ambrose Charpentier, Casement's GP in Uxbridge –

> *I have finished my examination of Sir Roger Casement. The X Rays exclude the presence of a calculus of the Kidneys, Ureters or Bladder. There are considerable osteophytic formations in connection with the intervertebral articulations of the lumber vertebrae, and an osteophytic outgrowth of the head of the femur on the left side. These evidences of arthritis are sufficient to explain the pains from which he is suffering.*
>
> *In regard to the original cause for these, I think they are practically always the result of absorption from the intestine. The treatment I would advise is as follows:-*
>
> *Give him Iodides as counter irritants, say a series of small blisters on any painful spot in the lumber spine and over the hip. Instead of this or following on after an interval, a series of radiant heat baths, say once a week for six weeks, and this followed later on with massage if he can stand it. He should be carefully dieted for his indigestion and I would advise intestinal antiseptics, such as calomel for 1/6 to 1/4 in pill each night, and you might give him liquid paraffin.*
>
> *All this will take some months and I have advised him strongly against returning to Rio de Janeiro where he cannot have any skilled treatment and where the diet and surroundings are quite unsuited for him.*[7]

In consequence, the Foreign Office granted Casement three months' sick leave. But despite the medical advice that he should avoid tropical climates and avoid being out of reach of surgical assistance, he quickly set off for Tenerife, going on from there to visit his brother in South Africa. All this merely forestalled his inevitable final departure from the consular service. After trying to get another two months' sick leave out of the Foreign Office, and wrangling over severance terms, he finally retired on health grounds in July 1913, with an annual pension of £421.

Casement was now free to pursue the nationalist cause as he wished – or in his own words, "henceforth and for aye I shall concentrate on Ireland alone".[8] He was able to express his views publicly for the first time and to write and publish articles under his own name rather than a pseudonym. On 24 October 1913, he made his first public speech as a nationalist at Ballymoney, Co Antrim. Sharing a platform with Alice Stopford Green, he argued against the exclusion of Ulster as a solution to the problem of Home Rule. Reporting the meeting the following day, *The Times* noted that Casement combined, "citizenship of the world with an enthusiastic attachment to romantic Nationalism".[9] It noted that in his speech he had been conciliatory towards Carsonism and that his proposition had been generally well received, though it also observed that the liveliness of the meeting in no way compared to that of the meetings being held by the Covenanters.

From this, he went on to become Treasurer of the thirty-strong Provisional Committee of the Irish Volunteers. Together with Eoin MacNeill, he co-wrote the Volunteers' Manifesto and went on a six-month recruiting drive around the country. His new status as an active nationalist was firmly cemented on St Patrick's Day 1914, when he reviewed the 1,000-strong Limerick Volunteers and marched at their head.[10] Then, in May 1914, following a meeting at Alice Stopford Green's house, he took Darrell Figgis and Erskine Childers to meet the London agent of an arms dealer to buy weapons for the Volunteers. With a total of £1,500 raised from Mrs Green, the Hon Mary Spring Rice, and the wife of Erskine Childers, they agreed the purchase of 1,500 rifles and 75,000 rounds of ammunition.[11] Recruiting for the Volunteers had meanwhile gone from strength to strength, so much so as to worry John Redmond, who saw it as a threat to the hegemony of the Irish Parliamentary Party. (Between the end of 1913 and July 1914, Volunteer numbers rose from 2,000 to 160,000.[12]) With the threat of setting up his own independent executive to which those Volunteers who supported the Irish Parliamentary Party would be asked to give their allegiance, Redmond demanded twenty-five places on the Provisional Committee for his own nominees. He rejected a counter-proposal suggested by Casement that the Provisional Committee should comprise a delegate from each county.[13] This left the Committee with little choice: to accede to Redmond's demands would mean losing control of the Volunteers, while rejecting them would lead to the movement being split. Their response was to go along with Redmond at the same time as privately ensuring that the arms they had on order would be allocated to those whom they trusted. While it was a pragmatic solution, Casement was subsequently to attract criticism from hardliners for apparently backing down.

Alongside his work with the Volunteers, Casement also became involved in late 1913 and in the early part of 1914 in a project to develop a tangible relationship with Germany, in pursuit of his now public call for "a friendly Union of Germany, America and Ireland".[14] This followed a decision by the White Star and Cunard lines to abandon calls at the Cork port of Queenstown (Cobh) on their transatlantic crossings. The decision was taken by the lines for their own commercial reasons, but it had an inevitable impact on the local economy. Casement and others campaigned to get the Hamburg-Amerika Line (HAL) to replace the lost service by directing its own ships to call at Queenstown on their transatlantic crossings. The signs looked promising, with HAL arranging to make its first call at Cobh on 20 January. But in what was to become a growing trait, Casement then displayed a serious lack of judgement and self-awareness and overplayed his hand. He organised a lavish civic reception for the docking of the HAL liner, including a formal lunch to be organised by the Harbour Board for the ship's captain and senior HAL management; for German flags to be flown by all ships in the harbour; for a brass band to play *The Watch on the Rhine*; and for a bagpipe band to attend from Belfast. In the prevailing international climate, the shipping company took fright at the prospect of offending British sensibilities,[15] and after asking for categorical assurances that there would be "no fuss" on the arrival of the new service, eventually backed out of providing the service altogether.[16]

*

Casement's next step was to go to America to encourage support and to secure further funds for the nationalists. On 20 July 1914, he met John Devoy, one of the leaders of *Clan na Gael* and editor of the *Gaelic American*, in New York. *Clan na Gael* was effectively the American wing of the IRB, devoted to securing Irish independence through physical force. According to Devoy, between 1871 and 1916, the IRB (or "reorganised Fenianism" as he called it in his memoirs) was maintained almost entirely by moral and material support from *Clan na Gael*.[17] The ground was therefore ostensibly fertile – according to the 1910 US census, there were at that time some 4.5m Irish-born citizens in the US.[18] While Casement had earlier written to Devoy about the Putumayo, enclosing two subscriptions for the *Gaelic American* (one for himself and one for his sister), and had occasionally sent small (but according to Devoy, "always very interesting") items of news relating to Ireland for publication, the two did not know each other.[19] And although Casement was an important member of the Volunteers' Provisional Committee, he was not a member of the IRB. When they met, Devoy's reaction was immediately negative because of the Provisional Committee's "surrender" to Redmond. Casement attempted to explain the background to the decision, only to be met with the response that –

> …*it did not require intimate local knowledge to enable one to understand the surrender; that it was a human proposition, a contest between men and principles that could be judged accurately whether the action was taken in Ireland, America or in any other*

part of the world; that it was an act of weakness that must produce bad results and that it was already cutting down the collection of money in America...[20]

According to Devoy, Casement "listened attentively ...and then in a calm and very friendly manner undertook to persuade me I was mistaken". Casement then wrote a lengthy, persuasive and conciliatory letter the following day, describing in detail all the events surrounding the Provisional Committee's decision. Devoy records that this letter was shown to the "Revolutionary Directory" and other men active in the movement, "and while they were not convinced by it that yielding control of the Volunteers to John Redmond was justifiable, all were impressed by the downright sincerity of the man [Casement], and it was decided to utilise his services in collecting funds for the purchase of arms".[21]

Casement then spent some time travelling between New York, Philadelphia and Chicago successfully raising funds. In this, he was helped in an unexpected way. The arms whose purchase Casement had helped instigate in May finally arrived in Ireland, being landed at Howth, just outside Dublin, and at Kilcoole, Co Wicklow, on 26 July. The events at Howth following the landing were to provide a major boost to support for the Volunteers and the nationalist cause in general. These were dispassionately recorded in the routine monthly Inspector General's Report to the Irish Chief Secretary –

...On Sunday the 26th of July a cargo of rifles and ammunition was run into Howth by an unknown yacht in the middle of the day. A large number of Irish Volunteers arrived simultaneously at the quay to land them. The ammunition and some rifles were sent off on motors, and the Volunteers to the number of 900 then marched towards Dublin each one carrying a rifle. There were only a few RIC at Howth, who could not prevent the landing. On

the road to Dublin the Volunteers were intercepted by a party of Dublin Metropolitan Police and Military and some twenty rifles were seized. The Military were afterwards attacked on their way to barracks in Dublin, and they fired on the mob. The incident aroused much resentment in the Country, and gave at once a great stimulus to the Volunteer movement. All this, however, was soon eclipsed by events on the Continent, and notwithstanding the incitements to disloyalty and rebellion published from time to time in the extreme Nationalist Press, Sinn Féin and Irish Freedom, it was manifest that the sympathies of the Irish Volunteers in the prospect of war with Germany were on the side of England…[22]

In terms of the facts, the report was concise and accurate. The police felt obliged to act in the face of gun-running taking place in broad daylight, and called out the troops in an attempt to disarm the Volunteers. While talks were taking place between the police and the Volunteers, the guns were spirited away, leaving the troops free to return to barracks. As they started to do so, they were accompanied by a jeering crowd. They then turned on the crowd at Bachelor's Walk and opened fire, killing three people and wounding thirty.[23] It is interesting that the Inspector General's report did not consider the details of the casualties worth mentioning, but the shooting at an unarmed crowd was to go down in nationalist memory. The memory was made even more bitter by the comparison between the large number of arms that the authorities had allowed the Ulster Volunteers in the north to accumulate and the heavy-handed treatment meted out in the south. Such was the outrage among Irish Americans within in the US that Casement was now feted as one of the instigators of the Howth gun-running and regarded as a hero rather than a villain as Devoy had implied. In a letter to Alice Stopford Green, Casement wrote in characteristic style, "…the Irish would make me into a demi-God if I let them".[24] His fund-raising efforts were met with immediate success, but this was short-lived due to the almost immediate outbreak of war in Europe, causing donations to dry up.

The outbreak of the Great War saw the beginning of the final chapter of Casement's career. According to Devoy, shortly after the outbreak a special committee of *Clan na Gael* members met the German Ambassador, Count von Bernstorff, at a reception at the German Club in New York. No secrecy was involved, but the delegation told Bernstorff that –

> ...*our friends in Ireland intended to use the opportunity presented by the war to make an effort to overthrow English rule in Ireland and set up an Independent Government; that they had not an adequate supply of arms, had no trained officers, and wanted Germany to supply the arms and a sufficient number of capable officers to make a good start, but that we wanted no money. We needed military help only.*

The *Clan na Gael* representatives went on to stress that by diverting British Army resources from the Western Front, such a rebellion would be to Germany's interest. Bernstorff undertook to send *Clan na Gael*'s request to Berlin, while the Clan reported the event to the IRB's Supreme Council in Ireland.[25] In the meantime, Casement had – it seems independently – prepared a formal address to the Kaiser. While the *Clan na Gael* approach had been that of practical men, Casement's occupied a higher philosophical ground, based on the view he had developed – as exemplified in the HAL incident – that the answer to conquering England lay in securing the freedom of the seas, and that England's control of the seas rested directly on its control of Ireland. His address no doubt surprised the hard men of *Clan na Gael*, but they signed it, with Devoy recording that, "we of the *Clan na Gael* would have worded some portions of it differently". The address was nevertheless despatched –

AFTER THE WILD GEESE

New York, August 25, 1914

To His Imperial Majesty, The German Emperor

Sire

The undersigned, representing many millions of the people of this country, either of Irish birth or Irish descent, desire very respectfully to place before Your Majesty what we believe to be the view of the vast majority of Irishmen not only in the United States but throughout the world.

In the first place, we seek to give voice to the feeling of Irishmen in America. That feeling is chiefly one of sympathy and admiration for the heroic people of Germany, assailed at all points by an unnatural league of enmity, having only one thing in common, a hatred of German prosperity and efficiency. We feel that the German people are in truth fighting for European civilization at its best and certainly in its less selfish form. We recognize that Germany did not seek this war, but that it was forced upon her by those jealous of her military security, envious of her industrial and commercial capacity, and aiming at her integrity as a Great World Power that was capable, if peace were maintained, of outdistancing the competition of all her rivals.

Since peace was essential to the fullest German development, and since in the realm of peaceful rivalry Germany could not be overcome, those who were jealous of her growing prosperity and were themselves incapable of matching it by peaceful means, determined to destroy by war what they could not meet by peace. This we believe to be the reason, and the sole reason, for the present combination of armaments against Germany. For this reason we assert that Germany is fighting the battle of European civilization at its best against European civilization at its worst.

We wholeheartedly hope for the success of the German people in this unequal struggle forced upon them. Just as they have overcome by peaceful means the competition of their trading rivals, so we pray they may now overcome by armed manhood the unfair combination those rivals have substituted for lawful effort.

This said on behalf of our countrymen in America, we would bring before Your Majesty the condition of our countrymen in Ireland, and draw Your Majesty's attention to the part that Ireland necessarily, if not openly, must play in this conflict and in every conflict where sea power is at stake.

The British claim to control the seas of the world, rests chiefly on an unnamed factor. That factor is Ireland. It is by the sole possession of Ireland that Great Britain has been able for two centuries to maintain an unchallengeable mastery of the seas and by this agency to convert a small trading community into the wholly arbitrary judges of war and peace for all mankind.

If Europe would be free at home, she must be free at sea. If Europe would have peace within her borders she must deprive Great Britain of the means to provoke or precipitate war whenever, as in the present case, it may suit the interests of that power to substitute war for peace.

There cannot be peace in Europe until Great Britain's claim to the mastery of the seas, that great highway of the Nations, has been finally disposed of.

We are profoundly convinced that so long as Great Britain is allowed to control, exploit and misappropriate Ireland and all Irish resources – whether of men, material wealth, or strategic position – she will dominate the seas. Thus the freedom of Ireland becomes of paramount, nay, of vital importance to the larger question of the freeing of the seas.

Hoping as we do that Germany will win this war so unrighteously forced upon her by a combination of assailants, each lacking the courage to act alone, we earnestly commend to Your Majesty's attention this fundamental fact that to restore the equilibrium of sea power so grievously injured by Great Britain, to the detriment of the whole world since the Napoleonic wars, Ireland must be freed from British control.

While the fortune of war may not bring German troops to Ireland, the hearts of thousands of Irishmen go out to the German shores today. Thousands of Irishmen are prepared to do their part to aid the German cause, for they recognise that it is their own.

Should God grant victory to the German people in this struggle of brave men to keep the freedom they have so dearly won, we hope that Ireland may be permitted to contribute something to the triumph of that good cause. We beg Your Majesty to reflect that a defeated Great Britain, still retaining Ireland, is really a victorious Great Britain.

We beg Your Majesty to reflect that an Ireland freed by German victory over Britain becomes the sure gage of a free ocean for all who traverse the seas.

On these grounds alone, did not natural sympathy and admiration for a people fighting against such heavy odds lead us to address Your Majesty, we should hope for a German triumph over an enemy who is also our enemy. We pray for that triumph for Germany; and we pray with it Your Majesty may have power, wisdom and strength of purpose to impose a lasting peace upon the seas by effecting the independence of Ireland and securing its recognition as a fixed condition of the terms of final settlement between the great maritime Powers.[26]

There is no indication of how this was received in Germany. If it actually ever got to the Kaiser, he would no doubt have been surprised to see the analysis that the key to British domination of the seas rested on Ireland. So far as *Clan na Gael* was concerned, it also seems clear that the style and form of the address – not to mention its content – also caused surprise (and perhaps some bemusement) even though they signed it. To what extent it reflected the views of Irish Americans (outside *Clan na Gael*) is also unknown, but the implication that it reflected the views of those in Ireland itself would undoubtedly have surprised and upset the majority of ordinary people there, who at that stage had heard little and knew little about Casement. Despite his success in raising funds from the nationalist community within the US, anti-German feeling within Ireland itself remained generally strong. It is true that following the Howth gun-running, the Inspector General's assessment was that the incident had resulted in a considerable feeling of unrest in Dublin and had increased support for the Volunteer movement there and in Meath and Tipperary (by September, the total strength of the Volunteers had reached 184,000). But he also reported that the view from Cork was that, "the attitude to the Volunteers towards the war is influenced by party politics, the Sinn Féin members [being] very extreme in their views and opposed to England, but the majority of the Volunteers are anti-German and the tone of the local Press strongly anti-German". And, "Sinn Féiners, and other extremists, are here and there making efforts to stir up anti-English feeling by the dissemination of seditious literature setting forth that "Ireland has no quarrel with Germany" and "England's difficulty is Ireland's opportunity". Nevertheless, he concluded that overall such literature had not yet affected the public mind to any extent and that there was "a general dread of a German invasion". Outside small Sinn Féin circles, "public feeling everywhere and in every class is strongly anti-German". Interestingly, he noted that, "It is highly probable that communications are passing between leading extremists in Ireland and the *Clan na Gael* in America, but there is no evidence to connect them with German Agents".[27] No mention is made of Casement but this was shortly to change. On 5 October, the *Irish Independent* printed a letter from Casement in America (dated 17 September) arguing that Ireland should not be involved in the war on the British side; it was the duty of Ireland as a Christian people to abstain from bloodshed, except in the cause of Ireland itself. Even if Home Rule were immediately granted, "it would still be the duty of Irishmen to save their strength and manhood for the trying tasks before them, to build up from a depleted population the fabric of a ruined national life".[28] This brought a swift response from the head of the British Foreign Office, who wrote to Casement reminding him that he was still liable in certain circumstances to be called upon to serve under the Crown and asking him to confirm whether he was indeed the author of the letter.[29] This was sufficient to make clear to Casement that any return to the United Kingdom would inevitably involve consequences.

Not only was Casement unable to return home, but he was also unhappy in America. As early as 11 August 1914, he wrote to Gertrude Bannister from New York, "Here I am marooned on a desert island – Manhattan! Surrounded by 5,000,000 of [sic] strangers! God save Germany!", and on 1 September, "I don't like USA. The more I see of it the less I like it – but it is a [indecipherable] country. The people are ignorant and unthinking and easily led by anything they read in the newspapers. The press is the worst in the world".[30] His answer was to go to Germany. Devoy records that he tried to discourage Casement from this when the matter had first been raised in early August, believing him temperamentally unsuited to dealing with the Germans, but Casement persisted and was in a hurry to go. The *Clan na Gael Executive* finally agreed to sanction the trip and to pay his expenses. Devoy also records that though this decision was subsequently endorsed by the IRB in Ireland, some members of the Supreme Council had shown reluctance. Having secured his own letter of introduction to the German Government from Count Bernstorff, Casement left for Germany via Norway on 15 October, together with 2,500 dollars in gold handed to him by *Clan na Gael* to cover his initial expenses in Germany. Notwithstanding his dislike of America and its people, and having known Devoy for barely three months, Casement wrote to him a typically emotional letter –

New York, 15 Oct.1914

My Dear Old Friend
I cannot go without a farewell word and grip of the heart. Without you there would be nothing, and if success come, or even a greater hope for the future, it will be due to you and your life of unceasing devotion to the most unselfish cause on earth.

May God keep you safe and well to see the first fruits of all your years of suffering and waiting and working. I shall not forget you. I am only sorry now I did not talk much louder that last evening for you to hear our final words.

But, please God, we meet again – and meantime we work and plan.

Good bye and au revoir where we both hope that meeting may be.

I leave in an hour; am still unshaved, but going to try it now, and wash my face with buttermilk to get a fair complexion.

Always in faith and hope and affection.

Your devoted
Roger Casement[31]

The references to shaving and complexion refer to Casement's intention to travel in disguise.

SIX

THE GERMAN IRISH BRIGADE

Sir Roger Casement's conduct consists in open betrayal of a Government which trusted him and a country which showered honours upon him. ...He has made his election with a quite incomprehensible perversity, and closed for ever by one foul blow an honourable career.

The *Evening News*, 2 December 1914

I have the honour to acknowledge receipt of yours of the 23rd instant, in which you lay before the German Government your proposal to form an Irish Brigade which will bind itself to fight only for the cause of Irish nationality. It will be composed of Irish prisoners of war who are ready to form such a Brigade.

Letter to Casement from Arthur Zimmermann, Secretary of State at the German Foreign Office, 28 December 1914

THE GERMAN IRISH BRIGADE

To save Ireland from some of the calamities of war was worth the loss to myself of pension and honours and was even worth the commission of technical "treason".
Letter from Casement in Germany to Sir Edward Grey, 1 February 1915

On embarking for his trip to Germany, Casement was about to enter into another episode demonstrating his lack of judgement. The *Findlay Affair* would, for reasons entirely of his own making, irritate and worry his supporters in the US at the same time as destroying any remaining credibility he might have within the British Government. It caused bemusement in Germany and caused him to lose focus on the job in hand.

The starting point of the affair was Casement's decision to take with him on the journey a twenty-four-year-old Norwegian seaman named Eivind Adler Christensen who, Casement claimed, he had met when strolling down Broadway on his first night in New York.[1] According to Casement, Christensen had spoken to him and they had subsequently become friends. His justification for taking Christensen with him (as his "servant") was that Christensen spoke Norwegian and (he claimed) German. A different version of their relationship was to be given much later by Christensen. In Christensen's version, the two had actually first met in 1906 at a hotel in Montevideo, when Casement had followed him into the lavatory. When they came out, they had had a drink together. Subsequently, Christensen had deserted his ship and remained in Montevideo for a month, during which time Casement had visited him in his lodgings. Christensen then left for America and before parting Casement had made him a present of money and jewellery to the value of about 900 dollars. Christensen said that he had not seen Casement again until their meeting in 1914 on Broadway.[2] Whichever version (if either) is true, Devoy was unhappy about Casement's decision to take Christensen with him. He subsequently wrote –

> *During our* [the Clan na Gael Executive's] *discussion, owing to my deafness, I missed one very important statement. That was Casement's announcement that he had decided to take with him as a servant or companion a Norwegian sailor named Christensen whose acquaintance he had recently made, but of whose character and antecedents he knew absolutely nothing, and of whom he had never heard before. …I heard enough of the talk to understand that he proposed to take a Norwegian along, but missed the fact that the acquaintance between the two was only of a few weeks' duration. Had I understood that, I would have objected strongly to Christensen going as Sir Roger's companion.*[3]

Casement and Christensen set off to travel to Germany via Norway on the Norwegian ship *Oskar II*, which arrived at Kristiania (previously Christiania and now Oslo)[4] on 29 October. Casement travelled first class with the passport and under the name of James Landy, an American citizen, while Christensen travelled second class under his own name. On arrival at Kristiania, they checked into the Grand Hotel, arriving there at 2 am. The next morning, Casement went to the German legation to hand in his letter of introduction from Count Bernstorrf and to make arrangements for onward travel to Germany. He was told to return the following morning to collect the necessary papers to provide safe passage to Berlin. He then told Christensen to go shopping and to return no later than 5.30 pm. When he did return, Christensen came out with a remarkable story. He told Casement that in going down to the hotel lobby, he had been approached by an English-speaking stranger who suggested that they should go out for a stroll together. Outside, he and the stranger had been met by a chauffeur-driven car which had taken them to some offices of the British Legation, where he had been questioned in a locked room. He was asked whether he had known a "tall dark Englishmen" on board *Oskar II*. Christensen had replied that he knew of no Englishman but he did know an American whom he had met in New York. The interviewer then said he would very much like to know the tall dark gentleman's name and address, to which Christensen replied that he had momentarily forgotten the man's name, and declined to give any further information. He said he had then been freed and had returned immediately to the hotel. Fearing that the British might in some way be able to interrupt his journey, Casement immediately sent Christensen to the German Legation with a note asking for an urgent meeting in order to secure agreement for him to travel to Germany the following day. A meeting was arranged for 7 pm at the German Consulate, where Casement met the German Minister Count Alfred von Oberndorff, who told him that he had telegraphed Berlin for instructions but had not yet received a reply. Casement was accordingly forced to return to his hotel, where he started to make plans to travel towards the German frontier by car. These were cancelled when he received further message from the German legation saying that a travel permit would definitely arrive in time for him to travel by train the following afternoon and that von Oberndorff himself would visit the hotel at noon to make the final arrangements. The following morning, Casement sent Christensen downstairs in the hotel to "keep his eyes open", only to be treated to another remarkable story when Christensen returned upstairs before midday. This time, Christensen said that he had again been taken to the British Legation and had again been interrogated in a locked room, this time by the British Minister himself, Mansfeldt de Cardonnel Findlay. Findlay told Christensen that he knew of Casement's identity and wanted a copy of his handwriting. He had gone on to say that Casement could expect no protection from the Americans because he had travelled on a false passport, and none from the Germans because he was neither a German subject nor an ally. In a remark that was to play a significant part in the subsequent story about the *Findlay Affair*, the Minister was then alleged by

Christensen to have commented that, "if someone knocked him [Casement] on the head he would get well paid for it", but in any case the British Government "would pay handsomely" anyone who helped secure Casement's capture. If Christensen was interested in the offer of a large reward, he should return to the British legation at 3 pm. In narrating this alleged train of events to Casement, Christensen presented 25 krone which he said had been given to him by Findlay as the first instalment for his services. When von Oberndorff arrived in Casement's room at noon as scheduled, all this was repeated to him.[5]

Logic dictated that Casement should put all this to one side and get on the train towards Germany as quickly as possible. Insofar as the stories put forward by Christensen were true, they could be quickly put behind him. Of course, the possibility of someone "knocking him on the head" might have been a worry, as might the thought that there could be a reward out for his capture. But looked at in his own terms, given the purpose of his journey, the safest place he could now be away from these threats was in Germany, only a few hours away. There were also some strange aspects to Christensen's various tales which would have aroused suspicion if presented to a more critical audience. The *Oskar II* had been stopped and held on its journey to Kristiania by the Royal Navy at Stornaway, ostensibly looking for German spies. Casement and Christensen both escaped attention, so an obvious question was why the British legation should have been suspicious of either of them when they finally disembarked at Kristiania. And if there were reasons for suspicion, why would the British have chosen to intercept Christensen at the hotel to ask him questions about Casement, rather than simply ask Casement himself? Casement's faith in Christensen also seems to have prevented him from noting the remarkable coincidence that every time Christensen went downstairs someone intercepted him. The upshot was that far from doubting Christensen, Casement decided to press home an advantage which he believed the British had presented to him and sent Christensen back to the British Legation at the time stipulated by Findlay. At this further meeting, Christensen was briefed to accept the offer of a large reward; in return, he would commit to persuading Casement to allow Christensen to travel with him on his journey to Copenhagen that same evening. The objective was to pin Findlay down on the details and terms of the reward for subsequent use by Casement against him. Christensen returned to the hotel with a 100-krone note – this time as the first instalment of his "large reward", which had been agreed at the meeting as £5,000 in gold. Christensen reported that for his part he had agreed to spy on Casement and provide details of his contacts in Ireland and America – for which he would be paid the going rate – so that the British Government could secure their arrest. To enable him to do this, Findlay had given him a contact address which he could write to anonymously, together with a system of code. To secure the £5,000 reward, Christensen would need to get "Sir Roger into his [Findlay's] power... If you get him to any place on the Skager-Rack or North Sea we shall have men-of-war ready and will take good care of him".[6] Christensen was subsequently to secure a handwritten note from Findlay, promising that, "if through information given by Adler Christensen, Sir Roger Casement be captured either with or without his companions, the said Adler Christensen is to receive from the British Government the sum of £5,000 to be paid as he may desire." And, "Adler Christensen is also to enjoy personal immunity and to be given a passage to the United States should he desire it".[7] Unbeknownst to Casement, Christensen also upped his demands with Findlay, arguing that Casement probably had large amounts of American money with him and, if that turned out to be the case, he would like this to be added to the £5,000 reward. The British Foreign Office agreed to the request, provided no harm was done to Casement. (The Foreign Office also told Findlay not to put anything in writing, but by then it was too late, as the note referred to above had already been handed to Christensen.)[8]

In Casement's mind, the interference by the British with his "servant" Christensen, and their attempts to provoke Christensen to be disloyal to his "master", were conduct unbecoming of any gentleman. Their offer of a reward for Casement's capture and, as he fixated upon, to murder him by "knocking him on the head", were criminal acts against international law. If these actions were generally disclosed, he believed, it would bring the British Government into grave disrepute, bring opprobrium on them from around the world, and thus help Casement's cause. He decided that before exposing the British Government, however, he would capitalise on the situation – along with Christensen, who would help him – by feeding misinformation to the British via the communication arrangements set up by Findlay. This would include false plans for delivering arms to Ireland and false details of movements by Casement and others. By the end of January 1915, enough had been done to cash in, and Casement prepared an "Open Letter to Sir Edward Grey" which he was confident would expose the British Government to the ridicule and disapproval which he thought it richly deserved. Copies were widely distributed, including to German representatives throughout Europe and America. But the response it generated was practically non-existent. In America, nothing appeared for six weeks until a copy was published in the *New York American*, generating little reaction.[9] In assuming that his letter would generate a "killer blow", Casement demonstrated how out of touch he was with the political and diplomatic world at large. The letter itself, sent from Berlin on 1 February 1915, was typically and inordinately lengthy and for that reason is often referred to but rarely reproduced in full. It is, nevertheless, key to understanding Casement's state of mind –

Sir

I observe that some discussion has taken place in the House of Lords on the subject of the pension I voluntarily ceased to draw when I set out to learn what might be the intentions of the German Government in regard to Ireland.

In the course of that discussion I understand Lord Crewe observed that "Sir Roger Casement's action merited a sensible punishment".

The question raised thus as to my action and your publicly suggested punishment of it I propose discussing here and now, since the final proof of the actual punishment you sought in secret to inflict upon me is, at length, in my possession.

It is true I was aware of your intentions from the first day I set foot in Norway three months ago; but it has taken time to compel your agent there to furnish the written proof of the conspiracy then set on foot against me by His Majesty's Government.

Let me first briefly define my action before proceeding to contrast it with your own.

The question between the British Government and myself has never been, as you are fully aware, a matter of a pension, of a reward, or a decoration.

I served the British Government faithfully and loyally as long as it was possible for me to do so, and when it became impossible, I resigned. When later, it became impossible for me to use the pension assigned me by law I voluntarily abandoned that income as I had previously resigned the post from which it was derived, and as I now proceed to divest myself of the honours and distinctions that at various times have been conferred upon me by His Majesty's Government.

I came to Europe from the United States last October in order to make sure that whatever might be the course of this war, my own country, Ireland, should suffer from it the minimum of harm.

The view I held was made sufficiently clear in an open letter

I wrote on the 17th of September last in New York, and sent to Ireland for public distribution among my countrymen. I append a printed copy of that letter. It defines my personal standpoint clearly enough and expresses the views I held, and hold, on an Irishman's duty to his country in this crisis of world affairs. Soon after writing that letter I set out for Europe.

To save Ireland from some of the calamities of war was worth the loss to myself of pension and honours and was even worth the commission of technical "treason".

I decided to take all the risks and to accept all the penalties the law might attach to my action. I did not, however, bargain for risks and penalties that lay outside the law as far as my own action lay outside the field of moral turpitude.

In other words, while I reckoned with British law and legal penalties and accepted the sacrifice of income, position and reputation as prices I must pay, I did not reckon with the British Government.

I was prepared to face charges in a court of law; I was not prepared to meet waylaying, kidnapping, suborning of dependents or "knocking on the head". In fine, all the expedients your representative in a neutral country invoked when he became aware of my presence there.

For the criminal conspiracy that Mr M de C Findlay, HBM Minister to the Court of Norway entered into on 30 October last, in the British Legation at Christiania, with the Norwegian subject, my dependent, Eivind Adler Christensen, involved all these things and more. It involved not merely a lawless attack upon myself for which the British Minister promised my follower the sum of £5,000, but it involved a breach of international law as well as of common law, for which the British Minister in Norway promised this Norwegian subject full immunity.

On the 29th of October last year I landed at Christiania, coming from America.

Within a few hours of my landing the man I had engaged and in whom I reposed trust was accosted by one of the secret service agents of the British Minister and carried off, in a private motor car, to the British Legation, where the first attempt was made on his honour to induce him to be false to me.

Your agent in the Legation that afternoon professed ignorance of who I was and sought, as he put it, merely to find out my identity and movements.

Failing in this the first attempt to obtain satisfaction, Adler Christensen was assailed the next day, the 30th of October, by a fresh agent and received an invitation to again visit the British Legation "where he would hear something good".

This, the second interview, held in the early afternoon, was with the Minister himself.

Mr Findlay came quickly to the point. The ignorance, assumed or actual, of the previous day, as to my identity, was now discarded. He confessed that he knew me, but that he did not know where I was going to, and what I intended doing, or what might be the specific end I had in view.

It was enough for him that I was an Irish Nationalist.

He admitted that the British Government had no evidence of anything wrong done or contemplated by me that empowered them either morally or lawfully to interfere with my movements. But he was intent on doing so. Therefore, he baldly invoked lawless methods, and suggested to my dependent that were I to "disappear" it would be "a very good thing for whoever brought it about".

He was careful to point out that nothing could happen to the perpetrator of the crime, since my presence in Christiania was known only to the British Government and that Government would screen and provide for those responsible for my "disappearance".

He indicated, quite plainly, the methods to be employed, by assuring Adler Christensen, that whoever "knocked him on the head need not do any work for the rest of his life", and proceeded to apply the moral by asking Christensen, 'I suppose you would not mind having an easy time of it for the rest of your days?'

My faithful follower concealed the anger he felt at this suggestion and continued the conversation in order to become more fully aware of the plot that might be devised against my safety. He pointed out that I had not only been very kind to him but that I "trusted him implicitly".

It was on this "implicit trust" Mr Findlay then proceeded to build the whole framework of his conspiracy against my life, my liberty, the public law of Norway and the happiness of the young man he sought to tempt by monstrous bribes to the commission of a dastardly crime against his admitted benefactor.

If I could be intercepted, cut off, "disappear", no one would know and no question could be asked, since there was no Government save the British Government knew of my presence in Norway and there was no authority I could appeal to for help, while that Government would shield the individual implicated and provide handsomely for his future. Such, in Mr Findlay's words (recorded by me) was the proposition put by His Majesty's Minister before the young man who had been enticed for this purpose into the British Legation.

That this man was faithful to me and the law of his country was a triumph of Norwegian integrity over the ignoble inducement proffered him by the richest and most powerful Government in the world to be false to both.

Having thus outlined his project, Mr Findlay invited Christensen to "think the matter over and return at 3 o'clock, if you are disposed to go on with it".

He handed him in Norwegian paper money twenty-five kroner "just to pay your taxi-cab fares", and dismissed him.

Feeling a not unnatural interest in these proposals as to how I should be disposed of, I instructed the man it was thus sought to bribe to return to the British Legation at 3 o'clock and to seemingly fall in with the wishes of your Envoy extraordinary.

I advised him, however, for the sake of appearance to "sell me dear" and to secure the promise of a very respectable sum for so very disreputable an act.

Christensen, who has been a sailor and naturally has seen some strange company, assured me he was perfectly at home with His Majesty's Representative.

He returned to the Legation at 3 o'clock and remained closeted with Mr Findlay until nearly 5 pm. The full record of their conversation will be laid before you, and others, in due course.

My follower pretended to fall in with the British Minister's projects, only stipulating for a good sum to be paid in return for his treachery. Mr Findlay promised on his "word of honour" (such was the quaint phraseology employed to guarantee this transaction) that Christensen should receive £5,000 sterling whenever he could deliver me into the hands of the British authorities.

If in the course of this kidnapping process I should come to harm or personal injury be done to me, then no question would be asked and full immunity guaranteed the kidnapper.

My follower pointed out that as I was leaving that evening for Copenhagen, having already booked my compartment in the mail train, he would not have any immediate chance of executing the commission.

Mr Findlay agreed that it would be necessary to defer the attempt until some favourable opportunity offered of decoying me down to the coast "anywhere on the Skaggerrack or North Sea", where British warships might be in waiting to seize me.

He entrusted my dependent with the further commission of purloining my correspondence with my supposed associates in America and Ireland, so that they, too, might participate in the "sensible punishment" being devised for me.

He ordained a system of secret correspondence with himself Christensen should employ, and wrote out the confidential address in Christiania to which he was to communicate the results of his efforts to purloin my papers and to report on my plans.

This address in Christiania was written down by Mr Findlay on a half sheet of Legation note paper in printed characters. This precaution was adopted he said "so as to prevent the handwriting being traced".

This document, along with one hundred crowns in Norwegian paper money given by Mr Findlay as an earnest of more to follow was at once brought to me with an account of the proceedings.

As I was clearly in a position of some danger, I changed my plans and instead of proceeding to Copenhagen as I had intended doing, I decided to alter my procedure and route.

It was then, with this secret knowledge of the full extent of the crime plotted by your Representative in Norway against me that I left Christiania on the 30th of October.

The rest of the story need not take so long in the telling.

You are fully aware of most of the details, as you were in constant touch with your agent both by cable and despatch.

You are also aware of the declaration of the Imperial German Government, issued on November 20 last in reply to the enquiry I addressed to them.

The British Government, both by press reports and by direct agents had charged Germany, throughout the length and breadth of Ireland, with the commission of atrocious crimes in Belgium and had warned the Irish people that their fate would be the same, did Germany win this war.

Your Government sought to frighten Irishmen into a predatory raid upon a people who had never injured them and to persuade them by false charges that this was their duty.

I sought not only a guarantee of German goodwill to Ireland, but to relieve my countrymen from the apprehensions this campaign of calumny was designed to provoke and so far as was possible to dissuade them from embarking in an immoral conflict against a *people who had never wronged Ireland. That Declaration of the German Government, issued as I know in all sincerity, is the justification for my "treason". The justification of the conspiracy of the British Government and its Minister at Christiania begun before I had set foot on German soil in a country where I had a perfect right to be and conducted by means of the lowest forms of attempted bribery and corruption I leave to you, sir, to discover.*

You will not discover it in the many interviews Mr Findlay had, during the months of November and December last, at his own seeking, with my faithful follower. The correspondence between them in the cypher the Minister had arranged tells its own story.

These interviews furnished matter that in due course I shall make public. What passed between your agent and mine on these occasions you are fully aware of, and you were the directing power throughout the whole proceeding.

Your object, as Mr Findlay frankly avowed to the man he thought he had bought, was to take my life with public indignity— mine was to expose your design and to do so through the very agent you had yourselves singled out for the purpose and had sought to corrupt to an act of singular infamy.

On one occasion in response to my follower's pretended dissatisfaction with the amount offered for betraying me you authorized your agent to increase the sum to £10,000. I have a full record of the conversations held and of the pledges proffered in your name.

On two occasions, during these prolonged bargainings your Minister gave Adler Christensen gifts of "earnest money". Once it was five hundred crowns in Norwegian currency; the next time a similar sum, partly in Norwegian money and partly in English gold. On one of these occasions, to be precise on the 7th of December last, Mr Findlay handed Adler Christensen the key to the back entrance of the British Legation, so that he might go and come unobserved and at all hours.

I propose returning this key in person to the donor and along with it the various sums so anxiously bestowed upon my follower.

The stories told Mr Findlay at these interviews should not have deceived a school boy. All the pretended evidence of my plans and intentions Adler Christensen produced, the bogus letters, fictitious maps and charts and other incitements to Mr Findlay's appetite for the incredible were part of my necessary plan of self defence to lay bare the conspiracy you were engaged in and to secure that convincing proof of it I now hold.

It was not until the 3rd ultimo that Mr Findlay committed himself to give my protector the duly signed and formal pledge of reward and immunity, in the name of the British Government, for the crime he was being instigated to commit, that is now in my possession.

I transmit a photograph of this document.

At a date compatible with my own security against the clandestine guarantees and immunities of the British Minister in Norway I shall proceed to lay before the legitimate authorities in that country the original document and the evidence in my possession that throws light on the proceeding of His Majesty's Government.

To that Government, through you, sir, I now beg to return the insignia of the Most Distinguished Order of St Michael and St George, the Coronation Medal of His Majesty King George V, and any other medal, honour or distinction conferred upon me by His Majesty's Government, of which it is possible for me to divest myself.

I am, sir, your most obedient, humble servant,
Roger Casement[10]

The enclosure with Casement's letter comprised a handwritten, undated note by Findlay on headed Legation notepaper –

> *On behalf of the British Government I promise that if through information given by Adler Christensen, Sir Roger Casement be captured either with or without his companions, the said Adler Christensen is to receive from the British Government the sum of £5000 to be paid as he may desire.*
>
> *Adler Christensen is also to enjoy personal immunity and to be given a passage to the United States should he desire it.*
>
> *M de C Findlay*
> *HBM Minister*[11]

Casement's jibe that the stories told by Christensen to Findlay "should not have deceived a school boy" obviously contained a grain of truth. Commenting on one of Findlay's regular reports to the Foreign Office on the intelligence provided by Christensen, one British official commented specifically, "This looks rather more like business but I fear all the time that it may fizzle out leaving Findlay looking an ass".[12] To be fair to Findlay, on the other hand, in many of his reports he acknowledged that the information being fed to him might not be genuine, while concluding that he believed that it was. Findlay also came to remark of Christensen that, "He is a dangerous criminal who needs to be watched". But he was more entitled to believe in Christensen than Casement gave him credit for, because although Christensen was indeed deceiving Findlay, he had also fundamentally deceived Casement. Contrary to Christensen's version of events on his and Casement's arrival in Kristiania, the official British record shows that it was Christensen who approached the British delegation there, rather than the other way round, and that it was Christensen who took the lead in offering to sell information. Francis (Frank) Lindley of the delegation records in a memorandum dated 29 October that an unknown Norwegian with an American accent had called that afternoon asking to see the Minister, but when told that the Minister was out on business, finally consented to see Lindley instead. The Norwegian stated that he had travelled to Christiania from the United States on the *Oskar II* with a "highly placed Englishman, a nobleman who had been decorated by King Edward". Lindley continued, "I understand that his relations with this Englishman were of an improper nature". The Norwegian had gone on to claim that he held letters from the German Embassy to Berlin in Washington on behalf of the Englishman, who was afraid of being searched. He showed copies of two of these to Lindley, who believed them to be genuine. The Norwegian had said that the Englishman was currently in Kristiania and was going to Germany "about trouble in Ireland", but he refused to give the man's name. In forwarding the memorandum to Sir Edward Grey, copied to the Prime Minister, McKenna, Lord Kitchener, Churchill and Birrell, Findlay suggested that Scotland Yard might identify the "nobleman" concerned, adding, "There cannot be many such blackguards in any class". At 5.25 pm the following day, 30 October, Findlay despatched a further telegram saying that Christensen had returned again that morning and had "showed me papers written by his English friend with whom evidently he has unnatural relations" – "The principal idea in the papers referred to was that invasion of England was extremely difficult but that a surprise invasion of Ireland by Irish Americans was practicable". After much pressing, Christensen had revealed that his friend was Sir Roger Casement and that he and Casement were to leave that afternoon for Berlin. At 8.10 pm the same evening, Findlay sent a further telegram reporting that Casement and Christensen had now left for Berlin, having been seen off by a person believed to be a member of the German Delegation. He noted that, "[the] scheme is to run some large steamships from America to Iceland [presumably a typo for Ireland] with arms and trained officers for nationalist rebels who would then rise." Findlay considered that this should be taken seriously and said that he had arranged that his informer (Christensen), "should let me know what passes in Germany and should be paid by results".[13]

All these manoeuvrings are the mirror image of the version relayed by Christensen to Casement and, as set out above, ultimately came to nothing. Casement unnecessarily wasted three months on an exercise which, far from advancing his cause, had worked against him. German officials had become irritated with him over his fixation with the affair, and Casement had become irritated with the German lack of interest in his machinations. While there is no indication that his letter to Grey had any major impact within the British Government, it could in no way have improved their longer-term attitude towards him. Casement's assumption that his letter would have widespread international repercussions showed yet again his serious lack of judgement – as Devoy put it, Casement's reaction to the affair caused him to lose "his sense of proportion for a time when the greatest war in history was going on".[14] More serious in practical terms was his lack of judgement in trusting Christensen, without whom the affair would never have happened. At the root of this was clearly his personal relationship with Christensen, a relationship confirmed in a statement given by the Chief Reception clerk at the Grand Hotel, Kristiania, to Scotland Yard in July 1916, in which he claimed that he had found Casement and Christensen in a compromising position when he had entered one of their hotel rooms without knocking.[15] The wording of the 1 February letter is clearly consistent with the fact that there was a relationship.

Christensen's activities as a go-between finally came to an end when he was found to have double-crossed the *Clan* in one of its endeavours, proving himself, in Devoy's own words, "a trickster and a fraud", leading to his summary dismissal.[16] But Christensen had one final hand to play in his catalogue of treachery and disloyalty towards Casement. Shortly before Casement's trial in June 1916, Christensen offered to testify. Interviewed by the Metropolitan

Police in Philadelphia on 23 May, Christensen gave a detailed account of his involvement with Casement, starting with their meeting in Montevideo, on to their journey to Christiania, where he had furnished documents to Findlay, and then on to their subsequent joint activities in Germany. Christensen described how he had also acted as a courier for communications between Casement and Devoy and had helped smuggle various people into Germany on Devoy's behalf. This work had ended when he and Devoy had seriously fallen out. Christensen's version of events was that Devoy had criticised him for his morals and personal behaviour, to which he had taken serious exception. According to the Metropolitan Police's report of the interview, this appeared to relate to Christensen's gambling and the fact that he had left his wife and was living with a woman that he had brought with him from Germany. In the process of the quarrel, the two had come to blows and Devoy had threatened to expose him. As a result, he had had no contact with Devoy since November 1915. His sole object in coming forward was "to get Devoy out of the way, as if his, Christensen's, career was made known to the American Police, he would probably get 10 years' imprisonment". Christensen said that he would be prepared to testify, provided the British Government paid an allowance of 15 dollars a week to his German "wife" while he was away, plus a payment to him of 200 dollars, with a guarantee that his liberty would not be interfered with. During the interview, Christensen also said that while in Berlin in May 1915, he had, at Casement's request, photographed a number of documents, among which was an Agreement signed by Casement and von Jagow, the German Foreign Secretary, about the use of Irish prisoners of war held in Germany to help the fight for Irish freedom. Christensen offered to produce a copy of the Agreement to the British Consul the following day. Reminiscent of his dealings with Findlay in October 1914, however, at the arranged appointment the following day, Christensen said that he had not brought the Agreement with him and had now decided not to pursue the matter, adding that he had been led on to say more than he intended. His failure to produce the copy of the Agreement put serious doubt on the veracity of his statement as a whole, which, together with his previous history with regard to the "*Findlay Affair*", brought matters to an end. The British authorities did not pursue his offer.[17]

*

While having wasted the best part of three months on the *Findlay Affair*, Casement had, nevertheless, made some progress on his core mission of securing German assistance in the nationalist cause. On arriving in Germany, he set himself up as self-styled Ambassador for Ireland, and within a very short time secured a significant position statement from the German Government. On 20 November 1914, having announced that Casement had been received in Berlin, the German Foreign Office issued the following statement –

> *The Imperial Government formally declares that under no circumstances would Germany invade Ireland with a view to its conquest or the overthrow of any native institutions in that country. Should the fortune of this great war, that was not of Germany's seeking ever bring in its course German troops to the shores of Ireland, they would land there as not as an army of invaders to pillage and destroy but as the forces of a Government that is inspired by goodwill towards a country and people for whom Germany desires only <u>national prosperity and national freedom</u>.*[18]

The German statement was circulated widely and while Casement's achievement in securing it impressed Devoy, it was met with almost universal condemnation elsewhere. While Irish nationalism remained firm in some quarters, there were many Irishmen fighting against Germany, and anti-German feeling in Ireland was still strong. Alice Stopford Green immediately ceased all communication with Casement.[19] Many in Ireland (and Irishmen elsewhere) had never heard of Casement and resented both his views and his claim to represent them. His personal position was made worse by a widely distributed pamphlet which he had written entitled, *The Crime Against Ireland and How the War May Right It*, in which he proposed a "German-American-Irish Alliance". Some thought Casement was mad. In a letter to the *Daily Chronicle* in November 1914, Sir Arthur Conan Doyle opined that Casement was, "a sick man …worn by tropical hardships, and he complained often of pains in his head", continuing, "Last May I had letters from him from Ireland which seemed to me so wild that I expressed fears at the time as to the state of his nerves. I have no doubt that he is not in a normal state of mind…"[20] The *Freeman's Journal* also nodded towards this in a report on 16 December 1914 that "Irish leaders in Boston today repudiated Sir Roger Casement's attitude towards Germany", continuing, "Sir Roger's action has evoked a widespread discussion. In a letter to the *London Daily Chronicle*, Sir Arthur Conan Doyle, the author, said that Casement must have been out of his mind".

But others did not accept this view. An earlier article in the *Scotsman* on 2 December had commented –

> *This eccentric gentleman, who his friends tell us is a man of the highest honour and of a full-souled chivalry rare in these modern days, before he took to trafficking with the enemies of Britain, and bartering away his patriotism for the favour of the German Emperor, was a not unimportant official in the British Consular Service.*

And on the same day, *the Evening News* summed up the situation as follows –

> *The very greatness of Sir Roger Casement's achievements in the service of his country heightens the offence of the crime he has committed, which admits of no palliation.*
>
> *Sir Roger Casement's conduct consists in open betrayal of a Government which trusted him and a country which showered honours upon him. …He has made his election with a quite incomprehensible perversity, and closed for ever by one foul blow an honourable career.*

On 30 December, a critical article in the *Daily Mail* noted that Casement's pamphlet was, "now being pressed into the hands of every American within reach of the Kaiser's far flung propaganda system". On 9 January 1915, *The Times* reported a speech by Lord Curzon which included the following –

> *…I am not going to deal with what has been said about Ireland, but I should like to mention the case of Sir Roger Casement, which is one in which I take a personal interest, for in the old days at the Foreign Office I was his official superior. This gentleman went to Germany after the outbreak of war, where he has been accused of disgraceful and disloyal acts. His friends wrote to the papers that not too much attention should be paid to those acts, as they were doubtful about his mental condition. Since then his proceedings seem to have been characterized by perfect possession of his faculties. The last thing of which we read is that he has prepared a pamphlet which has been printed by the German Government and circulated by the German Foreign Office pleading for an alliance between Germany and Ireland. I do not desire to comment upon it; it is unworthy of comment, but I wish to ask if this official who has received a title is to continue in the enjoyment of his pension.*

Casement's pension of £421-13s-6d was subsequently suspended on 4 February 1915.[21]

His next step in establishing an alliance with the German Government (as Curzon put it) was to secure their agreement to an "Irish Brigade" to be recruited from Irish prisoners of war in Germany. Despite his earlier criticism of the Irish Brigades in the South African War (and, by implication, of John MacBride) that no weapon had been untried, "to induce men loyal to their Queen to be false to their own allegiance, and to be false to themselves", Casement had met MacBride for lunch in 1913 and had been mesmerised by hearing a first-hand account of his experiences,[22] leading him to tell Alice Stopford Green that "he did splendid work there".[23] Casement had first put the idea of an Irish Brigade to the German Embassy while still in America in September, as well as suggestions as to how Germany might support nationalist movements in India and Egypt.[24] He now developed it as a formal proposal, which was accepted by Arthur Zimmermann, Under Secretary of State at the German Foreign Office, in a letter to Casement dated 28 December 1914 –

> *I have the honour to acknowledge receipt of yours of the 23rd instant, in which you lay before the German Government your proposal to form an Irish Brigade which will bind itself to fight only for the cause of Irish nationality. It will be composed of Irish prisoners of war who are ready to form such a Brigade.*
>
> *In answer, I beg to inform you that the German Government accepts your proposal, and the conditions under which the Brigade is to be formed as put forward in the plan laid down by you in your letter of 13th instant which are as follows.*[25]

The full agreement is set out below. Casement was to grandly refer to this as a "Treaty", which it was not, not having been ratified by either side. According to Devoy, Casement regarded it as "a crowning triumph of his efforts". The "Treaty" was published by *Clan na Gael* in the *Gaelic American* but – again according to Devoy

– none of the daily papers would agree to publish it.[26] The agreement is clearly the document which Christensen later failed to provide during his interviews with the Metropolitan Police in 1916 –

The Treaty

Article 1

> *With a view to securing the national freedom of Ireland, with the moral and material assistance of the German Imperial Government, an Irish Brigade shall be formed from among the Irish soldiers, or other natives of Ireland, now prisoners of war in Germany.*

Article 2

> *The object of the Irish Brigade shall be to fight solely in the cause of Ireland, and under no circumstances shall it be employed or directed to any German end.*

Article 3

> *The Irish Brigade shall be formed and shall fight under the Irish flag alone. The men shall wear a special, distinctively Irish uniform.*
>
> *As soon as Irishmen can be got for the purpose, either from Ireland or the United States, the Brigade shall have only Irish Officers. Until such time as Irish Officers can be secured German Officers will be appointed with the approval of Sir Roger Casement, to have disciplinary control of the men. But no military operation shall be ordered or conducted by the German Officers of the Brigade during such time as the men are under their control.*

Article 4

The Irish Brigade shall be clothed, fed and efficiently equipped with arms and munitions by the Imperial German Government on the clear understanding that these are furnished as a free gift to aid the cause of Irish Independence.

Article 5

It is distinctly understood and is hereby formally declared by the Parties to this agreement that the Irish Brigade shall consist only of Volunteers in the cause of Irish national freedom, and as such no member of the Irish Brigade shall receive pay or monetary reward of any kind from the Imperial German Government during the period he shall bear arms in the Brigade.

Article 6

The Imperial German Government undertakes, in certain circumstances, to send the Irish Brigade to Ireland with efficient military support and with an ample supply of arms and ammunition to equip the Irish National Volunteers in Ireland who may be willing to join them in the attempt to recover Irish national freedom by force of arms.

The "certain circumstances" hereby understood are the following:

In the event of a German naval victory affording the means of reaching the coast of Ireland, the Imperial German Government pledges itself to despatch the Irish Brigade and a supporting body of German officers and men, in German transports, to attempt a landing on the Irish coast.

Article 7

The opportunity to land in Ireland can only arise if the fortune of war should grant the German Navy a victory that would open, with reasonable prospect of success, the sea-route to Ireland. Should the German Navy not succeed in this effort the Irish Brigade shall be employed in Germany, or elsewhere, solely in such a way as Sir Roger Casement may approve as being in strict conformity with Article 2.

In this event it might be possible to employ the Irish Brigade to assist the Egyptian People to recover their freedom by driving the British out of Egypt. Short of directly fighting to free Ireland from British rule a blow struck at the British invaders of Egypt, to aid Egyptian national freedom, is a blow struck for a kindred cause to that of Ireland.

Article 8

In the event of the Irish Brigade volunteering for this service the Imperial German Government undertakes to make arrangements with the Austro-Hungarian Government for its transport through the Empire to Constantinople, and to provide with the Turkish Government for the recognition and acceptance of the Irish Brigade as a Volunteer Corps attached to the Turkish Army in the effort to expel the British from Egypt.

Article 9

In the event of the war coming to an end without the object of the Irish Brigade having been effected, namely, its landing in Ireland, the Imperial German Government undertakes to send each member of the Brigade who may so desire it, to the United States of America, with the necessary means to land in that country in conformity with the United States Immigration Laws.

Article 10

In the event of the Irish Brigade landing in Ireland, and military operations in that country resulting in the overthrow of British authority and the erection of a native Irish Government, the Imperial German Government will give the Irish Government so established its fullest moral support, and both by public recognition and by general goodwill will contribute, with all sincerity, to the establishment of an independent Government in Ireland.[27]

Devoy stresses that the Treaty was never ratified by any Irish body and that it had no influence whatsoever on the course of subsequent events. He does, however, single out Articles 7 and 8, postulating the use of the Irish Brigade in Egypt for particular condemnation, noting that, "we in America strongly objected to any such proposal, and our friends in Dublin were unalterably opposed to it. There was but one place for these men to fight, and that was in Ireland".[28]

From the German perspective, the agreement hardly represented a new departure. From the outset, they had recognised the potential for enlisting the support of the "enemy's enemy" by establishing a number of "Propaganda Camps" (or "seduction camps", as they were called by the neutral US camp inspectors), designed to persuade prisoners of war to change sides through special comforts and tailored propaganda. Among these camps was Zossen, 20 miles south of Berlin, a major camp initially housing Muslim, Indian and Black prisoners. In addition to enhanced living comforts, the camp included a mosque built in its centre "at the Kaiser's command". Facilities were provided to enable the practice of religious rights, including the provision of livestock for religious slaughter. The German officers at the camp were selected from those who had served in India and the East and who understood local languages and customs.[29] The objective was to "turn" the captives by offering them the opportunity to fight against the "occupiers" of their own country. For those from the Islamic states, this was sold as an opportunity to wage "Holy War". The arrangement clearly met with some success. The British intelligence files reveal plans to transport some 2,000 French, Indian and Russian Muslim volunteers from the prison camps to Turkey for this purpose in the early part of 1916.[30] While many on the German side had misgivings about what they saw as the dishonourable and possibly illegal practice of seducing prisoners of war to change sides, a secret note by the War Office in Berlin, dated 9 May 1916, included –

> *As for the view put forward that the work of German officers and soldiers in propaganda camps is incompatible with the sense of duty and honour of a German soldier, it may be remarked that the first suggestion to undertake such propaganda came from the highest quarters in the Empire, and, <u>moreover, with the knowledge of His Majesty the King Emperor.</u>*
>
> *As for the officers, all they have to do is to supervise the propaganda, whereas it is left to the professional propagandists to influence the opinion of prisoners-of-war...[31]*

In addition to "seducing" prisoners, the German Foreign Office were also actively engaged in what was to become known as the "Hindu-German Conspiracy", a scheme originally hatched by extremists in the US in early 1914 to secure revolt against British rule in India. (Though described as "Hindu", the project ultimately had the support of Buddhists and Muslims as well.) An "Indian Independence Committee" was set up by Zimmermann in Berlin, and in autumn 1914, Captain Franz von Papen, the German Military Attaché in Washington, was instructed to organise the purchase of arms and ammunition for 10,000 men. The arms were acquired and loaded onto a schooner in the US, the *Annie Larson*, for the first leg of their journey to India in March 1915, but a catalogue of complications followed, ending with the ship being seized at Hoquiam, Washington State, on 29 June. Little further progress was made, despite a constant flow of German money – it was reported, for example, that in one six-month period, no more than 200 pistols had been smuggled across the Pacific. The project was finally to come to an end in March 1917, when one of the Indian leaders in the US was arrested for violating its neutrality laws, leading to evidence of the whole plot being discovered.[32] At a federal trial in San Francisco held between 20 November 1917 and 24 April 1918, guilty verdicts were reached against over two dozen Indian nationals, German consular officials, and Indo-, German, and Irish Americans. (The trial gained lasting notoriety when, on its last day, one of the main defendants shot and killed another in the courtroom and was then immediately shot and killed himself by a US Marshall.) There is little historiography about the conspiracy, but it has been claimed that it was, in fact, an "Indo-German-Irish" plot, with Devoy, *Clan na Gael*, and Casement all playing a part. The evidence for this is slim, however, with Devoy making no mention of it in his otherwise comprehensive memoirs. Casement's direct contribution, if any, was probably limited to general conversations with those involved. While there was undoubtedly involvement by Irish Americans, this does not seem to have been to any meaningful extent centrally organised or directed.[33]

Even before Casement's "Treaty" had been agreed, preparations were under way to congregate all Irish prisoners (eventually totalling some 2,500) at Limburg Camp, near Frankfurt am Main, for recruitment into the Irish Brigade. From the outset, things went badly. When a Catholic bishop addressed 400 Irish prisoners at Sennelager on 30 November 1914, telling them about the impending move to Limburg, where they would be fed, clothed, treated better than other British prisoners and not required to work, they protested against being given special treatment. On 1 December, the senior NCOs of different Irish battalions drafted and signed the following letter to the Kaiser –

Sennelager, Dec 1, 1914

> Sir, – On behalf of the Irish Catholics now prisoners of war in the camp under your command, we, the undersigned, desire to tender to his Majesty the German Emperor our thanks for his consideration of our situation.
>
> We fully appreciate the kindness extended in (1) Grouping us together under one roof; (2) assuring us of better food; (3) decreasing the amount of fatigue work to be performed; but we regret we must beseech his Imperial Majesty to withdraw these concessions unless they are shared by the remainder of prisoners, as, in addition to being Irish Catholics, we have the honour to be British soldiers.
>
> We are, Sir, yours respectfully...[34]

Separately, Casement and his agents visited the camps at Güstrow, Döberitz, Wittenberg and Ruhleben, where they failed to secure any recruits. Then on 4 December, Casement visited Limburg, where he addressed an assembly of Irish NCOs and was met with a mixture of puzzlement and hostility.[35] Following the visit, he put on hold any further action until after the "Treaty" had been agreed, commenting, "I will not accept the responsibility for putting a couple of thousand Irish soldiers into the High Treason pot, unless I get very precise and sure promises both in their regard and for the political future of Ireland" – and, "From the point of view of the Irish Cause, I am not sure that the case against Findlay is not more telling than would be even the formation of an Irish Brigade. Of course, for the Germans, the Irish Brigade is the most important. It shames John Bull's Army and it knocks recruiting on the head in Ireland".[36]

These comments again demonstrate Casement's lack of judgement. The men he was trying to recruit were regular soldiers, many of whom had fought at Mons and had risked their lives in allegiance to the Crown. To assume that these same men, who had so recently lost comrades in battle, many of whom had been wounded and all of whom had been captured fighting the German Army, would now see Germany as an ally represented delusion on a grand scale. Even in Ireland itself, public sentiment was still at the time largely anti-German, fortified by the many reports of atrocities being committed by German troops in Belgium. Casement was to be faced with this reality when he returned to Limburg on a recruiting drive on 2 January 1915, after the Treaty had been agreed. Carrying a rolled umbrella over his arm, he arrived to face heckling from a crowd of about eighty men and addressed them for between fifteen and twenty minutes at an open meeting. According to an eyewitness who subsequently testified at his trial, Casement told them that he was going to form an Irish Brigade and asked them, 'Why live any longer in hunger and misery in this camp when you can better yourselves by joining the Irish Brigade which I am going to form? You will be sent to Berlin as the guests of the German Government.' He continued that in the event of Germany winning a sea battle, he would land the Irish Brigade in Ireland, and Ireland would equip them. They would free Ireland from England. If Germany didn't win, then they would be sent to America; they would get £10 or £20 of pocket money and a free passage. He was asked who he was, and he said he was Sir Roger Casement, the organiser of the Irish National Volunteer movement. Another eyewitness testified that Casement had received a poor reception and had been struck and pushed. Casement had swung his umbrella in response and someone had tried to grab it from him.[37]

Devoy subsequently blamed Casement's failure at Limburg on the way that he had handled the situation, arguing that he should have approached the prisoners individually with unsuitable candidates being filtered out first, rather than addressing them all at a meeting, "at which he delivered an address that went over their heads".[38] Support for this has been advanced from an unexpected source within the German Army, namely Joseph Zerhusen, Casement's interpreter during his stay in Germany. Zerhusen had not been present during Casement's visit to Limburg, so his assessment (written in 1966) was clearly based on discussions with prisoners who had been persuaded to join the Brigade, whom he met during the course of his duties –

> *Of course, when the idea of forming an Irish Brigade had been approved of by the German authorities, to begin with in my opinion the military people made an important mistake. Instead of going by the identity cards of the prisoners of war to select the soldiers of Irish nationality to put them into a separate camp, they let the men come on parade and then the order was given "All Irish to the right". Now, amongst the soldiers were, of course, a lot of well-seasoned men and these immediately smelt a rat, that there was something in this order. Therefore, quite a lot came forward although they were really no Irishmen and afterwards these very men were the stumbling block which practically handicapped Casement's adventure. When Casement and a few picked men went canvassing into the camp for the not-yet-formed Irish Brigade, the anti-Brigade men used their influence to deter them from joining the Brigade.[39]*

The package on offer, as put to the men in a leaflet subsequently distributed at Limburg on 9 May, was –

The German Offers

Irishmen

1. Here is a chance to fight for Ireland. You have fought for England, your country's hereditary enemy. You have fought for Belgium in England's interest, though it was no more to you than the Fiji Islands.

2. *Are you willing to fight for your country with a view to securing the national freedom of Ireland? With the moral and material assistance of the German Government an Irish Brigade is being formed.*
3. *The object of the Irish Brigade will be to fight solely for the cause of Ireland, and under no circumstances shall it be directed towards any German end.*
4. *The Irish Brigade shall be formed and fight under the Irish flag alone. The men will wear a special distinctive Irish uniform and have only Irish officers.*
5. *The Irish Brigade shall be clothed, fed, and officially equipped with arms and ammunition by the German Government. They shall be stationed near Berlin, and treated as guests of the German Government.*
6. *At the end of the war the German Government undertakes to send each member of the Brigade who desires it to the United States of America with necessary means to land.*
7. *The Irishmen in America are collecting money for the Irish Brigade. Those men who do not join the Irish Brigade will be removed from Limburg and distributed among other camps. If interested see your German company commander.*

Remember Bachelor's Walk
God Save Ireland[40]

Even if put person to person, it is hard to see how this could have attracted many recruits. It offered something for only committed nationalists. Even then, it needed to be seen against the background that the British Government had already committed to Home Rule at the end of the war. For many nationalists, that would (at that stage) have been enough. Taking up the offer would risk losing pay – and financial support being given to their wives in Ireland – and the possibility of never returning home.

Thoroughly chastened by his experience at the hands of the prisoners at Limburg, Casement wrote to a friend, "I will not return to Limburg to be insulted by a handful of recreant Irishmen".[41] And on 9 January, he had written to Count von Wedel, head of the English Department at the German Foreign Office –

> *I daresay a sham corps of sorts could be formed by tempting the men with promises of money; but an appeal to their patriotism is an appeal to something non-existent. ...<u>All thought of enrolling the men, I fear, must be abandoned</u> – they are mercenaries, pure and simple, and even had I the means to bribe them, I should not attempt to do so...*[42]

Casement left the camp after two weeks, thereafter leaving all further direct recruiting attempts to the leaders of those who had already volunteered and to three Roman Catholic priests for whom he had secured access. The final tally of all recruits was to come to a meagre fifty-four – comprising one sergeant-major, one deputy sergeant-major, three sergeants, three corporals, three lance-corporals and forty-three privates[43] – hardly a platoon, let alone a brigade.

At Limburg, the volunteers became an embarrassment to the camp authorities, both because of their ill-disciplined behaviour and because of the jeers and general opprobrium they attracted from other Irish, British and French prisoners at the camp. On 7 June, they were transferred to Zossen. In a report dated 20 August 1915, the Zossen Commandant's office noted –

> *The Irish are forming an Irish Brigade, which will be established after consultation between the Foreign Office and Sir Roger Casement, the champion of Irish independence...*
>
> *The members of the Irish Brigade are no longer German prisoners of war, but they wear an Irish uniform. The order is to be given that the Irish are to be treated as comrades...*

We try, as much as possible in the Camp here, to carry out plans for the promotion of their welfare, but where there are coloured people enclosed in the camp there are many unavoidable difficulties and dissensions. Also the German non. com. officer is not adapted for the special circumstances of the Irish.[44]

The Brigade's uniform, designed by Casement, consisted of a coat, stockings and cap, made of hunter's green cloth, with harp and shamrock decorations on the cap and collar.

*

The question of the leadership of the Brigade still needed to be resolved. Casement wanted someone holding the rank of colonel or above, both to give the post the right degree of prestige and to provide a contact at the right level with the German Government, who would not wish to negotiate directly with someone junior. It had not proved possible to persuade any Irish officer to join the Brigade, and the Treaty provided for the post to be filled by an Irishman or an Irish American. Devoy's response to a request for him to send an Irish-American officer was unhelpful –

I told him [Casement] *this was impossible; that American officers, and especially West Point graduates, had a very high sense of their own dignity, and that to ask them to take command of a body of fifty and odd men – and "deserters" at that – would be taken as an insult. Besides, we were convinced that President Wilson intended from the start to enter the War on the side of "The Allies", and that all retired officers would be subject to orders to rejoin the army. Casement, however, could not be brought to recognize these realities.*[45]

Devoy was finally able to provide help, however, in the person of Robert Monteith. Monteith was an ex-member of the British

Army, born in Co Wicklow in 1879. He had served in the Royal Horse Artillery in India and as a Bombardier in the Boer War with the South African Constabulary. Following his discharge in 1903, he had gone on to serve as an Army reserve until 1911, while taking on a job in the civil service working at the Ordnance Depot in Dundalk, Co Louth. In 1908, he moved to Dublin, where he held a variety of work placements before securing a job at the Ordnance Depot at Island Bridge. In November 1913, he joined the Irish Volunteers and was elected Captain of A Company, 1st Battalion of the Dublin Brigade, and acted as drill instructor. At the outbreak of war in August 1914, he was offered a Commission in the British Army, which he refused. This resulted in his dismissal from the Ordnance Depot, and a ban from living within the Metropolitan Police District of Dublin under the Defence of the Realm Act. He fled to Limerick, where he again acted as drill instructor with the local Volunteers.[46] On 2 August 1915, the day following O'Donovan Rossa's funeral in Dublin, Tom Clarke travelled to Limerick and discussed with Monteith the possibility of him joining the Irish Brigade. Monteith agreed to go, provided arrangements were made to look after his wife and family.[47] On 26 August, he secured agreement from the authorities for him and his family to leave Ireland for the United States.[48] From there, Devoy arranged for Christensen to smuggle him into Germany as a stowaway. He left the US on 7 October and arrived in Berlin via Norway and Denmark on 23 October.[49]

Monteith's diary provides a detailed account of his activities on arriving in Germany. He quickly met Casement and they travelled together to Zossen, where the men of the Irish Brigade were paraded and told by Casement that in future ("or until such time as a senior officer arrived from America"), Monteith was to be regarded as their commanding officer. Monteith then went to Limburg to take up recruiting for the Brigade from the Irish prisoners remaining there. His recruiting campaign lasted from 3

November until 23 November, and the daily entries in his diary show that hostility to joining the Brigade remained strong and was, if anything, greater than it had been at the beginning of the year. On the first day, he noted that the men "seemed indifferent and a lot of them absolutely impossible". Following entries included –

5/11/15 – Several men today asked what they would get for joining – a straight question. Pointed out I had nothing to offer except the honour of fighting for their own country. There was so to speak "nothing doing". A party of French prisoners today cried, 'Irish Traitors' as we passed.

7/11/15 – Recruiting. We now manage to get through about 50 men a day. Nearly all of them are satisfied with their present state, which is peculiar. All of them are loud in their statement that when the war is over they will be prepared to fight for Ireland. God help us! after the war. Their idea of fighting for Ireland seems to be to fight the people of the North. John Redmond seems to be a sort of tin God to these men, a constant cry is, 'Now we have home rule we are equal with England and it is our duty to fight alongside the English.'

9/11/15 – Recruiting. Men all satisfied with their present condition, most of these I find belong to the Special Reserve (i.e., Militia) can't see further than their nose and suffer no pain as long as their stomach is full.

10/11/15 – Noisy lot of men today who promised all sorts of kind things, such as shooting, hanging, etc....

18/11/15 – Recruiting. No change, men seem without interest in life, home, or future. It is so pitiful.

Monteith records that the German War Office would not give him permission to wear his Brigade uniform at Limburg, which he considered would "assist me in my work greatly". He also records at one stage that he had "up to now selected fifty-two men who will in all probability join us". But he goes on to complain elsewhere that, "The men selected by me are to be separated into separate rooms, consequently they will be under suspicion of every man in the camp – Irish, Russian and French. It will spoil everything". Whatever happened in the end, there is no record of any men actually transferring to Zossen to join the Brigade as a result of his efforts.[50]

At the end of November, Monteith was called back to Zossen by Casement because things were not going well there and the men were out of hand. He arrived at the camp to find them being treated as prisoners, with no leave allowed, no arms and no overcoats, in consequence of which they were in "an ugly humour". Alongside this, it seems that by now Casement had abandoned all his ambitions for the Brigade to fight to liberate Ireland itself, in favour of the fallback provided in the Treaty of the Brigade fighting to oust the British from Egypt. Accordingly, on 1 December, Monteith told the men that, "it is hardly probable that the invasion of the British Isles will take place" and asked them how they would feel about the idea, "of striking a blow at England by going to the Eastern Theatre of War and joining the Army for the invasion of Egypt and helping to free another small nationality which England strangely enough omits to free". He recorded, "Nobody seems very enthusiastic about the project".[51] Casement and Monteith then followed this up, interviewing the men jointly on 3 December, when thirty-eight men volunteered. Morale was then restored by a period of conventional training, including route marches, until on 22 December the German authorities ordered the withdrawal of arms from the men (which had been issued at the beginning of the month), resulting in a renewed period of belligerence and discontent, culminating in three fights on Christmas Day in the men's bungalow, with German soldiers having to quell the disturbance. There was more trouble on New Year's Day, when further fighting broke out after a German carelessly referred to Irishmen as English. (Zerhusen puts a slightly different spin on this: his version is that the Irish started to sing Irish songs, which the Germans present took exception to because they thought the songs were English.)[52] This disturbance resulted in the Brigade being confined to barracks, creating yet more ill-feeling.

Although Casement had unilaterally prepared for the bulk of the Brigade to fight in Egypt, it seems that he did not formally put the proposal to the German Foreign Office until the end of December. The idea was put to Enver Pasha, the Turkish leader, who agreed to the men fighting alongside Turkish forces, while the Foreign office agreed to the men being given weapons training. The Brigade's ill-discipline and poor behaviour continued, however, in consequence of which the project was finally vetoed by General von Lowenfeld, ADC to the Kaiser, who wrote on 10 February 1916 –

> *In view of the behaviour of the Irish – described in the report of the Commander of manoeuvres at Zossen on the 19th of January – consisting of individuals proving themselves addicted to drink and opposing the laws of military discipline and order, I agree that the proposal of Sir Roger Casement regarding the possession of rifles by the prisoners of war, which is supported by the Political Section of the General Staff, Berlin should be rejected. I consider it utterly inappropriate, even dangerous, that these undisciplined men, who because of far too lenient treatment are constantly proving guilty of the most grievous offences, should even be given weapons.*
>
> *I am unable to repose a great deal of confidence in a gentleman like Sir Roger Casement, who raises against the Government in whose service he has stood for many years, such grave charges; all the less so, as I cannot push aside the thought that the aforesaid propagandist might be guided by some sordid intentions.*[53]

Monteith was clearly never told of this final decision. On 14 January, Casement had been ordered on medical advice to a sanatorium, and had formerly put Monteith in sole charge of the Brigade.[54] He notes that from then on things went "badly" and his account becomes more general. He records various discussions and disputes with the German General Staff and notes that, despite writing a number of letters, he never received a reply. Monteith's German diary finishes on 10 April 1916, when he reports on his forthcoming trip to Ireland in advance of the Easter Rising –

> *We are cut off from communication with Ireland and America, and the whole transaction amounts to this, that I believe Sir Roger Casement, Sgt. Beverly* [later known as Bailey] *and myself are going straight to our death with our hands tied, without even hope of being able to raise a hand to defend ourselves, and fools think we cannot see through their treachery – or let me be charitable, want of foresight. We go well knowing what is in front of us, but we go without fear and without reproach.*
>
> *Without me and perhaps without Beverly the world will move along in the same way, but in Sir Roger Casement, the world loses one of her best and greatest men.*
>
> *R Monteith*
> *10/4/16 Berlin*[55]

SEVEN
RETURN TO IRELAND

...it became clear that I was being played with, fooled and used as by a most selfish and unscrupulous government for its own petty interests.
                              Casement on the German Government,
                                    15 February 1915 (MacColl, p.139)

To save my own countrymen from taking part in a great crime I should not sink from a hundred acts of "High Treason", or ever shirk from the consequences.
                    Casement writing from Munich, 30 October 1915

I will very gladly go to Ireland with the arms and do all I can to sustain and support a movement of resistance based on these grounds. For in this case it is far better for Irishmen to fight at home and resist conscription by force than to be swept into the

> *shambles of England's continental war and lose their lives in an unworthy cause.*
>
> Letter from Casement to German Foreign Office, 2 April 1916

The failure of the Irish Brigade project brought into question Casement's continuing role in Germany. It would have been surprising had the German authorities been prepared to put much more time and effort into a scheme that had promised tangible assistance to their war effort, only to produce so little by way of results – just over fifty men, "reckoned by the Germans to be disaffected, for the most part indisciplined, and certainly susceptible to drink".[1] They became less prepared to take Casement seriously. Some even suspected him of being a British spy. Casement, for his part, had become equally disillusioned with the German authorities, especially over what he saw as their lack of support over the outlandish *Findlay Affair*. Relationships therefore cooled, if they did not rupture, on both sides. Just as Casement had turned from full allegiance to the Crown to extreme dislike, he was now to completely overturn his view on things German, writing in early 1916 of German military officials –

> *...they are swine and cads of the first water – not one of them with the soul of a rat or the mind of a cur – They certainly deserve to be thoroughly well taught in the first rudiments of humanity and kindliness – for as they are, they are lower than the Congo savages in most things that constitute gentleness of mind, heart, or action.*[2]

Casement was not only disillusioned but his health was also deteriorating, especially his mental state. When Monteith first met Casement in October 1915, his diary records that, "Sir Roger looked very ill, despondent and nervous, and in a state of fretfulness".[3] Zerhusen's assessment of Casement in late 1915 amplified this –

> ...I also had the impression that he was not in very good health; that he seemed to be greatly troubled and dissatisfied. He often complained that he could not make any headway. German officials were so slow. They did not seem to fully realise the importance of the part Ireland did already play in the war by handicapping recruitment in Ireland. I think that Sir Roger was very disappointed that he could not get the interview with the Kaiser. As far as I know, the Kaiser personally was not in favour of a rebellion in Ireland. He believed too much in his reign by God's Grace and therefore could not fathom a rebellion against his royal cousin in England. And –
>
> But Sir Roger had one fault, if I may call it so. He was too trusting. People or the men, feigning an interest in Irish affairs agreeing to what he said, he would at once believe in their sincerity, and think them friends.[4]

By 12 January 1916, Casement's condition had got considerably worse. Monteith records in his diary, "SRC [Casement] very ill. I am afraid his mind is going, disappointment after disappointment has broken him, have tried to get him to see a mental specialist, wire for his doctor and go to Berlin to see some people, friends of his to whom I made known his condition". Elsewhere, Monteith noted that he had found Casement prostrate –

> ...his nerves had gone to pieces and his general breakdown was complete. He presented a deathlike appearance. His bronzed face had turned ashen colour, his features were pinched and haggard, and he lay so still his breathing was scarcely perceptible.[5]

After seeing a specialist on 14 January, Casement was admitted to a sanatorium in Munich, leaving Monteith in charge of the Brigade.

Devoy meanwhile had also become disillusioned with Casement. In May 1915, when the Military Council of the IRB were in the initial stages of considering a rising, they had sent one of its members, Joseph Mary Plunkett, to Germany to discuss the possible supply of arms. On his way, Plunkett met Devoy, who advised him not to involve Casement in those discussions, as had been intended. This resulted in the opening up of a direct line of communication with the German Government, bypassing Casement, further diminishing his role and, more crucially, his knowledge of what was going on in the movement. Devoy records that Plunkett laid out the military plans of the Irish leaders before the German General Staff who had approved them. Then in early February 1916, the IRB's Military Council notified *Clan na Gael* that they had decided on an insurrection and wanted arms from Germany to assist them after they had "risen". The arms were required to be delivered between April 20 and 23. This request was quickly passed to the German Embassy and transmitted by them to Berlin,[6] with Berlin replying that they would be able to send about ten machine guns, 20,000 rifles, ammunition and explosives.[7]

The first Casement heard about all this was when, on 6 March, Monteith was summoned to the German General Staff to be told that a rising was planned for Easter Monday and about the shipment of arms from Germany. It was left to Monteith to tell Casement, who was still in Munich recovering from his breakdown.[8] Casement was enraged at hearing this news, at first refusing to accept it. He had quite understandably believed that it was he who was leading the nationalist cause in Germany and that he had an agreed strategy as set out in his Treaty. He assumed that Germany were now simply finding a cheap and dishonourable way of escaping their responsibilities under the Treaty by providing arms without doing any of the fighting. It did not occur to him that it was his own side which were consciously leading on a unilateral rising, and that he had been deliberately kept out of the picture. While *Clan na Gael* had played no part in deciding on a rising, for his part, Devoy regarded the Treaty as peripheral to the job in hand, noting that, "We in America were convinced that our most important task was to furnish, to the utmost, means whereby the men in Ireland could arm and equip themselves".⁹ He knew that Casement would disagree and set out deliberately to prevent him interfering. In a letter to Laurence de Lacey, a former Volunteer and IRB member who had fled to America, Devoy later wrote on 20 July 1916, a few days after Casement's trial –

> *From our experiences of a year of his utter impracticability – he had been assuring us till we were sick that "there was no hope for the poor old woman" [Ireland] until the next war – we sent with the first note from home that we transmitted to Berlin a request that R* [Casement] *be asked to remain there, "to take care of Irish interests". We knew he would meddle in his honest but visionary way to such an extent as to spoil things, but we did not dream that he would ruin everything has he has done. He took no notice whatever of decisions or instructions, but without quarrelling, pursued his own dreams. The last letter I got from him, written last December, said the only hope now of making a demonstration that would impress the world was to send the "Brigade" to Egypt. To impress the world by sending 60 men to a place where they could do nothing. We had told him nearly a year before that we would not consent to this but he took no notice. He was obsessed with the idea that he was a wonderful leader and that nothing could be done without him. His letters always kept me awake on the night of the day I got them.¹⁰*

Casement's detailed response to the news of the rising is very fortuitously recorded in three letters he wrote to Count von Wedel, head of the English desk at the German Foreign Ministry, on 30 March and 1 and 2 April 1916. Casement handed copies of these to Princess Blücher in Berlin on 4 April, just before his final trip to Ireland, asking her to pass them on to Eoin MacNeill and E D Morel should anything happen to him. They resurfaced in February 1919, when Prince and Princess Blücher gave them to Major General Ewart, the head of the British Mission in Berlin, who immediately sent them on by hand with a "reliable French officer" to the British Delegation to the Royal Armistice Commission at Spa, from where they were passed to the War Office.[11] At their meeting with Ewart, it seems that little was said about the Blüchers' relationship with Casement, other than that when in Africa the Prince had met Casement at the time when he was British Consul at Delagoa Bay. In fact, they had had frequent contact over the years, with Prince Blücher (or Count Blücher as he was until the death of his father in 1916) acting as honorary treasurer to the Putumayo Mission fund, and Casement being a frequent visitor to the Count and Countess's home in London. At the outbreak of war, the Blüchers had moved to Germany as enemy aliens. In her subsequent memoirs, Princess Blücher records that at the end of November 1914, they were startled by the news of Casement's arrival in Germany – "We knew his anti-English feelings well, and his rabid Home Rule mania, but we did not expect it to have taken this intense form of becoming pro-German". She goes on to record that Prince Blücher had visited him and had, "tried to show him what a false position he had put himself in, and that he had better leave the country as quickly as possible, but it was no use. So after that we refused to see him or have anything more to do with him". As to his failure to secure recruits for the Irish Brigade, she went on –

> *He was not really successful anywhere. In fact, he soon became offended, because he said the Berlin Foreign Office did not trust him enough. We hinted to him that no one ever really trusted a traitor, at which he was greatly incensed, protesting he was not that; and he was hardly less so when others, trying to soften down the name, called him an Irish rebel. He did not like that either.*

> *His measure of success with the Irish prisoners may be summed up in the answer he got from one very raw Irishman whom he asked whether he did not hate England. The Irishman's reply was: 'Well, we may hate England, but that does not make us love Germany.'*[12]

Her opinion of Casement did not improve. She records that in October 1915, she saw him briefly when he came to Berlin from Munich, noting that, "People have very mixed opinions about him. Some think he is an English spy and only pretending to be a rebel, whereas others laugh at him as a man who has failed". She goes on to repeat a conversation with him where, "He tried, as usual, to talk me round about Ireland", concluding –

> *…when he begins airing his opinions in too self-satisfied a manner, it makes me want to repeat to him the words I had heard lately from the lips of a German lady about him, 'If you ask me,' she said, 'what I think of Roger Casement, I think him a blot on the earth.'*[13]

The dislike implied in these comments was by no means one way. When he first met the Blüchers in Berlin, Casement himself said of the Prince that, "Blücher's interest is solely in himself, and his chances of besting his unscrupulous old father".[14]

Casement's own diary is at odds with Princess Blücher's memoirs. These claim that she was very supportive of his mission, telling him that a rebellion in Ireland might help to bring the British Government to its senses.[15] But Casement's track record in being perceptive of the views of others is not great, and the Princess's own activities during the war give the lie to any suggestion that she might have been sympathetic either to Casement's cause or to his methods in pursuing it. She acknowledges that as an Englishwoman in Germany, her sympathies were divided, as were those of others in a similar position in her social circle. From the very early days of her stay in Germany, she took an active interest in the general welfare of British prisoners of war (among whom were some of her friends and close relatives) in conjunction with Princess Münster, daughter of George Hay-Drummond, 12th Earl of Kinnoull, and Princess Pless, the daughter of Colonel William Cornwallis-West of Denbighshire. The issue was naturally sensitive. She records that a request to see British prisoners was refused in September 1914 after Princess Pless had visited some prisoners without permission and on leaving had been heard to remark, 'Keep up your spirits,' which had been taken to imply support for Britain winning the war. But she goes on to record success in being able to buy *The Times*, remarking –

> *How I dread the sight of the casualty list in The Times. I shudder each time I read it, but it is a tremendous help to me, as in this way I am able to learn the names of all the regiments that have been sent out, and the whereabouts of their engagements, so that I can give every information when enquiring at the Central Office for missing and wounded. Good news from home so far.*[16]

In October 1914, she was accused of being pro-English for rebutting claims – widespread at the time – that the spikes in the clasp-knives issued to British soldiers were being used to scoop out the eyes of wounded Germans.[17] She also records being desperate at the number of reports of cruelty and bullying towards British prisoners – "We are sending accounts of brutality to the Foreign Office here, and I intend getting them reported at Headquarters, so that the perpetrators may be run to ground and punished, if not now, after the war".[18] She also became actively involved in controversy surrounding the treatment of submarine crews in early 1915, when Churchill ordered thirty-nine German submarine prisoners to be confined to naval barracks as "criminals" rather than prisoners of war, in response to Germany's campaign of unrestricted submarine warfare. The German authorities immediately imprisoned thirty-nine British officers with well-known names in reprisal, including Lieutenant Goschen, the son of the former British Ambassador to Berlin.[19] Having relations among the British officers chosen, Princess Blücher, Princess Münster and Princess Pless visited James W Gerard, the US Ambassador in Berlin, asking him to send a note that they had prepared to Princess Blucher's mother in England with a view to it being used to persuade Churchill to change his policy for the benefit of the British officers.[20] Her activities on behalf of British prisoners continued throughout the war, with many specific acts being recorded in her memoirs. As late as March 1918, she considered that, "there is still a great deal of bullying and ill-treatment of imprisoned British officers going on, and… too much personal authority is accorded to the officers in command of the camp".[21] And in January 1919, she records a visit from British officers helping to repatriate British prisoners.[22]

These activities do not, of course, rule out Casement's claim that she supported his mission, but it does seem unlikely that she would have much or any actual sympathy with his attempts to persuade British soldiers to abandon their allegiance. But whatever their exact relationship, it was to Princess Blücher that Casement turned before his departure from Germany. The circumstances are again fully described in her memoirs –

> *Berlin, April 4, 1916 – I was suddenly rung up on the telephone by Sir Roger Casement, saying he must see me at once. I was somewhat surprised, as I thought he was ill in bed in Munich. He was, a few days ago, when we heard of him last.*
>
> *However, although I was not keen on seeing him, I telephoned back to say that I would do so for a few minutes. Little did I think what a scene was before me.*

The poor man came into the room like one demented, talked in a husky whisper, rushed round examining all the doors, and then said: 'I have something to say to you, are you sure no-one is listening?'

For one moment I was frightened. I felt I was in the presence of a madman, and worked my way round to sit near the telephone so as to be able to call for help. And then he began: 'You were right a year ago when you told me that I had put my head into a noose in coming here. I have tried not to own you were right, and I did not like to tell you when you kept on urging me to get out of the country, that I realised from the moment I landed here what a terrific mistake I had made. And also I did not want to tell you that in reality I was a prisoner here. I could not get away. They will not let me out of the country.

'The German Foreign Office have had me shadowed, believing I was a spy in the pay of England, and England has had men spying on me all the time as well.

'Now the German Admiralty has asked me to go on an errand which all my being revolts against, and I am going mad at the thought of it, for it will make me appear a traitor to the Irish cause.'

And at these words he sat down and sobbed like a child. I saw the man was beside himself with terror and grief, and so I tried to get a few more definite facts out of him, and told him there is a way out of every difficulty if he would only tell me more.

But he said, 'If I told you more, it would endanger the lives of many, and as it is, it is only my life that has to be sacrificed.' I made all sorts of suggestions, but all he would say was: 'They are holding a pistol to my head here if I refuse, and they have a hangman's rope ready for me in England; and so the only thing to do is to go out and kill myself.'

I argued him out of this, and at last he went away after giving me a bundle of farewell letters to be opened after his death.

As he went to the door, he said: 'Tell them I was loyal to Ireland, although it will not appear so.'

He asked to see me again, but as I am watched like everyone else here, and as there was evidently some political intrigue on, I had to refuse.[23]

The bundle of farewell letters comprised those given to Major General Ewart referred to above. Casement's first letter, dated 30 March, is characteristically detailed and lengthy, running to some sixteen typed pages and about 6,500 words. It rehearses for Wedel in a blow-by-blow account his discussions with the German authorities, interspersed with emotional statements about his own position. In setting the scene, he notes that it is highly probable that he will shortly no longer be in Germany, but –

> *I am, in this, a passive agent, powerless to act according to my judgment, and with a course of action forced upon me that I wholly deprecate and by methods that I hesitate to characterise to you by the words that seem to justly apply to them.*
>
> *I am being used as a tool for purposes that are now very plain to me and of which I disapprove, by a species of pressure that I am powerless here to combat, since I am practically a prisoner with no means of communicating with my friends in America or Ireland, or stating the reasons that compel me to differ from the line of action they are presumably following, or of informing them of the character of the pressure being exerted to force me into actions against my judgment.*
>
> *But while I am deprived of the means of informing my friends in America of what I think, I feel it is my last duty to place on record here my view of the line of action forced upon me by the Gr. General Staff, and also to enter a vigorous protest against the involving of Lt. Monteith and some of the Irish soldiers at Zossen in the fate that threatens me.*

He then goes on to reiterate that since the beginning of the year he had been, "for the most part, in a 'health' cure at Munich" and rehearses the events surrounding Monteith's summons to the General Staff on 6 March. At that stage, he says, he had assumed that the decision to send arms to the Irish Volunteers was a response to his view that there would be advantage in arming the nationalists, to which there had previously been no reaction. In response to this development, he had drawn up a "brief memorandum giving my opinion of how best to ensure a safe landing of arms in Ireland" and had produced a second memorandum the following day, both of which were now with the General Staff. These memoranda had pointed out the importance of getting information from those in Ireland who would be receiving the arms and had suggested that he should go beforehand in a submarine, "with two of the men from Zossen I should pick out". Then on 16 March, he had had an interview with Captain Nadolny of the General Staff plus two of his colleagues from the "Political" section, where he was told that his proposal to go to Ireland by submarine had been rejected by the Admiralty. Furthermore, the project in hand was not simply to land arms but was part of a plan for a "rising" which had been communicated by Devoy. He had then been shown a letter from Devoy dated 16 February, asking for up to 100,000 rifles, cannon and, "above all officers and trained artillerymen". Nadolny went on to say that only 20,000 rifles, ten machine guns and five million cartridges could be sent and no German officers. Nevertheless, it should be possible for Casement or the "Irish revolutionaries" to dictate peace terms to the British Government and secure for Ireland "at least autonomy". He concluded that this presented, "the very opportunity for employing the 'Irish Brigade'", i.e., the fifty-five men at Zossen, urging Casement to take them all with him. In response, Casement had said that that would be a matter for Monteith, however –

> *...I thought it highly improbable that <u>under these circumstances</u> the whole body could be equally trusted, but that Lt. Monteith might be able to pick out a few tried men for working the machine guns on landing. The whole project really took my breath away. I had come prepared to discuss the best means of landing arms in Ireland and I found myself confronted with a proposal for a "rebellion" in Ireland I believed to be wholly futile at the best and at the worst something I dreaded to think of.*

Casement records in his letter that, "again and again", he insisted on the need to get to Ireland only to be told that the Admiralty would not hear of it. The next day he visited the Admiralty himself, where he was told that providing a submarine was not possible for technical reasons. At this point, he had proposed that he should himself send someone to Dublin to act as a messenger. For this task he chose an Irish American named John McGoey, a Volunteer who had been sent to Germany by Devoy several months earlier to help out. With Admiralty help, he despatched McGoey to Denmark on 19 March. (This project was in the event to fail when McGoey subsequently disappeared.[24])

As things stood, Casement writes that at this point he was committed to sail with Monteith and "a handful" of the Irish Brigade on 8 April. But he was still troubled –

> *I remained in the gravest doubt as to how to proceed. I foresaw the greatest difficulties ahead whatever I might do, and a tremendous responsibility being forced upon me in the dark and with wholly insufficient means of knowing what was the state of things in Ireland or in America. It was eleven months since I had had direct communication from Ireland and over three months since I had received any news from America.* And –
>
> *...I was confident that the value of the political services rendered by Irishmen in America to the German cause far*

transcended the value of any possible gift of arms Germany might make to Ireland.

I, therefore, had no scruples in assisting in the despatch of arms to Ireland. When it came to assisting an abortive outbreak, with wholly insufficient means, against British authority in Ireland, as the price of the belated gift, I was treading on other ground.

His letter went on to remind Wedel that he had always been greatly opposed to any attempted revolt in Ireland unless "backed up with foreign military help" as provided for in his Treaty. He was therefore becoming more and more concerned about the fate of his men who had, "committed treason on a distinct and formal promise, signed, sealed and delivered by the Imperial German Government" that if despatched to Ireland they would be supported by an ample German force. He now felt he was betraying both them and Monteith. He records that on his return to Berlin from Munich on 29 March, he first visited the Admiralty, where he had expressed concern about the possible conduct of the Irish soldiers should they be arrested *en route* to Ireland –

This particular fear was that these men, feeling themselves betrayed and deceived, might, as it were (and I think with perfect justice) turn "king's evidence" and establish a very damaging case against both the German Government and myself, the alleged "paid tool" of that Government.

He then records that following his visit to the Admiralty he had gone on to the General Staff, where the discussion quickly became acrimonious. Here, he had been reproached for his "underhand trick" in despatching McGoey to Ireland. He was threatened that unless he accepted conditions laid down by Nadolny, a telegram would be sent to Devoy cancelling the arms shipment and blaming Casement. At a further meeting the following day – 30 March –

the day of Casement's letter, Nadolny had made clear to him that the rising had been planned by the Irish themselves, that Devoy had asked for help, and that no responsibility for any of this fell on the German Government, which had responded with the offer of arms at considerable cost to themselves (£200,000). And while they were complying with Devoy's request, they, the German Staff, were not inspired by any "idealistic" interest. They were sending the arms in the hope that they would be used at once – "no revolution, no rifles". If Casement did not accept what was happening, Nadolny would telegraph Devoy in the following terms –

> *That the General Staff had made all arrangements for supplying the arms etc. promised, at the time and place agreed on, at Mr Devoy's request, but that owing to my opposition they were now declining to carry through the project and the entire responsibility for the non-delivery of the arms and the possible failure of or grave injury to the independence movement in Ireland fell upon me.*

The remaining six pages of Casement's letter comprise a lengthy exposition of the personal dilemma facing him and how he had decided to move forward. If implemented, Nadolny's threat would leave him looking a coward in the eyes of his fellow nationalists, at the same time as he was being denied the means to communicate with them. This left him with no choice but to go along with the project, "dead against my reason, judgment and intelligence". He would provide himself with poison, he said, to be taken in the event of the steamer taking him being seized by the British fleet *en route*. But he was not prepared to put the lives of members of his Brigade in danger by taking them with him, repeating his argument about the primacy of the Treaty –

> *My position is a hideous one. Let me restate it. First – entirely without consulting me and in opposition to my views, Mr Devoy*

and Irishmen decided to attempt some form of revolution in Ireland.

I have always opposed such a course unless assured of ample external military aid – an assurance wholly impossible today.

…The agreement with myself of 23–28 December 1914 is entirely ignored, although the prisoners of war who had been induced by its clear and specific pledge to abandon their allegiance to their Sovereign, are now to be employed as military agents in an enterprise at variance with the spirit, letter and whole scope of that Agreement, on whose supposed sanctity they have been induced by me to rely.

They are only to be told of what is intended from them when it is practically too late for them, as brave men, to refuse to accompany me and their officers.

Casement went on to say that if he refused to co-operate, the "fanatical enthusiasts" in Ireland who were going to attempt something "brave and foolhardy" the following month would not have the help of the German arms and –

…the reproach for having abandoned them to their fate and intervened to deprive them of the support <u>they themselves had asked for</u> from the German Government, will be laid upon me and my name will be cursed by future generations of my countrymen. I do not think anyone was ever put in a more atrocious position. Whatever I do must of necessity be wrong and must hurt some one no less than be contrary either to my reason, judgment or instinct.

My instinct, as an Irish nationalist, is to be with my countrymen in any project of theirs however foolhardy; to stand or fall with them!

He continued by reiterating his dilemma in different ways, while also remaining adamant, again and again, that he would not take the Brigade with him to Ireland. Arguing that the German

Government bore a share of the responsibility for the difficulty he was facing, and that they hoped to get some political or military capital out of the exercise, he then requested that they provide a party of a dozen or so men to cover the landing of the arms with machine-gun fire. Failing that, a submarine should be employed to oversee the landing. And whether all this was agreed or not, he would go with the expedition to Ireland alone –

> *This seems the best I can decide. While it is not all I would wish, it at least will leave my character as an Irishman safe in the final facts of my public career, and it will in no way damage or weaken the enterprise in Ireland or endanger the German vessel and her gallant crew. On the contrary, it will in certain possible eventualities (that must be apparent to you) render the position of her commanding officer and crew less dangerous and then the blame for "an attempt that failed" would always be lessened by the absence of the Irish soldiers.*

As his letter progressed, Casement displayed more and more of the mental stress he was under, commenting himself that he was very tired and by no means well but had one more point to raise later. In a footnote to the copy of the letter, he wrote – "The original was handed in person by Lt Monteith to Count Wedel who said he would attend to it at once. This was at 12.30 Saturday, 1 April 1916, a lovely summer day. I was sick in bed and with much medicine and the Dr at that very moment".

Casement's second letter, dated 1 April, was short and written from his sickbed. It simply repeated his wish to go on the journey to Ireland and noted that Monteith would probably want to come with him. He stated again that he could not "bring the men in", and said that they would need to be "looked after when I am gone". His third letter, dated the following day, 2 April, then marks a remarkable and complete turnaround in his position. He records here that he has now seen a copy of *Irish World* containing a speech given by Devoy in early March, which sets out the reasons why the Irish Volunteers want to act. These were – according to Casement's understanding – that the actions of the Irish Volunteers had forced the British Government to exclude Ireland from conscription and that the Government were determined to destroy the Volunteers as a result so that conscription could be reinstated. If this was the case, Casement was now anxious to help and welcomed the support offered by the German Government –

> *I will very gladly go to Ireland with the arms and do all I can to sustain and support a movement of resistance based on these grounds. For in this case it is far better for Irishmen to fight at home and resist conscription by force than to be swept into the shambles of England's continental war and lose their lives in an unworthy cause.*
>
> *Mr Devoy's speech removes some of the doubts that have troubled me.*

In light of subsequent events, it is difficult to know whether Casement had actually undergone a genuine conversion or whether he was simply trying to deceive the German authorities into letting him go to Ireland so that he could continue in his attempts to prevent the rising. Or perhaps he was set on having it both ways – getting to Ireland to attempt to stop the rising but being prepared to stand alongside the rebels if that failed. Nor is it clear whether, when the General Staff then decided on 7 April to allow him to go to Ireland after all,[25] this was in response to his apparent conversion or whether they were simply seizing the opportunity to be rid of him. Devoy records that the German General Staff allowed him to go to Ireland because he "deceived them into thinking that he wanted to participate in the fight".[26]

While the decision that he should go to Ireland had now been reached, the method chosen to get him there is also surrounded by confusion. The arms themselves were to be taken by the *Aud*, formerly the *Libau*, now disguised as a Norwegian merchant ship. Devoy states that the German authorities refused to allow Casement to travel on the *Aud*, but cites no reasons for that decision.[27] According to Reserve-Lieutenant Karl Spindler, the officer in charge of the *Aud*, "as Casement had expressed a very strong objection against accompanying us on the *Libau* [sic], it was finally decided to place a submarine at his disposal".[28] This fits in with Casement's repeated requests in his letters to Wedel, and may have been seen by him as a means to enable him to travel separately on arrival, and indeed to get to Ireland first, in order to get the rising called off. Whatever the reason, Casement left for Ireland from Wilhelmshaven on 12 April on the U-20 (the submarine that one year earlier had sunk the *Lusitania*), accompanied by Monteith and Daniel Julian Bailey, a member of the Irish Brigade. Bailey had been a reservist with the Royal Irish Rifles recalled at the outbreak of war and sent out with the BEF. He had been taken prisoner at the beginning of September 1914, and sent to Sennelager, subsequently moving to Limburg with the other Irish prisoners. He had joined the Irish Brigade in April 1915 under the name of D J Beverley, and had been made Sergeant. He recorded later that while at Zossen, Monteith had agreed that if he (Monteith) "ever got out" he would take Bailey with him.[29] It seems that he had been included in the party at Monteith's request.[30] Three days into the journey, the U-20 broke down and returned to Heligoland where the party transferred to the U-19, finally arriving off the Irish coast at the Bay of Tralee in the very early hours of Good Friday, 21 April.

The *Aud*, meanwhile, had left Lübeck for Ireland on 9 April. Its sailing plan was to arrive off Tralee on the night of Maundy Thursday, 20 April. This was in accordance with the original exchange between the German Foreign Office and *Clan na Gael*, when the delivery of arms had been promised between 20 and 23 April. Signals had been arranged for the *Aud* to notify its arrival and for the arms to be unloaded. But in early April, the IRB decided that a landing on Maundy Thursday would be too risky, as it would quickly become known to the British and give warning that something was about to happen. They decided instead to ask for the arms to be delivered after the insurrection had started at 6.30 pm on Easter Sunday, and sent Joseph Plunkett's niece, Philomena, to New York with the new instruction. But she did not arrive there until 14 April – after the *Aud* had sailed from Lübeck. When Devoy passed on the message to the German Admiralty, they told him that the *Aud* did not have wireless and that there was nothing they could do to get the message through. According to Devoy, he then sent someone to Ireland to pass the German message on, but this seems not to have been received.[31] This is borne out by the fact that it was not until Friday, 21 April, that Plunkett sent his agents down from Dublin to make the final arrangements to receive the arms, now expected forty-eight hours later.[32] The result was that when the *Aud* reached her destination on the afternoon of 20 April and signalled ashore at dusk, as planned, there was no response from the Volunteers, who should have been there to meet them. After anchoring overnight, Spindler decided the following day, Good Friday, 21 April, to cruise around Tralee Bay until nightfall, and then to make for Lisbon. During the course of this, however, he was intercepted by the Royal Navy and escorted by HMS *Bluebell* towards Queenstown (now Cobh) where, on entering the harbour on Saturday, 22 April, Spindler and his crew smartly ran up the German flag, abandoned ship and scuttled the *Aud*, together with its cargo.[33]

Whatever intentions Casement might have had about his actions on arriving in Ireland had already been taken out of his hands. According to Spindler, the U-19 had been instructed to put Casement and his party on board the *Aud* at a rendezvous in Tralee Bay, and Spindler was then to proceed under his instructions.[34] This seems far-fetched, as it takes away any logical reason why Casement would have been allowed to go by submarine rather than on the *Aud*. Devoy provides a simple and more plausible answer: Casement's trip and the journey of the *Aud* were separate, unconnected operations. On this basis, the commitment was simply to get Casement to Tralee, leaving him to sort out his role in the rising with the Volunteers themselves. Furthermore, the commander of the U-boat had been instructed specifically not to allow Casement and his party to land before 20 April, even if he got there earlier.[35] Thus, when Casement asked to be put ashore in Galway in order to reach Dublin at the earliest possible moment, the Captain of the U-19 insisted on continuing to Tralee Bay where, as noted above, the submarine arrived in the early hours of Good Friday, 21 April.[36] On arrival, and like the *Aud* before her, the U-19 failed to raise any response to its signals ashore; nor could it make any contact with the *Aud*. Eventually, the U-boat commander disembarked Casement and his party about 3 miles from land in an unpowered rubber dinghy, explaining that he could no longer risk losing his ship.[37] After some difficulty, they finally got ashore at Banna Strand at about 2 am[38], then needing to contact the Volunteers at Tralee. Casement was too weak following the journey to embark on a hike, so took cover at a spot called "McKenna's Fort", an old "rath" or earthen stronghold, while Monteith and Bailey made their way on foot to Tralee. On arriving there at about 8 am, they established their credentials by referring to "Mr Rice", Casement's agreed code name,[39] but were met with a clear lack of interest or urgency on the part of Austin Stack, the local commander of the Volunteers.

After some delay, Stack eventually organised a car to go out and look for Casement, but neither Monteith nor Bailey were able to provide proper directions, leaving them all driving round for a number of hours, suffering a puncture and being stopped by the police in the process.[40] By 1.30 pm, however, it was all too late anyway, as Casement had by then been arrested, following a tip-off by local inhabitants who had seen him and his party come ashore in the early hours. He was confined later in the day at the police barracks in Tralee. Meanwhile, having failed to find Casement, Stack arranged for Bailey to be put up overnight in an isolated farmhouse. One of Stack's men then visited him the following morning and directed him to nearby Ballyheigue Castle, where he was arrested while waiting as instructed. Monteith, meanwhile, had escaped completely, emerging in the United States some months later.

While being held in the barracks at Tralee, Casement was able to enlist the help of two people. At 6 pm on Good Friday, the police asked a local doctor – Michael Shanahan – to visit a prisoner who needed medical attention. While being examined in private, Casement told Shanahan who he was and that he wanted to get out – half a dozen men with revolvers could easily walk in and rescue him. As a supporter of the cause, Shanahan said he would do what he could and went to see the local Volunteers, who refused to help. They refused to accept that the prisoner was Casement (despite Stack's involvement in trying to find Casement earlier in the day), claiming that he was simply a Norwegian sailor. The second person Casement called on was a Father Ryan, the local parish priest. Casement had asked to see a priest, claiming that he was in need of spiritual guidance. The priest arrived at about 9 pm and, again speaking in private, Casement asked the priest to go to the Volunteers and, "Tell them I am a prisoner and that the rebellion will be a dismal failure, as the help they expect will not arrive". This time, however, according to Father Ryan, "He asked me to conceal his identity as well as his object in coming, until he should have left Tralee, lest any attempt should be made to rescue him. On the other hand, he was very anxious that I should spread the news broadcast after he had left".[41] Although Father Ryan gave this message to Stack, who arranged for it to be passed on to the organisers of the rising in Dublin, they not unsurprisingly ignored it.[42] Stack was to be criticised subsequently in many quarters for not attempting to rescue Casement, but his reasoning seems to have been that he had been given strict orders by the organisers that, to avoid alerting the British of impending action, "no shot should be fired until the agreed date for the rising".[43] In any event, later the same evening Stack and his deputy, Con Collins, were arrested. Stack was subsequently charged with conspiring to bring about a rebellion and trying to assist Monteith and Bailey to import arms for use in the rising. He was sentenced to death, subsequently commuted to life imprisonment, and released following a general amnesty in 1917.

A number of sources also claim that Casement somehow managed to get a message to Eoin MacNeill, Chief of Staff of the Volunteers, resulting in his well-known decision to cancel the Volunteer exercises arranged for Easter Sunday, which in turn resulted in the rising being postponed until Easter Monday and confined to the Dublin area only. Some of these sources refer simply to a "message", while Devoy goes further and refers to an actual letter. After recording the refusal of the commander of the U-19 to put Casement ashore at Galway, Devoy writes –

> *His letter to Eoin MacNeill was despatched promptly to Dublin and MacNeill's action on it came near to making the Insurrection an utter impossibility. The contents of that communication have never been published, but there is no doubt about their general purport. Casement impugned the good faith of the Germans, and asked that the Rising be postponed.*[44]

He then goes on to say that Casement's letter reached MacNeill on Easter Saturday, following receipt of which he despatched people to cancel the following day's manoeuvres. Devoy makes no previous reference to a letter, nor does he give details of how it was actually sent. But even if it existed, it seems unlikely that it would have been pivotal in determining MacNeill's actions. Like Casement, MacNeill had been kept in the dark about the plans for the rising. At a meeting called by MacNeill in February, agreement had been reached that there should be no insurrection unless an attempt were made to disarm the Volunteers. In early April, he agreed to manoeuvres being called for Easter Sunday but was not made aware by the Military Council that the plan was for these to form the basis of an insurrection. Then on Tuesday in Holy Week, the organisers of the rising deceived him yet again by producing a fake secret Dublin Castle document calling for the disarming of the Volunteers, resulting in MacNeill issuing a general order the following day telling all Volunteers to prepare for resistance. But the very next day, Maundy Thursday, he discovered that some Volunteers had received orders which could only relate to an impending insurrection. When challenged, Patrick Pearse, one of its organisers, finally admitted that a rising was to take place, in response to which MacNeill issued orders forbidding the Volunteers to take part in any offensive action. But his position was to change yet again the following day, Good Friday, when Pearse and others called on him to say that a German ship carrying arms was due to arrive on Sunday, in response to which MacNeill said he would not interfere. Ironically, that position was temporarily sealed the following day when the press reported that Casement had been arrested. MacNeill was to write later that this was decisive and that he agreed to take part in the rising because, "we were entitled to protect ourselves".[45] Thus, Casement's contribution in this narrative was directly opposite to that which he intended. It was not, of course, the end of the story. That came the same evening when the full account of the Military Council's duplicity towards MacNeill came out – including that over the false secret Castle Document – and he and Pearse parted company. MacNeill then issued his famous order cancelling all manoeuvres for Sunday, resulting in the rising being postponed until Easter Monday and effectively limited to Dublin.

Following his night at the Tralee police barracks, Casement was sent the following day to London, travelling overnight and arriving at Euston early on the morning of Easter Sunday, 23 April.

EIGHT
TRIAL, RETRIBUTION AND LEGACY

What I say I must act on. Some Irishmen are afraid to act, but I was not afraid to commit high treason.
    Casement at his interview on arrival at Scotland Yard

The English mob and vast majority of the people would like to see me hanged and want it badly. The British Government dare not hang me. (They don't want to either – as individuals I think.) But they simply dare not.
    Letter to Gavan Duffy from Brixton Prison, 14 June 1916

Old John Brown's body troubled the slave-owners all the more when they had nailed his coffin down.
    From a plea for Casement's reprieve by Miss Agnes Young,
                                                    Strathbally

On his arrival in London, Casement was met by police officers who took him immediately to Scotland Yard, where he was interviewed at 10 am. The interview was conducted by Basil Thomson, Assistant Commissioner of the Metropolitan Police, along with Captain Reginald Hall, Chief of Naval Intelligence, and others.[1] When asked his name, he replied that he would first like to see a friend who would be present at the interview and who would be someone Thomson would approve of. This turned out to be Sir William Tyrell, Private Secretary to Sir Edward Grey, who Casement had known during his consular days. That Casement should think that Tyrell would be prepared to accept his designation as a friend after all his activities in Germany, especially his letter to Sir Edward Grey about the *Findlay Affair*, and that Thomson would be impressed by this, demonstrates yet again how far he had become divorced from reality. When his request was refused and he was asked his name for the second time, he replied oddly, 'Officially, I am Sir Roger Casement.' He was then shown various items belonging to him that had been brought together following his landing – a sleeping car ticket from Berlin to Wilhelmshaven; scraps of a military code he had attempted to destroy following his initial arrest; and scraps of a personal diary which, in a crude personal code, recorded details of his journey to Ireland on the U-19 and U-20. While refusing to enter into a detailed conversation about these items, Casement acknowledged that they were his. The interview then went on to cover one of the many articles Casement had written criticising Britain's role in the war, causing him to note, "I have never concealed my opinions regarding the righteousness of England's war with Germany". But then he went further –

> *What I say I must act on. Some Irishmen are afraid to act, but I was not afraid to commit high treason.*

And –

> *I have done nothing treacherous to my country. I have committed perhaps many follies in endeavouring to help my country according to what I thought was best, and in this last act of mine in going back to Ireland I came with my eyes wide open, knowing exactly what I was going to do, knowing that you were bound to catch me.*

As the interview continued, he was asked whether he had ever received any money from the German Government, which he denied. As to his present attitude towards Germany, Casement drew a distinction between the German Government's early support for the Irish cause, where they genuinely believed that a rising might be successful, and their present attitude where, "they only wished to create a military diversion and cause bloodshed as an embarrassment to the British Government". Again, he reverted to the question of treason –

> *I never wanted to hurt your country as England but to help Ireland. I am a rebel. I committed high treason and I am prepared to take the consequences…*

There then came the question of the Irish Brigade, when Casement strongly refuted the claim that he had offered money to prisoners to "seduce them from their duty". He said he had made clear to the men that there would be no pay and what they were being offered was the opportunity to fight for Ireland. He had made clear that, "If they are going to commit high treason, they must do it with their eyes open".

As the end of the first day of his interview approached, Casement was asked, and refused, to give the names of the Nationalist leaders associated with him in Ireland. He had stuck steadfastly all day to the line that he was not prepared to betray his own countryman, remarking oddly at one stage, 'I am in terrible difficulties. I know more than you think I know.' He again asked to see Sir William Tyrell, who would act as a character witness to confirm that he would under no circumstances hurt any Irishman, a request that was flatly refused. In closing the session, Thomson told Casement that he would probably be charged with high treason, to which he simply responded, 'I hope so.'

The interview[2] resumed the following morning, Easter Monday, 24 April, after Casement had spent the night at Brixton Prison. Discussion now focused on the German arms shipment and the part he had played in it. He said openly that he had not travelled on the *Aud* because he wanted to arrive earlier than the ship so that he could warn the rebels that they had no chance of success. That had been prevented (he said and undoubtedly believed) by the delay caused by the breakdown of the U-20. He knew about the *Aud's* cargo and rehearsed in detail the arguments he had had with the German authorities about the whole affair, starting with the fact that it was Monteith who told him about the proposal for a rising, which had come to him "like a thunderclap". If there was to be any fighting in Ireland, he had decided that he must be there. But the German authorities had let him down by not providing any people to join in, and he had told them that he was not prepared to take the Irish Brigade with him because of the danger that that would put them in. Monteith had insisted on coming with him and it was he who had also wanted to bring Bailey. He was asked about the rebel leaders, to which he replied, 'I do not know the people's names concerned in this movement. I was not a member of any secret body at all. I was a member of the governing body of the Volunteers – an open organisation – and, although my intention was to get as many arms into Ireland as I could and to arm these men, I had no ulterior aim of any kind.' Late in the day – after the rising had started – Casement was recalled to interview to respond to reports that there was now a second arms ship on the way, which he denied. When the interview resumed on the third and final day, 25 April, Casement denied again that there was any prospect of a second ship coming behind the *Aud* – 'There is not, on my word of honour. None would come unless I telegraphed.' As the discussion widened out, Casement noted of the Germans – 'They could not understand me. They called me a dreamer.' And of the British Government – 'The Home Rule Bill is a lie. The Government never meant it to come off and they put it on the Statute Book solely to trap Ireland into arms.'

Even while Casement was being interviewed, the world at large was starting to put together its own version of events. On 25 April, *The Times* reported notification from the Admiralty that between the afternoon of 20 April and the afternoon of 21 April, an attempt had been made by a German auxiliary, in conjunction with a submarine, to land arms. As part of this, Casement had been taken prisoner along with others. The report went on to provide a brief account of Casement's activities in Germany, starting with the declaration he had secured from the German Government in support of an independent Ireland, on to views he had expressed in his pamphlet, *The Crime against Ireland and How the War may right it*, and then on to the accusations he had made about the *Findlay Affair* and his accusation that the Ambassador had offered money for someone to "knock him on the head".[3] The press generally concluded from all the evidence (understandably but falsely) that the whole project had been masterminded by Germany to further its own ends, was led by Casement and carried out by Sinn Féin. As *The Times* put it in a further article on 29 April, Ireland was quite simply being used as a "blackthorn" (cudgel) against the British – "It is quite clear that this modern Wolfe Tone, Roger Casement, was sent to Ireland in a German ship and that the revolt was planned by German brains". The objective, according to the newspaper, was to pin down British troops.[4] This is perhaps an echo of an earlier article in *The Times* of 17 April (while Casement was in the process of crossing to Ireland by submarine) which attributed to him the following quote –

> *The fact that England has not succeeded in extending compulsory recruiting to Ireland, and the admission that Ireland is exempt*

from doing military service for Great Britain or the British Empire, are the best justification for my visit to Germany.[5]

The Times reported that elsewhere there had been some interest in the affair in South Africa, where Casement was well known, with general opinion being that the British Government needed to take a firmer hand.[6] In Germany, there was, according to *The Times*, a "studied indifference", with newspapers supplying their readers with only a few "characteristic German summaries" of Irish history. The *Münchner Zeitung* reported the arrest of Austin Stack and "a man named Collins" for conspiring to land enemy arms in Ireland, while three days later, on 1 May, *The Times* reported comments from the *Hamburger Fremdenblatt* –

This, then, is the tragic fate of the bold Irish leader Sir Roger Casement, who tried to assist the liberation of his Fatherland from the century-long oppression by brutal English rule. He has fallen into the hands of his mortal enemies. It seems that he is an example of the fundamental characteristic traditionally attributed to the Irish people – boldness combined with a lack of prudence. For Casement should have been the last to venture into a war zone which made his capture by the English not impossible.[7]

American press coverage was also low-key. *The Times* reported from New York on 29 April that *Clan na Gael* had had information about Casement's capture twenty-four hours before the event, indicating that there must be communication channels between the US and Irish leaders,[8] and on 3 May that Irish loyalty had been tried and proved, quoting from the New York World –

If the British Government had staged a demonstration to prove that the great body of the Irish are pro-British so far as this war is concerned it could hardly have done so much for itself as the Germans have done for it. An Irish revolt made in Ireland can always command sympathy, whatever the issue. An Irish revolt made in Germany is another matter, especially an Irish revolt designed to encourage the Germans in the business of killing Irishmen who are fighting in the British Army to help Belgium and France, two countries with which the Irishman instinctively sympathises.

The article then continued with remarkably prescient advice which, had it only been heeded, would undoubtedly have changed the subsequent course of Irish history –

In the circumstances the British can afford to deal leniently with the misguided authors of this farce-tragedy. They have furnished the most convincing kind of proof that the Irish are not pro-German and that the Irish people still deserve as well at the hands of the British Government as they did the day the Home Rule Bill became the law of the realm. Instead of wrecking British prestige the Sinn Fein rebellion has strengthened British prestige, and Sir Roger Casement has managed to do for Great Britain what Great Britain has been unable to do for itself.[9]

The Government had a choice about how to deal with Casement. There was the option of a court martial, which could be quickly carried out with the minimum of public fuss or, like Arthur Lynch before him, a civil trial for high treason, completely open for all the world to see. For reasons that are unclear – but perhaps simply to allow for a court martial, which at that stage had not been ruled out – Thomson arranged for Casement to be transferred to the Tower of London and placed in military custody. Two days later, however, on 27 April, the Cabinet considered the position in Ireland in some detail, and out of concern that the rising might spread outside Dublin, decided to declare martial law over the whole of Ireland and to send General Sir John Maxwell there immediately to take charge. Asquith's report of the meeting went on to say that, "It was agreed that if civil proceedings could be resorted to and carried through as swiftly as those by Court Martial in the case of R Casement that course should be adopted".[10] No reason for this preference was given, and the caveat was odd since the respective procedures meant that a civil trial would inevitably take longer than a court martial. A civil charge of high treason (under a statute dating back to Edward III) involved three stages – a preliminary investigation, the presentation of a bill of indictment to a grand jury, and a trial at the Bar. *The Times* commented that many were concerned that at a time of war, "the nation should be burdened by the ancient inheritance of such an elaborate and dilatory procedure", and that unless the prisoner was having difficulty in getting together a defence, there was nothing to justify proceedings which would last for months. It went on to note how rarely the ancient statute had been used and its limited value – the last three cases having been against the "Young Irelander" William Smith O'Brien in 1848, where the death sentence had been commuted to transportation, against Arthur Lynch who had been pardoned, and against Nicholaus Ahlers, the German Consul at Sunderland in 1914. Originally German, Ahlers had become a naturalised British subject who, at the outbreak of war, had organised and assisted the return to Germany of a number of German nationals, claiming that he didn't know that war had broken out. He had been sentenced to death but the sentence had been quashed on appeal.[11] Despite the caveat at its meeting on 27 April, there is no evidence that the Cabinet considered the question of a civil trial versus a court martial again, though Sir F E Smith, the Attorney General, is on record as being "absolutely resolved" on a jury trial.[12] It is possible that the Government as a whole simply became more attracted to the benefits of satisfying public opinion, and possibly opinion in other States, by this method.

The preliminary hearing into the charges was fixed for Bow Street Police Court on 15 May. As the case had now become a civil matter, Casement was transferred back into custody at Brixton Prison rather than the Tower of London. The arrangements for his defence had quickly been taken in hand by his first cousins and nearest relatives in England, Gertrude and Elizabeth Bannister. They had contacted Alice Stopford Green, who suggested as his solicitor George Gavan Duffy, son of Sir Charles Gavan Duffy, the former Young Irelander. Duffy had offices in London at Gray's Inn and he and Casement knew each other. (The strength of feeling against Casement in England was so strong that the partners in Duffy's legal practice refused to continue working with him if he represented Casement, resulting in the partnership being dissolved.) Artemus Jones was appointed Casement's lead counsel, assisted by Professor J H Morgan, Professor of Constitutional Law at London University and Reader in Constitutional Law at the Inns of Court, who knew Casement from before the war. Sitting alongside Casement in court was Daniel Julian Bailey, it having been decided to charge them jointly. (Otherwise, according to the Attorney General, "the army would have been dissatisfied".)[13] *The Times* noted in reporting the first day that Casement looked more gaunt and thin than ever and appeared restless and ill at ease in both body and mind.[14] The charge before the court was that between 1 November 1914 and 21 April 1916, Casement and Bailey –

> ...*unlawfully, maliciously, and traitorously did commit high treason within and without the Realm of England in contempt of our Sovereign Lord the King and his laws, to the evil example of all others in the like case offending contrary to the duty and allegiance of them to our Sovereign Lord the King and against the form of the statute in such case made and provided.*

The nub of the case, as presented in court by the Attorney General, was Casement's activities at Limburg, where he had told prisoners he was Sir Roger Casement, the organiser of the Irish Volunteers, and –

> …that he was forming an Irish Brigade, and he invited all Irish prisoners of war to join him. He pointed out with emphasis that, in his opinion, everything was to be gained for Ireland by Germany winning the war, and that the Irish soldiers who were listening to his address had the best opportunity they had ever had of striking a blow for Ireland.

The Attorney General continued by stating that the plan had been to land the Irish Brigade in Ireland, in order to defend it against England. One of the prisoners at Limburg was Bailey.[15] The Attorney General then read out a statement given by Bailey while in police custody in Ireland on 23 April. In this, Bailey gave details of how he had joined the Irish Brigade at Limburg and had been made sergeant; of his journey to Ireland; and of the circumstances leading to his subsequent arrest. In the statement, Bailey distanced himself from any detailed knowledge of or participation in the operation in which he was involved. He claimed that it was only when the U-19 came round Shetland to the west coast of Ireland that he knew where he was going, and that it was only when the submarine got near Tralee that he gathered that the journey was "in connection with the Volunteer movement". His statement concluded that while he was on the submarine, he heard details of the proposed arms landing and also that Dublin Castle was to be raided. Witnesses for the Crown started with six ex-prisoners of war who had been repatriated from Limburg under a prisoner of war exchange scheme, who testified as to Casement's activities there. There then followed civilians from County Kerry who had witnessed the activities surrounding Casement's landing, and finally police witnesses from the Royal Irish Constabulary involved in the arrests and detention of both Casement and Bailey. The last of those to appear was the police sergeant who had arrested Bailey and who gave evidence that during interview, Bailey had offered information in exchange for protection and a deal as to punishment. At the end of the hearing on 17 May, both prisoners were formally charged and committed for trial.[16] On 25 May, after deliberating for an hour on an address given by the Lord Chief Justice, the twenty-three members of the Grand Jury of Middlesex and London agreed to their indictment on a charge of high treason, "by adhering to the King's enemies elsewhere than in the King's realm, to wit, in the empire of Germany, contrary to the Treason Act, 1351 (25 Edw III. Statute 5, Cap 2.)" The trial was set to start on 26 June at the Royal Courts of Justice. It would in the event last for four days, concluding on 29 June.

For the trial, Casement needed a lead counsel of sufficient stature to face Sir F E Smith for the Crown. This was troublesome because of a reluctance by those approached to act for the defence. A solution was found in the guise of Gavan Duffy's brother-in-law, Serjeant A M Sullivan, KC, of the Irish Bar, who said he would reluctantly take on the case, "provided I was handsomely paid", noting that the case would certainly run to three days, "on which basis I would want 150 guineas".[17] There then came the question of the defence, on which Casement had strong views. He had been particularly stung by the play made by the Attorney General at Bow Street on the fact that Casement had originally been a loyal servant of the Crown, and who had read out Casement's letter to Sir Edward Grey accepting his knighthood, describing it as fulsome. To the average onlooker, this might be regarded as a simple statement of fact, of no practical significance in relation to subsequent events. But his characteristic egocentricity led Casement to see this as a grave slight, impugning his integrity. As he noted in correspondence with Gavan Duffy, "the thing that troubles me is that I *ever* was a British official", and that he had desired to get out of the service "years" before the war. He claimed that his letter to Grey had been perfunctory; his real views were set out in the, "curt, rude letter I wrote Lord Lansdowne in June, 1905, when I was made a CMG and in my positive refusal to be invested by King Edward; and he had not been consulted about the knighthood and once it had been announced, "it was impossible, without giving *great offence* to King, Grey, the public, etc., etc., to refuse the honour thrust unsolicited at me. Had I done so, I should have been forced to resign my post also…"[18] As to the main line of his defence, again characteristically, Casement decided that he should himself admit full responsibility for inspiring the actions that had taken place, in relation to both the Rising and the actions of the German Government. There had been no German plot – the idea for the Rising had come from Irishmen themselves; it was a Sinn Féin rebellion. The German Government had only done what he had asked them to do. He had gone to Germany, "only to get guns and such help as was possible to allow of Irishmen at home fighting, instead of talking". Bizarrely, he then continued –

> *As it ended was probably the best. Had I got to Dublin, things might have been far worse, the rising more widespread, the attendant loss of life and inevitable failure more disastrous. Since the "blame" in the beginning was mine, the blame in the end was surely mine, and I shall admit of no attempt to put blame on the German Government… but I shall seek to establish the fact that it was my doing from first to last, and that it was I who "used" Germany and tried to drag her in a question that she knew nothing of and would have kept clear from.*
>
> *I succeeded in that. I did drag her in. The Treaty of 23–29 December, 1914, is an Act, a deed, something that forever must remain in the pages of History. I have committed Germany for all time to an Irish policy and to pronouncement in favour of Irish independence that, in all the centuries before, no other Power ever gave forth to any Irishman.*[19]

This was really no defence at all. Not only did Casement not deny any of the accusations against him but his "defence" went further in claiming responsibility for actions that had not been his. That approach found no favour with Serjeant Sullivan, who was looking to go to the other extreme. Sullivan, surprisingly, favoured the very same strategy adopted unsuccessfully in the case of Arthur Lynch in 1903, that is to say to get the indictment quashed on the grounds that the acts Casement was being accused of took place outside the realm and therefore did not constitute treason under the Edward III statute. If such a defence succeeded, no detailed rebuttals of the evidence would be needed. But Casement did not agree, arguing that not only did this approach seem "dishonourable", it would also deny him the opportunity to present his case to a wider audience. He concluded that the only course would be for him to conduct his own defence, writing to Duffy, "I owe it to Ireland, to the Irish in the USA, who so loyally helped, and to Germany, and even to my own wretched self to adopt the only course and conduct my case myself".[20] Both Duffy's and Casement's friends were horrified. Alice Stopford Green is alleged to have responded that Casement, "was desperately ill; that he was quite incapable of handling a court full of lawyers; the most he could do was the final speech after the verdict".[21] He was finally persuaded. The Sullivan defence would proceed, and if found guilty Casement would be able to make a speech from the dock. He would also have the opportunity to make an unsworn statement to the court on which he could not be cross-examined. The trial proceeded accordingly.

The Attorney General again opened with a statement on Casement's background and the fulsome letter he had written to Grey on being awarded his knighthood, noting that he had continued to draw his pension from the Foreign Office until October 1914 while he was on his way to Norway. He had then gone to Germany to seduce prisoners of war away from their allegiance. Those prisoners who refused to join had been punished by being placed on a lower ration scale. (This specific claim seems unlikely to have been true in the absence of any corroborating evidence.) Finally, Casement had arrived off the Irish coast. His arrival was obviously connected with the activities of the *Aud*. The Crown then produced the ex-prisoner witnesses from Limburg who, with one exception, testified that Casement had told them that they were not going to be asked to fight for Germany, only for Ireland. The exception was Private John Neil of the 2nd Battalion, 18th Royal Irish, who had not appeared at Bow Street. Unlike the others, Neill testified that in his speeches at Limburg, Casement had stated that when the Irish Brigade was formed it would first go to help the Turks against the Russians; then it would help the Germans against the British; and only then would they go and shed blood for Ireland.[22] Following the ex-prisoners, Irish civilian witnesses then testified as to Casement's landing at Banna Strand, with testimony from a member of the local Irish constabulary about events thereafter. This completed the case for the prosecution. Sullivan then rose to move that the indictment against Casement should be quashed. He noted that the 1351 Act under which Casement had been charged defined treason as, "levying war against the King or being adherent to the King's enemies in his realm giving them aid and comfort in the realm or elsewhere". This meant, Sullivan contended (as had Lynch's counsel many years before), that treasonable acts as defined by the statute must be carried out within the King's realm, whereas the charges against Casement were for acts committed outside the realm, i.e., in Germany. The charges were therefore bad in law.[23] After lengthy legal argument, the Justices rejected this view. At this point, Casement made his unsworn statement to the court, starting with the question of his knighthood and his Foreign Office pension – 'The pension I had earned by services rendered, and it was assigned to me by law. The knighthood it was not in my power to refuse.' He then refuted four "misstatements" that had been made in court. First, he had never advised Irishmen to fight with Turks against Russians, nor to fight with Germans on the Western Front. Secondly, he had never asked an Irishman to fight for Germany – 'I have always claimed that he has no right to fight for any land but Ireland.' Thirdly, he rejected the claim that prisoners of war at Limburg who refused to join the Irish Brigade were given starvation rations as a result. Lastly, he refuted any suggestion that he had ever received any money from Germany for his activities. Concluding his statement, Casement exhibited yet again the store he set by being regarded as a gentleman and a man of integrity, while at the same time being seemingly oblivious to the enormity of the many actions which he himself had described as high treason –

> *I trust, gentlemen of the jury, I have made that statement clearly and emphatically enough for all men, even my most bitter enemies, to comprehend that a man, who in the newspapers is said to be just another Irish traitor, may be a gentleman.*[24]

Serjeant Sullivan then commenced the defence's final address to the jury, giving rise to one of the most famous incidents in courtroom history. Sullivan started by appealing to the English sense of fair play, noting that Casement was not a fellow-countryman of the jurors, coming from a country that spoke differently and thought differently. He went on to argue that Casement had not intended treachery to the King. Here, Sullivan had to deal with the evidence given by Private Neill. It seems, surprisingly, that the prosecution had no knowledge of Casement's "Treaty" and its provisions to allow the Irish Brigade to fight with the Turks in Egypt. Casement admitted to Duffy that he had read out the provisions at a meeting with prisoners in April 1915,[25] and it seems likely that Neill's evidence was simply a garbled version of what he had heard there. But the point needed to be dealt with, as the main plank of Casement's justification for his actions had always been that he had never taken sides with the Germans against the British: the sole purpose of the Brigade had been to fight for Irish freedom. So Sullivan simply pointed out that no one except Private Neill, whom Sullivan regarded as untrustworthy, had heard Casement ask any Irishman at Limburg to fight for Germany – "Admittedly Casement recruited the Irish Brigade, but on the solemn undertaking that under no circumstances were they to be asked to fight for any country except their own". Casement was not a German and had no interest in what they might achieve through his actions. He then developed this into a new line of defence, arguing that Casement had intended to use the Irish Brigade in connection with the Irish Volunteer movement. The Ulster Volunteers had armed themselves, with German assistance, in order to resist Home Rule and thus the will of the King and the House of Commons. If the Government could not protect the constitutional rights of the majority against such resistance, citizens were entitled to take up arms to defend those rights themselves. This was the explanation for everything Casement had said and done. Sullivan was stopped by the judges from proceeding with this line of argument because it covered matters which were uncorroborated and which had not been admitted in evidence before the court. Sullivan duly apologised but lost his way in taking his argument forward, finally saying under obvious stress and before sitting down with his head in his hands, 'My Lords, I regret to say I have completely broken down.' The Court was immediately adjourned until the following day, when Artemus Jones reported that Sullivan had received medical advice that he should not continue. Artemus Jones accordingly concluded Sullivan's closing speech, following the line that Casement had gone to Germany, not to side with Germany but to form an Irish Brigade to fight the objectives of the Ulster Volunteers, as the elected British had chosen not to do that.

In his closing speech, the Attorney General dealt with the defence's arguments in crushing terms. On the argument that Casement had acted to protect Irish constitutional freedom in the face of the failure of the Government to control the Ulster Volunteers, he noted that had the acts taken place at the time when the Ulster Volunteers were fighting against Home Rule, that defence might have been relevant. But those controversies had been superseded by the advent of war, with no honest citizen now, "thinking or talking of whether or not there might at some future day be resistance to the Home Rule Bill"; that moment had passed. He went on to say that the question of why Casement had gone to Germany had still not been properly answered. The defence had argued that he had gone to recruit men to support the Irish Volunteers against the north of Ireland after the war. Had that really been the case, it would surely have made more sense for him to have stayed in Ireland and recruit men there. As it was, he had made no mention of this in his appeals and speeches to the prisoners at Limburg; it was all an afterthought.

The Lord Chief Justice's summing-up for the jury then included the following crucial direction, which distilled everything to a single basic question –

> ... *if he [Casement] knew or believed that the Irish Brigade was to be sent to Ireland during the war with a view to securing the national freedom of Ireland, that is, to engage in a civil war which would necessarily weaken and embarrass this country, then he was contriving and intending to assist the enemy.*

It took the jury just under an hour to find Casement guilty. Casement then joined the long line of Irish nationalists who had made famous speeches from the dock. Casement's version was typically verbose, sentimental and at times mawkish, replete with oratorical flourishes and often repetitive. It was pre-prepared and lasted for about half an hour. It was addressed to his fellow-countrymen rather than the court itself. Casement first of all argued at length that an English court had no right to try him, and he did not therefore accept its verdict. He then moved on to the argument that had been advanced by the defence about the Ulster Volunteers and the Irish Volunteers. The aim of the Irish Volunteers, he said, had been to win over the Ulstermen to the cause of a united Ireland. The fault lay with English politicians for inflaming passions against Home Rule, but as the Ulster Volunteers had armed themselves, it was necessary for the Irish Volunteers to do the same, so he had gone to America for help. When the war broke out and Irishmen were being told that it was their first duty to join the British Army, he considered he should do everything he could to keep Irishmen at home to safeguard their national existence. He concluded by saying that he had a natural right to be tried by his own countrymen rather than a foreign court in England.

The Times reported Casement's speech in generous terms, noting that he had at first been nervous but had soon become more confident –

> *When he was asked if he had anything to say on why he should not die, he leant across the dock rail and read a statement, which though mainly concerned with abstract doctrines, was listened to with great attention. He challenged the jurisdiction of the English court to try an Irishman, and he referred with considerable grace of diction to those political ideals which had already received a place in the oratory of his counsel. In all, he seemed to seek remembrance among that band of dreamers and patriot threnodists who have figured so conspicuously in the recent misfortunes of Ireland.*[26]

Other views on the speech have subsequently been varied, with some regarding it as among the best of its kind. Others have been less enthusiastic or muted in their comments. It is reproduced in full below –

My Lord Chief Justice, as I wish to reach a much wider audience than I see before me here, I intend to read all that I propose to say. What I read now is something I wrote twenty days ago. I may say at once, my Lord, that I protest against the jurisdiction in my case on this charge, and the argument that I am now going to read is addressed not to this Court, but to my own countrymen. There is an objection, possibly not good in law, but surely good on moral grounds, against the application to me here of this old English statute, 565 years old, that seeks to deprive an Irishman today of life and honour, not for "adhering to the King's enemies", but for adhering to his own people.

When this statute was passed in 1351, what was the state of men's minds on the question of a far higher allegiance – that of a man to God and His Kingdom? The law of that day did not permit a man to forsake his Church or deny his God save with his life. The "heretic", then, had the same doom as the "traitor". Today a man may forswear God and His heavenly kingdom without fear or penalty – all earlier statutes having gone the way of Nero's edicts against the Christians; but that Constitutional phantom, "The King", can still dig up from the dungeons and torture-chambers of the Dark Ages a law that takes a man's life and limb for an exercise of conscience.

If true religion rests on love, it is equally true that loyalty rests on love. The law that I am charged under has no parentage in love, and claims the allegiance of today on the ignorance and blindness of the past. I am being tried, in truth, not by my peers of the live present, but by the fears of the dead past; not by the civilisation of the twentieth century, but by the brutality of the fourteenth; not even by a statute framed in the language of the land that tries me, but emitted in the language of an enemy land – so antiquated is the law that must be sought today to slay an Irishman, whose offence is that he puts Ireland first! Loyalty is a sentiment, not a law. It rests on love, not restraint. The government of Ireland by

England rests on restraint, and not on law; and since it demands no love, it can evoke no loyalty.

But this statute is more absurd even than it is antiquated; and if it be potent to hang even one Irishman, it is still more potent to gibbet all Englishmen. Edward III was king, not only of the realm of England, but also of the realm of France, and he was not king of Ireland. Yet his dead hand today may pull the noose around the Irishman's neck, whose sovereign he was not, but it can strain no strand around the Frenchman's throat, whose sovereign he was. For centuries the successors of Edward III claimed to be kings of France, and quartered the arms of France on their royal shield down to the Union with Ireland on January 1st, 1801. Throughout these hundreds of years, these "kings of France" were constantly at war with their realm of France and their French subjects, who should have gone from birth to death with an obvious fear of treason before their eyes. But did they? Did the "kings of France" resident here at Windsor or in the Tower of London hang, draw and quarter as a traitor every Frenchman for four hundred years who fell into their power with arms in his hands? On the contrary, they received embassies of these traitors, presents from these traitors, even knighthood itself at the hands of these traitors, feasted with them, tilted with them, fought with them – but did not assassinate them by law.

Judicial assassination today is reserved only for one race of the King's subjects – for Irishmen, for those who cannot forget their allegiance to the realm of Ireland. The kings of England as such had no rights in Ireland up to the time of Henry VIII, save such as rested on compact and mutual obligation entered into between them and certain princes, chiefs, and lords of Ireland. This form of legal right, such as it was, gave no King of England lawful power to impeach an Irishman for high treason under this statute of King Edward III of England until an Irish Act, known as Poyning's Law, the tenth of Henry VII, was passed in 1494 at

Drogheda by the Parliament of the Pale in Ireland and enacted as law in that part of Ireland. But if by Poyning's Law an Irishman of the Pale could be indicted for high treason under this act, he could be indicted only in one way, and before one tribunal – by the law of the Realm of Ireland and in Ireland. The very law of Poyning, which, I believe, applies this statute of Edward III to Ireland, enacted for the Irishman's defence "all those laws by which England claims her liberty".

And what is the fundamental charter of an Englishman's liberty? That he shall be tried by his peers. With all respect, I assert this court is to me, an Irishman, charged with this offence, a foreign court – this jury is for me, an Irishman, not a jury of my peers to try me on this vital issue, for it is patent to every man of conscience that I have a right, an indefeasible right, if tried at all, under this statute of high treason, to be tried in Ireland, before an Irish court and by an Irish jury. This court, this jury, the public opinion of this country, England, cannot but be prejudiced in varying degrees against me, most of all in time of war. I did not land in England. I landed in Ireland. It was to Ireland I came; to Ireland I wanted to come; and the last place I desired to land was in England.

But for the Attorney General of England there is only England; there is no Ireland; there is only the law of England, no right of Ireland; the liberty of Ireland and of an Irishman is to be judged by the power of England. Yet for me, the Irish outlaw, there is a land of Ireland, a right of Ireland, and a charter for all Irishmen to appeal to, in the last resort, a charter that even the very statutes of England itself cannot deprive us of – nay more, a charter that Englishmen themselves assert as their fundamental bond of law that connects the two kingdoms. This charge of high treason involves a moral responsibility, as the very terms of the indictment against myself recite, inasmuch as I committed the acts I am charged with to "the evil example of others in the like case".

What was the evil example I set to others in the like case, and who were these others? The "evil example" charged is that I asserted the right of my own country, and "the others" to whom I appealed to aid my endeavour were my own countrymen. The example was given, not to Englishmen, but to Irishmen, and the "like case" can never arise in England, but only in Ireland. To Englishmen I set no evil example, for I made no appeal to them. I asked no Englishman to help me. I asked Irishmen to fight for their rights. The "evil example" was only to other Irishmen, who might come after me and in "like case" seek to do as I did. How, then, since neither my example nor my appeal was addressed to Englishmen, can I rightfully be tried by them?

If I did wrong in making that appeal to Irishmen to join with me in an effort to fight for Ireland, it is by Irishmen, and by them alone, I can be rightfully judged. From this court and its jurisdiction I appeal to those I am alleged to have wronged and to those I am alleged to have injured by my "evil example" and claim that they alone are competent to decide my guilt or innocence. If they find me guilty, the statute may affix the penalty, but the statute does not override or annul my right to seek judgment at their hands.

This is so fundamental a right, so natural a right, so obvious a right, that it is clear that the Crown were aware of it when they brought me by force and by stealth from Ireland to this country. It was not I who landed in England, but the Crown who dragged me here, away from my own country to which I had returned with a price on my head, away from my own countrymen whose loyalty is not in doubt, and safe from the judgment of my peers whose judgment I do not shrink from. I admit no other judgment but theirs. I accept no verdict save at their hands.

I assert from this dock that I am being tried here, not because it is just, but because it is unjust. Place me before a jury of my own countrymen, be it Protestant or Catholic, Unionist or Nationalist,

Sinn Féineach or Orangemen, and I shall accept the verdict, and bow to the statute and all its penalties. But I shall accept no meaner finding against me than that of those whose loyalty I have endangered by my example and to whom alone I made appeal. If they adjudge me guilty, then guilty I am. It is not I who am afraid of their verdict – it is the Crown. If this is not so, why fear the test? I fear it not. I demand it as my right.

This is the condemnation of English rule, of English-made law, of English government in Ireland, that it dare not rest on the will of the Irish people, but exists in defiance of their will: that is a rule, derived not from right, but from conquest.

But conquest, my Lord, gives no title; and, if it exists over the body, it fails over the mind. It can exert no empire over men's reason and judgment and affections; and it is from this law of conquest without title to the reason, judgment, and affection of my own countrymen that I appeal. I would add that the generous expressions of sympathy extended to me from many quarters, particularly from America, have touched me very much. In that country, as in my own, I am sure my motives are understood, and not misjudged – for the achievement of their liberty has been an abiding inspiration to Irishmen, and to all men elsewhere, rightly struggling to be free in like cause.

My Lord Chief Justice, if I may continue, I am not called upon, I conceive, to say anything in answer to the inquiry your lordship has addressed to me why Sentence should not be passed upon me. Since I do not accept any verdict in this Court, I cannot, my lord, admit the fitness of the sentence that of necessity must follow it form this Court. I hope I shall be acquitted of presumption if I say that the Court I see before me is not this High Court of Justice of England, but a far greater, a far higher, a far older assemblage of justices – that of the people of Ireland I sought to serve – and them alone – I leave my judgment and my sentence in their hands.

Let me pass from myself and my own fate to a more pressing, as it is a far more urgent theme – not the fate of the individual Irishman who may have tried and failed, but the claims and the fate of the country that has not failed. Ireland has not failed. Ireland has outlived the failure of all her hopes – and she still hopes. Ireland has seen her sons – aye, and her daughters too! – suffer from generation to generation, always for the same cause, meeting always the same fate, and always at the hands of the same power. Still, always a fresh generation has passed on to withstand the same oppression. For if English authority be omnipotent – a power, as Mr Gladstone phrased it, that reaches to the very ends of the earth – Irish hope exceeds the dimensions of that power, excels its authority, and renews with each generation the claims of the last. The cause that begets this indomitable persistency, the faculty of preserving through centuries of misery the remembrance of lost liberty – this surely is the noblest cause ever man strove for, ever lived for, ever died for. If this be the cause I stand here today indicted for and convicted of sustaining, then I stand in a goodly company and a right noble succession.

My counsel has referred to the Ulster Volunteer movement, and I will not touch at length upon that ground save only to say this, that neither I nor any of the leaders of the Irish Volunteers who were founded in Dublin in November 1913, had any quarrel with the Ulster Volunteers as such, who were born a year earlier. Our movement was not directed against them, but against the men who misused and misdirected the courage, the sincerity and the local patriotism of the men of the north of Ireland. On the contrary, we welcomed the coming of the Ulster Volunteers, even while we deprecated the aims and intentions of those Englishmen who sought to pervert to an English party use – to the means and purposes of their own bid for place and power in England – the armed activities of simple Irishmen. We aimed at winning the Ulster Volunteers to the cause of a United Ireland. We aimed at uniting all Irishmen in a natural and national bond of cohesion based on mutual self-respect. Our hope was a natural one, and if left to ourselves, not hard to accomplish. If external influences of disintegration would but leave us alone, we were sure that Nature itself must bring us together. It was not we, the Irish Volunteers, who broke the law, but a British party. The Government had permitted the Ulster Volunteers to be armed by Englishmen, to threaten not merely an English party in its hold on office, but to threaten that party through the lives and blood of Irishmen.

The battle was to be fought in Ireland in order that the political "outs" of today should be the "ins" of tomorrow in Great Britain. A law designed for the benefit of Ireland was to be met, not on the floor of Parliament, where the fight had indeed been won, but on the field of battle much nearer home, where the armies would be composed of Irishmen slaying each other for some English party gain; and the British Navy would be the chartered "transports" that were to bring to our shores a numerous assemblage of military and ex-military experts in the congenial and profitable exercise of holding down subject populations abroad. Our choice lay in submitting to foreign lawlessness or resisting it, and we did not hesitate to choose. But while the law-breakers had armed their would-be agents openly, and had been permitted to arm them openly, we were met within a few days of founding our movement – that aimed at a United Ireland from within – by Government action from without, directed against our obtaining any arms at all.

The Manifesto of the Irish Volunteers, promulgated at a public meeting in Dublin, November 25th 1913, stated with certainty the aims of the organisation, as I have outlined them. If the aims set out in that manifesto were a threat to the unity of the British Empire, then so much the worse for the Empire. An Empire that can only be held together by one section of its governing population perpetually holding down and sowing dissension among a smaller but nonetheless governing section, must have some canker at its heart, some ruin at its root. The Government that permitted the arming of those whose leaders declared that Irish national unity was a thing that should be opposed by force of arms, within nine days of the issue of our manifesto of goodwill to Irishmen of every creed and class, took steps to nullify our efforts by prohibiting the import of arms into Ireland as if it had been a hostile and blockaded coast. And this Proclamation of the 4th December 1913, known as the Arms Proclamation, was itself based on an illegal interpretation of the law, as the Chief Secretary has now publicly confessed. The Proclamation was met by the loyalists of Great Britain with an act of still more lawless defiance – an act of widespread gun-running into Ulster, that was denounced by the Lord Chancellor of England as "grossly illegal and utterly unconstitutional".

How did the Irish Volunteers meet the incitements to civil war that were uttered by the party of law and order in England? I can answer for my own acts and speeches. While one English party was responsible for preaching a doctrine of hatred, designed to bring about civil war in Ireland, the other, and that the party in power, took no active steps to restrain a propaganda that found its advocates in the Army, Navy, and Privy Council – in the House of Parliament and in the State Church – a propaganda the methods of whose expression were so "grossly illegal and utterly unconstitutional" that even the Lord Chancellor of England could find only words and no repressive action to apply to them. Since lawlessness sat in high places in England and laughed at the law as at the custodians of the law, what wonder was it that Irishmen should refuse to accept the verbal protestations of an English Lord Chancellor as a sufficient safeguard for their lives and liberties? I know not how all my colleagues on the Volunteer Committee in Dublin reviewed the growing menace, but those with whom I was in closest cooperation redoubled, in face of these threats from without, our efforts to unite all Irishmen from within. Our appeals were made to Protestant and Unionist as much almost as to Catholic and Nationalist Irishmen. We hoped that, by the exhibition of affection and goodwill on our part toward our political opponents in Ireland, we should yet succeed in winning them from the side of an English party whose sole interest in our country lay in its oppression in the past, and in the present in its degradation to the mean and narrow needs of their political animosities.

It is true that they based their actions – so they averred – on "fears of the Empire" and on a very diffuse loyalty that took in all the people of the empire, save only the Irish. That blessed word empire that bears so paradoxical resemblance to charity! For if charity begins at home, empire begins in other men's homes, and both may cover a multitude of sins. I, for one, was determined that Ireland was much more to me than empire, and, if charity begins at home, so must loyalty. Since arms were so necessary to make our organisation a reality, and to give to the minds of Irishmen, menaced with the most outrageous threats, a sense of security, it was our bounden duty to get arms before all else. I decided, with this end in view, to go to America, with surely a better right to appeal to Irishmen there for help in an hour of great national trial, than those envoys of empire could assert for their weekend descents on Ireland, or their appeals to Germany.

If, as the right honourable gentleman, the present Attorney General, asserted in a speech at Manchester, Nationalists would neither fight for Home Rule nor pay for it, it was our duty to show him that we knew how to do both. Within a few weeks of my arrival in the United States, the fund that had been opened to secure arms for the Volunteers of Ireland amounted to many thousands of pounds. In every case the money subscribed, whether it came from the purse of a wealthy man, or from the still readier pocket of the poor man, was Irish gold.

Then came the war! – which, as Mr Birrell said, "upset all calculations". It upset mine no less than Mr Birrell's, and put an end to my peaceful effort in America. A constitutional movement in Ireland is never very far from a breach of the constitution, as the loyalists of Ulster have been so eager to show us. A constitution, to be maintained intact, must be the achievement and the pride of the people themselves, must rest on their own free will and on their own determination to maintain it, instead of being something resident in another land, whose chief representative is an armed force – armed not to protect the population, but to hold it down. We had seen the workings of "the Irish Constitution" in the refusal of the Army of Occupation at the Curragh to obey the orders of the Crown. And now that we were told the first duty of an Irishman was to enter the army, in return for a promissory note, payable after death – a scrap of paper that might or might not be redeemed – I felt, over there in America, that my first duty was to keep Irishmen at home in the only army that could safeguard our national existence. If small nationalities were to be the pawns in this game of embattled giants, I saw no reason why Ireland should shed her blood in any cause but her own, and, if that be treason beyond the seas, I am not ashamed to avow it, or to answer it here with my life. And when we had the doctrine of Unionist loyalty at last – "Mausers and Kaisers, and any king you like", and I have heard that at Hamburg, not far from Limburg on the Lahn – I felt that I needed no other than that these words conveyed, to go forth and do likewise.

The difference between us was that the Unionist champions chose a path which they felt would lead to the woolsack, while I went a road I knew must lead to the dock. The difference between us is that my "treason" was based on a ruthless sincerity that forced me to attempt in time and season to carry out in action what I said in words, whereas their treason lay in verbal incitements that they knew would never be made good in their bodies. And so I am prouder to stand here today, in the traitor's dock, to answer this impeachment, than to fill the place of my right honourable accusers.

We have been told, we have been asked to hope, that after this war Ireland will get Home Rule as a reward for the lifeblood shed in a cause which, whomever else its success may benefit, can surely not benefit Ireland. And what will Home Rule be in return for what its vague promise has taken, and still hopes to take away from Ireland? It is not necessary to climb the painful stairs of Irish history – the treadmill of a nation, whose labours are as vain for her own uplifting as the convict's exertions are for his redemption, to review the long list of British promises made only to be broken – of Irish hopes, raised only to be dashed to the ground. Home Rule, when it comes, if come it does, will find an Ireland drained of all that is vital to its very existence unless it be that unquenchable hope we build on the graves of the dead.

We are told that if Irishmen go by the thousand to die, not for Ireland, but for Flanders, for Belgium, for a patch of sand in the deserts of Mesopotamia, or a rocky trench on the heights of Gallipoli, they are winning self-government for Ireland. But if they dare to lay down their lives on their native soil, if they dare to dream even that freedom can be won only at home by men resolved to fight for it there, then they are traitors to their country, and their dream and their deaths are phases of a dishonourable phantasy.

But history is not so recorded in other lands. In Ireland alone, in this twentieth century, is loyalty held to be a crime. If loyalty be something less than love and more than law, then we have had enough of such loyalty for Ireland or Irishmen. If we are to be indicted as criminals, to be shot as murderers, to be imprisoned as convicts, because our offence is that we love Ireland more than we value our lives, then I do not know what virtue resides in any offer of self-government held out to brave men on such terms. Self-government is our right, a thing born in us at birth, a thing no more to be doled out to us, or withheld from us, by another people than the right to life itself – than the right to feel the sun, or smell the flowers, or to love our kind. It is only from the convict these things are withheld, for crime committed and proven, and Ireland, that has wronged no man, has injured no land, and has sought no dominion over others – Ireland is being treated today among the nations of the world as if she were a convicted criminal.

If it be treason to fight against such an unnatural fate as this, then I am proud to be a rebel, and shall cling to my "rebellion" with the last drop of my blood. If there be no right of rebellion against this state of things that no savage tribe would endure without resistance, then I am sure that it is better for men to fight and die without right than to live in such a state as this. Where all your rights have become only an accumulated wrong, where men must beg with bated breath for leave to subsist in their own land, to think their own thoughts, to sing their own songs, to gather the fruits of their own labours, and, even while they beg, to see things inexorably drawn from them – then, surely, it is a braver, a saner and truer thing to be a rebel, in act and in deed, against such circumstances as these, than to tamely accept it, as the natural lot of men.

My lord, I have done. Gentlemen of the jury, I wish to thank you for your verdict. I hope you will not take amiss what I said, or think that I made any imputation on your truthfulness or your integrity when I spoke and said that this was not a trial by my peers. I maintain that I have a natural right to be tried in that natural jurisdiction, Ireland, my own country, and I would put it to you, how would you feel in the converse case – if an Englishman had landed here in England and the Crown or the Government, for its own purposes, had conveyed him secretly from England to Ireland under a false name, committed him to prison under a false name, and brought him before a tribunal in Ireland under a statute which they knew involved a trial before an Irish jury? How would you feel, yourselves, as Englishmen, if that Englishman was to be submitted to trial by jury in a land inflamed against him and believing him to be a criminal, when his only crime was that he had cared for England more than Ireland?[27]

Following the speech, Casement was sentenced to be hanged and was removed to the condemned cell at Pentonville Prison. Daniel Julian Bailey then entered the dock and formally pleaded "Not Guilty", but in a surprise move, the Attorney General said that he would be offering no evidence against him. Sir Frederick Smith said that he had given "deep consideration" to the case and had noted that in his statement Bailey had affirmed that he was not, and never had been, a traitor to his country, or to the army, and the only reason he had joined the Irish Brigade was by subterfuge to return to his country and the army. It was "hard to penetrate the mind of another", but he had looked at all the evidence and also at Bailey's service record, which was "extremely good". In the circumstances, he had, "taken the responsibility of deciding that the Crown will not contest the defence which the prisoner would have put forward" and would offer no evidence.[28] Bailey was accordingly acquitted and in due course returned to the army. Perhaps the authorities had simply had their pound of flesh. To expose and punish a former high-ranking official was one thing, to subject a mere army private to the same treatment was quite another. It had been the army that wanted him brought to trial, but the scale and nature of Bailey's crimes compared to those of Casement were quite different, even if in law they both constituted high treason. The incongruity of them being sent to the scaffold side by side could hardly have enhanced the prestige of the Government. Perhaps this was at least a part of the Attorney General's consideration.

On the day following his trial, Casement was stripped of his knighthood. On 3 July, he lodged an appeal, with the date for the hearing being subsequently fixed for 17 July to allow for Sullivan's return to full health. The main ground for appeal again focused on the meaning of the 1351 Act. Put simply, the question was whether the words of the statute – "adherent to the King's enemies in his realm giving them aid and comfort in the realm and elsewhere" –

meant that such adherence had to take place in the realm, as argued by the defence, or whether, as argued by the Crown, the words, "giving them aid and comfort in the realm", simply explained the meaning of being adherent to, as in, "adherent to the King's enemies in his realm, giving them aid or comfort in his realm, or elsewhere". After lengthy argument, the Justices decided in favour of the Crown –

> ...*we think a very good reason is to be found in this, that the subjects of the King owe him allegiance, and the allegiance follows the person of the subject. He is the King's liege wherever he may be, and he may violate his allegiance in a foreign country just as well as he may violate it in this country.*[29]

The appeal was rejected, leaving an appeal to the House of Lords as the only remaining judicial avenue open to Casement. Such an appeal was, however, contingent on there being a point of law of national interest to be decided. The sole arbiter of this was the Attorney General, who decided against allowing an appeal.

*

There can have been few who seriously believed that Casement would escape a guilty verdict for high treason. Carrying out the sentence was, however, a different matter. While on a number of occasions Casement had almost boasted that he had committed high treason, he himself did not believe that the death penalty would actually be carried out. Among other things, he was no doubt influenced by the precedent set by the case of Arthur Lynch. Writing to Gavan Duffy on 14 June (at just about the time when Lynch was visiting Maud Gonne in Paris following MacBride's execution), he said –

I write these remarks today in Brixton Jail, in case I may have no chance after the trial which is now impending in a few days. It must result in a verdict of guilty and sentence of death...

The English mob and vast majority of the people would like to see me hanged and want it badly. The British Government dare not hang me. (They don't want to either – as individuals I think.) But they simply dare not.

They would willingly now bring back to life poor Sean MacDermot, Connolly, Pearse, Colbert (and the other victims of their military autocrats of Easter Week), and they are assuredly not going to add to the roll of victims me. They know quite well what the world would say of that, and what America would say of it.

No – they are not men enough to hang me – as I hope to tell the Lord Chief Justice... The sentence will be "commuted" and I shall become a convict for life – possibly some day to be "pardoned" or released on ticket of leave (like Michel Davitt) if I live. The life of a British convict to me is far more dreadful to contemplate than death...)[30]

If Casement was influenced by the case of Lynch, he had – as so often – misjudged things badly. Lynch had been tried and sentenced some three years after events that had taken place in a faraway country, and he had been tried at almost his own insistence. The Government had had little appetite for the trial and commuted his sentence almost immediately after it had been passed. Casement, on the other hand, had committed acts directly against England at the height of total war. He was right to acknowledge the great strength of public feeling in England against him. By the middle of 1916, fighting on the Western Front was at its most fierce so far. The Battle of Verdun, involving mainly the French, had been raging since February and was to last until the end of the year, while the Battle of the Somme, along nearly 20 miles of the British line, had started on 1 July and was to last until November. Even in Ireland there were many who would see Casement as siding directly with the "enemy" rather than as their attempted liberator. One of the first reports in *The Times* of events on the Somme singled out the Ulster Division for special mention –

> Ulstermen played a great part on the opening day of the battle, charging through a devastating fire and taking five lines of enemy trenches. The Ulster Volunteer Force, from which the Ulster Division was made, has, says one who witnessed its gallant work, won a name which equals any in history.[31]

As for the south, 570 members of the 16th (Irish) Division were killed in the week of the rising at Hulluch, near Loos, in gas attacks staged between 27 and 29 April. Those in Ireland with relatives in either division would hardly have been pressing for Casement's reprieve. Nor would his case have been helped by the news of the execution of Captain Charles Fryatt, commander of the steamer *Brussels*, reported in *The Times* under the heading, *A New German Atrocity*. Fryatt had been instructed by the German submarine U-33 in March 1915 to stop, in response to which he had turned and headed towards the submarine, causing it to crash dive. Following the subsequent capture of the SS *Brussels* on 25 June 1916, Fryatt had been court-martialled at Bruges Town Hall on 27 July and executed the same day.[32]

Petitions for Casement's reprieve were organised almost immediately. Some signed for the traditional reason of Christian forgiveness. Among these was Cardinal Logue, the Catholic Primate, who agreed to sign, "from motives of mercy and charity".[33] W B Yeats wrote to Asquith saying that to execute Casement would be evil. Sir Arthur Conan Doyle secured the signature of a number of authors and journalists to a petition arguing that Casement's actions had been brought about by the severe strain placed upon him while he was a consul and the effect of several tropical fevers. The petition also argued that he had been "slandered" by the Crown during his trial. Signatories here included Arnold Bennett, John Galsworthy and Jerome K Jerome. A notable name who refused to sign was E D Morel. The strength of feeling against Casement was also manifest in the case of a petition organised by Gertrude Bannister, which Alice Stopford Green sent to about twenty influential people who all refused to sign, causing her to note that, "The upper classes are intensively hostile... the war has formed all minds into a single groove".[34] In a letter published in the *Manchester Guardian* (rejected by *The Times*) on 22 July, George Bernard Shaw argued in essence that Casement was a freedom fighter whose cause was just, drawing a parallel with the Serbs, who had fought for independence after five centuries of Turkish rule. In these circumstances, he should be treated not as a criminal but as a prisoner of war. Shaw also drew a parallel with the case of Christian de Wet, who in 1914 had taken part in the Maritz Rebellion by the Boers in South Africa. De Wet and others had received prison sentences of six or seven years plus a fine, but were released after two years. Shaw argued that if they were free and Casement was hanged, it could only be because he was Irish, as the two cases were exact parallels. The theme that Casement should be reprieved because of his mental condition gained particular traction. How else could his relatively recent erratic behaviour compared to his previous status as a humanitarian and high government official be otherwise explained? Questions about his sanity were to linger long after his death. In a letter dated 22 July 1916 to the Home Secretary, Reverend Canon Lyndsay of Christchurch, Malahide, County Dublin, thought that Casement should be sent to a lunatic asylum. He said that Casement had lived in his parish for several months in 1914, and –

The impression he left on me was that with much quick-witted intelligence, and experience of life, he was a crack-brained fanatic, and with such a distorted mind as to be scarcely responsible for his actions. He seemed to possess some strange psychic power, which fascinated and almost paralysed the minds of those he sought to influence and my wife thought him the most interesting and charming man she had ever met. But he had the habit of walking the roads bareheaded and swinging his arms in the air, so that the people thought him mad.

I have since been told that there is a strain of insanity in his family. This can be easily verified by enquiring in Co Antrim.

But looking at the case from the point of view of the welfare of Ireland, I am satisfied that to hang him, richly as his actions deserve it, would be to erect him into a possible hero, like Lord Edward Fitzgerald or Wolfe Tone, or the [indecipherable] *Martyrs.*

If possible, I would suggest that he should be certified to a criminal lunatic asylum. This would prevent invidious comparison with the fate of Captain Bowen-Colthurst.

(Captain Bowen-Colthurst had been convicted for the murder of Francis Sheehy-Skeffington following the Easter Rising and had been found guilty but insane.) In her petition to Asquith and the Home Secretary, a Miss Agnes Young of Brockley Park, Strathbally, Queens Co, had a different take –

In our opinion, Casement had not, up to the time of his trial, any serious hold on the Irish people. His nationalist writings were circulated in America, not in Ireland. His political projects, being those of an educated diplomatist, were too technical to be understood by such groups as the Republican Brotherhood and the irreconcilable section of Sinn Féin.

She urged against making him a national hero – "In the position of Mr Arthur Lynch and General De Wet, Casement will be harmless, disabled by his own failure. On a British scaffold he will do endless mischief", and, "There are multitudes who feel that the Knight-errant in the cause of suffering humanity in the Congo and the Putumayo cannot be treated as if he were on the moral level of a common murderer".[35]

Another strand in the arguments for clemency was the motive for Casement's journey to Ireland. Even before his trial, the substance of his meeting with Father Ryan at the Tralee police barracks on 21 April had been reported in the *Kildare Observer* and the *Dublin Evening Mail* on 20 May. Following the trial (and before the hearing of the appeal), the matter was raised again by the journalist Henry W Nevinson in a letter to the Editor of the *Daily News* published 12 July.[36] In outlining the story, Nevinson wrote –

> *Those who were acquainted with the facts have long known that Roger Casement had no personal connection with the "Sinn Féin" rising, except in so far as he came to Ireland in hopes of stopping it. For reasons which are appreciated by all who know him he refused to allow the truth about this to be put forward in his defence.*

On 17 July, the first day of the appeal hearing, Eva Gore Booth, a sister of the Countess de Markevitz, wrote in the same vein to Sir Edward Grey –

> *It seems quite clear from the priest's evidence that Casement really came to Ireland in a frantic attempt to dissuade the Sinn Féin leaders from what he considered the fatal mistake of the rising. It seems to me an intolerably ghastly idea that he should be hung as a result of this self-sacrificing and devoted effort, facing, as he did, almost certain death for the sake of preventing bloodshed and misery in Ireland. It would be impossible to exaggerate the feeling in Ireland on this matter, and the hopeless despair and bitterness*

with which the prospect of another execution is regarded – what they consider the deliberate and cold-blooded execution of a man who was not even in the rising, but whose generous and romantic personality has made him a favourite national hero.

Her letter concluded with a postscript saying that though not a member of Sinn Féin herself, she understood something of their point of view from her sister, Constance de Markevitz (who at the time of the letter was in gaol for her part in the Easter Rising). Grey's response to Eva Gore Booth's letter was to instruct that it should be acknowledged with a statement that the issue was nothing to do with the Foreign Office and that the papers had been passed on to the proper authorities; the reply should also comment that the matter should presumably have been referred to the defence counsel before the trial.[37] Sir Ernley Blackwell, the Cabinet's chief legal advisor, was dismissive of the whole argument, commenting in a memo on 21 July that, "The idea of saying that he had come with the intention and for the purpose of stopping the rising appears to have occurred to Casement only after his capture. It is at any rate entirely inconsistent with the proven facts". Blackwell attached in support of this an extract of the notes of Casement's interviews at Scotland Yard during which he had made no mention of the claim.[38]

Ordinarily, this might have ended the matter, but a letter dated 19 July to Sir Edward Grey from Michael Francis Doyle, an American solicitor who had been in attendance in support of the defence at Casement's trial, added a new dimension. Doyle said that he was writing "in a professional capacity as counsel for Roger Casement", claiming that the latter had not received a fair trial because it had been impossible for him to call any witnesses or produce any documents in support of his defence. He went on to claim that prior to his (Doyle's) arrival in the country on 12 June, Casement had applied to the Home Office for permission for Doyle to go to Germany to have these witnesses brought over and to obtain documents. Doyle listed fifteen facts which, he argued, the witnesses could have testified to with the result that, "in every likelihood", Casement would have been acquitted. Many of these points were of little practical consequence, such as how many times Casement had visited Limburg and whether he had actually seen some of the leaflets distributed ostensibly in his name. But they also included the claim, "That his [Casement's] intention in going to Ireland, which, however, he never expressed to any German official was to *prevent the rising* and inform the people that the expected assistance which they were promised would not be fulfilled". He then developed an argument that had indeed been of concern to the Government and had also been correctly identified as an issue by Casement – American public opinion. This was of especial concern due to the forthcoming US presidential election in November. Doyle commented –

> *I am most anxious, however, to call your attention to the effect that it will have on the United States of America. It is unnecessary for me to discuss the friendship of our Government to your country during this great war. Nothing would do more to destroy the friendly feeling of the American feeling towards Great Britain than Casement's execution under the circumstances. The shooting of the leaders of the late Irish uprising and Mr Sheehy Skeffington has caused a most profound effect in America, not merely upon those of Irish birth and extraction, but also on the entire American nation, and adding Casement as a victim would have a most serious effect upon the public opinion of our country, particularly when all the facts are known. I really believe that the coming Presidential election would be affected by it.[39]*

A similar letter from Doyle had been sent to the Home Office. This was replied to by Sir Ernley Blackwell on 24 July, who simply denied that any application had ever been made to the Home

Office by Casement or anyone acting on his behalf to bring over witnesses and documents as claimed by Doyle, nor had anyone ever told Doyle that that had been the case.[40] But the Foreign Office were nevertheless concerned. Sir Eric Drummond, Grey's Private Secretary, wrote to Lord Crewe, Lord President of the Council, on 26 July, saying that while the Home Office may well be right in their view that it would be a mistake to send Doyle a detailed reply, stories that Casement had gone to Ireland to stop the rising, and that he had been forbidden to procure evidence from Germany in his defence, were being widely circulated and were gaining considerable traction, including in Ireland and the United States. Drummond continued –

> *There is no doubt that, if Casement comes to be regarded as a martyr, it will be to some extent owing to statements such as these which have received no public contradiction. The Home Office have at their disposal evidence and facts which, if made public in concise and popular form, would entirely dispose of these assertions. To refuse to make any public statement because it is undignified or because there is no precedent seems to me in present circumstances to be both shortsighted and narrow-minded. It does not matter in what shape such a statement appears, provided it is made.*[41]

Within days, the Cabinet decided that this message should be got out by briefing the Press (possibly the *Morning Post* and the *Daily Chronicle*) unofficially, with details enabling them to refute the story in print. The briefing would pick out the fact that the *Aud* had been in close attendance upon Casement, and that Casement had come equipped with a military code as well as a large green flag; it had moreover been open to him to go into the witness box and offer the argument that he had come to stop the rising on oath. He had chosen not to do so. The Attorney General agreed with this approach but expressed doubts about whether any such article should be printed before Casement's execution. He was nevertheless persuaded by the Cabinet's view that it should be published at once.[42]

A final consideration regarding a possible reprieve centred around some private diaries that had been found at lodgings previously occupied by Casement in Ebury Street, Victoria. These diaries were found as part of a search during Casement's interviews at Scotland Yard and contained graphic details of paid-for homosexual encounters he had had, mainly with young teenage boys, starting in 1903. The diaries (which were subsequently to become widely known as the "Black Diaries") did not form any part of Casement's trial, though their existence did become publicly known, among other things as a result of a press conference called in May by Captain Hall following the interviews at Scotland Yard, where he had shown photocopies of selected extracts to newspaper editors – an act generally considered to be disreputable and intended to influence the course of any trial. In fact, before the eventual trial the prosecution offered the diaries to the defence, suggesting that they may help them in securing a verdict of "guilty but insane". When these were put to Serjeant Sullivan, he refused even to read them, saying that there was no question of Casement pleading guilty. (Sullivan subsequently said that he had taken this decision unilaterally, as he had considered death to be preferable to besmirching and dishonour.)[43]

*

There have been many suggestions that the eventual decision not to grant Casement a reprieve was driven by a specific agenda to make an example of him, and that he became, in effect, the object of a vendetta led principally by Sir Ernley Blackwell. But the official record shows this to have been far from the case, with the Government devoting a great deal of time deliberating on the matter in order to reach a properly considered decision. Between the end of his trial and his execution, the Cabinet considered the case on four separate occasions, taking into account all the issues outlined above in some detail. At its first discussion on 5 July, the question of the impact of an execution on public opinion in Ireland and America was discussed, and the possibility of a reprieve on the grounds of insanity. In his report of the discussion to the King, Asquith wrote –

> *The question arose as to the best way to deal with the Casement case. His diary is to be submitted to an Alienist* [psychiatrist] *for report. Several members of the Cabinet (including Sir E Grey and Lord Lansdowne) were strongly of the opinion that it would be better (if possible) that he should be kept in confinement as a criminal lunatic than that he should be executed, without any smirch on his character, and thus considered as a martyr in Ireland and America. Others took a contrary view. As Casement's sentence is under appeal, no immediate action is necessary.*[44]

Following the meeting, the Home Office obtained a report from Dr R Percy Smith MD FRCP, a leading physician for mental diseases and honorary consultant to military hospitals in London, and Dr Maurice Craig MD FRCP, a pioneer in mental illness, a member of the War Office Committee on Shell Shock, and later psychiatrist to Virginia Wolf and the future Edward VIII. Their report was based on entries in Casement's diary between 1 January and 31 December 1911. Their findings, dated 10 July, were inconclusive. While noting that Casement's condition was likely to have been longstanding and chronic, the Alienists found no evidence of delusion or general intellectual defect. They considered that he must be regarded as a mentally abnormal individual, with his absorption in the subject matter of his diary and his conduct suggesting much more mental disorder than was usually met in a person suffering only from a perverted instinct. On the evidence before them, however, they were unable to say that Casement was certifiably insane.[45]

The Cabinet next considered the matter on 19 July, in advance of which the Home Secretary circulated four memoranda, three of which were drafted by Sir Ernley Blackwell, and the fourth by Sir Charles Edward Troup, Permanent Secretary at the Home Office.[46] Blackwell's first memorandum set out for members of the Cabinet a resumé of Casement's career and the details of his trial, concluding with his overall assessment –

> *It is difficult to imagine a worse case of high treason than Casement's. It is aggravated rather than mitigated by his previous career in public service, and his private character – although it really has no relation to the actual offence with which he is charged – certainly cannot be pleaded in his favour.*

His second memorandum dealt with the principle of reprieve on the ground of insanity, noting that in many cases of murder, particularly those of a sexual character, there was a direct link between a mental abnormality such as that displayed in Casement's diaries and the crime that had been committed. In Casement's case, however, there was no such traceable link. He continued that no one who had read Casement's Putumayo Report, prepared at the same time as some of his diary entries, his speech from the dock, or any of his other writings could doubt that he was intellectually "very far from removed from anything that could properly be described as insanity". He concluded –

> *I do not believe that any tribunal of alienists who might be appointed to enquire into Casement's mental condition would be able on the strength of these diaries, and certainly not upon any*

other ground, to certify him insane, or even to express an opinion as to his enfeebled mental condition or impaired judgment which, having regard to the nature of his crime, would afford a legitimate excuse for the exercise of the prerogative of mercy.

Having dealt with the principle of exercising the prerogative on grounds of insanity, Blackwell then turned in his third memorandum to the wider question of exercising the prerogative on grounds of expediency, noting that while party political considerations were not allowed to influence decisions in this area, the situation was different where national issues were at stake. He then dealt with the position that had been taken by the Foreign Office, which considered that in order not to alienate more Irish-American sentiment, Casement could not safely be hanged unless the Government, "first published the fact of his private character as disclosed in his diaries". Blackwell then wrote words which have reverberated among historians and writers ever since –

> *There are obviously grave objections to any sort of official or even inspired publication of facts while the man is waiting trial or appeal, or even waiting execution. Perhaps I do not fully appreciate the danger which the Foreign Office see ahead in America if the law is allowed to take its course in this country, but the attitude adopted is rather a humiliating one.*
>
> *I see not the slightest objection to hanging Casement, and afterwards giving as much publicity to the contents of his diary as decency permits, so that at any rate the public in America and elsewhere may know what sort of man they are inclined to make a martyr of.*

He went on to comment that Casement's value as a martyr had already been largely discounted in any event, with his private character already being generally well known in London following comments on three occasions in the *Daily Express* declaring him to be a moral degenerate and citing his diaries as proof. If it were to be decided that execution would be inexpedient on national grounds, Blackwell questioned what it was hoped would be gained by setting up a statutory inquiry into Casement's sanity before a reprieve was announced. From the report already submitted by Drs Percy Smith and Maurice Craig, Blackwell concluded that Casement could not be certified as insane. If that were also to be the finding of an inquiry, Casement would have to be sent to penal servitude with a "stigma", "which he and his supporters say would be worse than death". There would then be a demand for the evidence on which the decision had been based and arguments that the diaries were forgeries. Vitally, all this also left out the question of public opinion –

> *The public know that Casement is not insane, as they understand insanity, and they will simply regard the inquiry as a subterfuge. It will be said that Casement has been reprieved not upon national but upon party grounds to further what has always been the policy of a section of the Cabinet on Irish matters.*

Rounding off this section of his argument, Blackwell concluded that there was nothing to be gained by reprieving Casement on one ground and pretending to have done so on another –

> *So far as I can judge, it would be far better to allow the law to take its course, and by judicious means to use the diaries to prevent Casement becoming a martyr.*

A final line of argument dealt with by Blackwell in his memorandum was the impact that hanging might have on the Irish question itself. Here, he observed simply that had Casement been arrested a few days later in Dublin, he would have been court-martialled and shot along with the other leaders of the rebellion. In Blackwell's view, however, it was the rising itself that had given greater impetus to support for Sinn Féin than the fact of the subsequent shootings.

In his memorandum, Sir Edward Troup agreed with Blackwell that Casement was perfectly sane. In Troupe's view, the only question was whether Casement's sentence should be commuted on expediency grounds because of its likely impact on Irish and American opinion. He doubted the strength of any adverse impact. In Ireland, Casement had never been regarded as a Sinn Féin leader and if he were reprieved, that would be taken as a sign of fear; alternatively, it would be taken as a reflection of the fact that he was an ex-Government official of the ruling class. If he were to be reprieved on grounds of expediency, the best course would be to say simply that there had already been enough executions in connection with the rebellion, and that the Government did not wish to add another to those who "had suffered the last penalty of the law". But Troupe then concluded damningly –

> *The difficulty of saying this in the case of Roger Casement is that he is both a worse offender in the matter of treason and disloyalty, and worse in personal character, than those who have already suffered death.*

Official details of the Cabinet discussion on 19 July are unknown. Asquith's report of the meeting to the King simply says that Casement's case was carefully considered and that it was the unanimous decision of the Cabinet that he should be hanged.[47]

The possibility of a reprieve was discussed for a final time on 2 August, the eve of Casement's execution. In his report to the King, Asquith says that the greater part of the meeting was taken up with a discussion of the matter in view of some further material and the urgent appeals for mercy from "authoritative and friendly quarters in the United States". (This seems to be a reference to the influential Republican Senator Henry Cabot Lodge, who was in favour of the United States entering the war in support of the Allies.) Again, the Cabinet decided that there were no grounds for reprieve. The Foreign Secretary drew up a note for Sir Cecil Spring Rice, the UK Ambassador in Washington, setting out reasons to be used in defending the Cabinet's decision.[48] Grey's note was telegraphed to Washington at 4 pm on the same day and circulated to the Cabinet.[49] It is worth setting out the substance of the note in full. Following the usual pleasantries, it said –

> The Government however feel that there is no ground except that of political expediency on which Casement can be reprieved and it would not be consistent with justice or tolerable to public opinion here to reprieve him on this ground.
>
> The Irish Rising began by the shooting of unarmed soldiers and policemen at sight and the greatest indignation is felt respecting those responsible for it. Casement is clearly proved to have done all in his power to instigate the rising with German aid; there is the clearest evidence that his object was absolutely hostile to this country and the ex post facto statement that he tried to stop the rising was not raised at the trial and is demonstrably untrue. His whole action in this matter was more peculiarly hostile and malevolent than that of any of the leaders, extreme though some of these were in Ireland.
>
> Irish soldiers, prisoners in Germany, who resisted Casement's solicitations of disloyalty were subjected to rigorous treatment by the Germans, some of them have since been exchanged as invalids and have died in this country regarding Casement as their murderer.
>
> There is nothing either in his public action or his private character that can be pleaded in extenuation of his action and in favour of mitigation of the sentence.
>
> Such material as might have been alleged to point to insanity, including extracts from his diary, was at the disposal of his Counsel, who never raised this plea on his behalf and Casement's

demeanour and proceedings throughout the trial gave no ground for suggesting insanity and indeed were sufficient to disprove it.

Under these circumstances a decision to reprieve Casement would be intensely resented by public opinion, both civil and military; the Government would be most strongly attacked for it and would have on grounds of fact and justice, have no defence.

The telegram ended by again setting out pleasantries in relation to Lodge, emphasising that the interest he had shown had been treated in the most friendly and considerate spirit. A reply from Spring Rice dated the same day, and received in the Foreign Office at 9.15 am on 3 August (fifteen minutes after Casement had been executed), noted that it had been announced that the US President had made no request for Casement's reprieve but that antagonism in the President's entourage and within the Democratic Party towards the British Government would now be greatly increased. Spring Rice suggested much good would now be done by a statement in Parliament along the lines of the Foreign Office telegram, especially if accompanied by an announcement that some of the other Irish political prisoners had now been amnestied. A further telegram from Spring Rice, received in the Foreign Office at 10.50 am, reported that the US Acting Secretary of State had emphasised to him that the US had made no official representations over Casement, but an announcement in Parliament as quickly as possible would be helpful. Spring Rice concluded –

> *There will probably be a considerable stir in Irish circles but he [the Acting US Secretary of State] hopes that it will now blow over especially if some act of grace is shown to other rebels: but he insisted that United States Government made no official representations on this subject. Lodge is most grateful for your message and agrees His Majesty's Government could take no other course.*[50]

*

A main concern had been resolved. While there had been much public and political pressure in the US in favour of a reprieve, the US Government had stood firm in refusing to become involved in what President Wilson insisted was a domestic matter for the British Government. As early as 2 May, Wilson had written to his Irish-American private secretary in relation to a plea for support for a reprieve from Michael Francis Doyle, "It is absolutely necessary to say that I could take no action of any kind regarding it".[51] In the UK, *The Times* reported the day after the execution (4 August), under three headings.[52] The first noted that shortly before his execution Casement had been received into the Roman Catholic Church. The report continued that a relatively small crowd of about 150 people had gathered outside Pentonville Prison before the execution, comprising mainly women and children from the immediate neighbourhood. These had been joined by about another one hundred spectators, many of them ammunition workers, when the breakfast hour started at local factories. As the minute bell began to toll following the execution, a group of workmen raised a cheer, while the women munition workers rushed back to their place of work. Five minutes later, the crowd had disappeared, with the street outside the gaol returning to normal. At the inquest on Casement's body held later that morning, Dr P R Mander, the senior medical officer of the prison, testified that death had been instantaneous. Noting that Casement had been under the doctor's observation in prison for a month, Gavan Duffy asked the doctor whether there was any truth, "in the suggestion of insanity that had been made in the Press", to which Mander replied, 'I saw no evidence of insanity.' *The Times* then went on to report an official statement that had been put out by the Government –

> *All the circumstances in the case of Roger Casement were carefully and repeatedly considered by the Government before the decision was reached not to interfere with the sentence of the law. He was*

convicted and punished for treachery of the worst kind to the Empire he had served and as a willing agent of Germany.

The Irish rebellion resulted in much loss of life, both among soldiers and civilians; Casement invoked and organised German assistance to the insurrection. In addition, though himself for many years a British official, he undertook the task of trying to induce soldiers of the British army, prisoners in the hands of Germany, to forswear their oath of allegiance and join their country's enemies. Conclusive evidence has come into the hands of the Government which explicitly provided that the brigade which he was trying to raise from among the Irish soldier prisoners might be employed in Egypt against the British Crown. Those among the Irish soldiers, prisoners in Germany, who resisted Casement's solicitations of disloyalty were subjected to treatment of exceptional cruelty by the Germans; some of them have since been exchanged as invalids and have died in this country, regarding Casement as their murderer.

The suggestion that Casement left Germany for the purpose of trying to stop the Irish Rising was not raised at the trial, and is conclusively disproved not only by the facts there disclosed, but by further evidence which has since become available.

Another suggestion, that Casement was out of his mind, is equally without foundation. Materials bearing on his mental condition were placed at the disposal of his counsel, who did not raise the plea of insanity. Casement's demeanour since his arrest, and throughout since the trial, gave no ground for any such defence, and indeed was sufficient to disprove it.

The new element in the Government's statement was the reference to the possibility of the Irish Brigade being employed in Egypt. It seems likely that this fact came to light as part of a process in which Casement transferred papers from his prison cell to Gavan Duffy. Such a transfer inevitably went through the censors. But it is a lasting surprise that the British authorities seem to have previously known nothing about Casement's Treaty, given that it had been published in the *Gaelic American*. Had this fact been known – and also the fact that some members of the Brigade had actively been preparing to fight alongside the Turks – the prosecution case would have been infinitely stronger. As it was, Casement (and his Counsel) made much of the inaccurate argument in defence that the Brigade would only ever have fought for Ireland. *The Times* concluded with a report on the "Feeling in Ireland". Their Dublin correspondent expected the execution to be violently denounced. While most of those who had campaigned for a reprieve had little sympathy with Casement's crime, they considered that enough blood had already been shed in the rebellion, and that, "the pardon of Casement would have had a good effect upon public opinion in this country". But at the same time, the correspondent also concluded that it was quite certain that, "if Casement had been reprieved the Nationalist Press would have hastened to compare that clemency with the severity of the executions in Dublin, and would have raised a new campaign against Sir John Maxwell. Nothing that the Government could have done with Casement would have satisfied the whole of Ireland". In practical terms, Casement's execution had few immediate consequences for the cause of Irish nationalism. As has been noted, few in Ireland had actually regarded him as a nationalist leader, while Irish-American public opinion quickly moved on, with *Clan na Gael*, if anything, playing down the significance of his execution. While Devoy was ultimately to note that Casement's name would, "ever have a revered place on the long roll of martyrs who gave their lives that Ireland might be free",[53] in a coded telegram on 1 August 1916, Spring Rice reported that in a conversation with Michael Francis Doyle, the latter had told him that *Clan na Gael* actually wanted Casement executed.

By any objective yardstick, Casement's career as a nationalist had been a practical failure. He had supported the cause ardently and had had a few successes, such as his work in fundraising and establishing the Irish Volunteers. But his attempted transition from consular official to self-styled diplomat was a step too far. Even as a consul, he had exhibited a flawed temperament, being unduly sensitive to criticism and over-conscious of his status and dignity. These traits became more exposed as time went on, as, for example, in the *Findlay Affair*. He was also extreme in his loyalties. However much he tried to play things down, there could be no denying the contrast between his obsequious letter of acceptance for his knighthood and his subsequent dismissal of the award as being of little account and something he had accepted because he had had no choice. He exhibited the same trait in the letters he wrote to Devoy at the same time as expressing his dislike of America in letters to Gertrude Bannister. This fickleness culminated with regard to Germany, where his initial view that the country could do no wrong turned into outright criticism that they had betrayed him. His overriding characteristic, as noted by Devoy, was that Casement believed he was always right and would brook no argument to the contrary.

But Casement's judgement was perhaps his most serious weakness. Given what he himself had said about MacBride and loyalty during the Boer War, it is astonishing that he should have seriously thought that Irishmen who had voluntarily joined the British Army, had fought the enemy, had in many cases been injured, and were now captives of the Germans, would want to transfer their allegiance to the enemy. Casement's claims that they would only be fighting for Ireland and not assisting Germany were not only too sophisticated for his audience but were pure sophistry, as the details of his Treaty spelled out. His judgement was also awry in setting so much store by his Treaty. Once his Irish Brigade failed to materialise, the Treaty meant nothing. In any event, it was flawed. Under the guise of self-styled Irish Ambassador, Casement had failed to get support for an alignment with Germany even from his fellow nationalists, as Devoy observed. He had also failed even to consider the implications for public opinion in Ireland prior to the rising. He appears to have given no thought at all as to whether the general population would have welcomed a treaty with the Germans, while so many were actually and actively part of a war against them, and while Home Rule had already been promised after the war. From the German perspective, the Treaty can have been of little significance. It was already their practice to enlist the support of prisoners from nationalist minorities to fight against their occupiers, and the Treaty potentially provided them with more manpower to fight the British. Any commitment from their side was negligible and could be easily rescinded, as events were to demonstrate.

Despite these obvious flaws, Casement has surprisingly gone on to become a hero in the eyes of many nationalists. While few among his supporters have chosen to defend his actions in going to Germany, many have argued that his execution, rather than the finding of guilt, was the result of a particular vindictiveness on the part of the British Government. Some, though not many, have argued that the trial itself was unfair, with the prosecution being led by the erstwhile staunch Ulster Unionist, Sir F E Smith. But there is no evidence that the prosecution acted improperly in any way, nor was this ever claimed by the defence. Many more have argued that following his distinguished career with the consular service, he had simply become insane. There is still a question mark over this in some quarters today. In 1930, Dr W K Anderson, an expert in tropical diseases, wrote to the Home Office asking – as a matter of "technical interest" – whether Casement's illness from malaria had been taken into account at the time of his trial, because in his view malaria was the cause of mental disturbances. He was told that the nature of the defence had precluded such an issue being raised but that "all relevant considerations regarding Casement's mental and physical condition were, of course, taken into consideration before the sentence was carried out".[54] And as recently as 2020, research has been undertaken into whether Casement's mental state might have been the result of neurosyphilis, though the evidence has so far proved inconclusive. In relation to his execution, however, the record is clear that this question was fully considered by the British Government, which consciously decided – though there were advantages in doing otherwise – that a reprieve on the grounds of insanity was not tenable. Sir Ernley Blackwell was surely right when he noted that nobody who had read the Putumayo Report or Casement's speech from the dock could conclude that he was insane.

The most serious and enduring controversy surrounding Casement is that of his private diaries, which became infamously known as the "Black Diaries". The basic charge is that the Government engineered the clandestine circulation of the diaries before Casement was executed in order to sabotage the campaign for his reprieve by turning potential influential supporters against him. (A subset of this argument, which started to develop at the time of Casement's execution, was that the diaries were either outright forgeries or had been written by Casement to describe in a coded form not his own activities but those of Armando Normand, a manager with the Peruvian Amazon rubber company. It was not until 2002 that the matter was finally settled when forensic tests commissioned by Professor Bill McCormack of Goldsmiths College, University of London, established beyond doubt that the diaries were genuine.[55]) Many of those who have advanced the argument about the deliberate "smirching" of Casement point the finger at Sir Ernley Blackwell. They claim that in various ways he demonstrated what was tantamount to a visceral hatred of Casement and cite in evidence his Cabinet memorandum stating that he saw nothing wrong in circulating the diaries after Casement had been hanged in order to show what sort of a man he was. But invariably, the same sources omit Blackwell's preceding comment that, "There are obviously grave objections to any sort of official or even inspired publication of the facts while the man is waiting trial or appeal, or even waiting execution". It is certainly clear from the record that Blackwell had no time for Casement and strongly disapproved of his actions, but his advice to the Cabinet and other writings were strictly forensic and have all the hallmarks of objective advice from a career civil servant. It was Blackwell himself who flagged the impropriety of circulating material in advance of execution and having done that, it is hard to conceive that he would engage in the skulduggery of doing just that secretly. But there is no doubt that there was some sort of campaign. In his biography of Casement written in 1931, Denis Gwynn attributed blame to "some mysterious agency in Scotland Yard", claiming that photographed pages from the diaries were shown in many of the London clubs, were handed around the House of Commons and in the press gallery, were shown to journalists who were known to be sympathisers of Casement, and were sent to some of his friends in America. Gwynn claims that after being confronted with the evidence, Redmond played no further part in Casement's defence. He also named one of the staff of the Ministry of Information, who had openly admitted that he had been responsible for having the diary copied.[56] But who exactly organised the campaign has never been established. At a meeting with F E Smith on 29 July 1916, Artemus Jones specifically raised the question of the diaries, referring to complaints by Casement's friends that attempts had been made to prejudice the press and members of the public against Casement by revealing the contents of the diaries. F E Smith assured them that "there was not a word of truth" in these complaints.[57] It is also reported that, at some stage, on hearing that the Foreign Office were proposing to circulate extracts from the diaries to influence opinion, F E Smith had told Grey that he thought it was "rather a ghoulish proposal", and Grey had agreed, saying that it would not be proceeded with without Cabinet authority.[58] It may be that the diaries simply fell into the Civil Service's wartime propaganda machine and were disseminated without any specific ministerial direction. But the campaign made its mark. Separately from its report on the execution, *The Times* raised the matter specifically in a leading article on the same day. The article accepted that justice had been done in carrying out the execution and acknowledged that Casement's trial had been conducted with "even exaggerated fairness". It went on to say that such agitation as there had been for reprieve had admitted that the case for clemency must turn purely on questions of expediency, which only the Government, having all the facts, could judge. But it continued –

> *It is in this conviction that we have absolutely refused during the last few weeks – in spite of some very curious pressure – to have the case retried in these columns. Newspapers have many and great responsibilities in these days, but the function of a final Court of Criminal Appeal is not one of them.*

And then, after remarking that the Government had been wise to make its own position perfectly clear in its statement following the execution, the article concluded –

> *On the other hand, we cannot help protesting against certain other attempts which have been made to use the Press for the purpose of raising issues which are utterly damaging to Casement's character, but have no connection whatever with the charges on which he was tried. These issues should either have been raised in public and in a straightforward manner, or they should have been left severely alone. The colour of his proved crime is deep enough by itself. It would have been fortunate, indeed, for everyone concerned, and the simplest act of justice, if he had been shot out of hand on the Kerry coast. But if there was ever a virtue in the pomp*

and circumstance of a great State Trial, it can only be weakened by inspired innuendos which, whatever their substance, are now irrelevant, improper, and un-English.[59]

Following the article, circulation of the diaries ceased in England and within a few weeks in America.[60] Damage to the reputation of the British Government had been done and, far from preventing Casement from becoming a martyr, the episode helped create an image of him as a victim among nationalists and supporters. To that extent, the strategy failed, though talking to MaColl in 1954, none other than Serjeant Sullivan took a pragmatic view of events. Sullivan recalled that Gavan Duffy had told him that the diaries had been shown to certain American correspondents in London before the trial – "The British Government of the day wasn't very particular about what they were prepared to do to damp down the pro-Irish and anti-British sentiment in America. I believe it [the dissemination of the diaries] was done at some time or other before the USA entered the war. What people do in war is unpredictable. Perfectly decent men will do perfectly shocking things in the prevailing hysteria".[61] As to whether it was justified to make use of the diaries for the purpose of "character assassination", McColl records that he discussed the matter with "various men of affairs" whose opinion he valued. These men had considered that since "what was then the greatest war in history was in full flood, it was justifiable to do so".[62]

The views of subsequent writers have varied, with Inglis arguing that the circulation of the diaries was the decisive reason for the failure of the reprieve campaign.[63] Dudgeon, on the other hand, must be right in his assessment that none of the petitions for reprieve was ever likely to succeed.[64] The arguments of those who think that Casement was treated harshly – and there are many – circle round the fact that his widely acclaimed humanitarian work in the Congo and the Putumayo should have been acknowledged in his final sentence; that his subsequent actions in Germany were a sign of insanity, or at best of mental imbalance, which again should have been recognised through clemency; or that he was victimised because of his sexual activities exposed in the Black Diaries. It is implicit in each of these scenarios that the default position of the British Government should have leaned towards clemency. From the British perspective, however, the default position lay in the opposite direction. Having been honoured for his many services to the British, Casement had chosen to defect to Britain's enemy and there to seduce British prisoners to abandon their allegiance to the Crown. He had done this at the height of a total war affecting all parts of the population and had spoken out consistently and loudly against his own country, himself acknowledging that his acts constituted high treason. In addition, on the best information available to the authorities at the time, Casement had been the leader most to blame for the Easter Rising, and to spare him when less important men had already been executed was considered not to be acceptable to public opinion.[65] So far as the British Government was concerned, the only serious argument for clemency was one of expediency – to avoid making Casement a martyr and avoid upsetting America. Having considered all the arguments at length, the Government had decided to bite the bullet.

It is ironic that Casement's enduring reputation as a nationalist should have finally rested on his association with the Easter Rising, a venture that he disapproved of and wanted to stop. Those such as Eva Gore Booth who petitioned for his reprieve on this ground were clearly doomed to fail, given that Casement had not used the argument in his own defence. He could hardly have done so without appearing to disassociate himself from the nationalist movement. Indeed, his instincts were to construct a defence falsely claiming full responsibility for the rising. Likewise, the British Government can hardly be blamed for so readily dismissing the claim, which appeared to contradict all the – admittedly limited – information that they had. Even from this distance, it is impossible to judge whether justice might have been better served if the Government had somehow contrived to grant a reprieve based on his motivation in going to Ireland. But as was so often the case, Casement's exact plans were unclear, with his final correspondence with the German authorities indicating a definite intention to stand alongside those taking part in the rising. And if Casement was hard done by in the matter of his intentions in going to Ireland, he was certainly not hard done by in relation to the possibility of using the Irish Brigade in Egypt, where had the truth been known at the time of his trial, his fate would undoubtedly have been sealed more speedily than it eventually was. While no one can be expected to incriminate themselves when on trial, Casement's insistence that the Irish Brigade would never have been asked to fight for anyone but Ireland betrayed the great store that he himself claimed to set by truth, honour and gentlemanly behaviour in his public statements.

The analysis subsequently provided by Serjeant Sullivan perhaps gives the explanation. Sullivan described Casement as a, "megalomaniac, a man with a fantastic estimate of his own importance", and noted that, "he [Casement] never consciously told a lie. He had all the instincts of a gentleman. He would tell you the most appalling falsehoods, and not only believe them himself – but make you believe them too".[66] An added explanation as to why Casement succeeded in his consular role but failed in his subsequent activities as a nationalist might also be found in a blunt, if somewhat cruel, summation given by his former friend Joseph Conrad in 1916 –

> *He was a good companion; but already in Africa I judged that he was a man, properly speaking, of no mind at all. I don't mean stupid. I mean that he was all emotion. By emotional force (Congo Report, Putumayo, etc.) he made his way, and sheer temperament*

– a truly tragic personality: all but the greatness of which he had not a trace. Only vanity. But by the Congo it was not visible yet.[67]

Perhaps the final word should go to Casement himself, from a farewell letter to his friend Richard Moreton, written from Pentonville on 28 July 1916 –

I made awful mistakes, and did heaps of things wrong, confused much and failed at much – but I very nearly came to doing some big things… on the Congo and elsewhere. It was only a shadow they tried on 26 June; the real man was gone. The best thing was the Congo, because there was more against me there and far cleverer rascals than the Putumayo ruffians.[68]

Roger Casement

Casement in the Congo

Roger Casement

Roger Casement arriving at Bow Street Magisrtates' Court

Robert Monteith – German Irish Brigade

PART THREE

NINE

DOWLING AND THE GERMAN PLOT – THE FINAL ACT

...there is absolutely no doubt in the mind of anyone who has examined it that there was a very serious conspiracy, in which powerful people in Ireland were engaged with the Germans to subvert British rule in Ireland.
                Prime Minister Lloyd George, House of Commons
                         Adjournment Debate, 25 June 1918

I need hardly tell you that the German Plot only exists in the panic disordered imagination of the English Government.
Letter from Maude Gonne, Holloway Prison, to W B Yeats, 14 June 1918 (The Gonne-Yeats Letters 1893–1938, p.395)

> ...*no ...early remission of sentence should be made, lest it be interpreted as an extenuation of the most heinous crime which a soldier can commit, viz. that of voluntarily serving with, and aiding, the enemy.*
>
> View of the Army Council, on remission of Dowling's sentence, 29 January 1924

After Casement's execution, the Irish Brigade ceased to have any real purpose or meaning. Following the decision to drop the charges against him, Bailey was transferred to the 3rd Wiltshire Regiment on 1 July 1916, and then on to the 3rd North Lancashires on 17 July, serving in Tanzania. On 9 March 1917, he transferred to the Royal Engineers at Alexandria before being finally discharged on 8 December 1919. He ended his career on a high note, having been mentioned in despatches in the *London Gazette* on 5 June 1919.[1] No reference to the treason charge is shown in Bailey's service record, but there is some evidence that despite being acquitted, his reputation remained tarnished. A letter from the Irish Women's Association to Sir Edward Henry KCVO, Commissioner of Police of the Metropolis, dated 7 June 1918, asked whether it was true that Bailey was now a captain in the British Army, as reports of this were "having a very bad effect on the men".[2] For his part, following his disappearance after Banna Strand, Monteith went on the run in the UK, evading all attempts to catch him (an anonymous report to the police in June 1916 that he was living in Paignton seems to have come to nothing[3]). He finally made his way to America via Liverpool, using false papers as a stoker, arriving in New York at the end of the year. His daughter, Florence Monteith Lynch, records, "December 1916, just a week before Christmas Bob Monteith climbed the steps of the old house on Third Avenue (the grapevine in Liverpool had provided him with the new address)".[4]

The exact details of what happened to the residual Irish Brigade following the departure of Casement and Monteith are unclear. What is known is that they had been moved by the end of June 1916 from Zossen to Danzig-Troyl, a large camp in West Prussia housing about 40,000 Russian prisoners of war.[5] A report by US Ambassador Gerard to Grey, dated 19 July 1916, recorded notification by the German Ministry of War that –

> *The Irishmen in question have been taken to the camp at Danzig-Troyl. These people may be talked with by the Ambassador or one of his representatives according to the wish of the Ambassador, in the presence of an officer from the Ministry of War. An interrogation of these people may only refer to their present condition and in no way to political matters.*

On 17 February 1917, Sir Horace Rumbold, HM Ambassador to Berne, wrote to Arthur Balfour, the Foreign Secretary, reporting that members of the Irish Brigade had been sent to Danzig to guard Russian prisoners of war.[6] According to Zerhusen, at Danzig the men had their own separate barracks and were given the freedom to go into neighbouring towns and villages and work there as free labourers if they wished, as well as having access to an English-speaking Catholic priest.[7] A more detailed and critical account is set out in a statement given to the British authorities in Cologne in 1921 by Michael O'Toole, formerly a private in the 1st Battalion Irish Guards. O'Toole had been a sergeant in the Irish Brigade and was widely regarded as one of its ringleaders, together with Private Michael Patrick Keogh, Royal Irish Rifles (Brigade rank CSM); Corporal Timothy Quinlisk, also Royal Irish Rifles (Brigade rank CQMS); and Lance Corporal Joseph Patrick Dowling of the 2nd Battalion Connaught Rangers (Brigade rank Sergeant)[8]. O'Toole's account of events at Zossen and Danzig-Troyl contains some clear inaccuracies, but the main points are consistent with other reports. According to O'Toole, when Casement left for Ireland, the men had refused to continue drilling. After attempting and failing to restore discipline, General von Schneider, the Zossen Camp Commandant, concluded that continuing to have the Brigade there was more trouble than it was worth, and so they were transferred to Danzig-Troyl. At Danzig-Troyl, the brigade members were given passes to leave the camp to visit a nearby public house, but they were not allowed to go any further. They were told that if they wanted more freedom they could go out to work and were given the option of agricultural work on the same basis as Russian prisoners, i.e., at 30 *pfennig* per day. When they refused to do this, they were allowed to go out and look for work on their own account, getting the same wages as German labourers. Those who refused to go out to work were forced to work in a gang under a sentry. O'Toole records that he went out to work in the lumber trade. He notes that this was the beginning of the scattering of the men, and the situation prevailed until November 1918, when Zerhusen arrived at the camp with passes, enabling them to travel freely throughout Germany.[9] The move to Danzig-Troyl had done nothing to improve discipline within the Brigade, or to improve its reputation for trouble-making. In a letter dated 20 May 1918 to Thomas St John Gaffney, former US Consul in Munich who had been recalled in 1915 because of his pro-German sympathies and who had now been appointed administrator of the Brigade, Zerhusen wrote –

> *In some towns the police and magistrates have begged us to take the Irishmen away, as there is always some trouble, swindling, debts, burglaries, selling stolen goods, beating policemen… found living with Kriegerfrauen when the husbands came home. …In some factories they will not employ Irishmen, because they work too irregularly, one day and the next day gone, or keep away in the afternoon, get advances on a week's pay and disappear. In short on the average they are a disgrace to the Irish.*[10]

But there was one final event in the long Irish Brigade tradition which O'Toole's statement fails to record, namely the landing by U-boat of Joseph Patrick Dowling in Ireland in April 1918, just two years after Casement before him. Dowling had been born in 1886 in Maryborough (Port Laoise), one of thirteen children by his parents John Dowling and Catherine Reddin. He became a carpenter and then joined the Leinster Regiment on 18 July 1904, transferring to the Connaught Rangers on 16 August 1904. He was put on the reserve list on 17 July 1907. At the outbreak of war, he was called up and posted as a lance corporal to the 2nd Battalion, Connaught Rangers, on 5 August 1914. He landed in France on 14 August 1914, reaching Mons on 23 August. After being separated from his regiment, he attached himself to the 306 French Regiment until he was captured on 3 September. He was then held at Sennelager until being moved with the other Irish prisoners to Limburg on 22 December. He then joined the Irish Brigade on 27 March 1915, taking an active part in the attempts to recruit new members.[11] The exact reason for Dowling's trip to Ireland has always remained unclear, though Zerhusen sets out some background. According to Zerhusen, at some unspecified date, which appears to be in early 1918, the Commandant at Danzig-Troyl was told by the War Office that they intended to send one of the Irishmen over to Ireland. They had in mind sending O'Toole and asked for advice. After consulting Zerhusen, the Commandant vetoed O'Toole on the grounds that he was untrustworthy. Instead, he suggested Dowling, as being, "of sufficient intelligence, courage and thoroughly patriotic for this dangerous job". In reply, the War Office wired on 15 March 1918 that Zerhusen and Dowling should proceed immediately in civilian clothes to attend the St Patrick's Day celebrations at the Hotel Adlon in Berlin. There they met an officer of the "secret service". Dowling agreed to go to Ireland and was instructed, "as to his behaviour in the use of secret inks, etc". The two then went to Hamburg, where Dowling stayed with Zerhusen at his house, from where he was taken to Wilhelmshaven and put on a U-boat to Ireland on 1 April. Zerhusen nowhere sets out the details of the "dangerous job" Dowling was being sent to carry out.[12]

The events following Dowling's arrival in Ireland were reminiscent of those of Casement before him. Dowling was put off the U-boat in a rubber dinghy off the coast of County Clare at between 2 am and 3 am on 12 April. He then landed the dinghy on the beach of Crab Island, an uninhabited island about half a mile from the mainland. Sometime later, probably around 6.30 am, Thomas Lynch, a local fisherman, saw a man waving a handkerchief in order to attract attention and get taken off the island. The man told him that his boat had been washed ashore and was broken. He said that other men had gone in another boat in a different direction. Lynch then gave the man a lift to Doolin Point on the mainland, in return for which he gave Lynch a 5-shilling piece. All this had been seen by Thomas Macnamara, a coast watcher, who intercepted the man he subsequently identified as Dowling on the pier at Doolin Point. He asked Dowling, as he was a stranger, for his authority for landing. Dowling replied that his ship, the SS *Mississippi*, had been torpedoed at about 9.30 pm the previous evening some 10 miles west of Crab Island. Macnamara then took Dowling to the local coastguard station and handed him over to the coastguard, Arthur Rouse. Dowling repeated his story about the *Mississippi* and told Rouse that his name was James O'Brien. Rouse then passed him on to Petty Officer William Henry Connell, to whom he made a statement. In this, Dowling elaborated that the SS *Mississippi* was painted grey and was on its way from Baltimore to Liverpool carrying foodstuff, but he did not know the Captain's name or that of the ship's owners. As the matter clearly required further investigation, Connell decided that Dowling should be seen by the Senior Naval Officer at Galway. Oddly, but perhaps believing his story about the

Mississippi and assuming that Dowling would want to co-operate in putting together the pieces over the alleged sinking, Connell told him to make his own way to Galway by rail from nearby Ennistymon. Dowling accordingly set off for Ennystimon, arriving there at about 10 am or 11 am, having hitched a lift from Martin Howley, a farm worker, who gave him a lift on his horse and cart. On arrival, he visited a boot shop, where he bought a pair of shoes and a pair of boots, paying £4 7s 0d in silver, and then went to the National Bank, where he exchanged £31 worth of silver for notes. Being a stranger, he was then approached in the street by Sergeant John Lawless of the RIC in the early afternoon. Again, he gave his name as James O'Brien and said he was from the South of Ireland, but refused to say from which part. As a result, Lawless, "took him by the shoulders and marched him to the barrack", where he was told that he was being questioned under the Defence of the Realm Act and was obliged to answer. He then said that he was from Mallow, County Cork, but had not been there for seven or eight years so did not know anybody. He repeated his claim that he had been torpedoed but now said that he had been on the *Niagara* as an engineer. He said that he was on the way to Galway to see the Senior Naval Officer there. Lawless noted that Dowling had taken "some drink" but understood his questions. Asked why, if he had been torpedoed, his clothes were very dry, Dowling replied that he had, "got a change of clothes". Thomas Flanagan, the Head Constable of the RIC at Ennistymon, witnessed Dowling's arrival at the barracks and also considered that he was under the influence of drink. According to Flanagan, Dowling said that he had been torpedoed on a voyage from America to visit friends before joining the US Army. After the ship was torpedoed, he had lowered himself into the water in a boat that was suspended from the deck of the ship. Shortly afterwards, the ship went down. He first said that the ship was the *Mississippi* but under questioning changed this to the *Niagara*. He said that he was in the electricity trade in

America and had worked some time at it. He said that before he went to America he had been an assistant in the railway station bars at Mallow and Ballybrophy. Another sergeant at Ennistymon RIC – Robert Walwood – then took a statement from Dowling at 4 pm on 12 April, noting that Dowling was by then normal – "He had drink taken previously but had settled down" –

James O'Brien – Statement 12 April 1918

> *Born March 1891. Left home 8 years of age and was first employed at Ballybrophy Railway Station Saloon. After that I went to Dublin aged about 12 years. Stayed there for 4 years with a farmer. Then went to Chicago. After 18 months went to New York. Played clarinet for Hennessey's Orchestra earning 16 dollars a week until 27 March this year. About 24 March, received notice that I would be called up. Before joining army wanted to see my relatives in Ireland. On 27 March left Chicago. Had about £54 plus a portmanteau of clothing. Left Baltimore on Steamer Mississippi, Captain's name was Hill. Ship was 3,500 tons with one funnel. The Captain gave me a job cleaning up and working with the cook. Went aboard on 1 April. There was the Captain and two Mates and a crew of 13. At 12.30am on Friday, 12 April, I heard a report. Head some of the men shout 'U-Boat.' Went on deck, no-one there. I assumed that they had left the ship. Got dressed, got money, and saw boat half lowered by two ropes. I cut the ropes and jumped in the boat. Reached land just before daybreak. Stayed there until saw fisherman at about 6am.*

Walwood then took Dowling to the Naval Base Office at Galway the following day, 13 April, where he was seen by the Senior Naval Officer there, Commander Francis Hannan. According to Hannan, Dowling said that he had left Baltimore on 2 April for Liverpool with a cargo of foodstuffs on government service, that the *Mississippi* had a crew of thirteen besides the Captain and two mates, and that the Captain's name was Hill (he didn't know his first name). There was one man called Jones, a seaman, and the cook he worked under was John (he did not know his other name). Hannan noted, "He [Dowling] seemed entirely ignorant to my mind of anything to do with a ship", and said that he had sent a trawler out to look for wreckage but so far as he was aware, none had been found. It was later confirmed by Major Charles Mullins of the RMLI that there was no record of a United States Steamer "*Mississippi*" of about 3,500 tons. Not (unsurprisingly) being satisfied with Dowling's various stories, Hannan then sent him overnight to London, escorted by Walwood, where he was handed over to Sergeant William McCormack of the Royal Defence Corps at the Cromwell Gardens Detention Barracks on 14 April. On 16 April, he was handed over to the Metropolitan Police. According to McCormack, he said, 'Come this way, Mr O'Brien,' to which the prisoner replied, 'Don't call me by that name again. My name is Dowling. They know all about me up there.'[13] Following a short stay at Cannon Row Police Station, Dowling was taken to be held at the Tower of London on 22 April.

It was agreed by the War Office, the Admiralty and MI5 that Dowling would be tried by court martial. In the period leading up to the trial, Dowling was subjected to a number of interrogations, mainly at New Scotland Yard, conducted by Basil Thomson, Assistant Commissioner of the Metropolitan Police, and Captain Reginald Hall, the Director of Naval Intelligence (both of whom had previously led the questioning of Casement), and Henry Curtis Bennett, King's Counsel, who had been brought in by Thomson because of his exceptional cross-examination skills.[14] Within days of arriving in London, Dowling had admitted his real identity and had given details of his arrival in Ireland broadly in line with the accounts given by the RIC and other witnesses. Crucially, Dowling now said that he had travelled to Ireland from Germany by U-boat.

He said he had arrived off the west coast at about midnight on 11/12 April, and after two attempts had landed ashore in a small rubber boat at about 2 am, thinking he had reached the mainland, only to find at daybreak that he was on an island. He had then signalled three fishermen in a motorboat to take him off the island and had given them £5 to say nothing. He was wearing an English lifebelt given to him by the commander of the U-boat and said that he had been torpedoed and washed ashore. When he was stopped by a police sergeant in Ennistymon, he had given information, "which was partly true and partly false" – 'They detained me thinking I am going to give them some useful information. I have told them nearly all the truth but not quite.' Dowling's explanation as to why he had been sent to Ireland was that he had been told to find out how things were going on there, as they had no recent information in Germany about Irish affairs. He said he had intended to see his brother, who was going to put him in touch with members of Sinn Féin. His statement concluded with an obvious nonsense about what was to happen next. He said that after he had obtained sufficient information to be able to go back to Germany the arrangement was that he should proceed to Liverpool and get a job on board a certain line of steamers. When it was known that one of these steamers was leaving, it would be torpedoed, and he was to be picked up on this torpedoed steamer by a U-boat and taken back to Germany. He said he would not give the name of the line.[15] When interrogated by Thomson, Hall and Bennett on 17 April, Dowling said that he had embarked on the submarine at Wilhelmshaven but did not know its number – 'I asked one of the chaps the number and he told me that they had no numbers now. I do not know whether this is true.' He did not know the Captain's name but would recognise him from a photograph. He said that he had volunteered for the mission because he wanted to get away from Germany and had been paid nothing for the job – 'I would not accept anything.' He said that the money he had brought with him – £50 – was all his own and represented money he had saved in Germany. The questioning then moved on to discussing in more detail the reason for his journey. He elaborated on his earlier statement by saying that the purpose of his mission was to find out "exactly what was going on in people's minds" – whether people were enlisting and about conscription. He was to write a letter – if conscription was going very badly, he was to say that things were going very well. The letter was to be sent to A J J Donley, a prisoner of war. When asked how he was going to get back to Germany, he now said that he was not going back: the fact was that he had simply been trying to get home. When asked whether, as in the case of Monteith, the plan was for him to go on to America, he said "not as far as I know". He claimed to know nothing about Casement's expedition other than that Bailey had said that they were going on a couple of days' pass and did not have time to say where.

At another interrogation on 20 April, the subject matter switched to a proposal that Dowling had made that he would be prepared to make a statement in return for a written undertaking that he would be let off. He was told, "If you would like to make a statement to us, do so by all means and we will take it down, and we should certainly recommend it in the proper quarter, but we cannot go further than that. It is for you to take or leave", and "… the point is you must make it in some way that there is no promise on our part, because we are not allowed to give any promise". Dowling responded by pointing out what had happened to Bailey, only to be told that Bailey had been given no promise –

> *The difference between your case and Bailey's is this – Bailey came over with Sir Roger Casement, they both got up for trial for high treason, not the same trial as you will have, because you will go to a Court Martial trial. He was put up with Sir Roger Casement and it was a question as to whether we should go on with Bailey's case and Bailey was looked on as having acted under Sir Roger*

Casement's orders, the case is different with you, because you came alone. Bailey did not really give any more information than you have. There was no promise at all to Bailey; in fact it was not decided until the very last minute that we should not proceed against him. The statement came from Sir Roger Casement who was afterwards executed, but there was no promise to either of them. In fact it was never done. Only in your case of course there is this, that if you told the truth and it was really of value, we should represent it to the proper quarters, but it would have to be given without any promise and it would have to be of value.

There then followed some further to-ing and fro-ing during which Dowling said that he did not want the information he had to be made public, but that he was nevertheless willing to give the information to those who might be interested – 'Any promise you can make as to my being overlooked they can answer me.' Again, the interrogators replied, 'They cannot. That is the whole point.' But Dowling persisted with a statement which was to be instrumental in setting the future turn of events – 'The Admiral himself told me that, if I told the truth'— at which point Captain Hall cut in, 'Yes, you did not tell me and I was obliged to turn you over to the authorities.' The conversation continued – Dowling: Anything I did tell you was the truth. Captain Hall: No. Now you are turned over to the judicial authorities, so that is neither here nor there.

The remainder of the interrogation centred around trying to find out the nature of the information held by Dowling that he was willing to trade. It was, he said, to do with Ireland, prompting the response, 'If you think by what you will say you will prejudice Ireland from having a successful rising I can tell you they will not have a successful rising. I think we all have the same views – we want to save trouble in Ireland,' to which Dowling replied, 'If you can do what I said, I am willing to meet you.'

DOWLING AND THE GERMAN PLOT - THE FINAL ACT

*

Even while Dowling was being interviewed, his arrival from Germany was assuming a wider dimension. His landing had come in the middle of growing unrest following the Government's decision to extend conscription to Ireland accompanied by a new attempt at Home Rule. The threat of conscription had resulted in widespread anger and threatened resistance by the Nationalist parties, the trade unions, and most worryingly by Roman Catholic bishops and priests. The bill to give effect to conscription had been published on 9 April, only three days before Dowling's arrival. On 13 April, Henry Duke, the Chief Secretary for Ireland, circulated a memorandum to the War Cabinet warning that a crisis was imminent.[16] And on 2 May, Arthur Samuels, the Irish Attorney General in Dublin Castle, wrote to the Prime Minister saying that Ireland was on the brink of civil war and there was no doubt about the existence of a "German intrigue". He reported that the people of Ireland were hoarding silver because they were being told that English paper money would be worthless when Germany won. Samuels enclosed with his letter a secret report from a Major Price, head of the Special Intelligence Branch at Army Headquarters in Dublin, which, deservedly or not, placed Dowling at the centre of what was to become known as the "German Plot". Price set out the details of Dowling's landing and claimed that his mission had been to talk to Sinn Féin leaders (who did not know of his coming and had not requested it) and that three weeks after his return to Germany, a German "expedition" would "set out". Price continued with vague reports of expected arms landings in Mayo and Galway and a report by a defecting Volunteer that he had received imported German arms. On 10 May, Samuels reported to the War Cabinet that there was now abundant evidence of hostile association by Sinn Féin with the Germans and they were daily organising effectively and "concocting rebellion". He argued that the leaders of Sinn Féin should be deported and interned. Walter Long, who had been empowered on the same day to act on the Cabinet's behalf in all Irish matters not requiring special attention, accepted the evidence provided by Samuels and Major Price without demur, merely commenting that a stern hand was needed to put down the "Irish-German conspiracy", which appeared to be widespread in Germany.[17] Accordingly, on the night of 17–18 May, seventy-three prominent leaders of Sinn Féin were arrested and deported to England. The list included Eamon de Valera, Arthur Griffith, Darrell Figgis, Count Plunkett, William Cosgrave, Thomas Dillon, Countess Markevitz, Maud Gonne and Mrs Tom Clarke. *The Times* reported that the Sinn Féin offices had been raided and that the deportees had left in a vessel from Kingstown (Dun Laoghaire), witnessed by a large crowd but with no accompanying disorder.[18]

The public justification for the arrests was set out the next day in a proclamation issued by Lord French, the Lord Lieutenant. This stated that "certain subjects" of His Majesty the King had "conspired to enter into, and have entered into, treasonable communication with the German enemy". On 23 May, the War Cabinet considered and approved a draft statement for publication which set out the reasons for the detentions in more detail. The statement opened as follows –

> *The revolutionary movement in Ireland, which culminated in the arrest of a considerable number of persons last week, consisted of two closely related series of activities:-*
>
> a. *The attempts of the German Government to foment rebellion in Ireland; and*
> b. *The preparations made in Ireland to carry those attempts into action.*

DOWLING AND THE GERMAN PLOT - THE FINAL ACT

> *The story of the active connection between the leaders of the Sinn Féin movement and the Germans, as disclosed by documents in the possession of the British Government, falls into two parts: the period prior to, and the period since, the abortive Irish Rebellion of 1916. The events of the first period can be told with some "detail", but the second period, which concerns recent events, permits no more than a "summary", as a full statement "of the facts and documents in the possession of the British Government" would disclose the names of persons who stood by the Government, and also the channels of communication through which the German was acting, and which it would not be in the public interest to reveal at present.*

Part 1 of the statement then proceeded to set out in detail information about the origins of the Easter Rising based on intelligence gleaned by the Admiralty from intercepted German messages – "The story begins as early as the 6th November, 1914, when Herr Zimmermann transmitted through Count Bernstorff a message from Casement asking if a messenger, if possible a native-born American, could be sent to Ireland with the word that everything was favourable". The statement went on to say that the plot had ripened at the beginning of 1916, when a despatch by Count Bernsdorff to an address in Rotterdam had included an extract from John Devoy, "to the effect that action in Ireland could not be postponed much longer, since he feared the arrest of the leaders. It had been decided, he said, to begin action on Easter Saturday, and he urged that arms and ammunition must be in Limerick by that date". And so the statement went on, setting out exchanges between America and Berlin, right up to the Rising. The point of Part 1 was to demonstrate that the Irish Volunteers had been, "in communication with the authorities in Germany and were for a long time known to be supplied by money through Irish-American societies". While the details may have been of interest to some, the main message was hardly new, as the Casement trial had amply demonstrated Irish, American and German connections.

Part 2 of the statement covered events following the Rising, starting with a message from Berlin to Washington on 17 June 1916, saying that Germany was prepared to give further help if the Irish, "would only say what form of help is required", and referring to a despatch by Bernstorff on 16 June 1916, stating that he had provided £1,000 for Casement's defence. The statement then reported a note dated 31 December from Zimmermann to Bernstorff, describing quantities of munitions which Germany were proposing to send to Ireland in February 1917, but at the same time making clear that it would not be possible to send German troops. In his reply to this on 18 January 1917, Bernstorff had said that, "the Irish Committee declined the proposal, as, without German troops, a rising would be useless". While communication channels had inevitably changed when America entered the war, it was clear, the statement said, that communications between Ireland and Germany were still continuing, citing as evidence a speech by de Valera given at a Convention of Irish Volunteers on 27 October 1917, in which he had said –

> *By proper organisation, recruiting, they could have 500,000 fighting volunteers in Ireland. That would be a big army, but without the opportunity and the means of fighting, it could only be used as a menace. There had already been too much bloodshed without success, and he would never advocate another rebellion without hopeful chances of success. They could see no hope of that in the near future, except through a German invasion of England, and the landing of troops and munitions in Ireland. They should be prepared to leave nothing undone towards that end.*

The statement went on to say that in January 1918, de Valera had also stated that, "So long as Germany is the enemy of England and England the enemy of Ireland, so long will Ireland be the friend of Germany". It continued by saying that in about April 1918, "it was definitely ascertained that the plan for landing arms in Ireland was ripe for execution, and that the Germans only awaited definite information from Ireland as to time, place, and date". The British authorities, it said, had been able to warn the Irish Command of a probable landing of an "agent from Germany from a submarine" and that the agent had duly landed on 12 April and had been arrested. In essence, the Government claimed that a new rising had been planned to follow a major German offensive on the Western Front, which would leave the British Army short of manpower. The rising would be dependent on munitions being landed from German submarines on the west coast of Ireland. There was evidence that the munitions were actually shipped on submarines at Cuxhaven at the beginning of May. Meanwhile, "according to documents found on his person, de Valera had worked out in detail the constitution of his rebel army, and hoped to be able to muster 500,000 trained men". According to the statement, plans for a rising following the German Spring Offensive were now "maturing" and a new shipment of arms from Germany was imminent. Finally, and clearly intended to keep America on side, the statement concluded –

> *An important feature in every plan was the establishment of submarine bases in Ireland to menace the shipping of all nations. In these circumstances, no other course was open to the Government, if useless bloodshed was to be avoided, and its duty to the Allies fulfilled, but to intern the "authors and abettors" of this criminal intrigue.*[19]

During discussion of the draft statement in the War Cabinet, George Barnes MP (and former leader of the Labour Party) expressed doubts as to whether public opinion would be satisfied by the claim of a plot until the matter had been tested before the courts. Following its publication, the "evidence" presented in the statement was certainly regarded by Nationalists as unconvincing. Writing from Dublin on 26 May, the correspondent of *The Times* reported that the nationalist press had been unanimous in declaring that the evidence of a "German Plot" was inadequate, that it would carry no conviction in Ireland, and that the Government's treatment of the deported nationalists was grossly unfair, having been described as "one of the most outrageous instances of injustice in the long history of British management in this country". The view of the nationalist press was that the prisoners should be given an immediate opportunity to vindicate themselves, with some newspapers suggesting that they should be put on trial in their own country before an Irish jury. The nationalist Joseph Devlin MP, was reported in the same article as saying that the British Government, in a "confused and panic-stricken state of mind", had got German plots on the brain and that, "arrests had been made on a wholesale scale of Irishmen and Irishwomen on vague charges, which the Government was unable to prove by trying them before a jury of their own countrymen". The Irish race, he said, would not believe one of those charges until proved before the only tribunal which lovers of justice and fair play recognised. But *The Times'* correspondent then went on to say that more moderate Irishmen, by contrast, did indeed believe firmly in the existence of a plot and that internment was a necessary act of public policy: it should be for the British to decide if and when the internees should be put on trial. The correspondent himself advised that if and when the question was raised in Parliament, "your readers will do well to remember that no sane man in Ireland has any doubts about the existence of the German plot". Many things had been hidden from the British public by means of censorship, he said: outrageously pro-German speeches had been made at public meetings; Sinn Féin had been systematically collecting arms and high explosives; and hundreds of Irishmen on the southern and western coasts could, "tell strange stories of the activities of German submarines". *The Times'* correspondent contended that the plot had been scotched just in time and that the Government itself could not escape criticism for being indifferent for too long to a serious danger. In the correspondent's view, "the best elements in Irish Nationalism recognise that Ireland's friends in all countries accept the Government's assurances about the plot, and that American and all Allied opinion is now marshalled solidly against sedition and the defenders of sedition in this country.[20]

The advent of the "German Plot" effectively killed off the twin policies of conscription and Home Rule. On 14 June, the Irish Committee of the War Cabinet concluded that, "…in view of the new information which has come into the possession of the Government as to the disturbed state of Ireland and as to the effects of priestly denunciations on the police, that the immediate enforcement of conscription is impossible. …The same circumstances destroy for the time being the chance of any agreed settlement of the Irish Government". This conclusion was endorsed by the War Cabinet on 19 June, subject to a decision to maintain the public position that the twin policies had been put on hold rather than abandoned.[21] This was followed up by a seven-and-a-half-hour Adjournment debate in the House of Commons on 25 June, where the Government attempted to defend its claim of a German plot and put the matter to rest.[22] Edward Shortt, the Chief Secretary of Ireland, told the House –

> *I have read in many papers, I have heard it said, and apparently there is a body in this House who also believe it, that the German plot is but a mere bogus invention intended by the Government in some way to injure Ireland and the Irish cause.*

He refuted that, again rehearsing the circumstances leading to the Easter Rising which he alleged had been "to some extent" financed by Germany. He told the House that in the lead-up to the present crisis written notices had appeared on walls saying –

> *Take no notice of the Police Order to destroy your own property, and to leave your homes if a German Army should land in Ireland. When the Germans come they will come as friends, and to put an end to English Rule in Ireland. Therefore, stay in your homes, and assist the German troops as much as you can.*

He continued to say that there had been incitement of the Volunteers – one internee had said that Germany had guaranteed them a Republic without more ado when she was victorious. In addition to such propaganda, "Our sources of information were able to warn us that an agent from Germany would be landed, as landed he was on 12 April on the West Coast of Ireland". Shortt denied claims that had been made that the agent had landed in a boat made for the British Navy and said that the Government knew that submarines were plying off the Irish coast where destruction of shipping could not possibly have been their aim; that the Government had been specifically warned that a rising was planned for the end of May; and that Germany would definitely land arms and attempt to land men at the same time – "Our duty was to strike, to strike hard, and we did so…". He went on to say that people were now coming on side, citing as an example Arthur Lynch, erstwhile Irish Brigadier from the Boer War –

> *In addition, there is another hon. Member of this House who at one time raised forces to fight against this country, aye, and at one time was sentenced to death for having done so, an hon. Member of this House who has never been afraid to speak his mind and has never been afraid to act on his convictions. That hon. Member has come forward, so convinced is he that this is Ireland's fight. He has received the commission of a colonel,* [technically this was not awarded until two days later, 27 June] *and, as some years ago when he thought we were in the wrong he raised a battalion to fight against us, today when he knows we are in the right, when*

> he knows the justice of our great cause, he is going to Ireland to raise a battalion to fight with us in this War.

The focus of contributors during the ensuing debate shifted between whether there actually was a plot and the merits of the conscription and Home Rule policies themselves. Lloyd George described the Irish problem as the most baffling ever to come before government. He defended the original policies on conscription, but then there had been the discovery of a very serious conspiracy to act in conjunction with Germany, "at a moment which it was anticipated would be a serious disaster for the Empire". Asquith considered the relationship between conscription and Home Rule "obscure and indeterminate". The mood in Ireland would make the pursuit of conscription fruitless: a voluntary recruitment scheme should have been attempted instead. He had no view on whether there was a German Plot – maybe there was a German Plot, but evidence for that existed a long time ago. For the Ulster Unionists, Sir Edward Carson focused on the question of conscription, arguing that Ireland should never have been excluded in the first place. His fellow Ulster Unionist James Craig favoured conscription and the exclusion of Ulster from Home Rule. In these circumstances, Ulster would be able to provide 50,000 men. The Conservative MP Sir Mark Sykes took a similar view to Edward Carson, reflecting that German involvement was nothing new, with contacts with Germany preceding the war. John McKean, the Independent Nationalist MP, was the only Nationalist to take part in the debate following the withdrawal of the Irish Parliamentary Party from Westminster earlier in the crisis. McKean considered the German Plot to be simply bogus. No complicity on the part of Ireland had been established – "You could not hang a dog upon the evidence which has been adduced in this plot", and, "The whole thing wears upon it the stamp of unreality, not to use any stronger word". A similar view on the Plot was put forward by the Liberal MP William Pringle –

I listened with the utmost care to the account of my right hon. and learned Friend of the change of situation which has made it necessary for the Government to abandon their policy of Home Rule. What is that change? The fact that there was a German plot! I make bold to say that no Member of this House has ever anywhere, not even in the course of a farcical comedy, heard an account as that which the Chief Secretary solemnly put forward in this Debate this afternoon.

Other MPs either professed support for the detention of the Sinn Féin internees, or argued that they should be quickly brought to trial. The overall mood of the debate was clearly, however, that while MPs had strong views on either side about the merits of extending conscription to Ireland and Home Rule, few actually believed in the existence of a German Plot.

Historians have since continued to debate the existence of a German Plot, or whether this was simply an invention by the British Government to further its own ends. The fact that the British Government never produced any hard evidence to back up its claim has led to a consensus that it was bogus, contrived either to halt the anti-conscription campaign or simply to get the troublesome leaders of Sinn Féin out of the way. In his recent work on British intelligence and Ireland, Paul McMahon has argued that the episode represented an apparent manipulation of intelligence by Hall and Thomson to prod the authorities into more forceful action following Dowling's landing, by persuading the Cabinet and Dublin Castle that a coup was imminent.[23] In another recent work, on the other hand, Seán Enright argues that the notion that the German Plot was fabricated has become a historical cliché without much factual foundation. According to Enright, the plot was "real enough" – at a crucial stage in the war, "the German High Command was desperate to land guns in Ireland but the insurgents were not ready for this step". Enright attributes the

Government's failure to provide evidence to the need to protect its intelligence source.[24] But against this, the record clearly shows that even at the time, Hall, as Director of Naval Intelligence, was unable to provide the War Cabinet with hard evidence of Sinn Féin complicity in any German scheme.[25] The most realistic conclusion must be that there never did exist a plot in the sense of a detailed conspiracy between Sinn Féin and Germany for an organised rebellion and that, just as he said, Dowling's mission was simply to make contact, establish local feeling and report back. As for the British Government, the distinction between a formal plot and unstructured communications between Sinn Féin and the German authorities would have hardly mattered. There was a crisis on the Western Front, a crisis in Ireland, and they had previously been caught out by the Easter Rising and German involvement. The intelligence they had received more than indicated a need to act firmly and quickly, and the term "German Plot" was simply useful shorthand.

*

While all the debate about the German Plot and Dowling's involvement in it was going on, he had still not been brought to trial. His General Court Martial finally took place on 8 and 9 July. It was, unusually, to be held in public and took place at the Middlesex Guildhall in Westminster, a venue providing easy access for the press. The trial was presided over by Lord Cheylesmore, with Sir Archibald Bodkin leading for the Prosecution, and Holman Gregory KC for the Defence. As with Casement before him, the main body of the case against Dowling rested on his membership of the Irish Brigade. Despite all that had been said elsewhere about the German Plot and Dowling's role in it, the formal charges restricted themselves to his landing in Ireland –

1. *That when a prisoner of war he voluntarily served the enemy in that he at Limburg Lahn Camp, in the Empire of Germany, between December 31, 1914, and December 31, 1915 joined and served in the Irish Brigade, a military body formed and sustained by Germany and fighting with the armed forces and on behalf of the enemy against the King.*
2. *Voluntarily aiding the enemy at Limburg Lahn Camp between the same dates, in that he voluntarily solicited, incited, and endeavoured to persuade certain British subjects, and members of military forces of this country who were prisoners of war, to forsake their duty and allegiance to the King, and to join the armed forces of the enemy to fight against the King.*
3. *That on April 10, 1918, he voluntarily departed from a certain unknown port in a German submarine, and that he was with divers naval forces of Germany with the object of landing in Ireland.*

Dowling pleaded "Not guilty" to each of the charges. In opening, Bodkin ran through Dowling's own background and the transfer of all Irish prisoners of war to Limburg at the end of 1914, where attempts were made by Casement and others to recruit them into the Irish Brigade. The most prominent among the others, he said, were the prisoners Quinlisk, Keogh, Bailey and Dowling. Testimony about the recruiting process at the camp was then given, as at Casement's trial, by ex-prisoners repatriated under exchange schemes.

One of the prisoners, John Cronin of the Munster Fusiliers, now living in Islington, had previously testified at Casement's trial. He now told the court about Dowling's role in recruitment for the Brigade at Limburg and how he had seen him being assaulted by other prisoners for his activities and having to be rescued by the German guards. Another witness, Daniel O'Brien of the 19th Royal Hussars testified that he himself had taken part in assaulting Dowling – 'We called him a dirty bastard, and said he was a traitor to his country,' for which, 'we got punished and our rations reduced.' James O'Sullivan, a corporal in the Dublin Fusiliers who worked as a post office corporal in the camp, told how he had a list of names of men in the camp in order to deal with their letters and parcels. After Casement visited Limburg, he had noticed in March 1915 that a number of names, including Dowling's, had the letters "IB" put against them. He told the men in the camp and he and others then struck Dowling as he came down some steps, calling him a traitor to his country, "and a number of other names which I should not like to express in Court". For this, he had lost his job and had been given fourteen days "in the dark cells". Another witness, John O'Sullivan, testified that Dowling had strolled about the camp "dressed in a light grey uniform with shamrocks on the shoulder and green facings" and that he had been given a rank in the Irish Brigade equivalent to a sergeant-major in the British Army, while the other prisoners starved.

Bodkin also described Dowling's landing in Ireland and called witnesses, including the fisherman who had rescued him from Crab Island and members of the RIC who had subsequently interviewed him, who testified as to his movements and the various stories he had given about how he had arrived there and what he was doing. Bodkin told the court that Dowling's claim that he had arrived in Ireland after being torpedoed on the *Mississippi* were untrue, calling on Inspector Barker of the CID, New Scotland Yard, to give evidence of a conversation he had witnessed between Dowling and his brother, John Thomas Dowling, in the Tower of London on 15 June. Barker said that permission had been given for that meeting on the condition that a police officer in addition to the military escort should be present. He had said to Dowling at the outset, 'Here is a young man who wants to speak to you; do you know him?', to which Dowling had replied, 'Yes, he is my brother.' Barker continued –

> *The two had a conversation lasting about 20 minutes or half an hour, chiefly relating to family matters, and then the prisoner said, 'This is a fine position to be in after being prisoner of war for three and a half years. I had a fine trip in the submarine – some trip.' The prisoner afterwards said to his brother, 'Did you get any news of my arrest?' And the brother replied, 'Not before it appeared in the newspapers.' The prisoner said, 'Oh, I suppose that is because I gave the false name of Thomas* [sic] *O'Brien.'*

Bodkin also called expert witnesses who testified that a collapsible boat found on Crab Island and which seemed to be the means used by Dowling to land there, was not of British, French or American manufacture and was likely to have come from a German submarine. The prosecution's contention was that Dowling could only have travelled by submarine with the full knowledge of the German authorities and that he had done so willingly. While it was not possible to know the nature of his actual mission, for the German authorities to run the risks of a submarine entering Galway Bay to land the prisoner meant that there was some important matter in hand commensurate with those risks. That matter would be for the benefit of Germany and implied treasonous activity on the part of the prisoner. All this needed to be seen in the context of the conditions in Ireland at the time.

The defence called no witnesses and when told that he could make a statement to the Court not under oath, Dowling replied after consultation with Holman Gregory, 'I have no statement to make.' Holman Gregory explained to the Court that, 'the diffidence of the prisoner in not going into the witness box should not be misunderstood or influence the Court against him. It was perhaps difficult for the Court to appreciate with what awe and trepidation an ignorant man like the prisoner approached a Court of this kind.' He told the Court that there was nothing to justify the conclusion that Dowling had acted voluntarily – 'These men were prisoners of war, living in most exceptional circumstances, starved or nearly starved, badly treated, ill-used, and were placed in a position where one witness himself had said that he had lost his memory and could not appreciate all that happened.' They had been told that joining the Irish Brigade was the only way to get out of Germany. This, he argued, represented the strongest and most cruel form of coercion – 'First there was ill-treatment; then better conditions; and then this suggestion of getting out of Germany.' So far as the boat was concerned, there was no actual evidence linking it to a German submarine or to Dowling. Finally, Holman Gregory then drew a parallel between the present case and that of Bailey, quoting from the Attorney General's statement at the Casement trial that Bailey had had no other motive than to return to his native country.

Dowling's defence was by any stretch unpersuasive. In summing up, the Judge Advocate drew a distinction between the cases of Dowling and Bailey: while Bailey had been prepared to swear that he had joined the Irish Brigade only to get back to his own country, Dowling had not taken the opportunity which was open to him of going into the box and saying why he had joined the Irish Brigade, and that he was in no way acting treacherously. There was practically no evidence on how Dowling had come to Ireland and when asked about this, he had made up a number of deliberately untrue stories. The question for the Court was why should the Germans have given Dowling money and land him on the coast of Ireland? Despite Dowling's army record showing him as being of good character, unsurprisingly Dowling was found guilty of all charges. On being asked whether he had any statement in mitigation of punishment, Dowling simply replied, 'No, sir.'[26] Almost inevitably he was found guilty on all counts and sentenced, "to suffer death by being shot". The formal submission to the King for confirmation of the finding and sentence, however, recommended that the sentence be commuted to penal servitude for life. The explanation for this is set out in a letter dated 26 July from Viscount Milner, the Secretary of State for War to the King's Private Secretary Lord Stamfordham –

> *In submitting to the King for confirmation the proceedings of the Court Martial held for the trial of Lance Corporal Dowling I have omitted to insert in the Submission the reasons which have moved the Army Council to recommend that the death sentence be mitigated to one of penal servitude for life. The circumstances, however, are as follows:-*
>
> *Previous to the trial by Court Martial and whilst Lance Corporal Dowling was being subjected to interrogation by the Intelligence Department, the Director of Naval Intelligence took upon himself to insinuate, if not to promise, immunity from the death penalty if he would, as it was put, "speak the truth" in connection with certain matters arising in the course of the interrogation. This promise subsequent formed the subject of an argument between Lance Corporal Dowling and the Director of Naval Intelligence, Lance Corporal Dowling alleging that he had spoken the truth and the Director of Naval Intelligence maintaining that he had not. I feel that in these circumstances it would not be proper to recommend to the King that the extreme penalty should be carried out and I have therefore submitted that the sentence be mitigated to one of penal servitude for life.*

The Adjutant General explained to the Secretary of State that this information had not been included in the formal recommendation to the King because he did not think that, "you would consider it desirable that a reflection upon an officer of the Admiralty should be contained in the submission".[27] Hall's apparent sabotage of the Dowling case had caused great irritation within the War Office and would continue to rankle in the future. An internal minute by Colonel Childs, the Director of Personal

Services at the War Office to the Adjutant General on 14 July, had included the statement that "without doubt" the Director of Naval Intelligence had either promised or insinuated to Lance Corporal Dowling immunity or at any rate protection if he would tell the truth. The man at the time said that he had told the truth but the Director of Naval Intelligence said that he had not. Childs continued, "I personally have doubts that the Director of Naval Intelligence was justified in making such a statement, i.e., that Dowling had not spoken the truth", and, "I am personally very much opposed to carrying out the death sentence in view of the behaviour of the Director of Naval Intelligence and I think it is very regrettable that the officer had anything whatever to do with the case and I fail to see in what way he was concerned". He went on to suggest that if it were decided that the sentence should be commuted, there should be a delay in telling the prisoner, who was no doubt preparing a petition for clemency. Keeping him on tenterhooks, as the DPS put it, might result in him revealing more than he already had in order to save his life. The Secretary of State agreed that the death sentence should be commuted but considered that if this were agreed by the Cabinet, it would be improper to withhold the information from Dowling, who should be told of the decision immediately. After the sentence had been commuted, Childs made an offer to the Director of Military Intelligence that he (Childs) should make representations to the Admiralty that the "indiscreet action by the Director of Naval Intelligence" had seriously compromised the case against Dowling and that Hall should be more circumspect in future (or "mind his own business"). But then the case against Hall crumbled when discussions with MI5 revealed that the occasion on which he had made his "offer" to Dowling was at an initial interview in his room at the Admiralty, prior to the formal interviews led by Thomson at New Scotland Yard. At that stage, Hall had been under the impression that Dowling had been arrested by the coastguards and in consequence was a naval prisoner; he had not been aware that Dowling was a soldier. In these circumstances, War Office criticism of Hall could not reasonably be pursued. Hall's actions had saved Dowling's life, but continuing resentment by the War Office would continue to make it difficult in the future.

The Times reported on 5 August that Dowling had been sentenced to death, commuted by the King to penal servitude for life. Its comment was brief – "When sentence was read at the Tower Dowling was present under escort, but he betrayed no emotion on hearing the judgment. He was afterwards conveyed to prison".[28] The official record refers to a petition submitted by him on 24 October 1918, without giving details. In a second petition dated 8 May 1919 from HM Prison Maidstone, Dowling argued that while a prisoner of war he had been given the opportunity to get home and had been forced to accept whatever means he was provided with – in this case a submarine. He had refused the offer to make a statement at his trial because, "on all other occasions when I was asked anything, I was told, I don't believe you". The prosecuting counsel had made much of this refusal, saying that had he stated that his intention was to get home, things would have been different – 'Well, I had no hesitation whatever at any time of making this statement, my intentions were to get home.' He concluded that it had now been four years and eight months since he had seen his parents and it would be too much to expect them to come to Maidstone for a visit of twenty minutes. The record notes that Private Dowling's conduct in prison had been good and "his general character and industry satisfactory", and that he was asking for a reduction in sentence, plus transfer to an Irish prison. The petition was rejected on 20 May.[29] A year later, on 7 June 1920, Dowling submitted a further petition, from HM Prison Portland, asking for a sentence reduction or a retrial. This time, he argued that his sentence was disproportionate to the evidence on which he had been convicted. He had "received an overdose of injustice". Having made his escape from Germany, he had been arrested just because of where he landed. He had been convicted of aiding the enemy, 'but I was one of a hundred who might be guilty of such a charge' ...'why can the others – men who escaped in German uniform, on German cargo boats and to my knowledge one in a German submarine – not be tried and convicted on the same evidence?' Dowling noted that other members of the Irish Brigade had now returned and that these could provide evidence to extricate him. He was, he said, "a political prisoner but I am not being treated as such". On 17 June, this petition was also refused.[30]

*

In 1922, Dowling's fate really did become political in the context of discussions that had taken place leading up to the Anglo-Irish Treaty agreeing an amnesty for political prisoners. No mechanisms were laid down for implementing this and it was left to both sides to put the agreement into effect. Dowling's case was to become a source of dispute between the two sides almost from the outset, with Irish opinion seeing Dowling as a natural candidate for release, the Colonial Office being sympathetic, but the British military being steadfastly resistant. On 6 May, L Curtis, Secretary to the Provisional Government of Ireland Committee of the Cabinet, wrote to the War Office asking for a decision on Dowling's future, as the Colonial Secretary, Winston Churchill, was having difficulty in justifying his continued detention, as others who had committed offences equally as grave as Dowling's had already been amnestied – "If this prisoner is released it will no longer be possible to argue that His Majesty's Government have in any way failed to apply the principle of amnesty for political offences to the fullest possible extent". He concluded –

> *Mr Churchill trusts therefore that the Army Council will now agree to the immediate release of the prisoner being notified to the Provisional Government in Dublin, who have repeatedly represented to him the grave embarrassment which they are being caused by political propaganda based on the continued detention of Dowling by His Majesty's Government.*

In a separate letter at official level on the same date, Curtis also wrote to Sir Herbert Creedy, the Permanent Secretary at the War Office, arguing that it was "almost impossible to frame intelligible reasons why this man should not be amnestied". Despite reminders on 14 June and 11 August, it took until 15 August for the War Office to reply, saying that their Secretary of State felt "unable to agree to Dowling's release". The background papers make clear that the War Office's advice to their Secretary of State was based on a continuing resentment of Hall's "interference" in Dowling's interrogation and the resulting commutation of his sentence –

> *He was found guilty of all charges and sentenced to be shot, but owing to a promise improperly made to him by Sir Reginald Hall, the DNI, it was considered necessary to commute his sentence into one of PS for Life, a most regrettable decision.*
>
> *This man was Casement's companion and chief supporter. I suppose it is possible to twist any offence into a political one, but this man was a deserter, a traitor, and I trust that you will oppose to the utmost either his release or any reduction in his sentence.*[31]

The question of Dowling's release then came up again later in the year, this time in connection with a bill to be introduced in the Dáil to indemnify members of HM Forces for acts done under martial law since the Easter Rising.[32] To help get the bill through, the Government of the Irish Free State represented that one of their greatest assets in meeting difficulties with the Anglo-

Irish Treaty was to be able to say that, for their part, the British Government had met all their undertakings with regard to the agreed amnesty. In this connection, they requested the release of about sixty Connaught Rangers who had been imprisoned for mutiny in India in 1920 following a protest about the activities of the British Government in Ireland. While the Army Council were predictably against this proposal, there was a clear British interest in the bill going through, and the Secretary of State for War warned the Council on 19 December that the Government might find it necessary to agree to the release on national policy grounds. In this case, their objections would be publicly acknowledged.[33] The matter was then considered by the Cabinet on 29 December, where it was agreed to send an emissary to the President of the Irish Free State agreeing to the release but on the strict condition that this would secure the passage of the Indemnity Bill through the Dáil. Further, the Emissary was to make clear that the same concession could not apply with regard to the release of Dowling, and if passage of the bill could not be secured without Dowling's release, the whole matter would come up again for consideration. Should this eventuality arise, the Cabinet noted the Prime Minister's strong view that in the last resort, Dowling should be released rather than risk losing the bill or increasing disturbances in Ireland.[34]

Loughnane, the Colonial Office representative in Dublin, accordingly consulted representatives of the Free State Government and telegraphed London on 1 January 1923 the result of discussions he had had with Tim Healy, the Governor General of the Irish Free State, W T Cosgrave, the President of the Executive Council of the Irish Free State, and others. In response to the Cabinet's position, Cosgrave had said that while the greatest pressure he was facing at present was the need to secure the release of the Connaught Rangers, the general feeling in the Free State was that achieving a satisfactory resolution of Dowling's case would inevitably follow as a corollary. The agitation that centred around Dowling was such that if he were not released, he might be run as a candidate against a certain minister to whose constituency he belonged and who had attracted considerable odium with the Republicans. The British Government's argument that Dowling's was a special case cut no ice with Cosgrave –

> *He [Cosgrave] and his Ministers have no sentimental interest in Dowling who is largely a mystery to them. They know nothing of his antecedents and they are regarding his case solely from the point of view of political expediency. He asks the British Government to take this view also and to subordinate entirely all considerations arising from the merits or demerits of the case.*

The response to this from Masterson-Smith, the Permanent Secretary at the Colonial Office, the following day, 2 January, started by noting that even the release of the Connaught Rangers was "hedged about with difficulty", with doubts existing in many quarters as to the suggested pardon of an act of mutiny, and that –

> *…the sole object that His Majesty's Government would have in advising a pardon in the case of the Connaught Rangers would be to relieve Mr Cosgrave from serious political embarrassment and enable him to secure a reasonably smooth passage for the Indemnity Bill.*
>
> *It would be on these grounds that the case for remission would be presented to Parliament and to the public here as an act of high policy directly related to the Irish settlement.*

The more closely Dowling's case was examined, he said –

> *"…the more difficult it becomes to maintain the view that it can be regarded as a case of which the main aspects are directly related to the Irish conflict. Dowling was a British subject, a member of*

> *His Majesty's forces, who for two years after the death of Casement persisted in a continuing act of gross treachery to the State. His case is strictly comparable with that of several other cases in which British subjects similarly circumstanced and guilty of less flagrant acts of treason are serving life sentences whose release has never been contemplated or suggested.*

Masterson-Smith concluded that if the release of the Connaught Rangers were sufficient to get Cosgrave over his problems, that could probably be secured, but if the cases of the Connaught Rangers and Dowling were to become intertwined, he could hold out no hope of an early decision, and asked Loughnane to put these considerations to Healy and Cosgrave. Loughnane replied to this the following day, 3 January, having talked to Healy and two ministers representing Cosgrave, who, he said, had been impressed greatly by the argument that Dowling's case was strictly comparable with that of several (non-Irish) other cases of men serving similar sentences whose continued detention the British Government would find hard to justify in Parliament if Dowling were released. They could not guarantee that a separate agitation would not grow "to formidable dimensions" during the passage of the bill, but they did not want to forego the chance that the release of the Connaught Rangers would give it sufficient impetus to carry it through safely.

The logjam having been broken, Masterson-Smith replied to Loughnane at 8 pm the same evening, asking him to tell the Governor General that the Connaught Rangers would be released the same night. At the same time –

> *In communicating this information to the Governor General, the Secretary of State* [now the Duke of Devonshire who had taken over from Churchill] *wishes you to impress upon him and through him upon Mr Cosgrave that the Cabinet have taken this decision upon the definite expectation conveyed in your telegram*

of today that the release of the Connaught Rangers alone would give a sufficient impetus to the Bill to carry it through safely and upon the assurance that the Free State Government would do their utmost to ensure its passage. The Secretary of State wishes the Governor General and Mr Cosgrave to be under no illusion as to the degree of embarrassment that would be created for His Majesty's Government if the expectation conveyed in your telegram were not realised and pressure were brought to bear upon them to reconsider the case of Dowling as a consequence of proceedings in the Irish Parliament during the passage of the Bill.[35]

The Free State Government did indeed manage to get the bill through the Dáil, but ran into difficulty in the Senate which passed a motion that no further progress should be made until HMG had released Dowling.[36] Cosgrave was, however, able to persuade the Senate to abandon this position and the bill was passed into law.

Agitation for Dowling's release nevertheless continued. On 12 January 1923, a Mrs H Fruhling of 28 Maitland Villas, Haverstock Hill, NW3, who claimed to be Dowling's second cousin, wrote pleading for his release. Though she had only met Dowling twice in her life, she felt sorry for his "poor mother". She received the familiar reply from Creedy that Dowling had been convicted of the most serious offence of which a soldier can be guilty, namely voluntarily aiding the enemy. Mrs Fruhling tried again, but to no avail –

I know little or nothing of the offence for which this man was convicted, I did not know of his existence but I cannot help feeling that it is strange that so many others are forgiven while he still languishes. He is little over 30 now, I believe, and must have been young at the time of his escapade.

We are all proud of the magnanimous treatment which England has meted out to the enemy, even the Kaiser is forgiven in a sense. May I again plead for clemency on behalf of this misguided man…[37]

In April 1923, the Labour MP Shapurji Saklavata wrote to the Under Secretary of State for War, referring to the fact that while various prisoners had been granted a free pardon following the settlement of the "Irish question", Dowling remained in prison, a situation which appeared unfair. Again, the War Office stuck to their line that Dowling was not a political prisoner and that he had been tried by court martial "for the worst possible offence". Saklavata's response that Dowling had not been interested in helping Germany but only and solely in fighting for Ireland got nowhere.[38] And on 23 May, Dowling himself submitted a further petition (officially recorded as his seventh) from HM Prison Parkhurst in which he asked for a copy of his court-martial proceedings "on repayment". This provoked internal correspondence about whether Dowling had the necessary £5 17s 8d to meet the cost, which was charged against the £35 17s 11d that had been taken from him on his arrest (though subsequently ordered to be repaid to him). Bizarrely, it was ordered that in the copy of the proceedings to be sent to Dowling, the names of members of the Court, the witnesses for the prosecution and all persons connected with the prosecution should be suppressed.[39]

In parallel with consideration of Dowling's petition, his case again became the subject of political interest. On 3 July, the Under Secretary of State at the Colonial Office wrote to the Secretary of State for War about new considerations that had arisen in the Dowling case, as set out in a private letter from Loughnane dated 5 June. This reported that agitation was now building up in the press, which was likely to be taken up by the Larkinites and Republicans. A debate in the Dáil was likely and the Irish Government would have to answer as to whether they had lodged a formal complaint with the British Government. While the Free State Government understood the arguments about the gravity of Dowling's offences under military law, it would be impossible for them to adopt the British line and it would damage their prestige to have to admit that they had failed in their protests to the British Government – "…they feel that the British Government's decision is placing them in a very false position with their own public". The Free State Government were not putting forward Dowling's case as that of a pure-minded patriot, Loughnane explained, but as a matter of pure political expediency. The covering letter from the Under Secretary of State at the Colonial Office noted that as Cosgrave had helped with the Indemnity Bill, the Duke of Devonshire considered that the release of Dowling would be a fitting gesture of thanks and asked whether the Army Council would be prepared to accept a recommendation to Cabinet that the remainder of Dowling's sentence be remitted. The day following this letter, the matter was raised again in the Irish Senate, under a motion calling for Dowling's release put down by Colonel Moore, a former lieutenant colonel in the Connaught Rangers and member of the National Volunteers. Moore had been active in raising a petition for Casement's reprieve in 1916, and his son, Ulick, had been killed on active service with the Connaught Rangers in March 1918. His motion was seconded by Sir Bryan Mahon, a former general in the British Army who had led the Relief of Mafeking in the Boer War and had succeeded Maxwell as Commander in Chief Ireland following the Easter Rising. (It had been Moore and Mahon who were responsible for the Senate motion calling for Dowling's release under the Indemnity Bill in January.) The ensuing debate, which took place on 4 and 5 July, predictably focused on the apparent injustice of Dowling's continuing imprisonment while others, including the Connaught Rangers, had now been released. A particular point seized on by Moore and other speakers was that in contrast to Dowling, none of the remaining members of the Irish Brigade had been tried or even charged, and had even been given back pay for the whole of the time they had been in Germany. There was also the inevitable comparison with Bailey, who had been reinstated in the army while Dowling had been left to languish in prison. Mahon made the point that the British Government had deliberately made political capital out of Dowling's arrest, making him out to be a more important person than he really was. First, he was imprisoned in the Tower of London, as nobles had been in the olden days, implying equivalence with them, and then he had been put up as a leading figure in the "so-called" German Plot, in relation to which numerous Irishmen had been arrested but none had been tried. He then went on to make the point that must have been obvious to most right-thinking people from the outset –

> ...Dowling is an illiterate man, and that being so it is hardly likely that a very intelligent and far-seeing nation like Germany would employ an illiterate soldier from the West of Ireland on a mission to this country, a mission demanding very great intelligence, a very difficult and complicated mission which was to organise a rising in Ireland.

The Labour Party and trade union activist Senator John O'Farrell argued succinctly that the attitude of the British Government risked a diplomatic rupture, "all for the sake of inflicting a mean and petty vengeance on one helpless man". Agreement on the unfairness of keeping Dowling in prison and the case for his release was effectively unanimous, but there was less agreement on the best way forward. As the Government of the Free State had already tried and failed to get the British Government to change its stance, there was concern among some senators that they should not appear to be criticising their own government. The final wording of the motion passed by the Senate was designed to reflect this –

> That the Government be requested to re-open with the British Government the question of the release or handing over to the Irish Government of Joseph Dowling, an ex-private of the Connaught Rangers, agreeably to the following resolution:-

That in the opinion of the Seanad the British Government should release or hand over to the Irish Government Joseph Dowling, an ex-private of the Connaught Rangers, of Irish nationality, arrested in Ireland, who is at present undergoing a life sentence of penal servitude in England in respect of an offence, political or quasi-political, committed prior to the Anglo-Irish Treaty, and that in passing this Resolution, the Seanad has in mind (1) the International and Constitutional aspect of the case, and (2) the adverse effect on the harmonious relations between Ireland and Great Britain produced by the continued retention of this prisoner.[40]

Neither Dowling's petition nor the Irish Senate's resolution could break the War Office's resistance. A letter from Creedy at the War Office to the Under Secretary of State at the Colonial Office on 7 July reiterated the Army Council's opposition to Dowling's release on the grounds that such a move would have a bad effect on the discipline of the Army, his offence having been, "the most serious of which a soldier can be guilty".[41] On 20 July, the Cabinet again decided against his release.[42] The matter was rounded off for the time being on 23 July, in response to an oral parliamentary question put down by Lieutenant Commander Kenworthy (10th Baron Strabolgi), the Liberal MP for Central Hull, who asked whether, and if so why, Dowling was still being detained. Tellingly, though the question had been addressed to the Under Secretary of State for the Colonies, it was answered by Lieutenant Colonel Guinness, the Under Secretary of State for War. Guinness gave a full reply setting out the background to Dowling's arrest, and the details of the offences of which he had been found guilty. He went on to refer to the amnesty, which had been extended both by the British and Irish Governments, "to the undisguised and regular supporters of the other party in our late domestic troubles". He continued –

> It is, however, obvious that a serving British soldier who not only leaves his own service, but who joins and takes an active part in that of an external enemy in a time of national peril cannot be placed in such a category. His Majesty's Government therefore, after giving the most careful consideration to the matter, have reluctantly come to the conclusion that they cannot advise His Majesty to vary the sentence imposed in this case.

When Kenworthy pointed out that many people had done much worse things than Dowling in Ireland – "murdered British officers in their beds and so on" – and had been liberated, Guinness fell back on the line that none of such crimes took place on active service, and "I do not think any of these peace-time crimes can compare in gravity with that of a man who deliberately goes over to the enemy, and tries to seduce other prisoners of war from their allegiance".[43]

But the matter would not go away. In September, a new government was formed in Ireland, while shortly afterwards in Britain a general election had been called for 6 December. On 13 November, the new Irish Minister of Defence, Richard Mulcahy, wrote to the Secretary of State for War, Lord Derby, asking him to secure Dowling's release before events became overtaken by work on the election. Derby simply ducked this, telling his officials on 16 November that he had not brought the matter to the Cabinet's attention, and asking them to tell Mulcahy that he had now "left for the North" and would answer the request as soon as possible, though it may be doubtful that there would be another Cabinet before the election. Derby's private Secretary duly wrote on 17 November – "Lord Derby has had to leave London for Lancashire, but on his return I will bring your letter to his notice". After the election, Derby noted that Mulcahy had been to see him "urging reconsideration of the release of Dowling", but in a letter dated 19 December to Devonshire, he said – "Further reflection has not induced me to think we should extend further clemency to this traitor and unless you have any objection I propose to inform the Minister of Defence that I cannot see my way clear to advise my colleagues to alter their decision". When the matter came up again in early January 1924, Baldwin refused to allow it to go to Cabinet in view of the fact that his government was unlikely to remain much longer in power and the matter would have to be decided by the next government.

The logjam would finally be broken when the new Labour Government came into office on 22 January 1924. On 26 January, James Henry Thomas, the new Colonial Secretary, set out the background to the Dowling case in a Secret Memorandum in advance of a special session of the Army Council to be held on 29 January. In this, he rehearsed HMG's agreement when the Anglo-Irish Treaty had been approved to release all political prisoners under a Royal Amnesty. Prisoners awaiting sentence of death for the murder of policemen had accordingly been released. HMG had at the outset refused to include the Connaught Ranger mutineers or Dowling in the category of political prisoners, though the Connaught Rangers had subsequently been released. Ever since the Treaty, the Free State Government had never ceased to press for Dowling's release in response to a demand from all parties in Southern Ireland. Thomas then moved on to the crux of the matter. The Committee of Imperial Defence now required an agreement with the Free State over the use of wireless stations in time of war, and responsibility for negotiating such an agreement with the Irish Minister of Defence rested with the Colonial Secretary. He continued –

> *I am given to understand that a satisfactory agreement in respect of wireless stations is, in the view of the Admiralty, absolutely vital to the safety of these islands in the event of war with a naval power. The requirements of the Admiralty are such as no other*

> *Dominion has ever been asked to concede, and will be extremely difficult for the Government of the Free State to concede. Even if the Free State Minister of Defence were able to agree to the conditions required by the Admiralty in respect of wireless stations, I fear that he may have great difficulty in getting them ratified by his colleagues in Dublin, unless the atmosphere has been previously cleared of this last outstanding grievance.*

To put the argument beyond doubt, Thomas only needed to conclude, "I am able to add, on information afforded to me personally by my predecessor the Duke of Devonshire, that not only he himself but also Mr Bonar Law when Prime Minister were in favour of Dowling's release on grounds of general policy".

Faced with no realistic choice, the Army Council had to back down, with Creedy writing to Masterson on 29 January that if only military considerations were involved, the Council would unanimously uphold the views of its predecessors that Dowling should not be released. The Council recognised, however, "that political considerations, which are not within their purview and on which they would not wish to offer any observations, may, in the opinion of the Government, render it desirable for other action to be taken". Creedy's letter also noted that, "You were good enough to say that you would try to arrange for the release to be effected with as little publicity as possible, at any rate this side of the Irish Channel... if any statement has to be made, the reasons for the release should be those of high policy". There then followed a wrangle about who should make the formal submission to the King for reprieve, with the new Secretary of State for War, Stephen Walsh, refusing to sign it in view of the background to the case. In the event, Ramsay MacDonald decided that Thomas should make the submission, which he duly did on 2 February, and Dowling was then released from Liverpool Prison on 6 February. The Free State sent someone to receive Dowling at the prison and take him straight to his home in Mayborough, from where he requested repayment of monies owing to him. On 15 February, the Regimental Paymaster at Warwick authorised the repayment to him of £28 0s 3d.[44] The arrangements to keep the news of Dowling's release low-key were successful, with *The Times* reporting simply on 9 February –

> *Joseph Dowling, the ex-British soldier who was arrested in Ireland in 1918 and charged with having landed from a German submarine, has been released from the prison where he was serving a life sentence in England. He is now with his parents at his home in Mayborough, Queen's County.*[45]

Dowling returned to London and on 23 October 1926 married Henrietta Hovenden, his second cousin and a retired London schoolteacher. According to the *News of the World*, he then lived an uneventful life in Hampstead following his trade of master carpenter. Apart from his wife, only the priest at his local church knew his true identity until his death on 1 August 1932.[46] In a brief article on 6 August, *The Times* noted that he was to be buried with Republican honours in Dublin the same day.[47] His coffin was met at Dun Laoghaire, by *Fianna Fail* representatives and members of the Dublin Brigade, IRA and *Cumann na mBan*, and was draped in the Irish tricolour with his Irish Brigade hat on top. Nearly a thousand people attended his funeral, including Michael Patrick Keogh and Michael O'Toole.[48]

It seems that the exact role that Dowling had been given by the German authorities following his landing in Ireland will never be known. All the evidence suggests, however, that his mission was simply to contact nationalist organisers about any plans they might have or opportunities they might see for a rising and to report back. Sending someone to Ireland on this sort of mission was part of normal German military thinking. In his account given to the British intelligence services in 1921, for example, O'Toole outlines details of specialist training that the German military had given to him for landing in Ireland carrying explosives – training which came to an end in July 1918, without the mission having actually taken place. Dowling's credentials as a nationalist were sound. Although he had fought in the British Army like his fellow captives at Limburg, he was one of the first to join the Irish Brigade and, according to O'Toole, comprised the nucleus of the Brigade together with Keogh and Quinlisk. He was sufficiently committed to show Casement's Treaty to O'Toole, who claims to have regarded it as amusing. But he appears not by any stretch to have been capable of either co-ordinating or organising what the British saw as a "German Plot". And if his claim that he had gone to Ireland simply to escape were true, that would in no way have been to his discredit as a nationalist. But whether this was the case or not, Dowling clearly saw what had happened to Bailey as a way out. Unfortunately, he did not have the intellect or skills to handle the situation well, and the British interrogators also handled things badly. The outcome of the muddle thus created saved Dowling's life, but at the same time ensured an enduring bitterness within the War Office, perhaps exacerbated by what had happened to Bailey before him when charges had been dropped unilaterally and at the last minute by the Attorney General. Reflecting general opinion in Ireland, the Free State Government fought for Dowling's release throughout while making clear (perhaps tacticly) that this was being done on the grounds of fairness rather than in relation to any role that had been played by Dowling as a nationalist. He had that recognition at his funeral, but it is hard not to agree with the claims that he had been simply used by the British Government in their propaganda over the German Plot, and that his lengthy imprisonment was due to a particular and personal vindictiveness on the part of the British military.

TEN
AFTERMATH

...the men who had given him the most trouble were those of the Casement Brigade who were very unwilling to return to England, not knowing what future might be awaiting there, or whether they might not be tried for their part in the Casement episode.
General Sir Richard Ewart, President of the Commission for the Repatriation of Prisoners of War, 3 February 1919

It is a sad (not to say ignominious as far as we are concerned) ending to a disgraceful incident.
War Office comment on the decision by law officers not to take proceedings against repatriated members of the Irish Brigade.

At the end of the war, the terms of the Armistice required the German Government to repatriate all Allied and US prisoners immediately. To facilitate this, the Allies set up a sub-commission on Prisoners of War of the Permanent International Armistice Commission. The sub-commission met at Spa and by 28 November 1918 had agreed a scheme for prisoners to be taken to nominated collection camps and from there to various ports where they would be allocated to individual transport vessels to take them home. Before these arrangements had been agreed, however, large numbers of prisoners had already started to make their own way across Europe. Many camp commandants had simply freed their prisoners immediately following the Armistice, or contrived to let them "escape" – in November 1918, Germany was starving, and not having to feed the prisoners meant more food for the local population. In other camps, where the authorities had tried to maintain discipline and carry on as before, they faced disaffection among the guards, many of whom had by now donned red armbands in sympathy with "the Bolsheviks".[1] Zerhusen records that when sitting outside a café in Danzig in November 1918, he saw a procession of "Reds" passing behind a red banner and there, "almost in the first rows", were "Sergeant Major" Keogh, "Sergeant" Kavanagh and a couple of Irish men –

> *They espied me at once, left the procession to welcome me and said, 'Oh what a good thing that you are here. Our present interpreter is quite incapable, but you know everything about us and according to our Treaty we have the same rights as any German soldier and are therefore entitled to send a representative to the Arbeit und Soldatenrat [Workers' and Soldiers' Council] and you shall be our representative. We want you to come tomorrow to the Camp to arrange this.'*

Zerhusen goes on to say that the next morning he went to the camp where the former Commandant told him that he had not been able to contact Berlin to find out what he should do with the Irishmen. He was then made their legal representative and undertook to sort things out without involving the Commandant. He says that he secured civilian clothes for the men, some money, and identity cards on which he would give each man a German name. He then arranged for the Irish Brigade prisoners out at work to be brought back to their camp while he and Kavanagh went to Munich to confer with the Bavarian Government and with a Dr Curry, an Irishman and erstwhile friend of Casement, to arrange for the men "to disappear for the time being". Those who went to Munich under this arrangement took refuge in monasteries and on the big estates of the Bavarian Catholic nobility. According to Zerhusen, a few days later, when English officers arrived in Danzig looking for them, the Commandant was able to say that all the Irishmen had left following the Revolution, he had no power to keep them, and he did not know where they were.[2]

Exactly how many men went to Munich is unknown. The special correspondent of the *Daily News* in Munich reported that on 29 November, "twelve former members of Roger Casement's Irish Brigade" had "waited on Kurt Eisner [head of the recently self-proclaimed "People's State of Bavaria"], explaining that they would be hanged if they returned to England, and asking for help from the Bavarian Government", a request which Eisner had "curtly refused, informing the deputation that they should address themselves to the Junkers and pan-Germans who had led them into their present plight". Most of the men who went to Munich subsequently appear to have drifted away, though it seems that Keogh and at least five other former members of the Irish Brigade went on to fight with revolutionaries in Munich in May 1919. Aside from those who went to Munich, a number of Brigade members made their own way around Europe after the Armistice, some eventually returning to Britain and others not. Some of those at Danzig actually chose as a group to accept voluntary repatriation, while others were rounded up by British forces. Not surprisingly, there was concern among the prisoners about how they would be treated following repatriation.[3] Princess Blücher recalls comments by General Sir Richard Ewart, President of the Commission for the Repatriation of Prisoners of War, made over dinner on 3 February 1919 –

> *Sir Richard, who was busy repatriating prisoners of war, said that the men who had given him most trouble were those of the Casement Brigade who were very unwilling to return to England, not knowing what future might be awaiting there, or whether they might not be tried for their part in the Casement episode. One of them, we heard to our great amusement, had been spending all his time last week shooting at the Bolshevists on the top of the Brandenburg Tor, which he seemed very much to prefer to returning home to the bosom of his family.*[4]

By 1 February 1919, the repatriation of Allied and US prisoners of war was complete.[5] On 2 February, Childs, at the War Office, wrote to the Judge Advocate General (JAG) raising the question of whether or not action should now be taken against the former members of the Irish Brigade. He recorded that the repatriation of these men had in no way been obstructed and nothing had been done to lead them to suppose that they were to be dealt with for their offences, but they had been terrified of what their reception would be in England and had been wondering ever since why nothing had happened to them. If they were to be proceeded against, there were two options – a court martial under the provisions of the Army Act, as in the case of Dowling, or a civilian trial for treason, as had finally been decided in relation to Casement. There were technical reasons why a court martial would be difficult, leading Childs to recommend that if action were to be taken against the men, the matter should be dealt with through the civil courts. The JAG agreed and passed the papers to Winston Churchill, the Secretary of State for War. Churchill wrote on 6

February, "I am strongly of the opinion that justice should be done upon these traitors to their allegiance", and agreed that civil proceedings were indicated. He directed that the law officers and the Lord Chancellor should be consulted both on law and policy, and that his views should be put before them.

But the Attorney General (Sir Gordon Hewart) was far from ready to agree to civil proceedings, possibly with an eye to the damage which might be done to Anglo-Irish relations through another "state trial" following that of Casement. A court martial would relegate the matter to a relatively low-key affair about army discipline, with the offenders still nevertheless being punished, rather than the whole power of the state being used against a few hapless private soldiers and NCOs.

This was indicated in a reply from the Director of Public Prosecutions to the War Office on 24 February –

> *This matter having been forwarded to me by the Treasury Solicitor, I have consulted the Attorney General thereon.*
>
> *The Attorney General requests me to state that as, in his view, a court-martial for offences under the Army Act would prima facie be a more appropriate and convenient tribunal for the trial of these men (or rather their ringleaders) than a civil court for high treason, he would be glad to be definitely informed before the case is formally submitted to the Law Officers as to whether a trial by court-martial is impossible and, if so, as to the reasons therefore: I accordingly return the papers…*

There then followed a protracted correspondence within the War Office on the technical and legal aspects of the matter. A key problem was that the Army Act barred trial by court martial for acts committed more than three years before. By joining the Irish Brigade, the prisoners could be charged with serving with or aiding the enemy, but in any such case it would be necessary to prove that the

Brigade itself was intended to serve or assist the enemy (as appeared to have been proved in the Dowling case), that the accused had joined voluntarily and that they had continued in it voluntarily up to a date not more than three years before the trial began. An alternative might be to court-martial them for treason, allowed under the Army Act because the offences had been committed abroad. In this case, the three-year limit would still apply. A final option in relation to trial by court martial would be to charge the men with desertion, in which case the three-year limit would not apply, as desertion was deemed to be a "continuing offence". But against this, it was difficult to see how a prisoner of war could be guilty of the offence of desertion when his absence from his duty was originally involuntary. None of these solutions was satisfactory, with the possibility of a court martial for treason being ruled out as potentially subject to legal challenge. The choice remained between a court martial, as adopted for Dowling, or a civil trial, as adopted for Casement. Whichever option was chosen, the problem of actual evidence remained, especially in relation to any acts committed by the men after April to May 1916. There was actually none, as set out in an internal minute by Major General Price of AG3 at the War Office 18 March –

> *The men who joined the German Irish Brigade were apparently moved to Zossen Camp in the summer of 1915, and were kept separate; so that no outside evidence is available as to their subsequent acts. According to statements of repatriated suspects, there was trouble at Zossen Camp on St Patrick's Day 1916, after which the German Irish Brigade was out of favour with the Germans. It was apparently broken up and the men sent to various mines, farms, etc. some three months afterwards.*
>
> *Casement, in his letters to Count Wedel... dated 30/3/16 and 1/4/16, writes of the 55 men (GIBgde) at Zossen and of his strong aversion to bringing any of them into serious danger by taking them with him in the projected trip to Ireland.*

> *I do not think that any definite evidence against these men, as to assisting the enemy as late as April or May 1916 can be produced: unless some of the repatriated prisoners (GIBgde) turn King's evidence against the ringleaders…*

At this stage, the War Office clearly had no idea of the moves to get members of the Irish Brigade to fight in Egypt, but even if they had, these activities ceased in February 1916 and would have fallen just the wrong side of the three-year barrier. The case was accordingly put to the law officers, whose subsequent opinion was as follows –

> *There cannot, in our opinion, be any question that if any of these persons is to be tried, the trial should take place before a Civil Court and not by Court Martial. With regard to the question whether any trial should take place at all, this must depend, in the first instance, upon the probability or otherwise of a conviction being obtained in the event of any one or more of these men being put upon this trial. The charge would have to be a charge of High Treason. We are of the opinion that it is highly improbable that a jury would convict anybody of this offence against whom it could only be said that he had joined the Irish Brigade. It would be open to any such person to say, and to say without the possibility of contradiction, that his reason for joining was not disloyalty to the Crown, but a desire to get a favourable opportunity to escape, or more lenient treatment from the Germans. The case of any man who could be shown to have attempted to get others to join the Brigade would be different, though even here the treatment which has already been meted out to Bailey and to Dowling leads us to deprecate the idea of putting anybody on trial who cannot be shown to have taken at least as prominent a part as these two took in endeavouring to get men to join the Irish Brigade. If the statements submitted to us are a fair sample of the evidence available, it fails entirely to show*

that any of the persons at present in this Country did more than to join the Irish Brigade themselves. It is true that Private Boland speaks of some of the four men at his Camp at Canterbury having spat in the face of other men who refused to join the Brigade and if action of this kind could be brought home to an individual we should be inclined to take a different view of his case, but Boland does not identify which of the four men it is whom he alleges to have acted in the way described, and even if he could identify the man we think it would not be desirable to put that man on trial unless some corroboration of Boland's statement could be obtained.

It follows that, upon the information before us, we do not advise that proceedings for treason should be launched against any of the repatriated members of the German Irish Brigade.

Sd. Gordon Hewart [Attorney General]
E M Pollock [Solicitor General]
G A H Branson [Junior Treasury Counsel]

Needless to say, the opinion was not well received in the War Office. In putting it to Churchill on 18 April, Childs commented, "I feel that the public generally will find themselves quite unable to understand why no action has been taken with a view to bringing these men to trial", before going on to suggest that all men who had joined the Irish Brigade should be discharged forthwith for misconduct, forfeiting their war gratuities and the twenty-eight days' furlough with pay and other advantages normally given to men on demobilisation. He concluded, "It is a sad – not to say ignominious as far as we are concerned – ending to a disgraceful incident".[6] The question of discharge was subsequently refined. In reply to a parliamentary question on 6 May, Captain Guest for the War Office said that as it had not been possible to proceed against repatriated Irish Brigade prisoners of war, they had had to be treated as any other prisoners. Only those who were "known to have accepted their release from the Germans shall be discharged from His Majesty's Service for misconduct". It is not clear precisely what this new definition meant, or whether anyone was ever discharged under its provisions. The parliamentary question implied that thirty-three Irish Brigade prisoners of war had been repatriated in all, a figure not contested by Captain Guest.[7] The final outcome does not seem to have been of any interest to the press.

ELEVEN
EPILOGUE

It was, surprisingly, World War II which provided the coda to the story of the Irish Brigades that had started with the flight of the Wild Geese. Although the Irish Free State (or Eire as it had been renamed in 1937) was now effectively independent and stayed neutral during World War II, the partition of Northern Ireland was still a fundamental source of resentment among hard-line republicans, giving rise to a major bombing campaign carried out on the British mainland by the IRA in 1938. In 1936, the IRA had been outlawed in the Free State, but as war approached, some republicans in both Ireland and America saw Germany as a potentially useful ally against the British, as in World War I. In the summer of 1939, British intelligence received casual information that the German Minister in Dublin, Dr Eduard Hempel, had been in touch with Seán MacBride and the Irish writer and republican activist Frances Stuart, the husband of Iseult Gonne.

Stuart and Hempel had got to know each other through Maud Gonne. Discussions among the three centred on organising and training a "Casement Brigade" recruited from Irish prisoners of war. Nothing further was heard about this scheme until January 1940, when with Hempel's assistance Stuart travelled to Berlin. In April 1940, Stephen Carrol Held, an Irishman of German origin with IRA connections, also went to Berlin to discuss proposals for the invasion of Ulster by 50,000 Germans assisted by 5,000 IRA men, with arms being landed for the use of the IRA. Held was unable to secure agreement to the supply of arms, but the German authorities were interested in the rest of the proposal. To take this forward, they despatched to Eire one of their agents, Herman Goertz, who was dropped by parachute on the night of 5/6 May. (Goetz had previously been deported from England in 1939, having served five years in prison for espionage.) Before leaving Germany, Goetz had talked to Francis Stuart and on landing made his way first to Stuart's home at Laragh Castle, Co Wicklow, where he was assisted by Iseult on his way to Held's house in Dublin. From there, he was put in contact with the IRA to discuss future co-operation between Germany and the IRA.[1]

Within Germany, steps were meanwhile being taken to identify suitable Irish POWs who might be prepared to join an Irish Brigade, or otherwise co-operate. Camps were visited for this purpose by Helmut Clissman, an NCO with the German intelligence service (the *Abwehr*). Clissman had studied in Ireland as a representative of the German Academic Exchange Board from 1933 to 1936, before going back to Dublin as the Exchange Board's secretary in 1938 and then returning to Germany at the outbreak of war. During his stay in Ireland he had married Elizabeth Mulcahy, a staunch Republican from Co Sligo.[2] Clissman invited Irish POWs to give their names with a view to transferring to a special camp that offered better conditions and possible release from captivity should they co-operate. Potential candidates were then moved first to Stalag IIIA at Luckenwalde, 50 kilometres south of Berlin and then, about eight weeks later, to Friesack Camp (Stalag XXA (301)), about 60 kilometres north-west of Berlin. Unlike the First World War, there were no attempts to enlist POWs via mass meetings. Instead, potential candidates were interviewed individually, not only to encourage them to change sides but also to weed out possible infiltrators and British informers. According to British intelligence, the IRA were directly represented in prison camps by Sean Russell, the former IRA Chief of Staff who had masterminded the 1938 bombing campaign, Francis Stuart and Frank Ryan, a former member of the IRA who had fought with the International Brigade in the Spanish Civil War. Ryan had been captured and ultimately given a thirty-year prison sentence before being released at the request of the Irish Government, supported by the *Abwehr*, on the condition that he never return to Spain.³ It seems that Ryan's participation in the recruitment process was reluctant and short-lived, with the suggestion that his own firm left-wing views made him fear being seen as a Nazi collaborator.⁴

The lead in handling Irish prisoners on the German side was then taken over by Jupp Hoven, a German staff officer, who was sent to Friesack in around March 1941. Hoven had longstanding connections with the IRA. British intelligence records show that as early as 1929, he had attended a conference of "revolutionary nationalists" where he had met leading IRA figures, and until 1939 had visited Ireland, both North and South, on behalf of Buro "J", the JAHNKE bureau, which collected intelligence outside Germany for von Ribbentrop, the Minister of Foreign Affairs.⁵ During the war, he belonged to a unit, "Sonderstab Herkules", involved in plans to penetrate Ireland. He already knew Clissman, having similarly been sent to Ireland before the war as an exchange student (studying anthropology). It is said that both of them had also become friendly with Ryan and had played a part in securing his release from Spain.⁶ Hoven records that as well as being given the task of sorting things out at Friesack, he also visited other POW camps to arrange for further suitable Irish prisoners to be transferred there. The objective he was given was to form an "Irish army unit", though further sorting also took place to identify men who might be suitable for training in sabotage and other activities. At Laufen Camp (Oflag VIIC), near Salzburg in Bavaria, he visited a Major McGrath, who had expressed a desire to take charge of the men. Testing his motivation, he asked McGrath whether this would not result in a conflict with his oath of allegiance as a British officer. McGrath had replied that he was an Irishman above all else and that given the opportunity he would fight for Ireland in the event of an actual invasion of Ireland on the Irish ports by British troops. Hoven notes that he did not mention anything about setting up an Irish Brigade to McGrath, his main purpose being to secure an Irishman "of such professed outlook" as Senior Officer in order to have the discipline of the men improved. Any doubts Hoven may have had being satisfied, he arranged for McGrath to be transferred to Friesack, where he arrived on 10 April 1941.[7]

McGrath had been born in Elphin, Co Roscommon in 1894. At the age of seventeen, he had moved to Lancashire where he joined the Officer Training Corps, subsequently securing a commission in the British Army and serving in Gallipoli and France during the First World War. He was promoted to Captain and wounded twice, the second time resulting in him spending the last year of the war in a military infirmary. After leaving the army in 1929, he returned to Ireland, managing cinemas and theatres before becoming the first manager of the Theatre Royal in Dublin in 1936. He was then recalled to the army as a reservist in 1939, and served with the BEF where he was given field promotion to Major before being captured on the retreat to Dunkirk in 1940.[8] McGrath states that over a three-month period in the prison camp at Laufen he was specially interviewed on several occasions with a view to him going to Friesack, but "he was downright in his refusal". He had then changed his position on the instruction of a senior British officer at Laufen, Brigadier Nicholson, who had famously conducted the British defence at the siege of Calais and had been captured on its fall. Nicholson told him to investigate what was going on at Friesack and to "smash" the attempts to seduce Irish prisoners.

At Friesack, McGrath took over from a Lieutenant Bissell, who had been unable to control the Irish prisoners there and who had been moved to another camp after preparations he was making to escape were detected by the camp authorities.[9] Just as Hoven had been suspicious of McGrath, so were the prisoners. To counter this, McGrath instigated a series of secret lectures where he told them explicitly that the Irish had been moved to Friesack so that efforts could be made to "suborn" them. For his part, he promised to stand by the men, "provided they were not influenced by the Germans to undertake anything behind his back". He successfully countered German criticism when they learned about this by saying that it would simply have been bad policy to appear unduly co-operative at the outset. He records that for their part, ninety per cent of the men were supportive of his comments. A large number of the prisoners considered that they had been trapped into something, stating that they had been misled into thinking that the camp had been formed to give preferential treatment to them because Eire was neutral. McGrath found that Friesack's designation Stalag XXA (301) was actually that of a large camp near Thorn (Torun) in Poland, and that it was being used to keep Friesack's existence secret. A consequence of this was that neither the Protecting Powers nor the Red Cross had inspected the camp to assess conditions, which he found to be bad. With the agreement of the camp authorities, he secured a regular supply of parcels from the Red Cross, telling them that a small sub-camp had been set up under the designation of Stalag XXA and that no parcels had been received. Concerts were arranged and a camp orchestra was formed.[10] While it was clear that some of the men were happy to collaborate with the Germans, others had pretended to co-operate simply in the hope of getting home. McGrath was prepared to sanction all this, in return for the men agreeing that on landing in Ireland or Britain they would immediately report to the authorities and have no contact with the IRA.[11]

Even without McGrath's attempts to frustrate the process, the notion of forming an Irish Brigade from among the prisoners was inevitably doomed to fail, for much the same reason as Casement had failed in the previous war. Irishmen who had voluntarily joined the British Army, especially at a time when Ireland had effectively gained its independence and was neutral, were the least likely to be prepared to abandon their oath of allegiance and fight alongside the enemy who had captured them. During McGrath's time at Friesack, the number of Irish prisoners in the camp reached a peak of 180 out of a possible total of 1,000 Irish prisoners held in the German camps as a whole.[12] Of the 180, the vast majority had no desire or intention to collaborate with the German plans. In those terms alone, the notion of raising a brigade was out of the question. The *Abwehr* began to recognise this and started to scale down its ambitions for Friesack, concentrating on training men for sabotage and espionage work rather than melding them into an independent fighting unit. Meanwhile, McGrath continued by various means his policy of frustrating the German plans, including encouraging prisoners not to agree to private interviews intended to persuade them to collaborate. Camp discipline also began to deteriorate, with prisoners burning German literature and cutting wires to loudspeakers used for relaying German propaganda. For McGrath, matters came to a head when he enlisted the services of an Irish priest, Father Thomas O'Shaughnessy, brought into the camp by the Germans to act as chaplain in July 1941.[13] O'Shaughnessy was supportive of McGrath and on returning to Rome agreed to take with him a secret written report from McGrath to the

British authorities on the situation at Friesack and the names of those undergoing training. It seems that the contents of the report became known to the *Abwehr*, perhaps through a wire-tap when the priest telephoned the Irish embassy before going to deliver the written report to them. McGrath was in consequence arrested by the Gestapo on 17 May 1942 and transferred to Sachsenhausen concentration camp before being moved to Dachau concentration camp on 13 February 1943, where he served out the rest of the war.[14] Friesack was then finally closed in 1943.

The story of the Irish Brigades thus came to an end. It is perhaps fitting that the final word on this final chapter should go to an Irishman and former member of the British Army, Brigadier W M T Magan, CBE. Bill Magan had been born in Athlone, Co Westmeath, to an Irish father and English mother. After a lifetime of service, mainly military in the Middle East, he joined MI5 in 1947. He died aged 101 in 2010. In 1962, he reviewed the file on the events surrounding Friesack and the attempt to establish a World War II Irish Brigade[15] from his desk, commenting –

> *I am sorry to have taken such a long time about reading this file. I have now done so. I doubt that it is of any current security value. It is, however, of greatest historical interest. It reveals clearly what I myself, and I dare say a great many other people probably, would consider incredible, that is that the Germans, despite a determined effort, had no success whatever in their attempt to wean Southern Irish prisoners of war from their loyalty, as members of the British forces, to the Crown. It is possible that what this file contains is not recorded anywhere else in the British war annals. History apart, it is perhaps not without some future security use as a guide to what might happen in comparable situations. I think the file should go to the archives.*

ENDNOTES

Prefix TNA represents the UK National Archives at Kew
Prefix NLI represents the National Library of Ireland, Dublin

Introduction
1 The Treaty of Limerick, 1691, Corpus of Electronic Texts, University College, Cork, at http://www.ucc.ie/celt/published/E703001-010/index.html [Accessed 16 December 2013].
2 Robert Kee, *Ireland* (1981), p.51.
3 *The Honourable Society of the Irish Brigade*, at http://home.earthlink.net/~rggsibiba/html/sib/sib4.html [accessed 8 June 2013].
4 G M Trevelyan, *A Shortened History of England* (1959), p.361.

1. Meagher and the American Civil War
1 Gary R Forney, *Thomas Francis Meagher: Irish Rebel, American Yankee, Montana Pioneer* (2003), p.20.
2 Thomas Francis Meagher, *The Sword Speech, 28 July 1846* (unabridged), from *Meagher of the Sword, speeches of Thomas Francis Meagher in Ireland*

1846–1848, ed Arthur Griffith, M H Gill & Son Ltd (1916), at http://en.wikisource.org/wiki/The_Sword_Speech [Accessed 3 January 2014]

3   F D, A M, and D B Sullivan, *Speeches from the Dock; or, Protests of Irish Patriotism* (1904), p.132.
4   Alan Downey, *The Complete Young Irelander: Thomas Francis Meagher* (1945), p.7.
5   Athur Griffith (ed), *Meagher of the Sword: Speeches by Thomas Francis Meagher in Ireland 1846–1848: His Narrative of Events in Ireland in July, 1848, Personal Reminiscences of Waterford, Galway, and his Schooldays* (1916), pp. viii, xi-xii.
6   Ibid, p.ix.
7   Forney, p.36.
8   *The Times*, 18 May 1948, p.5.
9   Forney, pp. 36-8.
10 Griffith, p.xiii.
11 National Flag, Department of the Taoiseach at www.taoiseach.gov.ie [Accessed 17 May 2017] and Fifteen facts about the Irish flag and 1916, *The Irish Times*, at www.irishtimes.com [Accessed 17 May 2017].
12 *The Times*, 17 May 1848, p.8.
13 *The Times*, 18 May, p.5.
14 *The Times*, 18 May 1848, p.5, and 19 May 1848, p.8.
15 *The Times*, 19 May 1848, p.4.
16 *The Times*, 20 May 1848, p.8.
17 *The Times*, 8 June 1848, p.8, 6 July 1848, p.5, and 11 July 1848, p.6.
18 House of Commons: Parliamentary Debates (Hansard), 22 July 1848, Cols 696-743.
19 T F O'Sullivan, *The Young Irelanders* (1945), p. 89, and Griffith, p.177.
20 Forney, p.41.
21 Ibid, pp 42-3.
22 TNA HO 45/2416.
23 Robert G Athearn, *Thomas Francis Meagher: An Irish Revolutionary in America* (1976), p.10.
24 Forney, p.45.
25 Robert Kee, *Ireland: A History* (1981), pp 105-6.
26 Ibid, p.106.
27 Griffith, pp.174-95 (from a narrative written by Meagher in Richmond Prison, Dublin, 1849, published in the *Nation*).
28 *The Times*, 11 October 1848, p.5. [This punishment meant death by hanging

following which the body was disposed of as described. Before law reforms in the 19th century, the punishment required the body to be taken down from the gallows *before* the prisoner had died – the sentence was, "To be drawn upon an Hurdle to the place of Execution and there hanged by the Neck but not until he is dead. But that he be taken down again and whilst alive his Bowels be taken out and burnt before his face. And that afterwards his head be severed from his Body. And his Body be divided into four Quarters and his Head and Quarters to be at the disposal of our Lord the King", file TNA DPP 4/36.]

29 The details of Meagher's trial set out in the text are generally taken from the reports of proceedings in *The Times* on 18 October 1848, p.5; 20 October, p.6; 21 October, p.3; 21 October, p.5; 23 October, pp. 2-3; 24 October, pp.6-7; and 25 October, p.4.

30 Captain W F Lyons, *Brigadier-General Thomas Francis Meagher: His Political and Military Career; With Selections from His Speeches and Writings* (1871), pp. 13-15.

31 *The Times*, 25 October 1848, p.4.

32 *The Times*, 18 October 1848, p.5.

33 *The Times*, 18 January 1849, p.5, 3 February 1849, p.7 and 12 May 1849, p.7.

34 *The Times*, 13 June 1849, p.8.

35 *The Times*, 19 June 1849, pp.3-4. The Bill was finally passed as the Transportation (Ireland) Act 1849, c.27.

36 O'Sullivan, p.89.

37 *The Times*, 11 July 1849, p.8.

38 Forney, pp. 58-9.

39 *The Times*, 26 April 1852, p.6.

40 Michael Cavanagh, *Memoirs of Gen Thomas Francis Meagher comprising The Leading Events of His Career* (1892), p.310.

41 Forney, pp.63-5.

42 John Keegan, *The American Civil War* (2009), p.51.

43 Keegan, p.40.

44 Cavanagh, pp.378-80.

45 Ibid, p.400.

46 Ibid, pp.409-412, 425 and 434.

47 Ibid, pp 427-32.

48 Daniel M Callaghan, *Thomas Francis Meagher and the Irish brigade in the Civil War* (2006), p.69.

49 Union Brigadier General Fitz-John Porter, cited in Callaghan, pp.85-6.

50　Callaghan, p.86.
51　Ibid, p.89.
52　Cavanagh, pp.451-8.
53　Callaghan, p.90.
54　Cavanagh, pp.459-62.
55　Forney, p.110.
56　Keegan, p.168.
57　Forney, p.24 and *The 28th Massachusetts Volunteer Infantry*, at http://www.28thmass.org/history.htm. [Accessed 3 March 2018].
58　*The Times*, 19 January 1863, p.12.
59　Cavanagh, pp.466-7.
60　Ibid, p.468.
61　Ibid, pp.470-1.
62　Ibid, Appendix pp.23-6.
63　Maldwyn A Jones, *The Limits of Liberty: American History 1607–1980* (1983), pp.220-1.
64　Clement Vallandigham, Ohio History Central, at http://www.ohiohistorycentral.org/w/Clement_Vallandigham. [Accessed 22 January 2018].
65　*The Times*, 13 October 1863, p.8.
66　D P Conyngham (Capt), *The Irish Brigade and its Campaigns* (1867), p.405.
67　Cavanagh, pp.451-2.
68　Rory T Cornish, *"Meagher, Thomas Francis (1823–1867)"*, Oxford Dictionary of National Biography, Oxford University Press (2004), at http://www.oxforddnb.com/view/article/18483. [Accessed 24 March 2014].
69　Callaghan, p.134.
70　Richard F Welsh, *America's Civil War: Why the Irish Fought for the Union*, at http://www.history.com. [Accessed 20 May 2014].
71　Callaghan, p.107-8.
72　Forney, pp.128-9.
73　Callaghan, p.175.
74　John E Carey, *Civil War Stories of Inspiration: Marsena Patrick, Provost Marshal General of the Army of the Potomac*, at http://civilwarstoriesofinspiration.wordpress.com/2008/09/20/. [Accessed 15 May 2014].
75　*The Times*, 1 February 1865, p.10.
76　Athearn, pp.137-8.
77　Cavanagh, p.493.
78　Keegan, p.273.

79 Conyngham, pp.402-3.
80 Ibid, p.399.
81 Ibid, pp.406-7.
82 Ibid, pp.408-11.
83 Ibid, pp.411-3.
84 Ibid, pp.413-4.
85 Ibid, pp.424-34.
86 Forney, p.133.
87 *The Times*, 13 October 1863, p.8.
88 Cavanagh, p.368.
89 Ibid, p.369.
90 Jones, p.229.

2. John MacBride and the Irish Transvaal Brigade

1   Lawrence William White and James Quinn (eds), *1916: Portraits and Lives* (2015), p.151
2   TNA CO 904/18, The National Archives, Kew.
3   Anthony J Jordan, *The Yeats-Gonne-MacBride Triangle* (2000), p.18.
4   Anthony J Jordan, *Major John MacBride, 1865-1916* (1991), pp.19 and 24-25.
5   Cited in Brian Barton, *The Secret Court Martial Records of the Easter Rising* (2010), p.210.
6   Manifesto dated 13 September 1899, cited by Donal P McCracken, in *Irish In The Boer War*, at www.blogstudio.com/woodgnome/irishboerwar.html [Accessed 25 June 2013].
7   Jordan, *Major John MacBride*, pp.24-5.
8   A S Snyman, *Blake's War*, at http://www.blakeswar.com [Accessed 30 August 2014].
9   John Blake, *A West Pointer with the Boers: Personal Narrative of Colonel J Y F Blake, Commander of the Irish Brigade* (1903), p.14.
10 Thomas Pakenham, *The Boer War* (1982), p.106.
11 Barton, p.210.
12 Pakenham, p.421.
13 *Irish volunteers fighting for freedom in the Anglo-Boer War*, at newhistory.co.za/irish-volunteers-fighting-for-freedom-in-anglo-boer-war [Accessed 1 July 2013].
14 Interview with MacBride in Paris, *The Times*, 16 November 1900, p.4.
15 *With the Flag to Pretoria* (1899–1900), Part 29, p.678.

16 *See* Pakenham, p.428.
17 Donal P McCracken, *MacBride's Brigade: Irish commandos in the Anglo-Boer war* (1999), pp.42-3.
18 *The Times,* 30 November 1900, p.10.
19 Barton, p.210 and *The Times,* 23 November 1900, p.4.
20 Copy on TNA CO 904/208, National Archives, Kew.
21 *The 1916 Rising: Personalities and Perspectives*, National Library of Ireland, at http://www.nli.ie/1916/pdf/9.4.-df [Accessed 27 July 2013].
22 Jordan, *Major John MacBride*, p.27.
23 Anna MacBride White and A Norman Jefferies (eds), *The Gonne-Yeats Letters 1893–1938: Always Your Friend* (1992), p.19.
24 Ibid, letter from Gonne to Yeats, 10 February 1903, p.166.
25 Anthony J Jordan, *The Yeats-Gonne-MacBride Triangle*, p.37.
26 *The Gonne-Yeats Letters 1893-1938: Always Your Friend*, p.168.
27 Ibid, p.172.
28 Ibid, p.186.
29 Jordan, *The Yeats-Gonne-MacBride Triangle*, pp.94-5.
30 *The Gonne-Yeats Letters 1893-1938: Always Your Friend*, pp.232-3.
31 *The Times,* 21 March 1900, p.5.
32 *The Times,* 2 January 1901, p.5.
33 *With the Flag to Pretoria,* Part 9, p.204.
34 Rayne Kruger, *Goodbye Dolly Gray* (1974), p.139.
35 Pakenham, p.213.
36 Ibid, pp.225-33.
37 Ibid, pp.357-8.
38 *With the Flag to Pretoria*, Part 20, p.483.
39 Elizabeth Longford, *Victoria,* (2011), p.606.
40 Correspondence on TNA CO 904/208, National Archives, Kew.
41 Ibid, Metropolitan Police Report dated 11 June 1903.
42 Ibid, note dated 29 November 1904.
43 Ibid, minute dated 29 December 1904.
44 House of Commons: Parliamentary Debates (Hansard), 20 June 1906, Col 189.
45 TNA CO 904/208, National Archives, Kew.
46 Barton, p.211.
47 House of Lords: Parliamentary Debates (Hansard), 4 July 1911, Col 155.
48 House of Commons: Parliamentary Debates (Hansard), 31December 1912, Cols 249-50.

49 House of Lords: Parliamentary Debates (Hansard), debate on Army Reinforcements, 8 January 1915, Cols 355-7. (Colonel Warburton is described by Viscount Midleton as a retired Royal Engineer who had written seditious articles in the newspaper *Sinn Féin*.)
50 House of Lords: Parliamentary Debates (Hansard), debate on The Sinn Féin Rebellion, 10 May 1916, Cols 955-1000.
51 TNA WO 71/350, National Archives, Kew.
52 Ibid, p.212.
53 TNA WO 71/350, National Archives, Kew.
54 Barton, p.213.
55 Ibid, p.216.
56 From the *Capuchin Annual 1966*, cited in Jordan, *Major John MacBride*, p.125.
57 Barton, p.216.
58 Ibid, p.211.
59 J B Lyons, *The Enigma of Tom Kettle: Irish Patriot, Essayist, Poet, British Soldier, 1880–1916* (1983), p.36.
60 Ibid, p.294.
61 Ellermann, Richard, *a long the riverrun: Selected Essays* (1989), p.241.
62 *The Gonne-Yeats Letters 1893–1938: Always Your Friend*, pp.374-6.
63 Ibid, letter to Yeats dated 8 November 1916, pp.384-5.

3. Arthur Lynch and the Second Irish Brigade

1 Oxford Dictionary of National Biography at http://www.oxforddnb.com [Accessed 17 August 2013] and Australian Dictionary of Biography at http://adb.anu.edu.au/biography/lynch-arthur-alfred-7270 [Accessed 10 August 2013].
2 TNA CO 904/18, p.681.
3 Anna MacBride White and A Norman Jeffares (eds), *The Gonne-Yeats Letters 1893-1938: Always Your Friend* (1992), p.64.
4 Donal P McCracken, *MacBride's Brigade: Irish commandos in the Anglo-Boer war* (1999), pp.77-8.
5 Donal P McCracken, *From Paris to Paris via Pretoria: Arthur Lynch at War*, Etudes Irlandaises, pp. 125-42 (2003), at www.persee.fr [Accessed 5 March 2021].
6 Statement by Lynch given at Bow Street Magistrates' Court, 1 August 1902, on file TNA J 17/650.
7 Arthur Lynch, *My Life Story* (1924), p.154.

8 House of Commons: Parliamentary Debates (Hansard), 9 February 1900, Cols 1041-2.
9 TNA J 17/650. (The original letter was in French. The English translation quoted at Lynch's trial was mistakenly and confusingly shown with the date 15 January 1901.)
10 Ibid, statement given by Lynch at Bow Street Magistrates' Court on 1 August 1902.
11 Lynch, p.157.
12 McCracken, *MacBride's Brigade: Irish commandos in the Anglo-Boer war* (1999), p.28.
13 TNA DPP 4/36, The National Archives, Kew.
14 McCracken, *MacBride's Brigade: Irish commandos in the Anglo-Boer war* (1999) p.95.
15 *The Times*, 21 October 1901, p.8.
16 Craig Wilcox, *Australia and the Boer War: the War in South Africa 1899–1902* (2002), pp.264-5.
17 Michael Davitt, *The Boer Fight for Freedom* (1902), pp.322-5.
18 *The Times*, 21 October 1901, p.8.
19 Wilcox, pp.264-5.
20 McCracken, *MacBride's Brigade: Irish commandos in the Anglo-Boer war* (1999), pp.98-101.
21 TNA DPP 4/36.
22 Statement by Lynch, 22 July 1902, on TNA DPP 4/36.
23 *The Times*, 21 October 1901, p.8.
24 House of Commons: Parliamentary Debates (Hansard), 16 January 1902, Cols 58-60 and 17 January 1902, Col 178.
25 *The Times*, 6 June 1902, p.10 and 7 June 1902, p.9.
26 Full details of the trial are set out in files TNA DPP 4/36 and TNA J 17/650.
27 *The Times*, 22 January 1903, p.10, 23 January, p.10, and 24 January, p.14.
28 Ibid.
29 Statements dated 22 July 1902 and 23 January 1903, TNA DPP 4/36.
30 TNA DPP 4/36.
31 TNA KB 33/47.
32 *The Times*, 27 January 1903, p.8.
33 *The Times*, 2 February 1903, p.7.
34 *The Times*, 31 January 1903, p.8. (Jameson and others involved were returned by Kruger to England after the raid, for which Jameson was given fifteen months in prison.)

35 Section 2 of the Act stated – "…if a person hereafter convicted of treason or felony, for which he shall be sentenced to death, or penal servitude, or any term of imprisonment with hard labour, or exceeding twelve months… [he] shall become and (until he shall have suffered the punishment to which he had been sentenced, or such other punishment as by the competent authorities may be substituted for the same, or shall receive a free pardon from the Her Majesty), shall continue thenceforth incapable of… being elected, or sitting, or voting, as a member of either House of Parliament…"
36 House of Commons: Parliamentary Debates (Hansard), 2 March 1903, Cols 1121-48.
37 *The Times*, 27 November 1903, p.6.
38 *The Times*, 25 January 1904, p.7.
39 TNA KB 33/48.
40 Hansard at http://hansard.millbanksystems.com/people/mr-arthur-lynch [Accessed 17 November 2013].
41 Oxford Dictionary of National Biography, *Lynch, Arthur Alfred (1861–1934)*, at http://www.oxforddnb.com/view/printable/34645 [Accessed 17 August 2013].
42 *The Gonne-Yeats Letters 1893-1938: Always Your Friend*, p.381.
43 TNA CAB 23/17.
44 Padraig Yeates, *A City in Wartime: Dublin 1914–18* (2012), p.251.
45 Ibid, p.285.
46 TNA WO 374/43377.
47 McCracken, *MacBride's Brigade: Irish commandos in the Anglo-Boer war* (1999) pp.94-5.
48 TNA DPP 4/36.
49 *The Times*, 26 March 1934, p.14.
50 Wilcox, Chapter 13.

4. Roger Casement – British Consul
1 Brian Inglis, *Roger Casement* (1973), p.135.
2 Ibid, p.115.
3 D George Boyce, *Casement, Roger David (1864–1916)*, Oxford Dictionary of National Biography, at http://www.oxforddnb.com [Accessed 8 January 2015].
4 Inglis, pp.27-32.
5 Angus Mitchell, *Casement's maps of the Niger Delta*, History Ireland Magazine, Issue 4 (July/August 2006), Vol 14, at http://www.historyireland.com [Accessed 17 January 2015].

6   Inglis, pp.38-9.
7   Rayne Kruger, *Goodbye Dolly Gray* (1959), p.37.
8   Inglis, p.53.
9   Kruger, pp.339-40.
10 Inglis, pp.54-5.
11 *The Times,* 1 October 1898, p.12.
12 Inglis, p.44.
13 *General Act of the Berlin Conference on West Africa, 26 February 1885*, at http://africanhistory.about.com [Accessed 28 January 2015].
14 *George Washington Williams's Open Letter to King Leopold on the Congo,1890*, at http://www.blackpast.org [Accessed 30 May 2016].
15 *Leopold II, E D Morel & The Congo,* at http://www.bouncing-balls.com/timeline/people [Accessed 18 April 2016].
16 Adam Hochschild, *King Leopold's Ghost: A Story of Greed, Terror and Heroism in Colonial Africa* (2012), p.112.
17 Inglis, pp.46-7.
18 Ruth Slade, *English Missionaries and the Beginning of the Anti-Congolese Campaign in England,* Revue Belge de Philosophie et d'Histoire, pp. 37-73 (1955), at www.persee.fr/doc/rbph_0035-0818_1955_num_33_1_1933 [Accessed 14 October 2018].
19 *Africa No 10 (1903), Despatch from His Majesty's Minister at Brussels respecting the Commission for the Protection of the Natives, instituted by the Government of the Independent Congo State under the Decree of September 18, 1896,* Cd 1754.
20 Africa No 10 (1903), Letter of Instruction dated 1 October 1896, pp.6-7.
21 Ordeal by poison describes a practice by the natives of administering the Calabar bean, or "ordeal bean" – *physostigma venenosum* – to persons accused of witchcraft and other crimes. When the poison killed the person concerned, it was believed that this was a sign of guilt. When it was rejected by the stomach, innocence had been proven. The bean was also used in a form of duelling. Here, a bean would be divided and taken by both parties to see who survived. Often, this resulted in both parties being killed.
22 Africa No 10 (1903), pp.13-4.
23 Slade.
24 Africa No 10 (1903), p.9.
25 Ibid, p.10.
26 Ibid, p.11.
27 Ibid, pp.20-1.

ENDNOTES

28 Ibid, p.22.
29 Ibid, pp.27-9.
30 Slade.
31 TNA FO 10/730, The National Archives, Kew.
32 Hochschild, p.180.
33 Inglis, pp.56-7.
34 Ibid, pp.50-1.
35 Ibid, pp.98-9.
36 Ibid, p.58.
37 TNA FO 403/338 Part II.
38 *Africa No 1 (1904), Correspondence and Report from His Majesty's Consul at Boma respecting the Administration of the Independent State of the Congo, February 1904, Cd 1933.*
39 Africa No 10 (1903).
40 House of Commons: Parliamentary Debates (Hansard), 20 May 1903, Cols 1289-332.
41 Jeffrey Dudgeon, *Roger Casement: The Black Diaries* (2002), p.129.
42 *Africa No 14 (1903), Despatch to certain of His Majesty's Representatives abroad in regard to alleged Cases of Ill-treatment of Natives and to the Existence of Trade Monopolies in the Independent State of the Congo,* October 1903, Cd 1809.
43 Africa No 1 (1904).
44 It seems inconceivable that the words quoted are not verbatim, but de Cuvelier's note implies that both statements were made by Chamberlain in the House of Commons on 6 August 1901 and 24 March 1903 respectively. Hansard indicates, however, that the Commons did not sit on 6 August 1901, and the quote for 24 March cannot be found in the business of the day.
45 Mitchell, p.91.
46 Africa No 1 (1904), Report by Casement to the Marquess of Lansdowne, 11 December 1903.
47 *The Times,* 7 December 1903, p.10.
48 Ibid, 16 December 1903, p.7.
49 Ibid, 22 December 1903, p.10.
50 Michael Holland, obituary, at www.jjhc.info/hollandmichaeljames1956.htm [Accessed 21 June 2018].
51 Ibid, 25 February 1904, p.10.
52 Ibid, 19 December 1903, p.7.
53 Ibid, 25 January 1904, p.4.
54 Africa No 1 (1904).

55 *Africa No 7 (1904), Further Correspondence respecting the Administration of the Independent State of the Congo [In continuation of Africa No 1 (1904)]*, HMSO, June 1904, CD 2097.
56 Ibid, 15 February 1904, p.6.
57 Ibid, 19 February 1904, p.4
58 Ibid, 22 February 1904, p.8.
59 Ibid, 21 April 1904, p.4.
60 Ibid, pp.96-7.
61 *Congo Reform Association*, at http://www.congoreformassociation.org [Accessed 26 May 2018].
62 *The Times*, 8 June 1904, p.3.
63 House of Commons: Parliamentary Debates (Hansard), 9 June 1904, Cols 1235-96.
64 *The Times*, 13 June 1904, p.7.
65 Tim Butcher in Introduction to Joseph Conrad, *Heart of Darkness and Youth* (2007), p.xi.
66 Joseph Conrad, *Heart of Darkness and Youth* (2007), p.42.
67 Dudgeon, *Roger Casement: The Black Diaries* (2002), p.144.
68 TNA FO 881/9761.
69 Miscellaneous No 8 (1912), *Correspondence respecting the Treatment of British Colonial Subjects and Native Indians employed in the collection of rubber in the Putumayo District*, HMSO, July 1912, Cd 6266, pp.7-24.
70 Ibid, pp.25-52.
71 TNA FO 881/9970.
72 TNA FO 881/9977.
73 Miscellaneous No 8, as above.
74 Inglis, p.195.

5. Casement the Nationalist
1 Brian Inglis, *Roger Casement* (1973), pp.128-9.
2 Angus Mitchell, *16 Lives: Roger Casement* (2013), p.129.
3 Geoffrey Dudgeon, *Roger Casement: The Black Diaries* (2002), p.402.
4 Inglis, pp.216-7.
5 *The Times*, 23 December 1908, p.8.
6 *The Times*, 5 March 1914, p.6.
7 NLI MS13,088/6 and W J McCormack, *Ambrose Edward Lea Charpentier (1861–1945), The Inaugural Griselda Stevens Lecture*, 27 March 2019.
8 Inglis, p.231.

9   *The Times*, 25 October 1903, p.10.
10 Roger Sawyer, *Casement: The Flawed Hero* (1984), p.114.
11 Dudgeon, p.419.
12 Ronan Fanning, *Fatal Path: British Government and Irish Revolution 1910–1922* (2013), pp.121-2.
13 Inglis, p.269.
14 Dudgeon, p.414.
15 Inglis, p.256.
16 René MacColl, *Roger Casement* (1965), pp.98-100.
17 John Devoy, *Recollections of an Irish Rebel* (1929), p.392.
18 Inglis, p.258.
19 Devoy, pp.407-8.
20 Ibid, p.410.
21 Ibid, pp.412-3.
22 TNA CO 904/94.
23 Charles Townshend, *Ireland: The 20th Century* (1999), p.67.
24 Inglis, p.277.
25 Devoy, pp.403-4.
26 Ibid, pp.404-6.
27 TNA CO 904/94.
28 Inglis, p.280.
29 Ibid, p.282.
30 NLI MS 13,074/9.i.
31 Devoy, pp.417-9.

6. The German Irish Brigade
1   Jeffrey Dudgeon, *Roger Casement: The Black Diaries* (2002), p.432.
2   TNA KV2/9.
3   John Devoy, *Recollections of an Irish Rebel* (1929) p.418.
4   Formerly Christiania, the Norwegian Government adopted the spelling Kristiania in 1877, though the former spelling often continued to be used after that date, including by Casement.
5   Denis Gwynn, *Traitor or patriot; the life and death of Roger Casement* (1931), pp.261-9.
6   Ibid, pp.269-72.
7   Devoy, p.424.
8   Brian Inglis, *Roger Casement* (1973), p.303.
9   Ibid, pp.313-4.

10 Devoy, pp.423-9.
11 Ibid, p.424.
12 TNA KV 2/6.
13 Ibid.
14 Devoy, p.431.
15 TNA HO 144/1637/311643/140.
16 Devoy, p.441.
17 TNA KV 2/9.
18 Dudgeon, p.448.
19 Inglis, p.294.
20 The Arthur Conan Doyle Encyclopedia, *Sir Roger Casement (article 30 November 1914), 7 July 1930*, at www.arthur-conan-doyle.com [Accessed 4 April 2019].
21 TNA KV 2/6. The decision to suspend Casement's pension was announced by Sir Edward Grey in the House of Commons on the same day, Hansard Cols 117-8.
22 Roger Sawyer, *Casement: The Flawed Hero* (1984), pp.110-1.
23 Inglis, p.299.
24 Ibid, pp.280-1.
25 TNA KV 2/9.
26 Devoy, p.432.
27 Ibid, pp.433-5.
28 Ibid, p.435.
29 John Yarnall, *Barbed Wire Disease: British & German Prisoners of War, 1914–19* (2011) pp.128-9.
30 TNA KV 2/9.
31 Yarnall, p.130.
32 Giles T Brown, *The Hindu Conspiracy, 1914–1917,* Pacific historical review, Volume 17 (1948).
33 Matthew Erin Plowman, *5 Irish Republicans and the Indo-German Conspiracy of World War I,* New Hibernia Review, Volume 7 (2003).
34 *The Times,* 27 October 1915, p.7.
35 TNA WO 141/9.
36 René MacColl, *Roger Casement* (1965) p.123.
37 Ibid, p.130.
38 Devoy, p.436.
39 Joseph Zerhusen, *Memoirs of Casement and the Irish Brigade,* NLI (1966), Roger McHugh papers NLI 31,728 (3)
40 *The Times,* 27 October 1915, p.7.

41 Martin Gilbert, *First World War* (1994), p.114.
42 McColl, p.131.
43 Yarnall, p.129.
44 TNA KV 2/9.
45 Devoy, p.438.
46 Florence Monteith Lynch, *The Mystery Man of Banner Strand: The Life and Death of Captain Robert Monteith* (1959), p.38.
47 Captain Robert Monteith, *Casement's Last Adventure* (1953), pp.57-8.
48 Florence Monteith Lynch, p.41.
49 Ibid, pp.50-2.
50 Ibid, pp.54-8.
51 Ibid, p.60.
52 Zerhusen.
53 MacColl, pp.149-50.
54 Florence Monteith Lynch, pp.60-6.
55 Ibid, p.68.

7. Return to Ireland
1 Jeffrey Dudgeon, *Roger Casement: The Black Diaries* (2002), p.450.
2 Ibid, p.462.
3 Florence Monteith Lynch, *The Mystery Man of Banna Strand: The Life and Death of Captain Robert Monteith* (1959), pp.53 *et seq*.
4 Joseph Zerhusen, *Memoirs of Casement and the Irish Brigade*, NLI (1966), Roger McHugh papers NLI Ms 31,728 (3)
5 Brian Inglis, *Roger Casement* (1973), p.321.
6 John Devoy, *Recollections of an Irish Rebel*, Charles D Young Co (1929), p.458-9.
7 Ibid, p.461.
8 René MacColl, *Roger Casement*, Four Square Books, London (1965), p.152.
9 Devoy, p.457.
10 TNA HO 144/1636/311643/53 (July 1916), letter from Devoy to Laurence de Lacey, 20 July 1916. Until December 1914, Laurence de Lacey had been the editor of *The Irish Volunteer* and an active Volunteer and IRB member. He fled to America in February 1915 after police discovered two men in possession of gelignite and seditious leaflets at his home. This letter was found at his home in San Francisco after he had been arrested by the US authorities.
11 TNA HO 144/1637194A.

12 Princess Blücher, *An English Wife in Berlin: A Private Memoir of Events, Politics, and Daily Life in Germany throughout the War and the Social Revolution of 1918* (1920), pp.42-4.
13 Ibid, p.87.
14 Dudgeon, p.266.
15 Inglis, pp.298-9.
16 Blücher, pp.29-31.
17 The belief that the spike in British clasp-knives was used to pick out the eyes of wounded Germans was widespread in Germany in 1914 – see John Yarnall, *Barbed Wire Disease: British & German Prisoners of War, 1914–19* (2011), p.80.
18 Blücher, p.40.
19 John Yarnall, *Barbed Wire Disease: British & German Prisoners of War, 1914–19* (2011), pp.91-6.
20 Blücher, pp.63-64.
21 Ibid, p.202.
22 Ibid, p.311.
23 Ibid, pp.130-1.
24 Denis Gwynn, *Traitor or Patriot: The Life and Death of Roger Casement* (1931), p.370. There has been much speculation about McGoey's disappearance without apparent trace. A recent researcher has added to the story by providing some evidence that McGoey eventually found his way via London to America where he died in 1924 – see http://www.irishbrigade.eu/other-men/goey.html [Accessed 29 October 2012].
25 Roger McHugh, *Casement and German help*, in *Leaders and Men of the Easter Rising: Dublin 1916* (F X Martin (ed), (1967), p.183.
26 Devoy, p.473.
27 Ibid.
28 *Dublin Fusiliers*, at www.dublin-fusiliers.com/Pows/casement/recruits/bailey.html [Accessed 4 April 2010].
29 TNA J 17/662.
30 Alan J Ward, *Ireland and Anglo-American Relations 1899–1921* (1969), p.102.
31 Max Caulfield, *The Easter Rebellion* (1963), pp.32-3.
32 W E Vaughan (ed), *A New History of Ireland VI, Ireland under the Union, II (1870–1921)*, F S Lyons, pp.200-3.
33 George Dangerfield, *The Damnable Question: A History of Anglo-Irish Relations* (1999), p.168.
34 *Dublin Fusiliers*, online as above.

35 Inglis, p.326.
36 Devoy, pp.472-3.
37 MacColl, p.158.
38 Dudgeon, p.468.
39 TNA J 17/662.
40 H Montgomery Hyde, *Famous Trials 9: Roger Casement* (1964), p.17.
41 Ibid, p.18.
42 Ibid, p.19.
43 Ibid, p.17.
44 Devoy, p.473.
45 Dangerfield, pp.170-3.

8. Trial, Retribution and Legacy

1   H Montgomery Hyde, *Famous trials 9: Roger Casement* (1964), pp.21-9.
2   Ibid, pp.31-40, and TNA CAB 37/147/7.
3   *The Times,* 25 April 1916, p.4.
4   Ibid, 29 April 1916, p.10.
5   Ibid, 17 April 1916, p.7.
6   Ibid, 27 April 1916, p.7.
7   Ibid, 27 April 1916 p.7 and 1 May 1916, p.7.
8   Ibid, 29 April 1916, p.10.
9   Ibid, 3 May 1916, p.7.
10 TNA CAB 37/146/20.
11 *The Times,* 15 May 1916, p.3 and 10 December 1914, p.5.
12 Montgomery Hyde, p.53.
13 Ibid, p.57.
14 *The Times,* 16 May 1916, p.9.
15 Ibid.
16 Montgomery Hyde, pp.58-65.
17 Ibid, p.68.
18 Ibid, pp.71-2.
19 Ibid, p.73.
20 Ibid, p.77-8.
21 Brian Inglis, *Roger Casement* (1973), p.341.
22 Montgomery Hyde, pp.94-5.
23 Ibid, pp.99-100.
24 Ibid, pp.101-2.
25 Jeffrey Dudgeon, *Roger Casement: The Black Diaries* (2002), pp. 508-9.

26 *The Times*, 30 June 1916, p.8.
27 *Roger Casement – Speech From The Dock, at* nootherlaw.com [Accessed 1 February 2022].
28 TNA J 17/662.
29 Montgomery Hyde, pp.130-1.
30 Ibid, p.81.
31 *The Times*, 7 July 1916, p.8.
32 Ibid, 29 July 1916, p.9.
33 Inglis, p.367.
34 Ibid, 371.
35 NLI MS 10,564/6/2/1 (1 and 2).
36 TNA HO 144/1636/311643/42.
37 TNA FO 800/112.
38 TNA HO 144/1636/311643/53.
39 TNA FO 800/112.
40 Ibid.
41 Ibid.
42 TNA HO 144/1636/311643/42.
43 Montgomery Hyde, pp.74-7.
44 TNA CAB 37/151/8.
45 TNA HO 144/1636/311643/40 (July 1916).
46 TNA CAB 37/151/35.
47 TNA CAB 37/152/1.
48 TNA CAB 37/153/11.
49 TNA FO 800/86.
50 Ibid.
51 *Roger Casement and America*, published on 1 April 2016, by Robert Schmuhl, University of Notre Dame, at https://breac.nd.edu [Accessed 4 April 2019], p.10.
52 *The Times*, 4 August 1916, p.3.
53 John Devoy, *Recollections of an Irish Rebel* (1929), p.478.
54 TNA HO 144/23432 (1930).
55 W J McCormack, *Roger Casement in Death or Haunting the Free State* (2002).
56 Denis Gwynn, *Traitor or Patriot; The Life and Death of Roger Casement* (1931), pp.16-20.
57 Montgomery Hyde, p.150.
58 Inglis, p.174.
59 *The Times*, 4 August 1916, p.7.

60 Montgomery Hyde, p.164.
61 René McColl, *Roger Casement* (1965), p.227.
62 Ibid, p.230.
63 Inglis, p.373.
64 Dudgeon, p.510.
65 Angus Mitchell, *16 Lives: Roger Casement* (2013), p.334.
66 McColl, p.227.
67 Séamas Ó Síocháin, *Evolution and Degeneration in the Thought of Roger Casement* (2002).
68 Montgomery Hyde, pp. 148-9.

9. Dowling and the German Plot – The Final Act

1 *Daniel Bailey, Irish Brigade Sergeant,* http://www.dublin-fusiliers.com/Pows/casement/recruits/bailey.html [Accessed 4 April 2010].
2 TNA MEPO 2/10668.
3 TNA MEPO 2/1069.
4 Florence Monteith Lynch, *The Mystery Man of Banna Strand: The Life and Death of Captain Robert Monteith* (1959), p.80.
5 *Zossen Prisoners of War Camp in WW1,* http://irishbrigade.eu/camps/zossen.html [Accessed 12 September 2020].
6 TNA WO 141/9.
7 Joseph Zerhusen, *Memoirs of Casement and the Irish Brigade,* NLI (1966), Roger McHugh papers, NLI Ms31,728(3).
8 TNA WO 141/9.
9 TNA KV 2/10.
10 Justin Dolan Stover, *The Afterlife of Roger Casement's Irish Brigade, 1916–1922,* (2016), https://breac.nd.edu/articles/the-afterlife-of-roger-casements-irish-brigade-1916-1922/ [Accessed 20 September 2020].
11 *Joseph Patrick Dowling, A member of Casement's Irish Brigade,* http://www.dublin-fusiliers.com/Pows/casement/recruits/dowling.html [Accessed 2 April 2010].
12 Zerhusen, pp.7-8.
13 TNA WO 141/72.
14 Seán Enright, *After the Rising: Soldiers, Lawyers and Trials of the Irish Revolution* (2016), p.45.
15 TNA WO 141/73.
16 George Dangerfield, *The Damnable Question: A History of Anglo-Irish Relations* (1976), p.284.
17 Ibid, pp.285-7.

18 *The Times*, 20 May 1918, p.7.
19 TNA CAB 23/6/38.
20 *The Times*, 27 May 1918, pp.9-10.
21 Ronan Fanning, *Fatal Path: British Government and Irish Revolution 1910–1922* (2013), pp.185-6.
22 Hansard, House of Commons, 25 June 1918, Cols 905-1015.
23 Paul McMahon, *British Spies and Irish Rebels: British Intelligence and Ireland 1916–1945* (2008), p.24.
24 Enright, p.46.
25 Fanning, p.184.
26 Details of Dowling's court martial are taken from TNA WO 141/73 and *The Times*, 9 July 1918, pp.7-8 and 10 July 1918, p.8.
27 TNA WO 141/73, Minute from the Adjutant General to the Secretary of State for War, 26 July 1918.
28 *The Times*, 5 August 1918, p.2.
29 TNA WO 141/65.
30 TNA WO 141/66.
31 TNA WO 141/67.
32 Saorstát Eireann, *Amnesty (British Military Bill)*, 1923, at data.oireachtas.ie [Accessed 8 December 2020].
33 TNA WO 141/92.
34 TNA CAB 72 (22), 29 December 1922.
35 TNA WO 141/68.
36 TNA WO 141/71.
37 TNA WO 141/68.
38 TNA WO 141/69.
39 TNA WO 141/70.
40 Seanad Éireann debate – Wednesday, 4 July and Thursday, 5 July 1923, https://www.oireachtas.ie/en/debates/seanad/1923-07-04/05 [Accessed 21 December 2020].
41 TNA WO 141/71.
42 TNA CAB 39(23), 20 July 1923.
43 Hansard, House of Commons, 23 July 1923, Cols 13-4.
44 TNA WO 141/75.
45 *The Times*, 9 February 1924, p.7.
46 *News of the World*, 7 August 1932.
47 *The Times*, 6 August 1932, p.5.
48 *Joseph Patrick Dowling, a Member of Casement's Irish Brigade.*

ENDNOTES

10. Aftermath

1 John Yarnall, *Barbed Wire Disease: British & German Prisoners of War, 1914–19* (2011), pp.174-7.
2 Joseph Zerhusen, *Memoirs of Casement and the Irish Brigade*, NLI (1966), Roger McHugh papers NLI Ms 31,728 (3) pp.9-10.
3 *After the end of the war,* http://irishbrigade.eu/camps/post-war.html [Accessed 12 September 2020].
4 Princess Blücher, *An English Wife in Berlin: A Private Memoir of Events, Politics, and Daily Life in Germany throughout the War and the Social Revolution of 1918* (1920), p.323.
5 Yarnall, p.177.
6 TNA WO 141/36.
7 *House of Commons Hansard*, 6 May 1919, Col 724.

11. Epilogue

1 TNA KV 3/345.
2 Carolle J Carter, *The Shamrock and the Swastika: German Espionage in Ireland in World war II*, Pacific Books, Palo Alto, California (1977), p.95.
3 Ibid, pp.114-5.
4 Tom Wall, *Dachau to the Dolomites: The Untold Story of the Irishmen, Himmler's Special Prisoners and the End of WWII*, Merrion Press, Newbridge, Co Kildare (2019), p.17.
5 TNA KV 6/79.
6 Wall, *Dachau to the Dolomites*, p.17.
7 TNA KV 3/345.
8 Wall, *Dachau to the Dolomites*, pp.199-201.
9 TNA KV 3/345.
10 Ibid.
11 Tom Wall, *The Truth and Colonel McGrath*, Dublin Review of Books (2017), at drb.ie [Accessed 25 November 2021].
12 Wall, *Dachau to the Dolomites*, p.18.
13 TNA KV 3/345.
14 Wall, *The Truth and Colonel McGrath*.
15 TNA KV 3/345.

BIBLIOGRAPHY
PRIMARY SOURCES

UK National Archives, Kew

File numbers –

CO 904/18
CO 904/94
CO 904/99
CO 904/194
CO 904/195
CO 904/208
DPP 4/36
FO 10/730
FO 115/2138
FO 383/39
FO 383/42
FO 383/43

FO 383/45
FO 383/296
FO 383/392
FO 383/396
FO 403/338
FO 403/351
FO 403/680
FO 600/6
FO 629/11
FO 629/12
FO 800/86
FO 800/112

FO 881/8315x
FO 881/8268
FO 881/8414
FO 881/9082
FO 881/9761
FO 881/9818
FO 881/9970
FO 881/9977
HO 45/2416
HO 144/1636/311643
HO 144/1636/311643/13
HO 144/1636/311643/20
HO 144/1636/311643/33
HO 144/1636/311643/40
HO 144/1636/311643/42
HO 144/1636/311643/44
HO 144/1636/311643/53
HO 144/1637/311643/67
HO 144/1637/311643/101
HO 144/1637/311643/105
HO 144/1637/311643/138
HO 144/1637/311643/140
HO 144/1637/311643/141
HO 144/1637/311643/148
HO 144/1637/311643/159
HO 144/1637/311643/181
HO 144/1637/311643/183
HO 144/1637/311643/191
HO 144/1637/311643/194A
HO 144/3444
HO 144/23432
HO 144/23465
HO 144/23467
J 17/650
J 17/662
KB 12/180
KB 12/218
KB 33/47
KB 33/48
KV 2/6
KV 2/7
KV 2/8
KV 2/9
KV 2/10
KV 3/345
KV 6/79
MEPO 2/10660
MEPO 2/10663
MEPO 2/10665
MEPO 2/10668
MEPO 2/10669
MEPO 2/10693
PCOM 9/2322
PCOM 9/2323
WO 32/8347
WO 71/350
WO 141/9
WO 141/15
WO 141/36
WO 141/49
WO 141/65
WO 141/66
WO 141/67
WO 141/68
WO 141/69
WO 141/70
WO 141/71
WO 141/72
WO 141/73
WO 141/74
WO 141/75
WO 141/92
WO 339/13445
WO 372/11/150278
WO 374/43377

PRIMARY SOURCES

Cabinet Papers and Minutes –

CAB 23/6, CAB 23/6/38, CAB 23/17, CAB 24/14, CAB 24/48/18, CAB 24/117, CAB 37/146/20, CAB 37/147/7, CAB 37/151/8, CAB 37/151/35, CAB 37/152/1, CAB 37/152/13, CAB 37/152/18, CAB 37/152/22, CAB 37/152/29, CAB 37/153/11, CAB 37/153/13, CAB 39/23, CAB 41/37, CAB 41/37/25 (and CAB 37/151/8), CAB 41/37/27, CAB 41/37/28, CAB 41/37/29, CAB 72 (22), CAB 77/152/4, CAB 128/33/44

Government & Parliamentary Publications

Command Papers

Africa No 10 (1903), *Despatch from His Majesty's Minister at Brussels respecting the Commission for the Protection of the Natives, instituted by the Government of the Independent Congo State under the Decree of September 18, 1896*, HMSO, August 1903, Cd 1754

Africa No14 (1903), *Despatch to certain of His Majesty's Representatives Abroad in regard to Alleged Cases of Ill-treatment of Natives and to the existence of Trade Monopolies in the Independent State of the Congo*, HMSO, October 1903, Cd 1809

Africa No 1 (1904), *Correspondence and Report from His Majesty's Consul at Boma respecting the Administration of the Independent State of the Congo*, HMSO, February 1904, Cd 1933

Africa No 7 (1904), *Further Correspondence respecting the Administration of the Independent State of the Congo. [In continuation of Africa No 1 (1904).]* HMSO, June 1904, Cd 2097

Miscellaneous No 8 (1912*), Correspondence respecting the Treatment of British Colonial Subjects and Native Indians employed in the collection of rubber in the Putumayo District*, HMSO July 1912, Cd 6266

Other

House of Commons and House of Lords: Parliamentary Debates (Hansard)

National Library Of Ireland

MS7879/9
MS10,564/1/2
MS10,564/6/9
MS10,763/2/2
MS10,763/2/5
MS13,074/9i/13
MS13,088/6
MS14,100/11
MS18,007/12
MS18,009/45
MS31,728(3)
MS36,204
MS36,204/1
MS36,204/2
MS36,205
MS36,207/2/1
MS36,207/3/4
MS44,674

Other Primary Sources

Austin Stack Papers, University College Dublin, Ref IE UCDA P149
Boehm/Casement Papers, University College Dublin, Ref IE UCDA P127
Blake, John, *A West Pointer with the Boers: Personal Narrative of Colonel J Y F Blake, Commander of the Irish Brigade*, Angel Guardian Press, Boston, 1903
General Act of the Berlin Conference on West Africa, 26 February 1885, at http://africanhistory.about.com [Accessed 28 January 2015]
George Washington Williams's Open Letter to King Leopold on the Congo, 1890 at http://www.blackpast.org [Accessed 30 May 2016]
Gerard, James W, *My Four Years in Germany*, George H Doran Company, New York (1917)
Tom Kettle papers (1880–1916), University College Dublin, Ref IE UCDA LA34
Lynch, Arthur, *My Life Story*, John Long Ltd, London (1924)

PRIMARY SOURCES

MacBride White, Anna and Jeffares, A Norman (eds), *The Gonne-Yeats Letters 1893–1938: Always Your Friend,* Hutchinson, London (1992)

McCarthy, Daniel J. *The Prisoner of War in Germany: The Care and Treatment of the Prisoner of War, with a History of the Development of the Principle of Neutral Inspection and Control*, Skeffington & Son Ltd, London (no publication dated given)

Meagher, Thomas Francis, *The Sword Speech, 28 July 1846* (unabridged), in *Meagher of the Sword, speeches of Thomas Francis Meagher in Ireland 1846–1848,* ed Arthur Griffith, M H Gill & Son Ltd (1916), at http://en.wikisource.org/wiki/The_Sword_Speech [Accessed 3 January 2014]

Seanad Éireann – Volume 1, 4 July 1923: *The Dowling Case – Motion by Senator Colonel Moore,* at https://www.oireachtas.i.e. [Accessed 8 December 2020]

Seanad Éireann – The Dowling Case, Debate, 5 July 1923, at https://oireachtas.i.e. [Accessed 21 December 2020]

Saorstát Éireann – *Amnesty (British Military Bill) 1923*, at https://www.oireachtas.i.e. [Accessed 8 December 2020]

The Treaty of Limerick, 1691, Corpus of Electronic Texts, University College, Cork, at http://www.ucc.ie/celt/published/E703001-010/index.html [Accessed 16 December 2013]

The private papers of F E Smith, the First Earl of Birkenhead

Audio and Video Recordings

Daly, Carrie, *Roger Casement Raving in Limerick*, https://www.rte.ie/archives/2016/0316/775381-roger-casement-contracts-malaria [Accessed 4 December 2019]

John Pilger, *The Outsiders: Seán MacBride,* interview with Seán MacBride, 1983, at http://johnpilger.com/videos/the-outsiders-sean-macbride [Accessed 13 August 2013]

BIBLIOGRAPHY
SECONDARY SOURCES

i) Reference

Australian Dictionary of Biography, National Centre of Biography, Australian National University, at http://adb.anu.edu.au/biography [Accessed 10 August 2013]

Oxford Dictionary of National Biography, Oxford University Press (2004), at http://www.oxforddnb.com [Accessed 17 August 2013 and 8 January 2015]

ii) Newspapers, periodicals and pamphlets

The *Freeman's Journal*
The Times, The Irish Times and other newspapers
The Times History of the War
With the Flag to Pretoria, Harmsworth Brothers, London (1899–1900)
Pamphlets relating to "Easter Week Rising 1916", NLI Ref IR94109

iii) Other

After the end of the war, http://irishbrigade.eu/camps/post-war.html [Accessed 12 September 2020]
Asquith, Margot, Michael Brock and Eleanor Brock (eds), *Margot Asquith's Great War Diary 1914–1916: The View from Downing Street*, Oxford University Press (2014)
Athearn, Robert G, *Thomas Francis Meagher: An Irish Revolutionary in America*, Arno Press, New York (1976)
Barker, A J, *Behind Barbed Wire*, B T Batsford Ltd, London (1974)
Barton, Brian, *The Secret Court Martial Records of the Easter Rising*, The History Press, Stroud (2010)
Birkenhead, The Second Earl, *The Life of F E Smith First Earl of Birkenhead*, Eyre and Spottiswoode, London (1959)
Blücher, Princess Evelyn, *An English Wife in Berlin: A Private Memoir of Events, Politics, and Daily Life in Germany Throughout the War and the Social Revolution of 1918*, New York, E P Dutton & Company (1920)
Bowman, Timothy, *Irish Regiments in the Great War: Discipline and Morale*, MUP (2003)
Brown, Giles T, *The Hindu Conspiracy, 1914–1917*, Pacific historical review, Berkeley, California, University of California Press (1948, Volume 17)
Callaghan, Daniel M, *Thomas Francis Meagher and the Irish Brigade in the Civil War* (McFarland & Company, Inc, Jefferson, North Carolina, and London (2006)
Campbell, John, *F E Smith: First Earl of Birkenhead*, Jonathan Cape, London (1983)
Carey, John E, *Civil War Stories of Inspiration, Marsena Patrick, Provost Marshal General of the Army of the Potomac*, at http://civilwarstoriesofinspiration.wordpress.com [Accessed 15 May 2014]
Carter, Carolle J, *The Shamrock and the Swastika: German Espionage in Ireland in World War II*, Pacific Books, Palo Alto, California (1977)
Casement recruiting of the Irish Brigade from Irish POWs, at http://www.dublin-fusiliers.com/Pows/casement/irish-brigade.html [Accessed 3 April 2010]
Caulfield, Max, *The Easter Rebellion*, Gill & Macmillan Ltd, Dublin (1963)
Cavanagh, Michael, *Memoirs of Gen. Thomas Francis Meagher comprising The Leading Events of His Career*, The Messenger Press, Worcester, Massachusetts (1892)
Clement Vallandigham, Ohio History Central, at http://www.ohiohistorycentral.org/w/Clement_Vallandigham.htm [Accessed 22 January 2018]

SECONDARY SOURCES

Conan Doyle, Arthur, *The Crime of the Congo*, Doubleday, Page & Company, New York (1909)

Conrad, Joseph, *Heart of Darkness and Youth*, Vintage Books, London (2007)

Conyngham, Capt D P, *The Irish Brigade and its Campaigns*, William McSorley & Co, New York (1867) at https://archive.org/details/irishbrigadeand00adgoog [Accessed 10 April 2014]

Coogan, Tim Pat, *The Twelve Apostles*, Head of Zeus Ltd, London (2017)

Cornish, Rory T, "Meagher, Thomas Francis (1823–1867)", *Oxford Dictionary of National Biography*, Oxford University Press (2004), at http://www.oxforddnb.com/view/article/18483. [Accessed 24 March 2014]

Costigan, *The Treason of Sir Roger Casement*, The American Historical Review, Vol 60, No 2 (1955)

Dangerfield, George, *The Strange Death of Liberal England*, Serif, London (1997)

Dangerfield, George, *The Damnable Question: A History of Anglo-Irish Relations*, Barnes and Noble Books, New York (1976)

Daniel Bailey, Irish Brigade Sergeant, at http://www.dublin-fusiliers.com/Pows/casement/recruits/bailey.html [Accessed 4 April 2010]

Daniel Bailey Trial, at http://www.dublin-fusiliers.com/Pows/casement/recruits/bailey/bailey-trial-evidence.html [Accessed 4 April 2010]

Davitt, Michael, *The Boer Fight for Freedom*, Funk and Wagnalls, New York (1902)

Devoy, John, *Recollections of an Irish Rebel*, Charles D Young Co (1929)

Doheny, Michael, *The Felon's Track: History of the 1848 Attempted Outbreak in Ireland*, M H Gill & Son Ltd, Dublin (1914) at http://www.slieveardagh.com/michael-doheny/ [Accessed 15/3/14]

Doerries, Reinhard R, *Prelude to the Easter Rising, Sir Roger Casement in Imperial Germany*, Frank Cass, London, Portland, OR (2000)

Doerries, Reinhard R, *Hopeless Mission: Sir Roger Casement in Imperial Germany*, The Journal of Intelligence History, International Intelligence History Association, Vol 6, Number 1 (2006)

Dowling, Joseph Patrick, A member of Casement's Irish Brigade, http://www.dublin-fusiliers.com/Pows/casement/recruits/dowling.html [Accessed 2 April 2010]

Downey, Alan, *The Complete Young Irelander: Thomas Francis Meagher*, Carthage Press (Waterford News Ltd), Waterford (1945)

Doyle, Mark, *Fighting like the Devil for the sake of God*, Manchester University Press, Manchester (2009)

Dudgeon, Jeffrey, *Roger Casement: The Black Diaries*, Belfast Press (Northern Ireland) Ltd (2002)

Durney, James, *James Crosby of MacBride's Irish Brigade*, Co. Kildare Online Electronic History Journal, at http://www.kildare.ie/library/ehistory/2010/05/james_crosby_of_macbrides_iris.asp [Accessed 2/7/13]

Ellermann, Richard, *a long the riverrun: Selected Essays*, Penguin Books, London (1989)

Enright, Seán, *After the Rising: Soldiers, Lawyers and Trials of the Irish Revolution*, Merrion Press, Co Kildare (2016)

Fanning, Ronan, *Fatal Path: British Government and Irish Revolution 1910–1922*, Faber and Faber Ltd, London (2013)

Fanning, Ronan, *A Will to Power: Eamon De Valera*, Faber and Faber Ltd, London (2015)

Ferriter, Diarmaid, *The Border: The Legacy of a Century of Anglo-Irish Politics*, Profile Books Ltd, London (2019)

Forney, Gary R, *Thomas Francis Meagher: Irish Rebel, American Yankee, Montana Pioneer*, Xlibris Corporation, USA (2003)

Garvin, Tom, *1922: The Birth of Irish Democracy*, Gill & Macmillan Ltd, Dublin (1996)

George Washington Williams's Open Letter to King Leopold on the Congo, 1890, The Black Past: Remembered and Reclaimed, http://www.blackpast.org/george-washington-williams-open-letter-king-leopold-congo-1890 [Accessed 30 May 2016]

Griffith, Arthur (ed), *Meagher of the Sword: Speeches of Thomas Francis Meagher in Ireland 1846–1848: His Narrative of Events in Ireland in July, 1848, Personal Reminiscences of Waterford, Galway, and his Schooldays*, M H Gill & Son Ltd, Dublin (1916)

Gwynn, Denis, *Traitor or Patriot; the Life and Death of Roger Casement*, Jonathan Cape and Harrison Smith (1931)

Hochschild, Adam, *King Leopold's Ghost: A Story of Greed, Terror and Heroism in Colonial Africa*, Pan Books, London, Basingstoke and Oxford (2012)

Inglis, Brian, *Roger Casement*, Hodder and Stoughton Ltd, London (1973)

Irish volunteers fighting for freedom in the Anglo-Boer War, at newhistory.co.za/irish-volunteers-fighting-for-freedom-in-anglo-boer-war [Accessed 1 July 2013]

Johnson, Paul, *Ireland: A Concise History from the Twelth Century to the Present Day*, Granada Publishing Ltd, London (1980)

Jones, Francis P, *History of the Sinn Féin Movement and the Irish Rebellion of 1916*, P J Kennedy, New York (1920)

Jones, Maldwyn A, *The Limits of Liberty: American History 1607–1980 (Short Oxford history of the modern world)*, Oxford University Press, Oxford (1983)

SECONDARY SOURCES

Jordan, Anthony J, *Major John MacBride, 1865–1916,* Westport Historical Society (1991)

Jordan, Anthony J, *The Yeats-Gonne-MacBride Triangle,* Westport Books, Dublin (2000)

Kee, Robert, *Ireland: A History,* Book Club Associates (Weidenfeld and Nicolson), London (1981)

Keegan, John, *The American Civil War,* Hutchinson, London (2009)

Kruger, Rayne, *Goodbye Dolly Gray: The Story of the Boer War,* Pan Books, London (1959)

Leopold II, E D Morel & The Congo, at http://www.bouncing-balls.com/timeline/people [Accessed 18 April 2016]

Longford, Elizabeth, *Victoria,* Abacus, London (2011)

Lyons, J B, *The Enigma of Tom Kettle: Irish Patriot, Essayist, Poet, British Soldier, 1880–1916,* The Glendale Press, Dublin (1983)

Lyons, Captain W F, *Brigadier-General Thomas Francis Meagher: His Political and Military Career; With Selections from His Speeches and Writings,* Cameron, Ferguson & Co, Glasgow (1871)

MacColl, René, *Roger Casement,* Four Square Books, London (1965)

McCormack, Mike, *Maude Gonne MacBride,* Ancient Order of Hibernians, at http://www.aoh.com/2013/04/10maude-gonne-macbride [Accessed 28 July 2013]

McCormack, W J, *Roger Casement in Death or Haunting the Free State,* University College Dublin Press (2002)

McCormack, W J, *Ambrose Edward Lea Charpentier (1861–1945),* The inaugural Griselda Stevens Lecture, delivered in the Edward Worth Library (1732), 27 March 2019

McCracken, Donal P, *Irish in the Boer War,* at www.blogstudio.com/woodgnome/irishboerwar.html [Accessed 25 June 2013]

McCracken, Donal P, *MacBride's Brigade: Irish commandos in the Anglo-Boer war,* Four Courts Press, Portland, OR (1999)

McCracken, Donal P, *From Paris to Paris via Pretoria: Arthur Lynch at War,* Etudes Irlandaises (2003), www.persee.fr [Accessed 5 March 2021]

MacGoey, John, http://www.irishbrigade.eu/other-men/goey.html and http://www.irishbrigade.eu/other-men/goey/1920-immigrant-usa/mcgoey-1920.html [Accessed 29 October 2012]

MacMahon, Paul, *British Spies and Irish Rebels: British Intelligence and Ireland 1916–1945,* The Boydell Press, Woodbridge (2008)

Mansergh, Nicholas, *The Irish Question 1840–1921,* George Allen & Unwin Ltd, London (1975)

Martin, F X (ed), *Leaders and Men of the Easter Rising: Dublin 1916,* Methuen & Co Ltd, London (1967)

Mitchell, Angus, *16 Lives: Roger Casement,* The O'Brien Press Ltd, Dublin (2013)

Mitchell, Angus, *Casement's Maps of the Niger Delta,* History Ireland Magazine, Issue 4, July/August 2006, Vol 14, History Publications Ltd, Dublin, at http://www.historyireland.com [Accessed 17 January 2015]

Monteith, Captain Robert, *Casement's Last Adventure*, Michael F Moynihan, Dublin (Revised Edition, 1953)

Monteith Lynch, Florence, *The Mystery Man of Banna Strand: The Life and Death of Captain Robert Monteith,* Vantage Press, Inc, New York (1959)

Monteith, the Officer in charge of the Irish Brigade, at http://www.irishbrigade.eu/recruits/monteith.html [Accessed 13 July 2011]

Montgomery Hyde, H, *Famous trials 9: Roger Casement*, Penguin Books, Harmondsworth (1964)

Nevinson, Henry W, *Last Changes Last Chances,* Nisbet and Co, London (1928)

Nowlan, Kevin B, *The politics of repeal: a study in the relations between Great Britain and Ireland, 1841–50,* Greenwood Press, Westport, Conn (1965)

O'Sullivan, T F, *The Young Irelanders,* The Kerryman Ltd, Tralee (1945)

Pakenham, Thomas, *The Boer War,* McDonald & Co (Publishers) Ltd, London (1982)

Pakenham, Thomas, *The Scramble for Africa,* Abacus, London (1992)

Parmiter, Geoffrey de C, *Roger Casement,* Arthur Baker Ltd, London (1936)

Plasman, Pierre-Luv and Thewissern, Catherine, *The Three Lives of the Casement Report: Its Impact on Official Reactions and Popular Opinion in Belgium*, published on 1 April 2016, Universite Catholique de Lovain, Belgium, at https://breac.nd.edu [Accessed 15 July 2018]

Plowman, Matthew Erin, *Irish Republicans and the Indo-German Conspiracy of World War 1*, New Hibernia Review (2003, Volume 7)

Plowman, Matthew Erin, *The British intelligence station in San Francisco during the First World War,* Journal of Intelligence History (2013), http://www.tandfonline.com/loi/rjih20 [Accessed 12 March 2013]

Recruits to Casement's Irish Brigade, at http://www.irishbrigade.eu/recruits-irish-brigade.html [Accessed 16 July 2011]

Royal Dublin Fusiliers forfeiting medals in Casement recruiting affair, at http://www.dublin-fusiliers.com/Pows/casement/rdf-recruits-casement.html [Accessed 3 April 2010]

Rudkin, David, *Cries from Casement as his Bones are Brought to Dublin,* British Broadcasting Corporation, London (1974)

Ryan, Dr Mark F: Life, Works, Criticism, References, Quotations, Notes, at http://ricorso.net [Accessed 23 August 2014]

Sawyer, Roger, *Casement: The Flawed Hero*, Routledge & Kegan Paul, London (1984)

Schmuhl, Robert, *Roger Casement and America*, published on 1 April 2016, University of Notre Dame, at https://breac.nd.edu [Accessed 4 April 2019]

Sinclair, Mick, *United in Arms, Divided in Dreams: James Connolly, Patrick Pearse and Easter 1916* (2013) [Kindle DX version]

Singleton Gates, Peter, Gerodias, Maurice, *The Black Diaries. An Account of Roger Casement's Life and Times, with a Collection of his Diaries and Public Writings*, Grove Press, New York (1959)

Síocháin, Séamas Ó, *Evolution and Degeneration in the Thought of Roger Casement*, Irish Journal of Anthropology (2002)

Sir Roger Casement, Article dated 30 November 1914, The Arthur Conan Doyle Encyclopedia, 7 July 1930, at https://www.arthur-conan-doyle [Accessed 4 April 2019]

Slade, Ruth, *English Missionaries and the Beginning of the Anti-Congolese Campaign in England*, Revue belge de Philologie et d'Histoire, pp 37-73 (1955), at www.persee.fr//rbph_0035-0818_1955_num_33_1_1933 [Accessed 14 October 2018]

Stover, Justin Dolan, *The Afterlife of Roger Casement's Irish Brigade, 1916–1922*, published on 1 April 2016, University of Notre Dame, at https://breac.nd.edu/articles/the-afterlife-of-roger-casements-irish-brigade-1916-1922/ [Accessed 20 September 2020]

Sullivan, F D, A M, and D B, *Speeches from the Dock; or, Protests of Irish Patriotism*, P J Kennedy, New York (1904)

Taylor, A J P, *Essays in English History*, Penguin Books Ltd, Harmondsworth (1976)

The 28th Massachusetts Volunteer Infantry, 4th Regiment, Irish Brigade, at http://28thmass.org/history.htm [Accessed 3 March 2018]

The 1916 Rising: Personalities and Perspectives, National Library of Ireland, at http://www.nli.ie/1916/pdf/9.4.-df [Accessed 27 July 2013]

The Putumayo Affair, at http://www.bouncing-balls.com/timeline/putumayo.htm [Accessed 18 April 2016]

To Make Men Traitors: Germany's Attempts to Seduce Her Prisoners-of-War (London, New York & Toronto: Hodder & Stoughton (1918)

Tóibín, Colm, *Easter 1916*, London Review of Books, Volume 38, Number 7, 31 March 1916, pp.11-23.

Townshend, Charles, *Ireland: The 20ᵗʰ Century*, Hodder Arnold, London (1998)

Trevelyan, George Macaulay, *A Shortened History of England*, Penguin Books, Harmondsworth (1959)

Vaughan, W E (ed), *A New History of Ireland VI, Ireland under the Union, II (1870–1921)*, Clarendon Press, Oxford (1996)

Walsh, Maurice, *The News from Ireland: Foreign Correspondents and the Irish Revolution*, I B Tauris, London and New York (2011)

Wall, Tom, *The Truth and Colonel McGrath*, Dublin Review of Books (2017), at drb.ie [Accessed 25 November 2021]

Wall, Tom, *Dachau to the Dolomites: The Untold Story of the Irishmen, Himmler's Special Prisoners and the End of WWII*, Merrion Press, Co Kildare (2019)

Walsh, Maurice, *Bitter Freedom: Ireland in a Revolutionary World 1918–1923*, Faber & Faber Ltd, London (2015)

Ward, Alan J, *Ireland and Anglo-American Relations 1899–1921*, Wedenfield and Nicholson, London (1969)

Welsh, Richard F, *America's Civil War: Why the Irish Fought for the Union*, at http://www.history.com. [Accessed 20 May 2014]

White, Lawrence William and Quinn, James (eds), *1916: Portraits and Lives*, Royal Irish Academy, Dublin (2015)

Wilcox, Craig, *Australia and the Boer War: The War in South Africa 1899–1902*, Oxford University Press, Melbourne (2002)

Yarnall, John, *Barbed Wire Disease: British and German Prisoners of War, 1914–19*, The History Press, Stroud (2011)

Yeates, Padraig, *A City in Wartime: Dublin 1914–18*, Gill & MacMillan, Dublin (2012)

Zossen Prisoner of War Camp in WW1, http://irishbrigade.eu/camps/zossen.html [Accessed 12 September 2020]

ACKNOWLEDGEMENTS

Most of the primary source material on which this work is based is held at the UK National Archives at Kew and at the National Library of Ireland in Dublin. The facilities at both these locations have been invaluable, as has the help given to me by their staff. I must also thank the staff at the UCD Archives for locating documents and making them available to me during a very successful visit, and similarly record my thanks to the staff at the Bodleian Library and at the British Library. I should like to record my special thanks to the late Lady Juliet Townsend for allowing me unfettered access to the papers of F E Smith, the First Earl of Birkenhead. My thanks also go to Dr Alastair Robson, real tennis colleague, friend and ex-student of Trinity College Dublin, who shared his knowledge of Irish literature and Irish history with me as well as introducing me to the sights and hospitality facilities of Dublin. Lastly, my love and gratitude go to my wife, Grace, for her encouragement and patience all along the way.

INDEX

Ahlers, Nicholaus, Consul, 228
Alverstone, Lord Chief Justice, 73,
Anderson, Dr W K, 273-4
Antietam (or Sharpsburg), battle of, 24-5
Arana, Julio Cesar, 133
Augustine, Father, 58
Asquith, H H, 57, 228, 254, 262, 266, 309

Bailey, Daniel Julian (also known as Beverly), 195, 214, 216-8, 224, 229-31, 251, 290, 299, 312, 315, 326-7, 333
Balfour, A J, 71, 81, 112, 291
Ballingarry, Battle of, 13
Bannister, Edward, 97

Bannister, Elisabeth, 229
Bannister, Gertrude, 154, 229, 255, 272
Bannister, Grace, 97
Barker, Inspector, New Scotland Yard, 313
Barnes, George (MP), 305
Bennett, Arnold, 255
Bennett, Henry Curtis, KC, 297-300
Bentley, William Holman, 97, 98, 102, 104, 107
Bernstorff, Count Johann Heinrich von, 154, 158, 303-4
Beverly, Daniel Julian (also known as Bailey), 195, 214
Birrell, Augustine KC, 172
Bissell, Lieutenant, 347

Blackwell, Sir Ernley, 258, 259, 261-6, 274-5
Blake, John, Colonel, Irish Transvaal Brigade, 41, 86
Blücher, Princess Evelyn, 200-2, 204-6, 337
Blücher, Prince Gebhard Leberecht, 201-2
Bodkin, Sir Archibald, 311-4
Boland, Private, 341
Botha, Louis, 66-7, 69
Bowen-Colthurst, Captain John, 256
Brunton, Sir Lauder, 142
Bryce, Viscount James, 53

Cabot Lodge, Senator Henry, 267-8
Cadbury, William, 128
Cambier, Father, 106
Carson KC, Sir E, Solicitor General, 73, 76, 86, 309
Casement, Roger, xi; family background, 96-7; in the Congo, 97-8; Niger Coast Protectorate, 98; Lourenço Marques and Luanda, 98-100, 108; Congo Free State, 108-9, 114; Congo Report, 116-32; 132; South America and the Putumayo Report, 132-8; retirement and award of a knighthood 138-9; disillusionment and the turn to nationalism, 141; in the US, 146; the Findlay Affair, 157-175, 197, 222, 225, 272; alliance with Germany, 175-8; the Treaty and the Irish Brigade, 178-95; disillusionment with Germany, 197-213, 339; return to Ireland and the Easter Rising, 213-20; interrogation and trial, 221-51; speech from the dock, 239-50; appeal, 251-2; the question of reprieve, 252-68, 326; execution and legacy, 268-80;
Casement, Roger (Sr), 96
Cecil, Lord Hugh, 81
Chamberlain, Joseph, 99,115
Chamberlain, Sir Neville, RIC, p.52
Chancellorsville, battle, 28
Charpentier, Dr Ambrose, 142
Chartists, 10
Cheylesmore, Lord, 311
Childers, Erskine, 144
Childs, Sir Borlase Elward Wyndham, Colonel (and later Major-General), 316-7, 337, 341
Churchill, Winston, 141, 203-4, 319-20, 337-8
Christensen, Eivind Adler, 157-175, 179,191
Clarke, Tom, 191
Clarke, Mrs Tom, 302
Cleburne, Patrick, Confederate General, American civil war, 27
Clissman, Helmut, 344-5
Colbert, Con, 253
Colenso, battle of, 42, 50, 64
Collins, Con, 218, 226
Commission for the Protection of Natives, 102-7
Conan Doyle, Sir Arthur, 128, 176, 254-5
Congo Reform Association, 128, 132, 141
Connell, William Henry, 294-5
Connolly, James, 253

INDEX

Conrad, Joseph, 98,128, 132, 279-80
Conyngham, D P, Captain, US Army, 32-3
Corcoran, Colonel Michael, 69th New York Militia, 22-3
Cornwallis-West, Colonel, William, 203
Cosgrave, William, 302, 322-3, 326
Craig, Captain James MP, 55, 309
Craig, Dr Maurice MD FRCP, 262-3, 265
Cranborne, Lord, 112
Creedy, Sir Herbert, 320, 324, 328, 331
Crewe, Lord, 163, 260
Cromer, Lord, 110
Cronin, John, 312
Curry, Dr Charles E, 336
Curtis, L, 319-20
Curzon, Lord, 177-8

Davitt, Michael, 45, 51, 68, 81, 82, 253
de Cuvelier, Adolphe, 105-6, 111, 114-6, 128
de Cleene, Father, 102, 106
De Lacey, Laurence, 200
de Lamartine, Alphonse, French Minister of Foreign Affairs, 7
Denison, Sir William, 21
Denny, T A, 127
Derby, Lord, 329
de Valera, Eamon, 302, 304
Devlin, Charles Ramsay (MP), 82
Devlin, Joseph (MP), 306
Devonshire, Duke of, 323, 326
Devoy, John, 51, 146, 148, 149, 154-5, 157-8, 173, 174, 175, 178, 182, 184, 186, 190, 198-200, 207-10, 213-6, 218-9, 271-3, 303
de Wet, Christian, 255, 256-7
Dilke, Sir Charles (MP), 111, 128
Dillon, John, 2, 6,13,15, 80
Dillon, Thomas, 302
Doheny, Michael,13
Donley, A J J, 299
Dowling, John, 293
Dowling, John Thomas, 313
Dowling, Joseph Patrick, xii, 291; background, 293; landing in Ireland, 293-297; interrogations, 297-300; the German Plot, 301-11; trial and sentence, 311-5; commutation, 315-8; petitions against sentence or conviction, 318-9; dispute over amnesty provisions of Anglo-Irish Treaty, 319-25; unsuccessful debates in the Dáil, 325-8; further pressure for release, 329-30; release, marriage, and conclusion 330-3
Doyle, Michael Francis, 258-60, 269, 271
Drummond, Sir Eric, 260
Dudgeon, Jeffrey, 277
Duffy, Charles Gavan, 2
Duffy, George Gavan, 229, 231-3, 235, 252, 269, 270, 277
Duke, Henry, 301
Dundee (Talana Hill), battle of, 42-3

Eetvelde, E D M van, 102
Eisner, Kurt, 336
Emmott, Alfred (MP), 129
Enright, Seán, 310-1
Epondo *(case of the native boy)*, 125

Ewart, General Sir Richard, 201, 206, 337

Fair Oaks, battle of 23-4
Farnham, Lord, 54
Figgis, Darrell, 144, 302
Findlay, Mansfeldt de Cardonnel, 159-175, 185
Finlay KC, Sir R B, Attorney General, 73-5, 81-2
First Battle of Bull Run, 22
Flanagan, Thomas, 295
Flight of the Wild Geese, ix
Fontenoy, Battle of, x, 96
Fox Bourne, Henry, 111
Fredericksburg, battle, 25-6
Fremont, US Major-General, 23
French, Lord, 302
Fruhling, Mrs H, Dowling petitioner, 324-5
Fryatt, Captain Charles, 254
Fussell, John (Chartist), 10

Gaffney, Thomas St John, 292
Galsworthy, John, 255
Gerard, James W, 204, 291
German Plot, 301-11, 327
Gettysburg, battle of, 30
Godert de Ginkel (1st Earl of Athlone), ix
Goertz, Herman, 344
Gonne, Iseult, 47, 343-4
Gonne, Maud, see *"John MacBride, Marriage to Maud Gonne"* 45-8, and 59-60, 64, 70, 84, 302, 344
Gore Booth, Eva, 257, 278
Gorst, Sir John Eldon (MP), 129
Goschen, Lieutenant, 204

Gosselin, Major Sir Nicholas, 63
Gregory, Holman, KC, 311, 314-5
Grenfell, George, 102, 103, 107, 109
Grey, Sir Edward, 131, 134, 137, 162, 172, 173, 222, 231-3, 257-8, 262, 267-8, 275-6, 291
Gribayedoff, Valerian, 78
Griffith, Arthur, 7, 40, 45-6, 302
Guest, Captain, 341-2
Guinness, Henry (Harry) Grattan, 107
Guinness, Walter, 1st Baron Moyne, 328-9
Gwynn, Denis, 275

Haldane, Lord 141
Hall, Reginald, Chief of Naval Intelligence, 222, 297-300, 310-1, 316-8, 320
Hancock, US General, 27, 30
Hannan, Commander Francis, 296-7
Hart, Major-General Arthur Fitzroy, Boer War, 50
Hay-Drummond, George, 12th Earl of Kinnoull, 203
Healy, Tim, KC, 323
Held, Stephen Carrol, 344
Hempel, Eduard, 343-4
Hencxthoven J, Father van, 102, 103
Henry, Sir Edward, KCVO, 290
Hewart, Sir Gordon, 338
Hindu-German Conspiracy, 183-4
Holland, Michael, 123
Hollywood, Edward, 6
Holt, John, 126-7
Horner, Francis (MP), 71
Hoven, Jupp, 345, 347
Hovenden, Henrietta, 332
Howley, Martin, 295

INDEX

Inglis, Brian, 277
Irish Brigade of the Wild Geese, x
Irish Confederation, 5-8, 10-13
Irish flag (tricolour), 8

Jagow, Gottlieb von, 174
Jephson, Anne, 97
Jerome, Jerome K, 255
Jones, Artemus, 229, 236, 275
Jones, Ernest, 10

Kavanagh, Sergeant, German Irish Brigade, 335-6
Kenworthy, Lieutenant Commander (MP), (10th Baron Strabolgi), 328-9
Keogh, Michael Patrick, 291, 312, 332-3, 335, 336
Kettle, Tom, 59
Kitchener, Lord, 172
Kossuth, Lajos, 96
Kruger, Paul, President, 41, 43-4, 59, 67, 80

Landy, James, 158
Lansdowne, Lord, 109, 112-4, 126, 128, 232, 262
Lawless, John, 295
Lee, Robert E, Commanding General, US Confederate Army, 27
Leopold II, King, 97, 100-3, 105, 107, 109, 120, 121, 122, 123, 124, 132, 141
Letelier, H, 78
Leyds, Dr W J, 64-5, 78, 79, 99
Limerick, Treat of, ix
Lindley, Francis (Frank), 171-2

Lloyd George, David, 84, 309
Logue, Cardinal, 254
Long, Walter, 302
Lonsdale, John (MP), 52-3
Lothaire, Captain, 101
Loughnane, N G, 321, 323, 326
Lowenfeld, General von, 194
Lynch, Alfred Arthur, xi; personal life, 63; Irish nationalist, 63; Second Irish Brigade, 64-70; nationalist politician, 70-3; trial and aftermath, 73-83; return to politics, 83; forms Irish Brigade in the British Army, 84-6; legacy, 86-8; 95, 227-8, 233-4, 252, 253, 256, 308
Lynch, John, 63
Lynch, Thomas, 294
Lyndsay, Reverend Canon, 255-6

MacBride, Dr Anthony, 39, 47
MacBride, John, xi, early life, 39-40; Irish Transvaal Brigade, 40-45, 48-51, 69, 70; marriage to Maud Gonne, 45-8; nationalist in Ireland, 52-6; Easter Rising and afterwards, 56-61; 81, 85-6, 87, 95, 96, 100, 178, 252, 272
MacBride, Joseph, 39-40
MacBride, Seán, 47, 48, 60-1, 343
McColl, René, 277
McCormack, Professor Bill, 274
McCormack, Sergeant William, 297
MacDermot, Sean, Sean, 253
MacDonald, Ramsay
McGhee, Thomas Darcy, 15
McGoey, John, 208, 209

McGrath, Major John, 346-9
McKean, John (MP), 309
McKenna, Reginald, 172
McMahon, Paul, 310
McManus (or MacManus), Terence Bellew, 14, 16, 19
MacNeill, Eoin, 144, 200, 218-20
McNeill, J G Swift (MP), 82
Macnamara, Thomas, 294
Magan, W M T, CBE, 349
Mahon, Sir Bryan, 326-7
Malvern Hill, battle of, 24
Mander, Dr P R, 269
Markevitz, Countess de, 257-8, 302
Masterson-Smith, Sir James, 322-3, 331
Maxwell, Major-General Sir John, 57-8, 228, 271, 326
Meagher, Thomas Francis, x; early life and education, 1-2; Young Irelander, 2-20, 45; Irish Brigade and US Civil War, 21-37; Acting Governor of Montana, 37; 87, 95
Midleton, Viscount, 55
Milner, Viscount, 316
Mitchel, John, 7, 9-11
Modderspruit (Modder River), battle, 42
Monteith, Robert, 190-5, 197-9, 207-9, 212, 214, 216-8, 224, 290, 299
Monteith Lynch, Florence, 290
Monteil, Colonel, 65, 78
Moore, Colonel, ex-Connaught Rangers, 326
Moore, Ulick, 326
Morel, E D, 107-8, 111, 127-8, 132, 200, 255
Moreton, Richard, 280

Morgan, Professor J H, 229
Mulcahy, Elizabeth, 344
Mulcahy, Richard, 329
Mullins, Major Charles, 297
Münster, Princess, 203, 204
Murphy, John B, 101

Nadolny, Captain, 207, 209-10
Neill, Private John, 234-6
Nevinson, Henry W, 257
Nicholson, Brigadier, 347
Nightingale, Florence, 141
Normand, Armando, 274

Oberndorff, Count Alfred von, 159-60
O'Brien, Daniel, 312-3
O'Connell, Daniel, and the Repeal Association, 2-5
O'Connell, John, 5, 20
O'Donaghue, Patrick, 14, 16-17, 19, 20
O'Farrell, Senator John, 327
O'Gorman, Richard Jnr, 6, 15, 21
O'Kelly, Sean, 57
O'Leary, John, 45
O'Shaughnessy, Father Thomas, 348-9
O'Sullivan, James, 313
O'Sullivan, John, 313
O'Toole, Michael, 291-3, 332-3

Palmerston, Lord, 96
Papen, Franz von, 183
Patrick, Marsena, US Provost Marshal, 30-1
Pearse, Patrick, 219-20, 253
Percy, Earl, 71, 130

INDEX

Phipps, Sir Constantine, 111, 128, 141
Pickersgill, W Clayton, Consul, 116
Pierson, J, 64
Pless, Princess, 203, 204
Plunkett, Count, 302
Plunkett, Joseph Mary, 199, 215
Plunkett, Philomena, 215
Powell, Annie, 63
Powell, Mrs Frances, 78
Price, Major General, War Office, AG3, 339-40
Price, Major, Army Special Intelligence Branch, Dublin, 301-2
Pringle, William (MP), 309-10

Quinlisk, Timothy, 291, 312, 333

Reddin, Catherine, 293
Redmond MP, John, 55, 80, 144-5, 146, 275
Redmond, William, 70-1, 81
Reilly, Thomas Devin, 15
Ribbentrop, von, 345
Ronslé, Mgr van, 102, 124
Rossa, Jeremiah O'Donovan, 82, 191
Rouse, Arthur, 294
Rumbold, Sir Horace, 291
Russell, Lord John, 10-12
Russell, Sean, 345
Ryan, Father, 217-8, 257
Ryan, Frank, 345
Ryan, Dr Mark, 39-40, 63

Saklavata, Shapurji (MP), 325
Samuel, Herbert (MP), 111
Samuels, Arthur, 301-2

Sarsfield, Patrick (1st Earl of Lucan), ix, x
Schneider, General von, 292
Scott, Robert, Major, US Army, 31
Shanahan, Dr Michael, 217
Shaw, George Bernard, 255
Sheehy-Skeffington, Francis, 256
Shields, US General, 23
Shortt, Edward, 307-9
Sims, Dr A, 102, 107
Sjöblom, E V, 102
Slievenamon, meeting, 12
Smith, Sir F E, Attorney General, 228, 231, 237, 251-2, 273, 275
Smith O'Brien, William, 6-9, 13, 14, 15, 17, 19-21, 228
Smith, Dr R Percy, MD, FRCP, 262-3, 265
Spindler, Karl, Reserve Lieutenant, 214-6
Spring Rice, Sir Cecil, 267-8, 271
Spring Rice, The Hon Mary, 144
Stack, Austin, 216-8, 226
Stamfordham, Lord, 316
Stanley, Henry Morton, 97
Stokes, Charles, 101
Stopford, Louisa Jane, 142
Stopford Green, Alice, 141, 142, 144, 148, 176, 178, 229, 233, 255
Stuart, Francis, 343-4
Sullivan KC, Serjeant A M, 231, 233-6, 251, 261, 277, 279
Sunday Rivers Bridge, fighting engagement, 75
Sykes, Sir Mark (MP), 309

Taft, William Howard, US President, 137

Taylor, Austin (MP), 129
Thomas, James Henry, 330-1
Thomson, Basil, Metropolitan Police, 222, 224, 227, 297-300, 310, 317
Thomson Walker, J W, 142
Tizon, Juan, 133-4
Troup, Sir Charles Edward, 263, 266
Trout Bartley, Christopher (MP), 80, 81
Tugela Heights, battle of, 50
Twain, Mark, 128
Tyrell, Sir William, 222, 223-4

Vallandigham, Clement, 28-9
Villebois-Mareuil, Count, 64-6, 74, 78, 79
Victoria, HM Queen, 50-1

Walsh, Stephen, 331

Walwood, Robert, 296
Washington, Booker T, 128
Wedel, Count von, 189, 200, 206, 209, 212, 214, 339
Williams, George Washington, 101, 107
Wilson, Woodrow, US President, 269

Yeats, John Butler, 59
Yeats, Lily, 59
Yeats, W B, 45, 46, 47, 59-60, 64, 84, 254
Young, Mrs Agnes, 256-7
Young Irelanders, 2

Zerhusen, Joseph, 187, 194, 197-8, 291-4, 335-6
Zimmermann, Arthur, 178, 183, 303-4